Failing the
Crystal Ball Test

Failing the Crystal Ball Test

The Carter Administration
and the
Fundamentalist Revolution in Iran

OFIRA SELIKTAR

PRAEGER

Westport, Connecticut
London

Library of Congress Cataloging-in-Publication Data

Seliktar, Ofira.
    Failing the crystal ball test : the Carter administration and the fundamentalist revolution
in Iran / Ofira Seliktar.
        p. cm.
    Includes bibliographical references and index.
    ISBN 0–275–96872–3 (alk. paper)
    1. United States—Foreign relations—Iran. 2. Iran—Foreign relations—United States. 3.
Islamic fundamentalism—Iran. I. Title.
    JZ1480.A57 I7   2000
    327.73055'09'047—dc21   00–022887

British Library Cataloguing in Publication Data is available.

Library of Congress Catalog Card Number: 00–022887
ISBN: 0–275–96872–3

First published in 2000

Praeger Publishers, 88 Post Road West, Westport, CT 06881
An imprint of Greenwood Publishing Group, Inc.
www.praeger.com

Printed in the United States of America

The paper used in this book complies with the
Permanent Paper Standard issued by the National
Information Standards Organization (Z39.48–1984).

10 9 8 7 6 5 4 3 2 1

To my sons, Yaron and Dror

Contents

Preface

On February 1, 1979, Ayatollah Khomeini arrived in Teheran. His tumultuous welcome provided the crowning touch to the revolutionary turmoil, which swept away the shah of Iran and the Pahlavi dynasty. The fundamentalist republic that Khomeini established was destined to send shock waves throughout the Middle East and the world. The impact was felt most keenly in the United States, where it contributed to President Carter's failure to get reelected and discredited the foreign policy vision of his administration.

The subsequent politics of Iranian fundamentalism have never left the headlines. International terrorism and the kidnapping of American hostages embroiled the Reagan administration in the Iran-contra scandal. The power vacuum in the region led to the prolonged Iran-Iraq war, which, in turn, served as a prelude to the Gulf War. The spread of fundamentalism in Algeria, the Sudan and Egypt are, at least, partially attributable to Iran's drive to promote Khomeini's political philosophy.

American experience with the Iranian revolution has been a subject of a long and passionate debate. The battle over "who lost Iran" and why has been fought along ideological, partisan, institutional and personal lines, with supporters and opponents of the administration arriving at diametrically opposed conclusions. Academic experts have focused on the role of human rights, the intelligence community, the structure of the administration and Carter's personality. Among the more theoretically oriented scholars, the events in Iran have rekindled an interest in uncovering universal laws of revolutionary change.

Although these perspectives are all valid, virtually all deal with narrow segments of the process that led the Carter administration to overestimate the endurance of the Pahlavi monarchy and underestimate the hold of the fundamentalists on the successor regime. It is only through the analysis of the complex process through which political change is conceptualized, applied to American foreign policy and used in the predictive endeavor, that a full understanding of the reasons for the Iranian calamity can be obtained.

This book provides such an understanding by offering a systematic analysis of the predictive failure at the paradigmatic, policy and intelligence levels. The theoretical framework analyzes the social science paradigms that were instrumental in determining the way in which political change was conceptualized. The applied chapters relate how these paradigmatic assumptions influenced the American approach to managing political change in Third World countries and permeated Carter's novel foreign policy philosophy, known as New Internationalism. A mixture of New Left imperatives and *moralpolitik* concerns for human rights, it framed the administration's approach to Iran and contributed to the policy and intelligence level debacle.

While the framework of this book was devised around the problems of the Iranian revolution, it can be used for the analysis of other forms of political change. Indeed, a decade after the Iranian revolution, communism in Eastern Europe collapsed under the pressure of democratically oriented movements. Though beneficial to American interests, few in the academic or policy community could foresee the speedy demise of the Soviet Union and its seemingly invincible empire. As the relatively stable Cold War situation gives way to a multitude of fragile international arrangements, the lessons of Iran can, hopefully, be used for anticipating changes that lie ahead.

A study of this scope would not have been possible without access to all the relevant documents. The classified documents seized during the takeover of the American embassy in Iran, and since published in seventy volumes by the Muslim Students Following the Line of Imam, provide a unique research opportunity. (These documents are cited in the text as Documents and full bibliographic information is cited in the references.) The documents are a treasure trove of information on the positions of the State Department, the embassy, the CIA, the Defense Intelligence Agency (DIA), the National Security Council and the academic experts who advised them. In addition, the National Security Archive used the Freedom of Information Act to declassify the White Paper—the State Department's own analysis of the predictive failure—and scores of related documents. Taken together, they provided a basis for creating a chronological narrative of the administration's perceptions and predictions from the beginning of 1977 to the seizure of the embassy in November 1979.

By analyzing the multifaceted nature of a predictive failure, this study has relevance to many fields of inquiry, including comparative politics, Middle East studies, American foreign policy, intelligence studies and business risk analysis.

Abbreviations

ACDA	Arms Control and Disarmament Agency
ACFPC	Arms Control and Foreign Policy Caucus
ACIR	American Committee for Iranian Rights
AI	Amnesty International
ARMISH-MAAG	U.S. Army Mission Headquarters–Military Assistance Advisory Group
AWACS	Airborne Warning and Command Systems
BERI	Business Environment Risk Index
BI	Business International
CAIB	*Covert Action Information Bulletin*
CALC	Clergy and Laity Concerned
CAP	Commercial Action Plan
CARI	Committee Against Repression in Iran
CDI	Center for Defense Information
CDP	Center for Development Policy
CIA	Central Intelligence Agency
CIP	Center for International Policy

CNFMP	Coalition for a New Foreign Policy
CNS	Committee for National Security
CNSS	Center for National Security Studies
COHA	Council on Hemispheric Affairs
DIA	Defense Intelligence Agency
ECLA	Economic Commission for Latin America
FISA	Foreign Intelligence Surveillance Act
HUMINT	human intelligence
IADL	International Association of Democratic Lawyers
ICA	International Communication Agency
ICJ	International Commission of Jurists
IDCFHR	Iranian Committee for the Defense of Freedom and Human Rights
IIM	Interagency Intelligence Memorandum
ILHR	International League for Human Rights
INR	Intelligence and Research
IPS	Institute for Policy Studies
IR	International Relations
IRP	Islamic Republican Party
JAMA	*Jonbesh-e Mosalmanan-e Mobarez* (Movement of Combatant Muslims)
KDPI	Kuridistan Democratic Party of Iran
LMI	Liberation Movement of Iran
MAAG	Military Assistance Advisory Group
MCPL	Members of Congress for Peace Through Law
MERIP	Middle East Research and Information Project
MNCs	multinational corporations
MPLA	Popular Movement for the Liberation of Angola
MPRP	Muslim People's Republican Party
NACLA	North American Congress on Latin America
NATO	North Atlantic Treaty Organization
NDF	National Democratic Front
NF	National Front (Iran)
NIE	National Intelligence Estimate
NIEO	New International Economic Order
NSC	National Security Council
NVOI	National Voice of Iran
OC-5	Organizing Committee for the Fifth Estate
OPEC	Organization of Petroleum Exporting Countries

PD	Policy Directive
PD	Presidential Directive
PG	Provisional Government
PIN	Party of the Iranian People
PLO	Palestine Liberation Organization
PRC	Policy Review Committee
RD	relative deprivation
SANE	Committee for a Sane Nuclear Policy
SAVAK	secret police in Iran
SCC	Special Coordinating Committee
SDECE	Service de Documentation Extérieure et de Contre-Espionnage
SFLI	Students Following the Line of the Imam
SMGATB	Society of Merchants, Guilds, and Artisans of the Teheran Bazaar
SOPs	standard operating procedures
SORO	Special Operations Research Office
TNI	Transnational Institute
WIP	World Indicators Program

Introduction: The Theory and Practice of Predicting Political Change

The fall of the shah of Iran, along with the Communist takeover of China and South Vietnam, ranks as one of the greatest setbacks to American foreign policy since World War II. The fundamentalist revolution has loomed even larger in the pantheon of intelligence failures. The debacle set off a deep and bitter debate about the way the United States had predicted and managed political change.

Prediction and effective foreign policy making are closely intertwined. Consciously or subconsciously, policy decisions rest on predictions of the likely course of future events. One observer noted that "even the naïve practitioner who insists that he makes every decision solely on the facts at hand operates with an implicit conception of what the future will be like" (Rothestein 1972, 159). Henry Kissinger (1981, 283–284) equated foreign policy with "our ability to perceive trends and dangers before they become overwhelming." Officials must act on "judgments about the future that cannot be proved true when they are made." He added that "when the scope for action is greatest, the knowledge on which to base such actions is often the least; when certain knowledge is at hand, the scope for creative action has often disappeared."

Given the high cost of missing important changes, an enormous intellectual effort to identify sources of predictive failures has been afoot for more than half a century. Following the pioneering work of Roberta Wohlstetter (1962) on Pearl Harbor, a large literature has focused on military-strategic forecasting. Work on political forecasting is less prevalent, but equally important. As Roger Hilsman (1967, 565) argued, "effective foreign policy depends on the capacity to predict events in the social affairs of men and a better capacity to predict would mean better and more effective foreign policy."

While forecasting military-strategic change and political change focus on different dimensions of international reality, they are both susceptible to the same types of predictive errors. Logically conceived, prediction is comparable to a form of statistical inference. In every predictive episode, evidence is assessed and probability is assigned to the "hypothesis" that change will or will not occur. Prognosticators run the risk of committing two types of statistical errors. They can either reject a "true hypothesis," that is, decide that a change will not take place when, in fact, a change is going to occur, or accept a "false hypothesis," that is, decide that a change will take place when it will not occur. Experts have worked to eliminate both types of errors, but instances where adverse change was not predicted have, understandably, attracted the most attention.

Failures range from minimal to fundamental and are grouped in four categories. In the first two—known as residuals and errors—the actual prediction of the event is successful, but the time frame is off by a certain margin. The failure in these categories does not necessitate any changes in basic theory and/or predictive methodology. In the third category the miss is known as an outliner—the error is large enough for the methodology and the applications to be revised, but the basic theory is still viewed as adequate. In the last category the miss is so great that, in terms of philosophy of science, it becomes an anomaly. An anomalous case casts doubts not only on the methods and applications used by the community of practitioners, but also on the underlying theory. In such cases, the subsequent debate about the misdiagnosis leads to a major revision of the predictive process at the level of procedures and organization. More important, a fundamental failure triggers a revision of the *epistemic level of knowledge*, often referred to as a paradigm.

There is little doubt that the revolution in Iran fits the model of a fundamental failure that occurred at the *paradigmatic, policy and intelligence dimensions of the predictive process*. Zbigniew Brzezinski (1983, 397), the national security adviser in the Carter administration, claimed that the "failure is not so much a matter of particular intelligence reports or even specific policies . . . [b]ut a deeper intellectual misjudgment of a central historical reality." Academic observers seem to agree that the failure was a fundamental one. As one of them noted, it was a "conceptual crisis, a sort of theoretical glaucoma" (Milani 1988, 22). Another described it as "one of those catalytic events . . . that shook American beliefs in their own perception of what was going on in other countries" (Shiels 1991, 84).

Such fundamental failures can be best understood in terms of Thomas Kuhn's analysis of revolutionary changes in knowledge. In his famous work on the structure of scientific revolution, Kuhn postulated that during routine times a set of agreed upon fundamental concepts are used to analyze a situation. These deep-seated concepts known as master-theories or paradigms dominate the field of a given intellectual endeavor and dictate the standards of rational inquiry. They form the "entire constellation of beliefs, values, technologies and so on shared by the members of a given community" (Kuhn 1970, 175). The dominant paradigm ordains what questions will arise, what forms of explanation will be accepted and what interpretations will be recognized as legitimate. As long as the paradigm is not challenged, its normalcy is accepted widely. But in the wake of a severe crisis, the dominant paradigm is questioned and overthrown. These paradigmatic battles, which are fought at the very frontiers of rationality, dictate how the community of practitioners looks at the relevant reality. When the new paradigm wins, the novel and "revolutionary" perceptions become routine and "normal."

Although Kuhn was primarily concerned with the scientific community, his work can be applied to the study of intelligence failures. The assumption here is that foreign policy practitioners use paradigms to analyze the political reality of countries in their purview. A study of American Third World policy contended that without such paradigms—a set of rules and standards for evaluating facts—the "policymaker is lost . . . all problems, approaches, facts and possible courses of action seem equally plausible" (Shafer 1988, 34).

Still, discerning how paradigms shape the view of changing international reality is not easy. Traditional models of foreign policy decision making do not focus explicitly on the epistemics of "understanding" that are crucial to such an endeavor. The rational choice model, the bureaucratic politics model and the crisis behavior model have either emphasized the political, environmental and structural dimensions of policy making or have analyzed the process through which a collective understanding of a situation is reached.

The cognitive approach is closer to the issue of epistemology: a popular scholar compared the belief system of foreign policy practitioners to a "set of lenses through which information concerning the physical and social environment is received" (Holsti 1962). But even the leading researchers in the field have failed to agree on how the two elements in the "cognitive map" of actors— broad fundamentals and the more narrowly proscribed instrumental beliefs— interact in discerning changing realities. A perusal of the cognitive belief literature hints at the source of these difficulties. A dominant assumption of this model is that key decisionmakers in charge of appraising the situation can be identified readily and that their beliefs and perceptions can be deduced through cognitive mapping, simulation or other analytic devices. Yet from an epistemic standpoint, this assumption is too static and limited. Studies on how bureaucracies "think" reveal that a collective understanding of a situation is arrived at as a result of the performance of a large number of individuals who apply concepts from an "analytic communal inventory." Such inventories are formed through complex and ill-defined intellectual interactions among foreign policy actors, bureaucratic experts, scholars and journalists.

Studies of the American foreign policy culture offer an alternative for tracking paradigms used in discerning political change. This large literature shows how enduring patterns of thought, symbols and values affect foreign policy deliberations and inform perception of the future. Although direct empirical links between prevalent intellectual trends and foreign policy practices are hard to demonstrate, they are necessarily pervasive. One scholar used an image from Indian cosmology to describe how fundamental beliefs affect policymakers: "[t]he table at which policymakers sit is like the platform . . . on which the world stands: under it is a pyramid of arbitrary assumptions, untested and indeed un-testable hypotheses and imprecise measures" (Staniland 1991, 275–276). While undoubtedly true, this definition is too broad to capture the paradigmatic as-sumptions that underlay a given forecasting episode.

To go beyond these limits requires a more dialectically oriented psychologi-cal, sociological and ethnographic approach. Ralph Pettman (1975), an authority on epistemology of foreign policy, argued that the search for the paradigms that determine how practitioners conceive of foreign societies should involve the *entire community of discourse on a given issue*. More recently, Giandomenico Majone (1989, 161–164), in his *Evidence, Argument and Persuasion in the Policy Process* formalized this proposition. The book, which is fast setting stan-dards for the discipline, focuses attention on the discourse of the *policy com-munity* defined as all those who share an active interest in a certain policy domain, that is, political actors, professional analysts, interest groups, academics and journalists. Majone argued that the discourse that surrounds a given policy issue is highly dynamic and dialectic. Because a policy community is jointed loosely and its members have different professional, ideological and intellectual commitments, the focus of inquiry should involve the *entire discourse* rather than select participants.

Using the discourse community as a model for understanding how forecasting of political change occurs makes it possible to combine the features of the more traditional approaches to decision making with elements of political culture and the epistemology of collective concept-use. Unfortunately, like many sociolog-ical constructs, a discourse community is a somewhat loose set of assumptions and concepts. The complexity and opacity of the process of discourse poses a considerable analytical problem. In particular, the influence wielded by academ-ics and intellectuals on policymakers is seldom direct or measurable. As Smith (1993, 49) put it, "ideas are not a consumer good shipped from intellectual warehouses . . . to be retailed in executive branches or Capitol Hill." Tanter and Ullman (1972, 3) asserted more bluntly that policymakers "have seldom given much heed to the writings of theorists." Still, other observers noted that the "thinking professions" have a major, albeit indirect and diffuse impact on policy making; they create a "climate of ideas," define the situation and mold the perspectives of policymakers. Over time, these ideas come to amount to an "almost rigid, congealed, mass of conventional wisdom" (Etzioni-Halevy 1985, 26). Given their pervasiveness, it would be naïve to assume that practitioners can diverge significantly from such views of reality. In fact, "academic pens leave a mark . . . policymakers' basic understanding of the world seldom differs fundamentally from social scientists" (Shafer 1988, 12).

A discourse community approach is useful especially in analyzing American perceptions of Third World countries, which were heavily shaped by academic paradigms. Indeed, this book is based on the assumption that a dialectical relation exists between intellectual ways of thinking about political change and the way in which such collective concepts inform politicians, bureaucrats and intelligence officials. To restate the Kuhnian proposition, the paradigm or paradigms developed in the relevant branches of social knowledge influence the epistemology of foreign policy practitioners who are in charge of predicting and managing political change. In turn, political practices will influence the structuring and restructuring of the paradigms. This interaction essentially is inseparable, but for analytical purposes we can isolate the elements of such a process.

First, this study will discuss the theories of political change that were popular before and during the Iranian revolution. Political change in Iran, like in other revolutionary situations, was precipitated by a *crisis of legitimacy*. Such a crisis occurs when fundamental societal norms are discarded and new ones adopted. The idea that alterations in legitimacy formulas precede political change is certainly not new. All political life is based on principles of legitimacy: These norms and values are embedded in the *collective belief system* and can be identified by tracking the societal legitimacy discourse, or more precisely the process of legitimation and delegitimation. As norms and values of society change, so do its more tangible political edifices such as processes and institutions. Successful prediction of impeding change must involve an early identification of changing collective beliefs and especially the indices of delegitimation (Horowitz 1979).

In spite of its obvious advantages, tracking changes in a collective belief system is not easy. Unlike indicators of performance, legitimacy norms are amorphous and ill-defined. Scholars have been divided deeply over the concept of legitimacy and the companion question of how and why societies embrace and drop political norms. A major cause of these disagreements stems from the fact that, in analyzing how norms of legitimacy change, social scientists rely on different ontological and epistemic assumptions about social reality and embrace a sharply divergent view of human nature. These root assumptions form different paradigms for discussing political change, whether observers are aware of it or not. Paradigms form the basis for predictive formulas about the cause, the timing and direction of political change. Since paradigms are themselves normative in character, they dictate what norms and values *should be considered legitimate*. Locked into their respective paradigms, observers tend to project their own sense of legitimacy onto the belief system of the society they analyze. What is more important, these normative projections tend to inform their predictions of when and how political change will occur and what direction it will take.

Indeed, starting in the 1950s, much of the work on Iran was dominated by the developmental paradigm, also known as modernization theory. Gabriel Almond, one of the leading developmentalists, once explained how developmentalism could help American efforts to induce change in underdeveloped countries. He declared that "our foreign policy must be informed . . . by a sound theory of social and cultural change. . . . Without this kind of social science thinking, we will be unable to effect the course of change in the Third World in directions favorable to the preservation and spread of our own culture" (quoted in Shafer 1988, 13).

However, the failure of the underdeveloped world to follow this prescriptive path and the Vietnam War discredited the tenets of developmentalism and popularized the dependency paradigm. Known also as *dependencia*, the new paradigm was derived from a neo-Marxist critique of modernization theory. It acknowledged that linear progress takes place, but asserted that, ultimately, societies would legitimize an enlightened, egalitarian distributive justice system. When applied to Iran, the two formulas produced striking different visions of political change. Whereas developmentally inspired scholars held that the collective belief system in Iran is following in the footsteps of Turkey, then considered the hallmark of modernization, dependency oriented observers predicted a shift toward an Indian or even Yugoslav model. By the midseventies the intellectual pull of dependency became so strong that increasing numbers of observers developed doubts that Iran would ever follow the Western path. Ironically, both paradigms failed to fathom a religiously driven "regressive" revolution that resulted in an Islamic theocracy.

Second, this book will analyze how these two paradigms affected American foreign policy. Since the discourse community approach involves cross-fertilization between practitioners and larger intellectual trends, it was only natural that the developmental paradigm would become part of the Cold War attempt to contain communism. However, the war in Vietnam, the rise of the civil rights movement and the spread of the counterculture delegitimized many notions of modernization. Inspired by neo-Marxist assumptions of *dependencia*, the New Left contended that Third World societies are in the process of moving toward egalitarianism and away from Western market principles. Viewed from this angle, American efforts to contain leftist movements put her on the "wrong" side of history. In order to put the United States on the "right" side of political change, the New Left developed a novel vision of foreign relations. Known as New Internationalism, it was a mixture of *moralpolitik* concerns for human rights and needs, egalitarianism and antimilitarism. As long as *realpolitik* dominated American foreign policy under Nixon and Kissinger, New Internationalism remained a marginal phenomenon. However, an opportunity to mainstream the new vision presented itself when Jimmy Carter, under pressure from the left wing of the Democratic Party, embraced many of its tenets.

Third, this work will demonstrate how New Internationalism guided the Carter administration's efforts to manage political change in Iran. Because of its strategic importance, starting with Truman, consecutive American administrations tried to keep Iran within the Western sphere of influence. Using developmental prescriptions, Iran, under the leadership of Mohammed Reza Pahlavi, was turned into a laboratory of modernization. However, by the time Carter arrived in the White House the shah's record, affected by the dependency critique, became controversial. The moralpolitikers in the administration and Congress were eager to stir Iran into the direction proscribed by New Internationalism. As planned change turned into revolutionary chaos, paradigmatic thinking coupled with policy and intelligence problems led the administration to overestimate the strength of the shah and misunderstand the nature of the successor regime.

The organization of the book reflects the research strategy developed above. Chapter I provides a theoretical framework for discussing the process of legitimization and delegitimation of a collective belief system. Chapter 2 describes how the developmental paradigm and its dependency rival conceptualized these constructs and offers contrasting views of the direction of change. Drawing on the dependency view of political change, the chapter also analyzes the intellectual origins of New Internationalism. Chapter 3 details the efforts of President Carter to apply tenets of New Internationalism to Iran and the deep divisions it created between the moralpolitikers and realpolitikers in his administration. Chapter 4 provides a thematic-chronological account of the politics of the predictive process during the first phase of the revolution, which culminated in the collapse of the monarchy. Using the same thematic-chronological approach, chapter 5 details the administration's misperceptions of the successor regime in Iran and its failure to evaluate correctly the strength and strategies of the fundamentalists that led to the seizure of the American embassy in Teheran. Chapter 6 provides a systematic analysis of the predicative failures of the Carter administration at the paradigmatic, policy and intelligence levels and offers some suggestions for improving the predictive process.

1

Theories of Political Change and Predictions of Change: Methodological Problems

Starting with Aristotle and Plato, the search for principles that underlay political change has been a staple of Western philosophy. One scholar wrote that "ideologies stand for centuries and then one day the temples are empty" (Boulding 1962, 281). Much of such change is precipitated by a crisis of legitimacy, defined as an alteration in the core values of the collective belief system of a society. Socrates speculated that alterations in legitimacy formulas precede political change, setting off a long quest to uncover how communal norms crystallize into a collective belief system and a corresponding political structure. This search has been problematic, prompting Huntington (1991, 46), a leading authority on political change, to note that legitimacy "is a mushy concept that political scientists do well to avoid." Indeed, there are a number of problems that face students of legitimacy.

METHODOLOGICAL PROBLEMS OF TRACKING CHANGES IN A COLLECTIVE BELIEF SYSTEM

Tracking legitimacy norms poses considerable methodological problems. An important issue is the unit of analysis, that is, the question of who are the *ideational bearers* of the collective belief system. Ontologically, the answer divides political science into macrosociological *holism* and microsociological *individualism*. The former holds that a society is a whole and cannot be reduced to the sum of its individual parts; the latter postulates that a collective is a sum total of individual beliefs. A related question deals with the kind of knowledge that should be used to probe for political beliefs. Epistemologically, the division runs between *positivism*, an assumption that the only admissible knowledge is based on scientific methods of investigation and *antipositivism*, which holds that such knowledge is essentially subjective, relativistic or spiritual.

Thinkers as diverse as Karl Marx and Emile Durkheim subscribed to the holistic approach, but macrosociology is most prominently associated with the "sociology of knowledge" approach of Karl Mannheim (1955, 264–311). Macrosociologists insist that the collective belief system should not be confused with the arithmetic sum of "individual consciousness" of a group. However, there is less clarity as to what the appropriate unit of analysis should be. One extreme view conceives of a "belief carrier" as an abstract, almost metaphysical "supersocietal" entity resembling the "general will" of the Enlightenment. The Marxist notion that a self-appointed intellectual vanguard should represent the "general will" offers a somewhat different solution. Indeed, left-wing intellectuals as varied as Herbert Marcuse and Andre Gundar Frank had emerged as spokesmen for the "collective consciousness" (Valenzuela and Valenzuela 1978; Kammen 1980, 24–25).

Reacting to the difficulties posed by holism, the rival school of *ontological individualism* is committed to the view that the beliefs of individuals are the only legitimate unit of analysis. This microsociological approach holds that political change can be predicted by the study of individual political beliefs. Among its early proponents were behaviorally oriented political scientists who sought to obtain "hard" empirical data of political change. Almond and Verba (1965, 13), the foremost spokesmen for microsociological individualism, defined political culture as the "particular distribution of orientations toward political objects among the members of the nation." In other words, a collective belief system can be described in terms of statistically derived psychological modalities of a given population.

In spite of its popularity, ontological individualism has not escaped serious criticisms. One prevalent complaint is that microsociologists neglect the distribution of power in a society (Converse 1987; Frey 1985). A popular solution to the problem of power disparities is to assume that elites represent the collective beliefs system more faithfully than rank and file. This notion has a long intellectual tradition, spawning a number of research strategies. By far, the most popular is the study of "images" or "cognitive maps" of leaders.

On the surface, this approach is ideal for solving the many ontological and epistemic problems associated with prediction of change. Elites are easier to track than masses; in close societies they are the only accessible members of the community. However, elites do not always represent the values of the rank and file. Following elite beliefs may be occasionally misleading because of what Elliot and Schlesinger (1979) called the "circular effect." Elites define the parameters of the collective belief system, invest in it psychologically and are normally last to acknowledge new norms that can delegitimate their rule. In Iran a popular challenge to the Pahlavis went undetected because much of the re-

search was based on elites. Preoccupation with elites has served poorly Sovietol-
ogists, who were overtaken by events when communism collapsed.

The inadequacies of the macrosociological and microsociological approaches
bred the *interactionist* perspective. Interactionism is based on the assumption
that neither the group nor the individual can be accorded "unqualified primacy"
and both are "mutually constitutive" in the ongoing process of creating social
reality. Interactionism can be traced to the work of George Simmel and George
Herbert Mead, who argued that the societal belief system constitutes complex-
symbolic sets; they should be seen as a product and a determinant of individual
beliefs generated through continuous social interaction (Burrell and Morgan
1979, 69–78; Seliktar 1986).

The interactionist perspective has gone a long way toward recasting the original quest for the ideational bearers of the collective. In this view changes in
legitimacy norms can be best discerned by following the *discourse* of a society.
Proponents of the interactionist tradition argue that "cognitive maps" of a group
discourse are a better approximation of the collective belief system than either
the cognitive map of elites or mass beliefs. Among others, they look for "concrete language practices to identify the actors and parameters of discourse (Shapiro, Bonham and Heradstveit 1980).

THE DIMENSIONS OF A COLLECTIVE BELIEF SYSTEM:
EXISTENTIAL IMPERATIVES AS VALIDITY CLAIMS

Much of the insight into discursive practices comes from anthropological
studies. Linton (1945) postulated that in order to survive, a group legitimizes
parts of its perceptional-ideational beliefs into an all-encompassing worldview.
Such a collective belief system forms the parameters of the social order in a
given society at a given period of time. Once a collective belief system is legitimized, it gives rise to social roles, structures and processes that hold a society
together.

Douglas (1992, 43, 133–134) conceived of this process as a normative debate
or discourse, in the course of which the collective works out its existential
imperatives. The three dimensions that require some type of a consensus are
rules for gaining membership, principles for establishing an authority system
and rules for distributing wealth. This discourse produces *normative validity
claims*, that is, "reasoned elaborations" intended to persuade individuals that
they need to obey the legitimizing principles of political practice (Matheson
1987; Misztal 1996, 251). Once legitimized, these validity claims are used to
construct the three axes of the collective belief system. The first axis is hori-
zontal and comprises the principles of group boundary—criteria for granting
membership and acquiring territory—known as *group membership/territorial*
legitimacy. The second axis is vertical and denotes the principles upon which
the authority system rests—*authority system* legitimacy. The third axis is di-

agonal and articulates the principles of distributive justice and binds group members and the authority system together—*distributive justice* legitimacy.

Membership/territory legitimacy has evolved from the *Gemeinschaft* community where validity claims were based on kinship, into *Gesellschaft* associations which ties members through a "feeling of interdependence" and a "community of fate." Nationalism, a set of principles that put loyalty to the nation-state above primordial ties, became increasingly popular. As long as a relatively ethnically homogenous group occupies a well-defined national territory, few challenges to such validity claims occur. However, in cases of *polycentric nationalism*, where disparate groups were brought under one national roof, tensions are never far from the surface. A dominant group may treat members of other groups as inferior or try to "homogenize" them by suppressing ethnic expressions. Religious divisions have added vast complications to the membership formulas. Since religion was a common base for conferring membership status, individuals belonging to a minority religion have been often relegated to the status of "second-class citizenship."

Authority system legitimacy comprises a set of validity claims that justify the creation of a system of controls over a group. Since controls involve the exercise of power, validity claims help to ensure members' compliance. Max Weber's analysis of authority systems is well known. He identified three pure types of validity claims: (1) rational grounds—a belief in the legality of rule of authority and the right of those chosen under these rules to command, (2) traditional grounds—based on the sanctity of traditions and the legitimacy of those who exercise authority according to traditional tenets and (3) charismatic grounds—resting on the commitment to a certain individual and the order revealed to him.

Weber's taxonomy has generated an enormous critical literature, including suggestions for updating his categories. Rigby (1982) sought to differentiate among authority systems based on contract, custom and command figures. Herz (1978) distinguished between *numinous-traditional* validity claims and *civic* claims. The former is based on claims of divine origin or other supernational rights and is conferred on the bearer in either the remote past or in the present. Civic legitimacy is derived from the consent of the members of the collective and is contractual in nature, hence involving procedural or rational-legal validity claims. There has been a considerable debate as to the appropriate procedural rules required to establish and maintain rational-civic legitimacy. The democratic regime-based on the experience of Western democracies is one obvious answer. However, historically, the vast majority of states that have claimed rational-legal legitimacy were authoritarian or downright totalitarian. Fascist rulers have often evoked a mystic mandate from the people. In the Communist command-structure, the legitimacy of the authority system was based on goal achievement or "goal rationality" rather than on the application of rules (Epstein 1984; Thompson 1976; Rigby 1982).

To further confuse matters, regimes have used a bewildering combination of validity claims to legitimize their rule. Mixes of charismatic, numinous-traditional and legal-rational claims have been the rule rather than the exception in Third World countries. In patrimonial and neopatrimonial regimes, such as monarchial Iran, the authority system was based on divine grace as well as on legal-rational principles. Regimes based on a charismatic "maximum leader" have enhanced their legitimacy through "ritualistic" elections, a practice equally common in the Communist command system.

Distributive justice is part of a larger domain of social justice, defined as a series of principles for assigning particular things to particular individuals (Galston 1980, 5). Distributive justice pertains to the more limited question of "who distributes to whom, in virtue of what criterial characteristics, by what procedures, with what distributive outcomes" (Lane 1986). To satisfy the requirements of social justice, distributive schemes have been based on a number of validity claims. Three "pure" types can be identified: (1) ascriptive-traditional claims that underpin traditional economies, (2) utilitarian-productive claims that underlie market economies and (3) egalitarian principles that inform communist economies.

Ascriptive claims, based largely on birthright, have been prevalent in traditional societies whose constitutive domain was noneconomic. With the refocusing of the constitutive domain on economics, the principle of efficiency rather than birth generated a utilitarian-productive validity claim. Economically meritorious individuals, defined as those who possess scarce factors of entrepreneurship and skill, were deemed worthy of receiving a share of resources commensurate with their contribution. Popularized by Adam Smith's *Wealth of Nations*, this *equity* principal had become widely accepted in Western market economies. Although capitalism has been highly efficient in generating wealth, market economy created large inequalities among social classes and "boom and bust" cycles to which the poorer strata were particularly vulnerable. It was left to Marx, in his well-known critique of capitalism, to argue that general principles of justice demand an egalitarian distribution of resources. At a later stage, Marx envisaged a distribution based on *human needs*, a notion that various neo-Marxist thinkers developed more than a century later.

The discursive perspective holds that norms of legitimacy that emerge in the collective discourse are internalized in the minds of group members and translated into action through a repetitive performance of roles. In due course these roles crystallize into structures—institutions and processes—that shape and bind the collective through an endless stream of policies. The widely used concept of *regime*, meaning a set of governing arrangements that include networks of rules, norms and procedures, reflects this idea most closely. Political change at the structural level occurs only after old norms have been delegitimized and new ones adopted.

THE PROCESS OF LEGITIMIZING A COLLECTIVE BELIEF
SYSTEM: THE DISCURSIVE APPROACH

The legitimation discourse serves as the arena for an exchange of symbolic and substantive arguments in favor of accepting or rejecting validity claims. However, efforts to predict change by tracking an amorphous and ongoing discourse are difficult. To begin with, there is little argument as to how broadly based a collective belief system is. The Marxist and neo-Marxist tradition holds that the collective belief system reflects the "dominant ideology" and a "hegemonic culture." Jurgen Habermas (1975), in his pioneering discussion of the communication society (*Kommunikationsgemeinschaft*), argued that political discourse rewards linguistic competence that is correlated with power and class structure. Others, like Durkheim hold that collective belief system represents the conscience collective of the entire society. This is probably true in relatively homogenous societies where norms are widely shared. Other societies are more fragmented and correspond to what Weber called the "elective affinity model," where a particular world view can be best understood in terms of the experience of the assorted groups.

To enhance the predictive capacity, a good understanding of the dynamics of the discourse is necessary. In particular, three questions need to be addressed. The first one pertains to the *locus* of the discourse. Much of the research on political communication reflects the habit of equating discursive practices with Western-style "rational" and institutionalized political procedures (Nimmo and Sanders 1981). Critics have blamed the twin tradition of Parsonian structuralism and historical "objectivism" for trivializing the role of cultural, non-"rational," symbolic and mythical elements. Such an approach is especially detrimental in following the discourse in "diglossiac" societies, where there are large differences between the "high" language of elites and the "low" language of the masses (Weinstein 1979).

But following broader cultural trends may be confusing since there are precious few *rules of recognition* that would allow observers to determine well in advance the probability that a given intellectual idea will alter an important legitimacy formula. Turner and Killian (1972) articulated such rules of recognition in the "emergent norms" theory, which holds that normative challenges emanate from an individual or a group and "chain out" to larger and larger segments of the population. Applying the "emergent norms" methodology to Iran might have helped to spot the growing popularity of the fundamentalists.

The second question pertains to the identity of the participants in the legitimacy discourse. Theoretically, all members should be counted among the "ideational bearers" of their respective society. In reality though, crucial elites form "ideational clusters" that have a disproportional impact, a fact well recognized by political scientists who have scrutinized formal political elites. However, such an approach excludes "nonconstituted" leaders such as writers, poets, activists, students and other free-floating intelligentsia. These "confrontational" elites often challenge extant legitimacy norms and the political institutions that are built around them (Tucker 1981, 7). These elites, as well as, religious heretics and ideological apostates carry the seeds of a *challenge belief system* that, under proper conditions, can replace the dominant belief system. At the very least, they can incrementally change key parts of the extant belief system (Said 1971; Coser 1964; Brinton 1965, 39).

Widening the search for potentially crucial elites and their beliefs is methodologically complex. As one observer wrote; "it is easy retrospectively but difficult prospectively to identify which specific publics are strategically critical to a regime's legitimacy" (Rothschild 1979, 59). The various "legitimacy" taxonomies offer a promising solution. One such taxonomy groups people into "members," "contenders" and "challengers." "Members" are most closely identified with the dominant belief system and have vested interests in its continuation. "Contenders" pool their resources to influence selective validity claims, but do not reject the overall system. The "challengers," mostly antiestablishment and disaffected groups, strive to replace the entire belief system of their society (Tilly 1978, 52; Moshiri 1985, 188). Another taxonomy identifies "ruling," "accepting" and "opposition" groups. Whether the collective belief system moves into any particular direction—authoritarianism, liberalism, market economy, socialism—depends on how the "ruling" and "opposition" elites play the large amorphous middle group (Chalmers and Robinson 1982). Research indicates that it is possible to list conditions under which the interplay of elites would move the collective into a market direction as opposed to socialism (Wildavsky 1986).

The third question deals with the time span of an ideational challenge, which is normally time-lagged. As will be clear from later chapters, fundamentalist ideas circulated in Iran for at least three decades before the revolution. However, few observers considered them credible enough to threaten the monarchy, thus relegating them to background "noise." The Iranian case demonstrates that a successful forecast needs not only separate "noise" from signals, but "bet" on the "correct" trends and the elites that proclaim them. Unfortunately, this type of calculus is susceptible to personal biases and paradigmatic assumptions of observers; what some consider a marginal or deviant trend, others view as a harbinger of a new order. Indeed, the then-prevalent paradigms viewed fundamentalism as marginal "noise." By the same token, paradigmatic assumptions can overstate the representatives of a "crucial elite," as the lionizing of the Latin American leftist intellectuals in American academia demonstrates (Vargas Llosa 1992).

Even if the "ideational bearers" in the discourse can be traced, it is essential to understand how norms of legitimacy operate as individual mental constructs. Apter's (1965, 391) old comment that "legitimacy is too complex, related as it is to personal identity, and ultimately, to individual needs for meaning and purpose" is still relevant.

At the core of the problem are two conflicting views of how people form and maintain feelings of legitimacy. In their classic study, French and Raven (1959) argued that legitimacy is something sentimental; it derives from a sense of obligation and duty toward the group and the authority system, but is independent of performance. Easton (1965, 273) added that legitimacy is experienced by individuals as a "strong inner conviction of the moral validity of the authority system." Experts assume that such feelings develop early in life and transform into "diffuse support" (Fraser 1974). The opposing view is based on the much quoted study of Hollander and Julian (1970), who found that feelings of legitimacy are strongly related to the performance of the system. This so-called "functional legitimacy" approach derived from rational choice theories, which stipulated that the types of rewards individuals obtain from the system shape their perceptions of legitimacy. Fear of coercion may also affect feelings of legitimacy. This line of research has found that individuals engage in a complex calculus of rewards and punishments when considering what is legitimate and what is not (Muller 1979; Wrong 1980; Tyler 1990).

Given the lack of consensus, it is probably safe to assume that neither generalized sentiments nor self-interest or fear of coercion alone can explain how individuals legitimize societal beliefs. Boulding (1962, 79) postulated that in forming a view of what is legitimate, individuals are guided by a mix of three perceptual systems: *integrative system*, based on social consensus, *threat system*, based on coercion and *exchange system*, based on functional considerations. In other words, perceptions of legitimacy are shaped by normative expectations that people have with regard to what constitutes a fair or reasonable amount of consensus, coercion and functional performance. Still, trying to discern how changes in this complex formula trigger a process of delegitimation poses considerable problems.

THE PROCESS OF DELEGITIMATION: THE SYSTEMIC AND INDIVIDUAL LEVEL VIEW

The division between macrosociologists who study change at the level of macrosystems and the microsociologists who look at individual psychology complicates the analysis of delegitimation (Nisbet 1969, 288). Since interactionism incorporates both holistic and individual perspectives, a short overview of both approaches is in order.

Systemic Level Mechanisms

Systemic level mechanisms have a long intellectual history. They derive from what Karl Popper called historicism, or the idea that human history has a discernable way of evolving. Much of this "social physics" approach was influenced by the physical sciences, most notably Newtonian physics. The Newtonian analogy is predicated on the view of the universe as a regulated automation.

The movement of historical mass was conceived as taking place in a perfect closed system—stable, timeless and deterministic. Since change here is synonymous with acceleration and deceleration, the resultant laws of change were expressed in term of trajectory. In Newtonian linear progression the "initial state" is used to predict all the other states that the system passes in a time sequence (Nagel 1979, 447).

Finding its way into positivism, "social physics" resulted in a view of society as a series of structures and processes moving in an orderly and predictable way from a lower to a higher state. Talcott Parsons (1951) adopted this structural-functional framework to the study of political change. The four functional parts of the system—pattern maintenance, integration, goal-attainment and adaptation—were assumed to preserve the homeostatic characteristics of the system. This "scientific" depiction of politics attracted David Easton (1953, 1965) and other political scientists eager to find laws of change. The newly developed cybernetic theories further boosted the deterministic view of change. Karl Deutsch (1963), an early enthusiast, postulated that the deterministic properties of the system would make it easy to predict change by tracking empirical indices.

In spite of the fact that the works of Parsons and Easton were "missionary," with little empirical validation, the system approach became *de rigueur* in political science. The all but mandatory use of system terminology created the impression of an orderly and deterministic political universe and was bolstered by a variety of linear methodologies for measuring political change. A large number of "handbooks" of political change replete with indices came to dominate the field.

Because of the paradigmatic status of macrosystemic theories, little attention was paid to the problems of applying the notion of a closed system to social reality. Ludwig von Bertalanaffy (1956) sounded one of the few cautionary notes at the time. He warned that social organizations, like other living organisms, may be better represented by an open system analogue. An open system differs from a closed one in two important aspects: it maintains an exchange with the environment and has the property of "equifinality," that is, the final state cannot be deduced from many initial conditions. Other critics charged that the Parsonian-Eastonian approach was ill equipped to handle forms of political change that led to "system disintegration, disappearance or destruction" (Burrell and Morgan 1985, 65–67).

In spite of these warnings there was little appetite for abandoning the mechanistic notions of change. The behavioral fervor that gripped the discipline in the 1960s put a premium on linear-deterministic models and the high predictability that they offered. Gabriel Almond (1966) noted in his presidential address that such exactitude was "exhilarating." The quest for an easy linear model of change was also related to the increased role of political scientists in the "technostructure" of the American government where system analysis, first developed in the military, was at a premium. As one critic put it: "system methods have served them [social scientists] not only as public relation devise, but as centralizing power instrument of the first order" (Lilienfeld 1978, 267).

Individual Level Mechanisms

While less abstract, the analysis of political change at the individual level is by no means well understood. A perusal of literature reveals three explanatory traditions. The first is loosely based on Emile Durkheim's notion of anomie, which is said to afflict individuals in transitional situations. Stress generated by anomic states affects emotional homeostasis, defined as people's ability to cope with demands of daily life. Although the ability to cope is partially idiosyncratic, it is also social in the sense that need satisfaction is informed by the collective belief system. Anomic states create ambiguities in what is a legitimate need satisfaction: when disoriented individuals fail to meet their confused expectations, they proceed to delegitimize collective norms (Homans 1961, 214–219). Among others, anomic state theory was used to explain the experience of the Weimar Republic.

The second explanatory perspective is derived from the work of Neil Smelser (1962) and others students of social stratification. Known as "normative strains" analysis, the theory postulates that societal roles are based on "determinants" derived from their value to the group. This *expediency*—or usefulness—varies across time; as economic conditions change, some roles are "demoted" and others are "promoted." When the social status of the role bearers is not adjusted accordingly, it can trigger powerful demands for change. Smelser asserted that the increasingly important middle class in France delegitimized the validity norms that underpinned the aristocratic authority system and the largely ascriptive distributive justices system, triggering a revolution.

The third explanatory perspective is based on cognitive psychology. Briefly put, cognitive theories assume that individuals feel uncomfortable when they are faced with two dissonant elements. In order to reduce the feeling of discomfort, a person will proceed to eliminate the source of dissonance by adjusting beliefs, information or feelings (Festinger 1957). Developed in the context of individual psychology, notions of cognitive dissonance have been applied to values change in group settings. Rescher (1969), a pioneer in social forecasting, argued that when new values are introduced in the course of a societal discourse, people either adjust their attitudes or reject the discordant norms. Over time, such a process on an individual level may lead to far-reaching alternation in collective norms. By way of illustration, Rescher pointed out that a century ago workers expected minimum remuneration when considering "economic justice," more recently this norm came to mean "quality of life" or "good life."

While popular, cognitive theories did not escape criticism. Anthropologists have long argued that ambiguities and contradiction are embedded in a traditional belief system (Ellul 1958). Converse (1964), in his seminal work on mass beliefs, found that most people harbor contradictory and dissonant beliefs. Others noted that there is no universal logic which dictates which two elements "will be perceived as being consistent or inconsistent" (Billig 1976, 142–143). Comparative studies indicated that some cultures have a high tolerance for contractions between beliefs and daily praxis (Ajami 1981). The most important challenge to cognitive consistency comes from attribution theory. Studies demonstrated that people tolerate dissonance because of errors in causal inference and other lapses in reasoning (Nisbett and Ross 1980, 169–192). *Belief perseverance* is apparently widespread because of "human propensity to cling to initial opinions, attitudes and theories" (Anderson 1983). Some scholars charged that peoples' political thinking harbors ignorance and inconsistencies (Lamber et al. 1988).

Both cognitive and attribution theory poses problems for understanding how people delegitimize extant norms. Indeed, one scholar asserted that "to fail to accord legitimacy, to delegitimate an established institution or process runs contrary to many natural psychological processes" (R. E. Lane 1979, 68). Worse, authorities can manipulate individual beliefs through a combination of socialization and coercion. In certain traditional-authoritarian regimes, many of the political norms were considered "sacred." When a discrepancy between a stated value and a reality occurred, only the authorities were allowed to draw the "right" inference and make the "appropriate" revisions (Boulding 1962, 288).

Despite these difficulties, it is possible to combine insights from the three explanatory perspectives to offer an understanding of how delegitimation occurs at the individual level. According to rational choice theory, when people make decisions they use a mechanism known as *validation*, which links beliefs about reality with the behavioral outcomes of these beliefs. Validation, in turn, is filtered through the sense of *eudemonics*, that is, well-being (Strumpel 1972). Well-being is a multivariate concept: *it simultaneously depends on the state of self, the well-being of the reference group and some general norm of what well-being should be.* In spite of its notorious fuzziness, there are certain elements that affect the sense of well-being of individuals. Economics have an important and fairly universal impact on social eudemonics and the resultant evaluation of the legitimacy of the political system. Declining economic performance would cast doubts on the distributive justice system and may eventually affect other dimensions of legitimacy, even to the point of delegitimizing a democratic authority system. Conversely, good performance may bolster an authoritarian or a totalitarian regime. According to a pioneering study the fascist regime in Spain enjoyed a fair amount of legitimacy because it delivered economic benefits (McDounough, Barnes and Lopez Pina 1986).

The Spanish study, as well as other research, indicates that the three axes of legitimacy-group membership, authority system and distributive justice—are intertwined in peoples' minds. The very complex nature of eudemonic considerations, coupled with the not entirely predictable way in which members of a group alter their views of what is legitimate, cast doubt on linear theories of change. If anything, the analysis of change at the individual level illustrates why linearity cannot be assumed. Evidently, the numerous ways in which people can alter the legitimacy formulas account for the "choices" that the system makes. Since each delegitimation can be represented as a policy choice between contradictory alternatives, that is, tribalism vs. nation-state, democracy vs. authoritarianism, market economy vs. socialism, the systemic level can register a series of bifurcations. One observer described this process as "whole complex moving forward, irreversibly, with period arrivals at point of substantial change" (Jones 1981).

ACTIVATING THE PROCESS OF DELEGITIMATION: TRIGGER CONDITIONS OF CHANGE

In order to facilitate prediction, it is important to identify the trigger conditions for such legitimacy altering events. The significance of finding trigger conditions is self-evident; if general categories of triggers can be isolated, prediction of upcoming change and its direction can be made as easy as forecasting physical phenomena. As indicated, belief systems persist because people, habituated to the role scripts that reflect these norms, take them for granted. But consensus can erode when legitimacy claims are challenged in the course of a public debate. However, scholars are not entirely clear what can trigger delegitimizing challenges. Boulding's (1962, 280) old query as to "why one set of symbols seems to fire the imagination of large bodies of people at a certain stage of history," only to be abandoned later has remained essentially unanswered. Literature reveals five generations of explanatory perspectives that, not surprisingly, reflects the continuous debate between macrosystemic and individual levels view of political change.

The first generation is based on the natural history school of Crane Brinton, Pitrin Sorokin and others. These scholars investigated revolutionary patterns but failed to provide a theoretical perspective. Brinton (1965) set the standard in his analysis of the French and Russian revolutions and many of his ideas found their way into later generation theories.

Second generation scholars, eager to create testable hypothesis of change, used Parsonian-Eastonian notions of input-output equilibrium to argue that certain types of imbalances affect the "authoritative allocation of values." When systems become incapable of responding in a satisfactory manner to new demands, a legitimacy crisis develops. Change was said to occur when the system reached a "ceiling condition" beyond which it could not take effective action (Apter 1974, 110; Parvin 1973). But critics argued that concepts such as "threshold conditions" and "breaking point" are too vague and not grounded in empirical reality.

In an apparent effort to correct these shortcomings, third generation theorists tried to look for trigger conditions in the psychological states of individuals. Riding the crest of the behavioral revolution, scholars were confident that empirical work would lead to predictive theories (Kochanek 1973). By and large, psychological explanations were anchored in the "frustration-aggression" theory of John Dollard. For instance, the popular J-curve theory of Davies (1962) held that, during periods of economic prosperity, peoples' expectations rise commensurably. When economic fortunes decline, these raising expectations cannot be met, leading to frustration.

Gurr (1968; 1970; 1973) provided a more complex view of psychological triggers. He used the concept of relative deprivation (RD) to argue that frustration sets in when there is a discrepancy between an actor's value expectation and value capability. Other scholars suggested alternative routes through which feelings of relative deprivation are formed. At its height the RD movement represented one of the most prominent empirical effort to predict political change (Gillespie and Nesvold 1971; Feierabend, with Feierabend and Nesvold 1971). Along the way, RD spurred research into conditions of economic inequality that were largely ignored by second-generation theorists. A number of scholars set out to find a correlation between land tenure patterns—a common source of inequality in Third World countries—and political strife. Southeast Asia and Latin America—two of the then-troubled regions of the world—featured heavily in this effort (Russet 1964; Alker and Russet 1966; Mitchell 1968; 1969; Paige 1970; Russo 1972).

However, in spite of the enormous effort, the RD models failed to produce a universal measure of discontent. Critics pointed out that the process of collectivization of discontent is influenced by a complex and interactive pattern of comparisons, including temporal comparisons (between past and present) social comparisons (with other members of the group) and vertical comparison (with other societies). Even more problematic was the definition of value expectation in a given society. Since individual expectations are derived from what the collective belief system considers to be legitimate needs and wants, there is no one good way of estimating them (Dubnoff 1986). Other critics complained that RD is focused too heavily on economic factors to the neglect of other issues, including ethnic and religious grievances (Horowiz 1973).

Reacting to these problems, fourth generation theories probed structural preconditions of delegitimation. Barrington Moore (1966), who was influenced by Marxist notions of structural change, inspired much of this approach. His disciple, Theda Skocpol (1979), firmly rejected the notion that "idea systems deployed as self-conscious political arguments by identifiable political actors" play a role in triggering political mobilization, a prelude to delegitimation. In her opinion the crucial triggers are structural: the weakening and progressive incapacitation of the administrative and military machinery of the state.

Tilly (1973; 1978) and Gamson (1975) pursued a different avenue of fourth generation inquiry. They argued that even acute relative deprivation does not automatically trigger delegitimation and neither, for that matter, do structural weaknesses. In their view it is "resource mobilization"—elites that can articulate grievances, solidarity networks that bind potential participants together and coalition building among aggrieved elements—that provide the necessary triggers. While Tilly viewed the role of elites as only one of the elements of mobilization, Dunn (1972, 15) considered ideational leaders crucial because of their impact on the discourse. However, it was only the Iranian revolution that made the cultural approach popular.

Indeed, fifth generation theories focused squarely on the role of ideology in triggering delegitimation. Much of the new approach derived from the withering critique of Skocpol's structuralism. Although Skocpol (1982) subsequently admitted that the Iranian revolution changed her mind, her detractors continued to hammer her. They accused her of a Marxist disregard for human agency and of creating sweeping generalizations (Sewell 1985; Colburn 1994, 9). In what became the standard of the fifth generation, one scholar wrote that the focus on culture is essential because "it provides an ideational foundation for structure and institutions" (Kimmel 1990, 190).

THE NATURE OF THE DELEGITIMATION DISCOURSE: SYMBOLS AND SUBSTANCE

While enormous energy has been expanded on defining trigger conditions, little attention has been devoted to discursive practices. Research indicates that the legitimacy discourse proceeds on two distinctive levels: the concrete and the symbolic. Symbolic meanings are much more difficult to understand than the more "tangible" ones because "every symbol stands for something other than itself." *Condensation symbols*, which condense "patriotic pride, promises of future greatness" and other esoteric messages are particularly difficult to decipher (Edelman 1985, 6–12).

Discerning symbolic meaning can be especially vexing for outside analysts. Symbols are steeped in foreign culture or indigenous subculture and can create an impression of "irrationality." American observers have often wondered why groups nurture what seems like obscure historical grievances or revoke a glorious mythical past. Action based on symbols can be equally difficult to interpret. As one scholar noted, meaning may be situated in "any number of historical sequences from the recollected past of the agent, so that different features of that action may be responses or sequels to quite different pasts" (MacIntyre 1973).

The discursive practices of delegitimation can include symbols of more than one ontological community. These "enclave" groups, as Douglas (1992, 108) called them, are either pushed into a marginal position or can work through subterranean processes to undermine the dominant belief system. Much of Christian proselytizing was accomplished behind the pagan edifice of Rome (Gieryn 1983). The spread of fundamentalism in Iran went virtually unnoticed because its symbolic cues escaped observers who were focused on the study of the "rational" cognitive realm of discourse.

Students of symbolic politics offer a number of strategies for decoding an evolving legitimacy crisis. One strategy calls for a closer scrutiny of what is frequently written off as the "irrational" aspects of discourse. After analyzing sources of predictive failure, studies found that experts enforce their own sense of competence by discarding seemingly "irrational" information. This habit stems from the Western instinct to assume that truth is "hierarchical, unidirectional" and based on "homogenistic" logic (Michael 1985; Maruyama 1973; 1974). Another strategy calls for a focus on deceit, deception conspiracy theories and other "irrational" elements that exist in many cultures or subcultures. None of these phenomena are easily discernable since deceit, deception and bad faith are linguistically "nonmarked," that is, they use the same linguistic code as truthful communication. Even if there is a commitment to fidelity, distortions can set in because facts and interpretations are routinely mixed in narration of political reality (Anderson 1986; Sexton 1986).

Such communication lapses explain how fanciful information spreads in a society. Whether originating in bona fide news or stemming form deliberate lying or forgery, sensationalism and gossip spread it around. Conspiracy theories are particularly common in societies afflicted with powerful historical traumas; they also appeal to powerless minorities. Experts caution that outside observers may have a difficult time dealing with such cultural undercurrents. The so-called "emic," namely native explanations of political reality are rooted in particularistic chains of causation that make little overt sense. Dismissing them as "irrational" may obscure vital elements in the legitimation discourse as the Iranian case demonstrates.

A third strategy involves tracking political affairs and scandals. Such occurrences are normally studied in their historical context, but methodologically, affairs and scandals are *nonroutine* power struggles, which occur when individuals or a group violate core norms. A frequently used example, the Dreyfus affair, although ostensibly dealing with anti-Semitism, reflected the efforts to delegitimize religiously based membership norms in France (Yanai 1990). Corruption scandals reflect a growing reluctance to regard public positions as remunerative means for personal enrichment. At a deeper level, they may indicate the growing acceptance of legal-rational legitimacy that calls for a separation between the private and public spheres. Scandals that involve executive secrecy and wheeling-dealing signal a tightening of norms over the process of governance and, ultimately, a distrust of the authority system.

Two variants of this strategy are particularly fruitful in tracking the legitimacy discourse in closed societies. One is the analysis of witch-hunts and purges, which are akin to medieval persecutions against those who challenged the "sacred" dogma. The "unmasking" and purge seek to remove the actual or potential carriers of the offending norms. Paradoxically, the attendant controversy often helps to spread the challenged beliefs (Goodin 1981). The other involves an examination of sanctioned and non-sanctioned debates among academics and intellectuals. It is now clear that the "*glasnost*" period in the Soviet Union was ushered in by a seemingly obscure academic debate about problems of communism. Instead of the orthodox explanations of economic difficulties as "vestiges of capitalism," corruption, poor management and antagonism between workers and the party were acknowledged. In an equally esoteric development, the Soviet Academy of Science formally rehabilitated Nikolai Kondratieff, the brilliant economist whose work on the long cycles theory of capitalism sent him to the Gulag. At that time virtually no one noticed that a sacred Marxist dogma was revised to allow for the possibility—as Kondratieff had argued—that capitalism is "self-regulating rather than self-destructing" (Fuhrman 1988).

THE TIMETABLE OF THE DELEGITIMATION DISCOURSE: CONTINUOUS AND REVOLUTIONARY CHANGE

The spirited debate about triggers of delegitimation has touched only indirectly on the timetable of change. *Continuous* change is easier to predict, especially in an open society. Such change is associated with the epistemic notion of a "teleological generation," defined as people similarly located in the historical process who share a unifying experience. As new generations come of political age, this common experience becomes fragmented and new norms and values are introduced. Most of this change is subterranean, giving rise to the concept of a "silent revolution." Key (1955), in his classic study, found that "critical" and realigning elections are driven by "teleological generations," which replace each other. In what is perhaps the most sophisticated study of its kind, Butler and Stokes (1971) demonstrated how consecutive cohorts in Britain "morphed" the party system from a conservative to a liberal-socialist mode.

Spatial theories of electoral behavior explain how such movements occur. Accordingly, parties occupy a space, i.e. a cluster of normative claims and their operational policies in one or more dimension of the legitimacy matrix (Budge, Crewe and Farlie 1976). As norms change, parties that are associated with a "losing space" shrivel or disappear, whereas others reformulate their position to fit more closely the new beliefs. Still other parties are created around newly legitimized claims. Conservative parties that were in a long decline have recently revived because norms of redistributive egalitarianism had waned. To compete for the newly opened "conservative" space, socialist parties had to reconfigure as the New Democrats or New Labor. Green parties sprung up around the claims that validate environmental integrity.

In contrast to incremental transformation, revolutionary change is telescoped into a relatively short and dramatic period. LaBarre (1971) used Kuhn's concept of a scientific revolution to explain that during a revolution, key legitimizing principles are discarded and a new paradigm is formed. Swidler (1986) described the two modes as "settled" and "unsettled lives." In the former, the dominant belief system, though changing in increments, serves as a guide for role scenarios and actions. In the latter, a competing vision emerges, forcing the society to make paradigmatic choices between the old and the new. One scholar wrote that during revolutionary times, "the intellectual framework that sustains a pre-vailing system is widely scrutinized" (Colburn 1994, 90).

These and other studies have analyzed the actual onset of revolutionary ac-tivity. The discussion of trigger conditions makes clear that psychological dis-comfort matures overtime, leading to the "spark and cinder" stage. The "spark," or more precisely the accelerator, is generated by a variety of incidents, either planned or accidental, which range from acts of symbolic defiance by individuals to natural and man-made disasters. Common accelerators involve food rioting in wake of austerity measures, mass religious celebrations, famines, earthquakes and wars (Bienen and Gersovitz, 1986; Betts and Huntington, 1985–86). The resulting unraveling of the social order leads to the questioning of the compe-tence of authorities and facilitates the assault on the ancien regime.

Once disturbances begin, mass mobilization plays a large part in the process of change. At the most visible level, crowds act as a catalyst for delegitimation. Starting with Gustav LaBonne, studies of mob behavior have noted that crowds act in a seemingly chaotic, "irrational" and "nonnormative" way (Kimmel 1990, 67–68). However, this chaotic destructiveness is aimed at the "representative images" of the collective belief system (Canetti 1962, 19). Rational choice schol-ars observed that mob settings encourage high-risk taking, which, in turn, en-hance the credibility of the challengers.

Revolutionary developments alter the usual rules of discourse in two ways. First, there is a change in modes of social learning. During normal times social learning is slow, or "single looped:" during turbulent times it becomes fast and creative, or "double looped" (Argyris and Schon 1978). Not incidentally, the "double loop" learning is also present during panics, fashion fads and other mass "crazes." Second, the revolutionary discourse upsets the natural balance between the cognitive and affective elements of peoples' relation to the political order. Normally, both cognition and affective loading color the way individuals per-ceive the regime. During a revolution affective loading in the discourse in-creases, the cognitive parts become simplistic, negative rather than positive goals are emphasized, formulaic solutions are offered and complex issues are reduced to catchy slogans. The struggle is often represented as the battle between the forces of light and the forces of darkness (Green 1984; Farhi 1990). Some refer to this discursive pattern as "collective effervescence," a category that fits events as disparate as messianic movements and the French Revolution (Schmookler 1984, 208).

Others describe it as a period of *liminality* which occurs at points of transition where "all previous standards and modes are subject to criticism." A feeling of "communitas"—a state of perceived equality—where roles and status are free-floating enhances liminality (Pilskin 1980, 13). Liminality explains why crucial elites can mobilize large masses of people in a relatively short period of time. Charismatic leaders are especially effective in "short-circuiting" the cognitive components of the discourse and manipulating emotions and symbols. Such charismatic legitimacy causes a "group of people or an entire nation to fall under the binding spell of a leader," who presents himself as "God or Savior" (Willner 1984, 20). What is more, the actual ideology of such crucial elites may or may not have a true popular following. As Dunn (1972, 236) put it, "revolutions are supported by many who would not have supported them had they had a clear understanding of what the revolution were in fact to bring about."

Given these dynamics, prediction in a revolutionary period is next to impossible. One observer likened revolutions to an avalanche, "the release of enormous forces moving vast masses through space" (Dunn 1972, 3–4). Finding a way to model such events engaged scholars who were critical of the linear approach. Drawing on the behavior of complexity, instability and randomness, Prigogine and Stengers (1984, 106) argued that certain types of thermodynamic processes may provide a reasonable analogy of social reality. Thermodynamic systems include the concept of entropy, which is at the core of a process of conservation and reversibility. Growing entropy in the system indicates an increase of disorder. At a certain point, known as the "threshold of stability," the system reaches a "bifurcation point," that is, a stage in which it has to choose between two spatial distributional paths. In political terms, such a bifurcation results in a stochastic choice between diametrically opposed directions (Cnudde 1973; Ward 1983).

Another promising analogue comes from *progressive biological systems* theory. A progressive system is built on *homeorhesis*, a pattern of change through flow. In a homeorhetic system there are numerous pathways, or *chreods*, each with a different type of stability built into it. Changes start from a single chreod, depicted as a valley that branches further down the road, creating new chreods. This process will repeat itself, creating an *epigenic* landscape full of branched pathways. It is normally impossible to predict the time and the direction of chreodic branching. What is more, just before the actual branching occurs, there is a brief *competence period*, when the system is competent to bloc change. Once this brief window of opportunity closes, uncontrollable branching will start (Waddington 1977).

A third model is based on *catastrophe theory*, developed in the 1970s to account for sudden and dramatic changes in the behavior of systems, which previously functioned in a continuous and smooth way. Mathematical modeling indicates that, as a result of unnoticed stimulus, the behavioral surface reaches a cusp where the system becomes bifurcated. It is in this zone that the behavior of the system becomes "inaccessible," that is, impervious to control and susceptible to dramatic changes that can result in diametrically divergent paths of developments (Adelman and Mihn 1982; Landsberger and McDaniel 1976).

These complex models of change have two important implications for tracking political discourse in revolutionary situations. First government intervention, normally in the form of coercion, can only be successful during a certain brief period, before the system becomes "inaccessible." But this window of opportunity is often only recognized *post hoc*. Second, estimating the swirl of ideological debate is very hard. There is little consistency and plenty of contradictory and antagonistic actions. Since in the liminal stage power relations are fluid, estimating the distribution of power is difficult, and quite often misleading. The initial coalition of contenders (moderates) and challengers (radicals) breaks up and branching can occur in a multitude of directions (Farhi 1990, 84; Shain and Linz 1995, 31).

The contours of the new collective belief system will emerge only at the end of the revolutionary process. This end product is normally referred to as consolidation, but from the discursive perspective it can be viewed as *transvaluation*.

THE PROCESS OF TRANSVALUATION: REFORMIST AND RADICAL

Unlike delegitimation, transvaluation has received little attention, resulting in some hazy formulations. Apter (1965, 65–66) described transvaluation as retraditionalization; after a period of flux, "a new coherence of values, institutions and organizations" is expected to emerge. Thoenes (1966, 127) stated that demarcating the border between the old and the new system involves a certain degree of arbitrariness. Essentially, it requires a judgment about how much of the legitimacy matrix has changed. The large literature on "continuity and change" is a testimony to the problem. Revolutions normally result in a total transformation: a change of power relations, structures, processes and actors (Brecher and Jones 1986). As the Iranian case makes clear, such radical alterations follow change in one or more dimensions of legitimacy. The more recent collapse of the Soviet Union was predicated on changing norms of membership/territory, the authority system and the distributive justice system.

Radical transvaluation presents methodological problems. Revolutionary leadership is normally quick to transform the legal and institutional structure of the society and pursue other structural goals. Transforming peoples' attitudes is more difficult, especially since the revolutionary discourse masks a divergence of norms and values. Intense efforts to create a widespread allegiance for the new belief system take the form of mass resocialization. The Bolshevik drive to create a "new Soviet man," Kamal Ataturk's efforts to destroy religious beliefs and the campaign of Iranian fundamentalists to instill piety come to mind. Yet, given the somewhat esoteric nature of the collective belief system the true extent of transvaluation is difficult to assess. Selbin (1993, 20, 23) warned that a postrevolutionary ideological consolidation should not be conflated with legitimacy or hegemony. He proposed to use a legitimacy continuum that runs from a complete and enthusiastic adoption of the new norms to a grudging and tacit acceptance.

The absence of agreed upon norms for assessing the true hold of validity norms, and—by implication—the legitimacy of regimes, have engendered a heated debate. Many scholars take the Weberian position that as long as the population regards the regime as legitimate, it is legitimate. On the surface, this approach assures objectivity because in Weber's term it amounts to an *objective* report about peoples' beliefs. However, others argue that the ability of external observers to make an objective report on the legitimacy of a system is limited. As one scholar noted, observers make *judgments* about beliefs in legitimacy of norms (Beetham 1991, 13). Because legitimacy norms vary across time and space, social scientists have no universal standards of evaluation. As a result, scholars tend to project their own normative-paradigmatic expectations on the discourse of the societies that they study. Such expectations are both subtle and powerful; they shape the field of inquiry and dictate the research strategies. The next chapter will demonstrate that prediction of political change prior to the Iranian revolution was shaped by two powerful paradigms: developmentalism and dependency.

2

Paradigmatic Views of Political Change: Developmentalism vs. Dependency

Even before the United States emerged as a superpower following WWII, the foreign policy community showed a great interest in the study of the future. In fact, post-war planning started a few months after Pearl Harbor. This future orientation was linked to what one observer described "as a kind of unconscious or premonitory sensation that the burden of decisions regarding the future world order" would rest on Washington (Santoro 1992, 34). Forecasting became part and parcel of the perceived need for managing political change around the globe.

As the Cold War took hold, there was an increased sense in Washington that political change in Europe and the underdeveloped world might breed instability and provide an opening for the Soviet Union. The key assumption in American efforts to block communism was that political and economic conditions are linked, thus putting a premium on prosperity and stability. As one senator put it: "with God's help, we will lift Shanghai up, ever up, until it is just like Kansas City" (quoted in Campbell 1971, 178). In the first application of this principle, the State Department devised and executed the Marshall Plan.

While there was confidence that economic aid would stabilize Europe, planners were not entirely sure that a Marshall Plan–style approach would work in underdeveloped countries. The Truman administration enlisted a large number of academics to study economic and political development. Spurred by such seminal figures as Max Milikan and Walt W. Rostow, this collective effort generated the developmental paradigm. Alternatively referred to as modernization theory, the paradigm focused on the process of nation building and the stages of economic development. It found its way into President Kennedy's Alliance for Progress plan for Latin America and the counterinsurgency policies in Southeast Asia, among others. Indeed, critics often charged that developmentalism was "increasingly perceived as an arm of American foreign policy" (Gendzier 1985, 23).

However, by the end of the sixties the turmoil in the Third World challenged the premises of modernization. As the failure to predict these adverse trends mounted, the early enthusiasm of foreign policy practitioners was turning into skepticism. One senior State Department official described as "hubris" the nation-building notion "that professors could make bricks without the straw of experience" (Ball 1982, 183). Another critic noted that "we assume à la Hegel, Marx, or W. W. Rostow that the non-Western world would inevitably follow the same development path as us" (Wiarda 1985, 11).

However, it was the *dependencia* movement that offered the most systemic critique of the developmental paradigm. Generated by a group of Latin American scholars, the dependency paradigm was a loose amalgam of Marxist, Leninist and nationalist ideas, which assumed that, once liberated from capitalist and imperialistic constraints, Third World countries will develop into "authentic" and socialist societies. As the agitation over civil rights and the war in Vietnam grew, dependency ideas entered mainstream political science. By the mid-1970s *dependencia* displaced modernization as the main paradigm for analyzing political change.

The following chapter will discuss the contending views of political change embedded in these two paradigms. The choice of the term paradigm, used here interchangeably with "approach," "school of thought" and "movement," does not imply a complete unity of thought. Still, despite the intense divisions that plagued both paradigms, they represent distinctive metatheoretical assumptions as well as ontological and epistemic claims about the nature of political reality and political change.

THE DEVELOPMENTAL VIEW OF CHANGE: LINEAR PROGRESSION TOWARD THE WEST

The developmental paradigm was part of the behavioral movement in American political science. Philosophically, behaviorism was rooted in the Western tradition of historicism, that is, *nomothetic* knowledge that sought to develop general laws for deterministic-repeatable events. The companion assumption held that extrapolating from past trends could predict the future. As one critic noted, the ultimate dream of historicists was to emulate the hard science: "just as astronomy can predict eclipses, it will be possible for sociology to predict revolutions" (Popper 1966, 3).

Such prospects exhilarated the postwar generation of political scientists. Lerner and Laswell (1951) were among the first to stipulate that political scientists would need to anticipate political changes and urged them to develop predicative methods. Other enthusiasts of forecasting would later argue that universities and think tanks are the "nerve centers of society," forming a "consultative commonwealth" of experts that can foresee problems and intervene ahead of time (Dror 1975). Confidence in developing a general theory of political change had run especially high among IR specialists. Singer (1961) contended that such a theory should accurately depict events that have taken place, explain why they took place and be prepared to predict under what conditions similar events will occur in the future.

The developmental paradigm shared with behaviorism a number of simplifying assumptions about political reality. Ontologically, the assumption was that reality is external to people and can be broken up into discreet parts made up of concrete events that are amenable to statistical treatment. Hence, variables that represent change were thought to reside in a particular section of social reality and could be easily isolated. The companion epistemological assumptions held that the political realm is understood and communicated among members of society in the form of "hard" knowledge.

Developmentalists assumed that such knowledge forms a fairly autonomous realm of attitudes that can be readily identified, mostly by manipulating sociologically meaningful categories of experience such as levels of education, income or occupation. As for human nature, they postulated that environment shapes individuals in a mechanistic and even deterministic way.

Three related meta-assumptions were at the core of developmental theory. First, it was held that universal laws of change could be developed because human beliefs are based upon certain cognitive processes that are invariant in all societies. Among them were the linguistic concepts of conjunction, disjunction and negation, which—along with notions of implication and equivalence— form the backbone of formal logic (D'Amico 1988). Second, it was surmised that all humans share the Newtonian concept of time. Characteristic of the secular West, this concept envisages time as spatialized, its passage symbolized by movements along a continuum that forms a linear progression from an initial state to an open future. However, such a model was not well suited to traditional societies whose perception of time, as in the Chinese case, is cyclical. The Judeo-Christian model is conceived in linear terms, but has a closed future; the time trajectory has a profound moral significance, as it leads to Redemption in Judaism and the Second Coming in Christianity (Sivin 1966; Falk 1988).

Third, there was an assumption of universal rationality. Logic or rationality is at the core of the predictive behavior: It involves *postulated rationality*, that is, ideas about how people would act, if they were rational. The mathematician and philosopher Danielle Bernouli pointed out that "if all men, being rational would behave in the same way under similar circumstances," it would be possible to deduce the fundamental laws which govern human behavior (Miller and Starr 1967, 47).

Unfortunately, universal rationality is difficult to square with cultural-religious traditions. Judeo-Christianity, as well as Islam, equates rationality with the human capacity to ask questions about the meaning of self and how it relates to an "ultimate reality" derived from God and the Truth (Cauthen 1969, 75). It is much closer to the Enlightenment philosophy, which created a vision of an autonomous individual cast upon a morally unpurposive environment. To meet this new existential contingency, Enlightenment invested people with a "natural rationality"; by using scientific methods they were said to understand the vast but fundamentally ordered and empirically available universe. Paul Tillich (1977, 71) described this secular rationality as a type of initiation into the human race—"human beings become human by participating in universal reason." When used to predict change, this rationality was translated into "reasonableness" and took on the paradigmatic assumptions of the scholars.

It was this secular definition of rationality that scholars used to predict political change. There was a particular prejudice against religious beliefs that were often considered "irrational." To conform to the tenets of epistemic realism, any reference to a supernatural reality was expunged or treated as a pathological aberration.

Given such simplifying assumptions about reality it was not difficult for developmentalists to postulate that societies move from "primitive" (underdeveloped) stages to more "advanced" form patterned on the secularized, democratic and industrialized Western nation-state. The Parsonian-Eastonian system theories greatly facilitate this view. The West was considered to be a positive agent of change, with new technologies, skills and values "diffusing to developing societies." Change was said to be incremental and, according to the well-financed Committee on Comparative Development of the Social Research Council, orderly and peaceful (Binder et al. 1971).

Since the problem of nation building was high on the developmental agenda, scholars tackled the issue of membership/territory legitimacy first. By and large, tribalism and ethnic sensitivity were consigned to the "residual category" of traditional society. Deutsch (1953; 1963) linked levels of socieconomic development to a decline in primordial forms of attachment to measure the actual progress in nation building. Deutsch devised a series of quantitative indices such as levels of literacy, rates of communication and industrialization. Another measure was derived from Lijphart's (1968) celebrated work on consociational democracy in the Netherlands. Lijphart asserted that deeply divided societies like Cyprus and Lebanon were moving in the direction of a consociational nation-state.

Developmentalists were also greatly interested in the norms that undergird the authority system of different societies. Because of their secularism, scholars surmised that societies would shed traditional-numinous legitimacy and accept a rational-legal one. During the heydays of behaviorism it became common to view this progress as inevitable. Leading liberal theologians added weight to this outlook. For instance, Harvey Cox (1965, 63) argued that modern man is becoming pragmatic and profane and wastes no time thinking about "ultimate or religious questions." By the time Stark and Glock (1968) published their influential book on the subject, the notion that numinous-religious legitimacy, especially of the fundamentalist variety, was "primitive" and doomed to pass from history had become widespread. According to one observer, fundamental-ists were treated as a "bizarre" spectacle and "denizens of the zoo" (Warner 1979).

Fired by their nomothetical zeal, developmentalists turned these ideas into a linear law of transition. One Middle East expert used the metaphor of "shattered glass" to describe the break with traditional legitimacy; he asserted that the Arab professional classes were articulating new rational-legality claims (Halpern 1963). Another leading scholar, in a book about legitimacy in Arab countries published a year before the Iranian revolution, found evidence of the growing "irrelevance of Islamic standards and criteria" (Hudson 1977, 17). In a 1963 conference sponsored by the American University Field Staff, American scholars overrode some Islam experts who argued that religious sentiments in the Middle East were still strong, to officially conclude that the "secularization process is fundamental" (Silvert 1964, 103).

There was less agreement whether this linear progression would lead to a civic-democratic authority system. In their famous study Almond and Verba (1965) purported to show that societies go through stages of parochial, subject and civic cultures, a view that was popular among other developmentalists (Lip-set 1960). But some observers were less sanguine. Geertz (1964) cautioned that traditional-numinous and parochial norms might successfully resist the process of rationalization inherent in modernization. Huntington (1968) challenged the notion that political development is linear. He warned almost prophetically about the decay and chaos to come. These and other critics pointed out that, histori-cally, there have been numerous "mosaic" regimes, which have reflected mixed validity claims. Turner (1974, 151, 168) drew attention to the fact that the con-cept of rationality and rationalization is uniquely European, and warned of the increase of religious sentiments in Turkey.

Finally, there were scholars who espoused the "corporatist" model of political change. After looking at the economic roots of regimes, these observers con-cluded that the "peculiar set of circumstances" which led to the emergence of liberal democracies in Europe no longer exist in the twentieth century. Schmitter (1971), a leading exponent of corporatism, argued that many countries, espe-cially in Latin America, which industrialized late, are stuck in the "corporatists" model of political development.

The heated debates on the authority system focused attention on the principles of distributive justice. Initially, scholars believed that Third World countries would evolve a market economy. Rostow (1964) the author of the developmental "Bible," *The States of Economic Growth*, argued that this phase would follow the so-called "take-off" stage. In terms of legitimacy discourse, the assumption was that, as societies progress along a linear trajectory, ascriptive claims would be dropped in favor of market meritocracy. From the American perspective, markets offered the best antidote to the high levels of inequality that existed in ascriptive-traditional societies. In making this assumption experts were encour-aged by the pioneering work of Kuznet (1955), who showed that, as the level of development rises, inequality declines. Kuznet's research spurred a virtual cottage industry of studies that sought to analyze the relation between stages of development and social inequality. In the end, the debate among experts became so complex that, depending on the data and the study, it was possible to find support for the seemingly contradictory conclusions that increased equality was either a precondition for a market economy or its product (Lenski 1966; Azar and Farah 1981; Kanbur 1979; Elsenhans 1983).

The feverish effort to eradicate inequality was spurred by the growing concern that large social differences were conducive to Communist-inspired upheavals. There was also an underlying desire to prove that markets can deal with the problem of nonequitable distribution of wealth. While the debate between capitalism and communism was certainly not new, the emergence of the dependency paradigm in the sixties put the developmentalists on the defensive.

THE DEPENDENCY VIEW OF CHANGE: LINEAR PROGRESSION TOWARD A SOCIALIST UTOPIA

The dependency paradigm was developed by a number of largely Latin American scholars who sought to discredit developmentalism and the American foreign policy that powered it. Raul Prebish, a Latin American economist associated with the Economic Commission for Latin America (ECLA), is credited with developing the dependency perspective, along with Fernando Henrique Cardoso, Andre Gundar Frank, Enzo Faletto, Samir Amin and others. Dependencia is not a coherent body of theory and its constituent elements—orthodox dependency, unorthodox dependency, analytical dependency, heretical dependency, bargaining dependency and world-system—occasionally clash and contradict each other (Packenham 1992, 11).

On the common side, Marxist and neo-Marxist concepts heavily influenced dependency scholarship's view of political change. The dependencistas reversed the evolutionary equation: Rather than considering Western democracies as a source of progress worth emulating, they regarded them as the roots of Third World "peripheral" position and economic backwardness. Dependencistas noted that "terms like 'distorted,' 'backward' and 'peripheral' described a Third World that was not simply a rung or two below the West on the evolutionary ladder, but whose very configuration was a product of the West's action" (Barnett 1996, 112).

Dependency advocates posited that true development could be achieved only by undermining the American view of economic policy and distributive justice. As one of them put it, the American-European view of "economic growth first, redistribution later" does not fit Latin American desire to assure that growth should bring equity in income distribution (Coleman 1977, 7–8). These arguments were based on the view that socialism, not capitalism, is the ultimate destiny of human change. Thus, to the doubt that the Western path to development is a desirable one was added the deterministic view that it is not a possible one (Brown 1985).

What enabled dependency scholars to take such a stand were their paradigmatic core assumptions, a somewhat incongruent mix of *radical structuralism* and *radical humanism*. Ontologically, radical structuralism is essentially positivist and nomothetic. But, unlike behaviorism, this view assumed that human behavior cannot be understood by a simple examination of "individual motives and intentions." Rather, radical scholars followed the Marxist notion that once structures are established, people unconsciously reproduce them "in spite of their repressive characteristics" (Little 1985). In this sense, capitalism and its global projections, colonialism and imperialism, were forms of "false consciousness," which were destined to disappear.

Radical humanism was based on a subjective ontology of nominalism. It was assisted by an antipositivist epistemology and buttressed by a voluntaristic rather than deterministic view of human nature. Methodologically ideographic, radical humanism relied heavily on subjective states of "consciousness" and "potentiality" as the basis for radical critique of society (Burrell and Morgan 1985, 34–35). Dependency scholars frequently attacked developmentalists as "butterfly collectors" who set up categories and laws, and denounced the idea of cumulative social science (Cardoso 1977; Packenham 1992, 254). Paul Feyerabend (1975), who developed an elaborate neo-Marxist critique of positivism, called it a "rebellion against method." By embracing this rebellion, dependency scholars "liberated" themselves from an empirically based social inquiry. One critic noted that "a moralist need no evidence other than his senses to judge something right or wrong, and no elaborate scientific calculus to ascertain what the proper course of action should be" (Kadushin 1974, 163).

Unencumbered by empirical concerns, dependency scholars used a Marxist inspired historical-structural analysis that purported to illuminate basic historical trends. Applied to the Third World, the forecast asserted that change could only occur in two forms: transformation from one kind of dependency to another kind of dependency and from dependency to socialism. The premise here was that, ultimately, all countries are destined to reach a socialist "golden age" (Cardoso and Faletto 1979, 173–177; Cardoso 1977). Cuba was most often mentioned as a possible model for such a socialist utopia, followed by China and, sometimes, Vietnam (Packenham 1992, 30; Fagen 1978, 299).

These assertions were impossible to refute because dependency scholars used *epistemic holism*, or *nonfalsification* to ward off criticism. In this view, empirical data could be used to support dependency claims, but never to reject its postulates, which were held to be "true by definition." Not incidentally, Marxism considers it "vulgar" to falsify theories through empirical observations. This created double standards: dependency advocates demanded that their scholarship be evaluated in the context of its "place in the historical struggle," but all criticism, "no matter how nonpolemical and accurate" was accused of being hostile and politically motivated (Packenham 1992, 15, 225). That dependency should adopt epistemological holism was not surprising given the fact that it also advocated the politicization of scholarship. In contrast to behaviorism that strove to separate scholarship and politics, dependencistas followed the Gramscian imperative that scholarship is "an agent of struggle" to be applied to the discursive venues of a society, primarily by bringing a moral advocacy to bear on the prevalent norms of legitimacy.

The formidable dependency apparatus was used to debunk the developmental analysis of political change. On the membership/territory issue dependencistas criticized Western scholarship for the notion that primordial allegiances are at the heart of modern day cleavages in traditional societies. They suggested that primordial rivalries were manufactured by Western colonial powers. Galtung (1971) contended that "imperialism is a system that splits collectivities and rearranges their parts according to its own interests." Others held colonial "administrative penetration" responsible for inflaming primordial sentiments (Newbury 1983). World-theorists implied that once capitalism and imperialism were eliminated, people would legitimize inclusive norms of membership to form a world alliance (Wallerstein 1975; Falk 1976b). To prove the validity of this contention, dependency scholars pointed to the absence of ethnic strife in communist societies.

In terms of authority system, dependency theorists shared the conviction of the developmentalists that traditional-numinous validity claims are outmoded and destined to fade from history. However, they showed little enthusiasm for the belief that such a linear process will result in a Western-style democratic rationality. On the contrary, many described the apparatus of democracy—elections, political parties and legislatures—as mere "formalism," or worse, an elite mechanism to oppress the masses. As befits holism and radical humanism, dependencistas were fond of vague schemes of popular participation. They spoke of "real democracy," "institutions and processes that serve people" and of channels to "express authentic beliefs." Conversely, they doubted that parliamentary representation could reflect the deeper human need for "consciousness formation" (Evans 1979, 48; Cardoso and Faletto 1979, xxiv; Galtung 1976). Revolutionary upheavals, most notably in Cuba, were seen as a "radical humanistic underpinning of participatory democracy" (Vogelgesang 1974, 32).

While casting doubts on democratic formalism, dependency writers extolled the virtues of "substantive democracy," a euphemism for a society where egalitarian principles of distributive justice would triumph. However, their vision of social justice went beyond the standard precepts of Marxism to embrace the human needs philosophy. Johan Galtung (1976) and John Burton (1979; 1985), leading human needs advocates, argued that, in addition to equality and social justice, personal growth and fulfillment, nonalienating work, ecological balance and other "quality of experience" factors should be emphasized. Galtung drew this list from a World Indicators Program (WIP) project established by the In-

ternational Political Science Association in 1973 to counter developmental reliance on purely economic indicators of growth (Lawler 1995, 136).

Dependency advocates described how this socialist end game would be
achieved. To begin with, they rejected the "realist" view of international relations in which actors can choose their future economic and political direction.
Galtung (1964; 1971), in his highly influential theory of structural aggression,
accused the West of practicing "cultural imperialism" against the less developed
countries. Far from being sovereign and free, these societies were said to have
validated capitalist norms under coercion. Dependencistas pointed out that the
North-South division of labor not just perpetuates but increases the large social
inequalities in the Third World.

A number of studies that found a "consistent and significant" correlation between international dependency—defined as investment penetration, reliance on
foreign capital and operation of multinational corporations (MNCs)—and the
level of income inequality provided empirical support for this assertion (Chase-
Dunn 1975; Bornschier and Chase-Dunn, 1978). Indeed, these and others scholars considered the multinational corporations largely responsible for the dependency relations between North and South. Cardoso (1973, 146–149) wrote that
the MNCs had changed the "dynamic basis of the productive system" and gave
"groups expressing the basic interests and modes of organization of international
capitalism" a disproportional amount of power."

To eradicate these inequalities, a number of strategies were offered. American
Marxist scholars argued that domestic revolution should be followed by expropriation of Western investment (Baran 1957; Baran and Sweezy 1966). Others
wanted to change the international economic order, which, in their view, was a
"multi-headed octopus with powerful tentacles constantly sucking wealth from
the weakened peripheries" (Banks 1985). Prebish wanted to establish the New
International Economic Order (NIEO) to challenge the principles of "global
economic liberalism associated with the North," thus affirming the basic conflict
between the North and South (Packenham 1992, 193; Kubalkova and Cruickshank 1981, 98). Prebisch suggested that the MNCs should sell their equity to
local investors, but other dependencistas recommended nationalization. One
scholar wrote that property should be seen as enjoyed conditionally, upon fulfillment of terms specified by the state (Coleman 1977, 16).

Initially, dependency scholarship was limited to the fringes of American political science. However, within two decades the dependency paradigm penetrated mainstream political science. Observers noted that dependency changed
"substantive and epistemological parameters of scholarly thinking" on Latin
America, development theory and other topics. This influence was so profound
that one scholar wrote that the "concept of development is now widely scorned"
and that "many writers doubt that the Western path is a desirable path" (Brown
1985; Payne 1984, 1; Packenham 1992, 238).

HEADED TOWARD CONVERGENCE: REDEFINING THE
DIRECTION OF POLITICAL CHANGE

The spread of dependency ideas should be seen in the context of the larger societal and foreign policy crisis in America. Developmental theory was a projection of American optimism that political change could be managed and molded into a "desirable," that is, Western direction. However, by the late sixties it became quite clear that none of the paradigmatic assumptions worked: tribal and ethnic rivalries were tearing many societies apart and brutal dictatorships sprouted where democracy was expected to flourish. By 1976, just in Latin America alone, most of the countries were under military rule. One commentator observed that it became obvious that American effort will not create "a lot of little Americas around the world" (Campbell 1971, 181; Farcau 1996, 14). The economies of Third World countries were also in trouble; state controls, corruption, nepotism and mismanagement by *kleptocrats* had stifled market-merit legitimacy (Ben-Dor 1974).

The fact that developmentalism failed in its predictions triggered widespread and often devastating criticism. One of the detractors decried what one scholar called the "projective fallacy," the idea that "our experience describes the likely course others will follow" (Shafer 1988, 68). Another criticized the "eight pernicious myths of the 19th century science" which enabled political scientists to assume that "social change" takes societies through easily identifiable stages of development (Tilly 1984). Yet another lamented that in the Third World we "expected democracy" and "merit" and got authoritarian regimes and ascriptive economies instead (Wiarda 1985, 29). These and other observers felt that Americans were ethnocentric and naïve, and that they had a misplaced faith in modernity whose "roots are shallow in many societies." One critic wrote that Americans believed that "transplanting Lockean institutions was like rooting ivy from cuttings—quick and simple" (Bull 1966; Der Derian 1996; Hatcher 1990, 297).

Perhaps the most corrosive critique came from the intellectual left. Herbert Marcuse, Max Horkheimer and others member of the critical theory group associated with the Frankfurt School attacked the positivist philosophy that underpinned the behavioral movement. Critical theorists viewed American social sciences as "naïve," "pedestrian," "hypnotized by facts" and "intellectually lazy." They mocked the idea that data is "out there" ready for "immediate interpretation" and ridiculed the myth of scientific objectivity (Diggins 1992, 347; Hughes 1983).

Unable to withstand such harsh criticism, the developmental paradigm succumbed to dependencia. In a subtle but powerful shift in mainstream political science the behavioral tradition of "value free" science was put on the defensive and social advocacy took over. Bay (1965) was one of the first to urge the study of human needs and dignity, followed by Easton's (1969) call to make the discipline more relevant to "real" political concerns. In an extraordinary about-face, Easton, who conceded that behaviorism conceals "an ideology based upon empirical conservatism," called for a "postbehavioral revolution;" he urged his colleagues to focus on "contemporary needs" rather than methodological sophistication. Alvin Gouldner (1970, 192), a leading critic of mainstream sociology, welcomed such views since, in his opinion, they sought to invalidate the Parsonian ban on addressing the question of "where moral norms themselves come from."

Dependency thinking began to alter some of the most cherished notions of the developmental era. First to be reexamined was the systemic notion of political change. Gouldner (1959; 1970, 351–352) used Marxist concepts to attack the Parsonian social system with its "endless capacity" to deny radical change. Dahrendoff's (1959) old work on class and class conflict became a favorite in the "order-conflict" debate, which made such staples of radical sociology like "contradictions," "modes of domination" and "deprivation" common fare in political science (Burrell and Morgan 1985, 10–19).

The issue of economic direction was especially affected. As noted, developmentalism assumed that, in spite of a certain amount of social inequality, market principles were a legitimate, and, indeed, a desirable direction of political change. This is not to say that capitalism was universally accepted. Following the New Deal, Keynesian views of what distributive justice should be had pervaded American academy (Root 1955, 246, 255–264). Antimarket sentiments were further inflamed when John K. Galbraith (1957) published his *Affluent Society* and David Bazelon (1963) followed with *Paper Economy*. Both of these influential works maintained that capitalism had become morally unacceptable because it served the "haves" and neglected the poor. The Christian theologian Harvey Cox (1965) wrote that the Protestant ethic of "work-duty-money-salvation" should be discarded and basic income guaranteed for everyone so that people would be able to enjoy the "play" principle. However, it was left to John Rawls in his immensely popular work *A Theory of Justice* (1971) to boost the legitimacy of dependency-inspired notions of distributive justice. Although Rawls did not advocate socialism, he felt that economic growth should be regulated so as to maximize the well-being of the poorest members of the society. Rawlsian principles, which spread rapidly in the discipline, imposed an important normative limit on what should be a *morally acceptable level of inequality*.

The perception that egalitarian norms are more legitimate than other forms of wealth distribution spurred a large empirical effort to find how "real people" view this issue. An early round of studies seemed to bear out the assumption that people considered the equality of outcomes more fair and thus more legitimate than equality of opportunity (Deutsch 1975; 1985; Jasso and Rossi 1977; Jasso 1980; Florig 1986). Undoubtedly, the most celebrated piece of evidence came from what Kinder and Kiewiet (1979) called *sociotrophic* voting, namely that, in casting their vote, people respond to larger social concerns rather than narrow self-interests. Whether consciously or not, many of these studies also reflected the view that support for redistribution principles will continue to increase. A review of voting studies found that all top experts predicted that Johnson's election in 1964 would usher in a new Democratic realignment (Sundquist 1983, 2). This consensus was so strong that Kevin Phillips (1968), who predicted a repudiation of egalitarianism and a Republican realignment, was virtually ignored.

The effort to prove that "real people" had legitimized egalitarian notions of distributive justice reflected the then-popular theme of the "coming legitimacy crisis of capitalism" popularized by Jurgen Habermas (1975), a neo-Marxist thinker. The German philosopher, who became highly influential in the United States, asserted that, once capitalism runs out of "pay-offs," people would turn against it and embrace socialism. A number of highly pessimistic studies on "democratic overload" seemed to bear out this prediction (Crozier, Huntington and Watanuki 1975; King 1975). More to the point, there was a growing agreement that market tenets should not be applied to developing countries. Scholars noted that the concept of a "rational market man" was a product of the Anglo-Protestant ethic and could be offensive to other cultures (Palmer 1985, 112; Visker 1988). India, which preferred egalitarianism to growth, was seen by many as an appropriate model for Third World development (Frankel 1978).

With the growing emphasis on economic equality, there was a subtle but fundamental shift in the way political scientists evaluated the legitimacy of authoritarian regimes. The new orthodoxy called for a distinction between authoritarian rulers who presided over ascriptive or capitalist economies and those who strove to create a more egalitarian system. The former were often labeled "reactionary" or "coercive," whereas the latter were described as "progressive." Packenham (1973, 275–276), a self-described dependency follower-turned-critic, argued that any Third World regime which promotes "substantive economic and social egalitarianism" should be regarded as legitimate, even if democratic standards are absent. Thus, it became common to consider Castro or Nasser as more legitimate than Somoza or the shah of Iran. One critic observed that Cuba was perceived as a "human society" that had conquered the curse of money and " 'bourgeois' legality" (Diggins 1992, 237). Another critic contended that "moral endorsement of the coercive politics of the Castro regime was predicated on the ... belief that it was designed to remove inequalities" (Hollander 1992, 137).

This shift was accompanied by the growing disenchantment of American academics with their own democratic polity. Barrington Moore (1966, 505–506) was the first serious scholar to introduce a Marxist perspective into developmental theory. His highly acclaimed *Social Origins of Dictatorship and Democracy* argued that Western liberalism had begun "to display many symptoms of obsolescence" and warned against exporting "ethnocentric" systems to other societies. Veteran developmentalists like Apter (1965) took to arguing that "mobilization regimes," "guided democracies" and "people's democracies" should be considered legitimate equivalents of the Anglo-Saxon model.

Not surprisingly, dependency also affected the way in which the legitimacy of communist regimes was evaluated. During the early phase of the Cold War, American scholars denounced totalitarian communism as illegitimate (Friedrich and Brzezinski 1956). To use a then-popular taxonomy of legitimacy, such regimes were considered as "fully repudiated," a reference to their coercive nature (Rose 1969). However, Tucker (1961), a leading Sovietologist, was one of the first to argue for a more "expansive" view of legitimacy. He asserted that, in spite of the fact that the Soviet system is not Western, it enlists "masses of people" into various politically meaningful, albeit guided activities. By the early 1970s, the perceived legitimacy of the Soviet Union became even more nuanced. Hough (1973, 164–165; 1977) asserted that the "complex system of checking and counter-checking" involves a good deal of citizens' participation in administrative life. What is more, he believed that this participation had the same relatively "narrow class base it has in the West." Hough, an influential Soviet expert, claimed that under Brezhnev the "Soviet leadership almost seems to have made the Soviet Union closer to the spirit of the pluralistic model of American political science that is the United States."

In a volume devoted to the issue of communist legitimacy, a co-editor wrote that legitimacy should not be equated simply with "positive acceptance or support of the regime" (Rigby 1982, 15). A contributor explained that communism enjoys an "egalitarian-patronage" legitimacy, adding that it provides "centrally defined and guaranteed life strategies for the individual" as well as job security and equitable distribution of wealth. All in all, he found communism to be a "powerful new mode of legitimation accepted by large masses of people in Eastern European countries" (Feher 1982, 65, 74–75). Another study asserted that in the Soviet Union the "values and beliefs of the working class are generally congruent with those of the political elite" (D. Lane 1979). A reviewer chided the authors of a book about blue-collar workers in Eastern Europe for neglecting to emphasize the "high degree of real economic egalitarianism" and full employment policies in the region (Bradley 1983).

Communist regimes in China and the developing world received an even more enthusiastic evaluation. The Committee of Concerned Asian Scholars gave China high marks for its egalitarian ethos. A popular text found that "except for occasional unrest and disaffection, the engagement of individuals in this grand effort of national Communist self-liberation was deep and genuine (Merkl 1967, 485). Many experts asserted that Albania, Vietnam and Yugoslavia enjoy an "authentic" legitimacy (Bialer 1983; Denitch 1976). Above all, it was Cuba that garnered the most rave reviews (Hollander 1981, 251–253).

The spread of dependency thinking in political science did not go unchallenged. Almond (1990, 13–19), a frequent target of dependency advocates, called his critics "ideological propagandists." Other scholars, true to the spirit of behaviorism, tried to test dependency-driven hypotheses. There was a special effort to find whether developing countries had become impoverished under market conditions, or whether American foreign policy promoted the exploitative policies of multinational corporations (Bratton 1982; Weede and Tiefenbach 1981; Gowa 1985). Moreover, studies of Japan and Pacific Rim countries indicated that market economy can be adapted to diverse cultures and even made morally appealing, as the case of Japan demonstrated (Dore 1983).

The failure to verify dependency assertions did little to damage the credibility of the new paradigm. On the contrary, because of the heightened politicization, critics of dependency were often attacked. Soviet experts like Zbigniew Brzezinski and Richard Pipes who refused to accept the legitimacy of communism were labeled "right-wing" or "émigré scholars," a euphemism for personal bias (Barron 1985, 17–21). The dependency imprint was especially strong in Latin American studies, but research on black Africa was also influenced by paradigmatic consideration. Since the continent was high on the "victims quotients" of colonialism, scholars were reluctant to discuss such topics as ethnic violence, corruption, mismanagement and a tradition of political brutality.

The repeated glorification of socialism and the vilification of capitalism and, by implication, Western democracy left the latter holding the unhappy end of the equation. A growing number of studies held that a democratic system masks gross social inequalities and serves only the interests of the few (Parenti 1983). Lane (1985) argued that there was a "doctrinary tension" between democracy and capitalism and worried that the distributive justice system that it represents might be repudiated by people on moral grounds.

Along with the doubts about democracy and market values came the theory that capitalism and socialism are destined to converge. Bogdan Denitch (1979, 8), a leading socialist scholar, contended that the "general optimism [about capitalism] . . . is replaced by an increasing fashionable pessimism." Wolfe (1971; 1978), another convergence advocate, predicted that social democracy would become the only historically inevitable choice. Horowitz (1977, 361) declared that there is "already a common consensus that the ultimate moral goal" of the United States and the Soviet Union are "roughly parallel." In his view, both countries represented an extension of the philosophy of "Enlightenment and Christian rationalism." Others ventured that public ownership in America "is no longer seen as evil" and expressed optimism that social ownership of corporate business will result in greater equality (Stauber 1975; Yunker 1986). The new consensus was so strong that even reluctant observers like Brzezinski and Huntington (1971, 12) surmised that the Soviet Union and the United States would enter into a phase of "mutual discovery." Ironically, the still lingering spirit of behaviorism helped to turn such normative predictions into new "scientific" laws of change. Olaf Helmer (1986), the inventor of the Delphi technique and a top authority on forecasting, was bullish on convergence. He predicted that the Russians would adopt some limited features of market economy and that the Americans would legitimize a broader egalitarian vision.

Observers contended that the spread of a marginal Marxist movement was nothing short of extraordinary. A large number of mainstream scholars were urging openness toward the new paradigm and praised its intellectual virtues

(Packenham 1992, 260; Biersteker 1987, 287–288; Smith 1985). Even those who opposed dependency were resigned to its influence. Holsti (1978), who complained that dependency has more in common with Marxism than International Relations (IR), called for "bridge building." Many commentators credited the intellectual strength of dependency scholarship for its rapid spread in the discipline. Others noted that political scientists were personally susceptible to left wing ideologies.

LEANING TO THE LEFT: THE MYTH AND REALITY OF THE OBJECTIVE SOCIAL SCIENTIST

From the inception of the discipline, social scientists professed their adherence to the Weberian ideal of values-free research and "disinterested motivation." Writing many years later, Shklar (1984, 131) repeated the conventional wisdom that scholars are guardians of the public good and keepers of common rationality.

Yet this idealized self-image has been challenged by a long line of research into political beliefs of social scientists. As early as the twenties, studies found that social scientists were less religious than the general population and were more likely to champion left-wing causes and vote for left-wing candidates. Studies also demonstrated that leftist trends were most pronounced at top academic institutions (Lipset 1959; Ladd and Lipset 1973, 21; Lipset and Ladd 1972a; Lipset and Ladd 1972b; Lipset and Dobson 1972; Ladd and Lipset 1971; Ladd and Lipset, 1975; Wynn 1972; Lipset 1982; Rothman and Lichter 1996). A survey of sociology textbooks in the 1940s found a leftist bias "which was not justified on the basis of scientific data" and a heightened concern for social inequalities (Hobbs 1951, 17, 82, 87, 128–129). Such leftist sentiments were hardly dampened by the McCarthy crusade. One critic noted that, "it was more dangerous for the career of an academic to be a public supporter of McCarthy than a bitter opponent" (Lipset and Dobson 1972, 163). Moreover, the McCarthy backlash stifled legitimate misgivings about communism abroad and neo-Marxism at home, contributing to what became known as the "anti-anti-communism" phenomenon among the American intelligentsia (Lewy 1992).

The expansion of the universities, in which the overall numbers of professors more than doubled between 1960 and 1975, provided positions for a large number of New Left activists. As the number of leftist professors grew, many political science departments developed a pronounced anticonservative bias. Even if the number of openly Marxist and neo-Marxist instructors was much lower that the 10,000 estimated by conservative organizations, "hard core radicals" were said to have secured a respected space on the academic spectrum. By contrast, even moderate conservatives were considered "beyond the pale" (Hollander 1992, 153–154).

Personal beliefs colored academic research in many different ways. First, political scientists tended to portray conservatism as an aberration or feeble mindedness. McClosky (1958, 35), a noted political psychologist, argued that "conservative beliefs are found most frequently among the uninformed, the poorly educated and so far as we can determine, the less intelligent." Others argued that conservatives are "frustrated, maladjusted" or unable to deal with a complex and sophisticated modern world. The possibility that conservatives may have a legitimate grievance against communism or the redistributive policies of the New Deal was not even considered (Nash 1975, 138). The sociologist Daniel Bell (1962) famously predicted the "end of ideology," implying the passing away of religion and conservatism.

Second, many social scientists exhibited a deep commitment to egalitarian norms. They agreed with Michael Harrington that equality and a relatively class-less society should be a desired goal of the political process (Lipset 1959; Becker and Horowitz 1972). Some tried to demonstrate that a classless society is feasible (Spence 1978, 2, 23). The new line of thinking was extremely effective in changing the public discourse on distributive justice. As Majone (1989, 148–149) demonstrated, with little difference in the actual distribution of wealth, in the mid-1960s poverty became a major concern and market-created disparities were criticized.

Third, there was a concerned effort to delegitimize the norms of market economy. Capitalism was critiqued on several grounds: It was seen as a creator of injustice and inequality, promoter of global inequality, destroyer of human bonds and a deformer of the spirit and dignity of the individual (Hollander 1992, 54). The antibusiness Democratic Socialists attracted a large following of political scientists and sociologists, including three former heads of the American Political Science Association and their three counterparts in the American Sociological Association (Lipset and Ladd 1972b; Etzioni-Halevy 1986). Cooperation and egalitarianism were extolled as a more "humane" way of life and one that was more "natural" for people the globe over. A book about a workers' commune in Spain claimed that such a cooperative environment fulfills human needs and could serve as a universal model (Lutz and Lux 1988). The working of the market was especially castigated because of its perceived inability to address ingrained injustices like race discrimination. One critic commented that many social scientists were nourished on the tradition of "immoral wealth and saintly poverty" (DeMott 1989).

There is little doubt that the growth of dependency-driven ideas had a major impact on the general societal discourse in America. The academics formed the base of the so-called New Class, whom Lipset (1979, 67) defined as "socially liberal or radical, highly critical intelligentsia." Together with noninstitutional intellectuals, the New Class used its power of symbolic formulation to "restructure man's concept of himself and his society." One observer argued that the New Class turned the rational-distributive society into a "model of civilization" while the "ideological, scientific and artistic intelligentsia . . . produces, perpetuates and disseminates the culture and ethos of distribution" (Lipset 1979, 79; Konrad and Szelenyi 1970, 148–149). Galbraith (1985, 298) provided a blueprint for action by urging academics to use their skills to put forward "seemingly implausible" suggestions for social reforms. As they gained adherents, these suggestions would emerge "as grave needs" and finally, as "human rights."

Indeed, many of the egalitarian norms found their way into the "war on poverty" of the Kennedy and Johnson administrations. The definition of poverty of welfare recipients was changed to "standards of decency," designed to assure self-esteem, personal dignity and social worth (Smolensky 1971). Academics were also in the forefront of the affirmative action movement and the effort to organize "low-influence" people like homosexuals and the welfare population (Beauchamp 1977; Horowitz 1977, 377–397; Glazer 1972, 157–161).

Under normal circumstances, the impact of the leftist New Class would have been balanced by conservative voices. However, religious and market forces had been on the retreat since the thirties. The war in Vietnam had further eroded the standing of the conservatives. It was through this unique set of circumstances that dependency tenets penetrated American foreign policy. While it may be difficult to pinpoint a specific policy, they have created the "conceptual frameworks" in which foreign and military policies were constructed (Etzioni-Halevy 1985, 27; Banks 1985). Nowhere was this influence more dramatic than in the advocacy of a moralpolitik-based, egalitarian international order.

FROM REALPOLITIK TO MORALPOLITIK: THE INTELLECTUAL BASE OF NEW INTERNATIONALISM

Political realism, or realpolitik, was at the core of traditional IR theory, which emphasized a state-centric view of international relations and a corresponding belief that states aggressively pursue their self-interests. Although developmentalists thought that morality and expediency could be reconciled, American global interests were never far from the surface of the academic discourse. By the late 1960s, the realpolitik approach began to falter under a radical critique that combined the anti-Americanism of the dependency paradigm and a neo-Wilsonian idealism. In due course this critique would evolve into New Internationalism, a unique New Left vision of international relations.

The new approach attacked the notion that power is at the center of international relations and emphasized peaceful relations and goodwill among states. One enthusiast listed "humanism . . . social consciousness, generosity and openness . . . world mindedness" as part of the new international system (Hughes 1975).

The claim that power politics contributed to world conflicts lead many scholars to denounce deterrence as an acceptable principle of international relations. A large number of studies demonstrated that cooperation is not only morally superior but also empirically feasible. Much of this evidence was derived from workshops in which academics acted as "political practitioners" engaged in solving global conflicts (Azar and Burton 1986). As Billington (1987) argued, the "ban power" crusade was reinforced by an academic generation that gained tenure: "It legitimized the notion that power is bad and American power is the worst." In a sign of the times, some futurologists refused to consider violence as a legitimate subject of prediction (Kaye and Solem 1974). Scholars who clung to deterrence were accused of "moral blindness" and conflict mongering (O'Neill 1982). The debate became so heated that one prominent IR theorist compared the radical critique to Orwell's *Animal Farm* (Singer 1976).

The intractable nature of the war in Vietnam helped the academic moralpolitikers. Even the staid Council on Foreign Relations, long a bastion of the foreign policy establishment, entered a period of "soul-searching" (Ricci 1993, 51, 75, 143; Gershman 1980; Destler, Gelb and Lake 1984, 91). A group of academics and foreign policy specialists, including Paul C. Warnke, Leslie Gelb and Anthony Lake established *Foreign Policy*, a new journal dedicated to reexamining the premises of international relations. A founding member declared himself to be "positively euphoric" that a new "liberal-populist coalition" was emerging in foreign policy. He urged the United States to abandon its hegemonic ways and mend relations with a "radically altered world" (Hughes 1975).

Reorienting American foreign policy was also high on the agenda of the Trilateral Commission established by the Columbia professor Zbigniew Brzezinski. Brzezinski, a Soviet expert, wrote about many of the same issues that were raised by the dependencistas. He was especially concerned about the growing schism between the First and Third World and urged to put North-South relations on the agenda. Brzezinski (1971, 1972, 1973) described the plight of the underdeveloped countries as the "moral problem of our time" and even conceded that the Planetary Humanists—his term for New Internationalists—are right in stressing the acute inequalities between rich and poor nations.

Brzezinski asserted that the realpolitik approach, as exemplified by the Nixon doctrine, could not cope with egalitarian changes taking place around the globe. He predicted that the world is moving toward a "new international order" where American capitalism was becoming isolated by notions of equality, "which is increasingly the underlying mode and the felt aspirations in an increasingly congested world." Echoing the convergence theme, he predicted that the American system, "resist as it may," will be compelled to accommodate itself to the "new Internationalist context" (1976). However, Brzezinski's conversion seemed to be motivated by old Cold War considerations and more than a dollop of realpolitik, most notably the fear that the new egalitarian legitimacy would facilitate Soviet expansion. To avert this, Brzezinski (1968) urged a major Western effort to help the economically depressed South.

With much of the academic bona fides of moralpolitik established, it was left to a group of radical scholars and intellectuals to take the attack on realpolitik into the political arena. At the core of this group was the Institute for Policy Studies (IPS) established by Marcus L. Raskin and Richard J. Barnet in 1963. The IPS founders were disaffected administration officials, who were joined by the historian-activist Arthur Waskow and other radical academics. Raskin and Barnet believed in the power of ideas to affect social change. The latter noted that "what we've done is point out what's irrational in society at a time when an issue is widely unpopular—before it becomes part of the conventional wisdom" (quoted in Yoffe 1977, 16; Kelley 1976; Seligman 1982). Waskow wrote that radicals need to experiment in order to discover at what point their ideas are "neither smashed nor ignored," but create enough change to move society" (quoted in Dickson 1971, 278). The mission of challenging societal paradigms was also emphasized in official IPS reports. One of them spoke of a "longer and deeper struggle, a struggle over the underlying principles and future directions of the . . . ideas and assumptions now governing America" (quoted in Hollander 1992, 12).

To further this campaign the IPS established in Amsterdam the Transnational Institute (TNI) under the Chilean communist Orlando Letelier. The openly Marxist TNI advocated leftist revolutions in Third World countries and its organ, *Race and Class* favored the Cuban and Soviet backed Popular Movement for the Liberation of Angola (MPLA) in Angola and the leftist guerrillas in Mozambique. Saul Landau, who succeeded Letelier as director, was a personal friend of Fidel Castro. Fred Halliday, a TNI fellow, devoted his writings to undermining right-wing regimes allied with the United States, including Iran. TNI published material highly critical of multinational corporations (Isaac and Isaac 1983, 113; Muravchik 1984–85; Judis 1981; Stang 1976).

In addition to their attacks on realpolitik, radical scholars asserted that the world is evolving toward socialism and argued that the United States should move to the "right" side of history. Even if not everyone agreed with Castro's forecast that "capitalist nations will pass into the trashcan of history," many mainstream scholars seemed to echo this theme. Bayless Manning (1976), the president of the Council on Foreign Affairs, took to warning that the United States had repeatedly "wound up on the wrong side of that historical evolution" and others talked about "swimming with the tide rather than against it" (Bull 1979). To make America march in step with history, radical scholars urged Washington to embrace revolutionary change. Barnet (1968, 5; 1969, 45) noted that "the revolutionary idea—that radical change is necessary, that is inevitable . . . has steadily grown." Gurtov (1974, 213) added that the "United States should be identifying with those groups or governments that are . . . working toward equality of social and economic justice and personal freedom."

Out of this core notion of political change other imperatives of New Internationalism evolved. Perhaps the most important was historical revisionism. Revisionist scholars like William Appleman Williams and Gabriel Kolko and Joyce Kolko argued that American capitalism, not Soviet expansionism, were to blame for the Cold War. They declared that "capitalist society" based on a grossly inequitable distribution of wealth and income had to fight the "ascendancy movement of change" (Williams 1969, 5; Kolko 1969, 9; Kolko and Kolko 1972, 3). These and other scholars posited that American fears of the Soviet Union were highly exaggerated or "invented" for the sake of the "American military complex" and big corporations (Baran and Sweezy 1966, 184; Raskin

1979, 32–34; Barnet 1971). In their first book Barnet and Raskin (1966) called the U.S. effort to develop NATO "obsolete and dangerous." Both the IPS and TNI staged seminars on the "myth of the Soviet threat" (Train 1980). Over time, such views became quite common among mainstream Soviet experts. Garthoff (1978), a well-known authority on Soviet strategy, accused those who still believed in Soviet aggressive intentions of being politically motivated. One critic explained that the reevaluation of Soviet motives became conflated with the rejection of threat and violence in international relations (Pipes 1977).

The assumption that the Soviet Union is peaceloving led New Internationalists to develop the "doctrine of equanimity," a belief that the United States had little to be concerned about concerning Soviet international behavior (Gershman 1980). For those who were not persuaded by "equanimity" there was the "moral equivalency" thesis, the idea that the United States is as bad as the Soviet Union (Garson 1996, 34; Hollander 1992, 188–189; Kadushin 1974). Still, New Internationalists normally depicted Moscow as more eager to pursue peace. Such sentiments were destined to persist until the very end of the Cold War. Praising Gorbachev, Falk commented that "it is Moscow, not Washington that is providing the peoples of the world with some basis to hope for the avoidance of warfare and nuclear destruction, for a safer and more equitable world" (quoted in Hollander 1992, 461).

Closely related to Cold War revisionism was the switch from globalism to regionalism in the analysis of international conflicts. Globalists viewed local conflicts as growing out of communist, mostly Soviet, efforts to exploit tension and expand into new geostrategic areas. By embracing a dependency definition of change, regionalists came to stress indigenous causes of conflict (Doran 1989). In what became a standard regionalist argument, one advocate asserted that "the 'unrest' in the contemporary world has not been 'caused' by Soviet power but by conditions of injustice and human degradation" (Dellums 1983, xxii). There was also corresponding celebration of "nationalism," an umbrella term for anti-American regimes with an egalitarian bend. The radical humanism of dependency imbued such societies with a "measure of innocence and wholesome simplicity" that contrasted with the United States. Algeria, North Korea, Cambodia, Tanzania, Mozambique and even Albania were frequently included in this category. One New Internationalist wrote: "due to its principled struggle, the small Albanian people has become a focus of interest . . . for oppressed elements elsewhere" (quoted in Hollander 1981, 143, 275).

Not accidentally, the regionalist vision was also construed as a critique of American intervention in Third World countries. Galtung (1990) accused the United States of appropriating the Biblical metaphor of God's Chosen People. He explained that the "New Israel" America felt justified in subjugating Third World countries, the contemporary equivalent of "Canaanites." Others, like Barnet (1969) explained that there is a connection between the "capitalist war machine" and American interference around the globe. According to the New Left, much of this intervention was aimed at safeguarding the interests of the MNCs, an argument popularized in *Global Reach*, a virtual best seller co-authored by Barnet and Muller (1974). The MNCs were held responsible for the peripheral status of the developing countries and the United States was portrayed as a repressive and exploitative force, which "bears the lion's share for the suffering of the poor" (Hollander 1992, 29).

Cold war revisionism and regionalism went hand in hand with the antimilitarism of New Internationalism. High on the New Left agenda was America's nuclear weapon program. As Falk (1977, 82) explained, there was a need to "connect nuclear policy with the wider search for stability and equity in the world." But there was also a strong sentiment against conventional armaments and a demand that Washington stop military sales to its Third World allies and withdraw its troops from abroad. Perhaps the most ardent attack was directed against CIA operations in the Third World. Ostensibly, the concern stemmed from the fact that the CIA was perceived as an "invisible government," a theme of a then highly popular book (Wise and Ross 1964). However, for most New Internationalists the CIA was a major impediment to the unfolding process of egalitarian change. Barnet (1968, 45; 1969) claimed that the CIA had, on average, intervened against a revolution or native insurgency once every twenty months. Falk (1975, 93; 1976a) urged to dismantle the agency's covert capability and to "oppose all impulses" toward intervention.

The New Internationalists also attacked the special relations between developmental scholars and the intelligence agencies. During the fifties and sixties, many academics worked for the CIA and the State and Defense Departments where they helped to develop the anti-insurgency and low intensity conflict theories used in Vietnam and Latin America. New Internationalists accused these scholars of being "mandarins" and part of the "academic-military-industrial complex" who serve as "mouthpieces" for the status quo (Chomsky 1969; Feldman 1989). Much of this scorn was reserved for Project Camelot, which was conceived by the Special Operations Research Office (SORO), an Army think-tank. Camelot's objective was to apply social science theories in order to predict change in Latin America and elsewhere. In 1965 Johann Galtung, who was at the time in Chile, publicized the story (Dickson 1971, 133–136; Deitchman 1976, 144–165). Camelot created a shock wave in the academic community; one scholar dubbed the cooperation between social scientists and government the "unholy alliance" (Horowitz 1977, 398).

A critique of realpolitik was only part of the New Internationalist philosophy. Providing an alternative vision of what American foreign policy should be was another. At its core was an expanded vision of human rights, which, in contrast to the traditional emphasis on civil rights, focused on *substantive* human rights, akin to the human needs concept championed by Galtung, Burton and others. According to this view, satisfying the fundamental right to work, to food, to shelter and to education takes precedence over the narrowly defined civil rights of procedural legitimacy of democracies (Muravchik 1984–85). Not incidentally, the expansive vision of human rights enhanced the legitimacy of socialist regimes that were able to meet the new criteria, even though they repressed civil rights. Denitch (1979, 18) complained that the civil rights are "parochial and clearly flawed" because they neglect "quality of life" criteria pioneered by socialist states. Another advocate called the civic based view "arrogant" and explained that many Third World countries "decided to place collective betterment ahead of respect for individual rights against the states" (Shirk 1977–78).

While highly popular in academic and intellectual circles, New Internationalism had yet to make an impact on actual policies. Such an opportunity presented itself during the Carter administration. The war in Vietnam and the Nixon tenure discredited much of the traditional foreign policy establishment and the realpolitik philosophy, which underpinned it. As the new generation of foreign policy activists moved into the political vacuum they carried the moralpolitik vision of New Internationalism into the center of American foreign policy.

3

Road Testing New Internationalism: The Iran Policy of the Carter Administration

Faced with the prospect of Soviet expansion to Iran, the Truman administration, under the policy of containment, decided to help the pro-Western shah, Reza Pahlavi, to modernize his deeply traditional country. The task mobilized the foreign policy community and scholars. Bringing academic paradigms to bear on foreign policy was common practice in postwar Washington but in the case of Iran, which was virtually "terra incognita," practitioners were particularly dependent on experts. This proximity to power fueled a nascent activism in the field.

As long as the Cold War dominated American foreign policy, controversy over Iran was muted and nuanced (Ladjevardi 1983). The assumption that the country was modernizing successfully was sustained by the seeming legitimacy of the monarchy and underpinned by an impressive array of economic indicators. Even those who had doubts about the legitimacy of the regime were ready to dismiss them in the name of realpolitik. However, the victory of Carter made New Internationalism the official philosophy in Washington, triggering a bitter debate on American policy regarding its long-time ally and strategic bastion in the Middle East.

The following chapter will analyze the impact of New Internationalism on the shaping of Carter's Iranian policy.

CRUSADING AGAINST REALPOLITIK: MAINSTREAMING THE NEW INTERNATIONALISM VISION

The war in Vietnam bolstered the New Left efforts to create a network for disseminating its foreign policy ideas. The Institute for Policy Studies (IPS), with its high anti-Vietnam profile, led the way. One effective strategy was to link leftist lobbies such as the Committee for a Sane Nuclear Policy (SANE), the Peace Through Law Education Fund, the Council for a Livable World, the pro-Marxist North American Congress on Latin American (NACLA), the Council on Hemispheric Affairs (COHA), Mobilization for Survival, Coalition for a New Foreign Policy (CNFMP) and others. Another was to create an interlocking system of centers and groups, some of them spun off from the IPS. Among them were the Center for National Security Studies (CNSS), the Committee for National Security (CNS), the Center for Development Policy (CDP), the Center for International Policy (CIP) and the Center for Defense Information (CDI). These centers tracked the human right record of American Third World allies, monitored Latin American policy and offered a radical critique of Washington's military policy (Tyson 1981, 48–49; Powell 1987, 371–376; Muravchik 1986; Isaac and Isaac 1983, 125, 129; Isaac 1980).

The leftist network was buttressed by a large number of alternative media outlets. The IPS was involved in the Dispatch News Service, which provided antiwar information, the Pacific News Service and a number of periodicals like *In This Time, Mother Jones* and the Middle East Research and Information Project (*MERIP*). The Organizing Committee for the Fifth Estate (OC-5), launched by Philip Agee, a CIA defector, published *CounterSpy* and *Covert Action Information Bulletin* (*CAIB*), which specialized in exposing clandestine operations of the CIA. In addition, IPS fellows and others published widely in more mainstream journals like *Nation, Progressive* and wrote numerous op-eds for the *New York Times* and the *Washington Post*. In an annual report, the IPS described its own respectability; it noted that Leslie Gelb from the *New York Times* called the Institute "one of the three pre-eminent centers for foreign policy perspective" (Institute for Policy Studies 1980).

Congress constituted the most important target of the IPS and other New Left groups. In the late 1950s, Marcus Raskin, who worked for Robert W. Kastenmeier (D-Wis.) organized *The Liberal Papers*, an ambitious project to bring leftist social scientists in contact with Congress. Mindful of the failure of the project, Raskin and Barnet set out to create a more effective way to influence legislators. This Gramascian prescription included educating legislators in the rudiments of Marxism-Leninism, as IPS fellow Philip Brenner explained (1983, viii). The novel lobbying effort was highly successful in identifying sympathetic lawmakers. A series of IPS seminars in 1966 led to the creation of Members of Congress for Peace Through Law (MCPL), later renamed Arms Control and Foreign Policy Caucus (ACFPC). House members associated with MCPL-ACFPC, known as "The Group," supported arms limitation, the development of a global economic order and the abolition of war. IPS assisted sympathetic members in drafting proposals, amendments and resolutions (Powell 1987, 21, 28, 41).

The leftist caucus was greatly enhanced when, between 1970 and 1974, 201 new representatives took their seats. Many of this Vietnam and Watergate "class" became ardent supporters of New Internationalism. In addition to Kastenmeier and the veterans of the *Liberal Papers* project, there was Philip Burton (D-Calif.), Donald M. Fraser (D-Minn.), Don Edwards (D-Calif.), Tom Harkin (D-Iowa), William Fitts Ryan (D-Calif.), Robert Drinan (D-Mass.), Alan Cranston (D-Calif.), John Culver (D-Iowa), Gaylord Nelson (D-Wis.), Thomas Eagleton (D-Mo.), Helen Mayner (D-N.Y.), Gerry Studds (D-Mass.) and others. Burton, first elected in 1964, was the leader of the radical antiwar wing of the Democratic Party. Legislators from the Congressional Black Caucus—Charles C. Diggs (D-Mich.), John Conyers (D-Mich.), Gus Savage (D-Ill.), Ronald V. Dellums (D-Calif.), George Crocett (D-Mich.) and Parren Mitchell (D-Mass.)— were also early followers. James Abourezk (D-S.D.) became an enthusiastic supporter; George McGovern (D-N.D.) Mark Hatfield (R-Ore.), Edward Kennedy (D-Mass.) Walter Mondale (D-Minn.) and Frank Church (D-Id.) were in tune with many of the New Internationalist themes.

Many of these legislators were on important committees. At one point, out of the 23 Democrats on the Foreign Affairs Committees, 14 belonged to ACFPC. Others occupied positions on subcommittees that dealt with human rights and foreign aid. Fraser led the human rights crusade, Harkin played an important role in reforming foreign aid along the lines of human needs, Ryan helped to block American covert intervention, Diggs pushed for better relations with socialist black Africa (Powell 1987, 21, 22, 76, 248–249, 261; Radosh 1996; Kristol 1987).

In addition to lawmakers, the IPS targeted congressional staffers. During the early 1970s the number of congressional aides expanded dramatically and their functions multiplied, leading one senator to note that "this country is basically run by the legislative staff" (quoted in Franck and Wiesband 1979, 228–229). Many of them were antiwar activists who fitted the New Class profile and were attached to IPS seminars and its Washington School, a permanent outreach for policy makers, journalists and other foreign policy "influentials." William G. Miller, who became the influential head of staff on the Senate Select Committee on Intelligence, was one of the unofficial leaders of the progressive aides. Miller, an outspoken critic of American foreign policy, later became involved in the antishah crusade. Other aides ran for Congress, enhancing the leftist-liberal lobby. John Culver, an assistant to Ted Kennedy, was elected to Congress in 1964; his aide, Richard Clark, was elected to the Senate in 1972. Toby Moffet and Richard Nolen—aides to Walter Mondale—won congressional seats in 1974.

A number of legislative aides were directly associated with IPS and other leftists groups. Gar Alperovitz served as an assistant to Senator Gaylord Nelson and Carl (Rick) Inderfurth and Gregory Treverton ended up on the Senate Intelligence Committee. Miller and David Aaron, an aide to Mondale, were involved with the Center for International Policy, a group that included Orlando Letelier. George Miller hired Cynthia Arnson, an IPS associate fellow; Mark Schneider, a friend of Letelier, was on Ted Kennedy's staff (Dickson 1971; Powell 1987, 22).

All along, the leftist lobbies were trying to reshape the foreign policy of the

Democratic Party. Raskin, Barnet and Allard Lowenstein, a veteran civil rights activist, organized the "dump Johnson" movement in the party. Their candidate of choice, George McGovern, a former professor of history, was an early revisionist. He deplored the American role in the Cold War, wanted to cut NATO forces by half and criticized the campaign against progressive regime. Described as the "kingpin in the Cuba lobby," McGovern asserted that "Castro does not seem to be a dictator for his own sake, but a convinced revolutionary, who is popular with his own people" (McGovern 1977, 284; Horowitz 1978, 60; Radosh 1996, 166).

Helped by the McGovern wing of the Democratic Party, the leftist network strove to implement key provisions of New Internationalism. Changing congressional attitudes toward multinational corporations was high on the list. As noted, the MNCs were held responsible for marginalizing Third World countries, and Frank Church's Subcommittee on Multinational Corporations sought ways to control their activities. Equally important was the human rights campaign, which was spurred by the defeat of Salvador Allende in 1973. Don Fraser and other MCPL members initiated hearings on human right abuses in Chile; subsequently, the administration was forced to adopt a general human rights policy. Harkin, with the help of Abourezk, introduced the 1975 amendment to the Federal Assistance Act that prohibited aid to countries that violated human rights.

Linking foreign aid to human rights proved a boon for the New Internationalists, who publicized human right abuses in right wing regimes allied with the United States. In addition to Chile, their "short list" included Iran, South Korea, Indonesia, Uruguay and Argentina. The National Council of Churches focused on South Korea, whose government combined a vigorous capitalist economy with a strong anticommunist stand. Clergy and Laity Concerned (CALC), IPS and TNI waged a strong campaign against the shah of Iran. Virtually all groups denounced the apartheid regime in South Africa.

The focus on human rights was part of a larger strategy of mainstreaming the philosophy of human needs. Dependency advocates were especially successful in influencing United Nations organizations dealing with economic needs. In the United States they received an unexpected boost from Robert McNamara (1995, 311–312) who, deeply humbled by the war in Vietnam, was determined to embrace the novel approach after his appointment to the World Bank. Over the bitter objection of the Nixon and Ford administrations, Congress adopted the view that American aid should ameliorate poverty rather than spur growth.

Encouraged by this success, the New Internationalists mounted an attack on American military posture around the globe. The Coalition for New Foreign and Military Policy, working closely with the Foreign Policy Caucus in Congress, sponsored a number of initiatives to curtail military transfers to American Third World allies. In a successful showdown, Dick Clark, the chairman of the African Affairs subcommittee in the Senate, blocked the administration's efforts to send arms to a pro-Western faction fighting a Marxist government in Angola. Clark who visited Angola in 1975, declared that "values of human rights and racial equality that America shared with the nations there" will solve the problem (quoted in Isaacson 1992, 685).

More important, the New Left mounted a major effort to curtail the intelligence community. Raskin and Barnet were among the first to advocate the elimination of the CIA. In 1972, the IPS established the Project for National Security, which was subsequently spun off as the Center for National Security Studies (CNSS). Under the energetic leadership of Robert Borosage and Morton Halperin, CNSS became a driving force in the anti-intelligence crusade. In a highly publicized conference on Capital Hill in 1972 the CNSS put the CIA "on trial." The proceedings were published in *The CIA File*, a book that was said to influence the "popular attitudes on intelligence for "next half a decade" (Constantinides 1993, 91; Falk 1976a).

The campaign bore fruit when, in 1975, the Senate voted to establish the Select Committee on Intelligence. Frank Church, who had a personal rapport with Barnet and warmly reviewed his book *Global Reach*, chaired the committee. He appointed William Miller and David Aaron, a protégé of Walter Mondale, another important member of the committee, to key positions. Gregory Treverton and Rick Inderfurth, two intelligence critics with ties to leftist lobbies were also hired (Powell 1987, 61). To make the New International view better known, the CNSS published *The Lawless State*, which detailed intelligence abuses. The widely read book advocated a charter for the CIA, dismantling of covert operations and the elimination of human espionage (Halperin et al. 1976). These and other critics posited that human espionage corrupts the process of intelligence gathering and wanted to replace it with "clean" technical intelligence, an updated version of "New View" intelligence (Rees 1981).

Conservatives and traditional Democrats tried to prevent the mainstreaming of New Internationalism. They accused the New Left of advocating foreign policy friendly to the Soviet Union and international communism. IPS, which bore the brunt of the attacks, was denounced as a front for the KGB (Crozier 1979). However, these charges did not hurt the popularity of the New Left. On the contrary, because of the Vietnam backlash, the public discourse seemed to favor the moralpolitik flavor of New Internationalism. With the Nixon doctrine in tatters, the 1976 elections provided an ideal opportunity for a referendum on key tenets of New Internationalism.

THE UNLIKELY CRUSADER: JIMMY CARTER AND THE EMBRACE OF NEW INTERNATIONALISM

After McGovern's landslide defeat in 1972, the New Left pinned its hope on a number of progressive candidates like Morris K. Udall, whom McGovern endorsed for president, followed by Frank Church and Fred Harris, the populist senator from Oklahoma. The ascendancy of Jimmy Carter was an unwelcome surprise; his "conversion" to human rights was of a recent vintage and Carter's putative security adviser, Zbigniew Brzezinski, in spite of his concern for

"North-South" relations, was considered a closet hawk. Worse, Brzezinski, like Carter, was associated with the Trilateral Commission, which the leftists accused of "imperalist" sentiments (Block 1979).

To make sure that Carter implemented the New Internationalist vision, the New Left mounted a major campaign during the Democratic Party convention in June 1976. The IPS presented its own platform written by Marcus Raskin. The Platform Committee, dominated by leftist New Politics activists, insisted on moving American foreign policy into the regionalist mold. They extracted a promise from Carter to cut military spending and oppose the B-1 bomber (Muravchik 1981; McGovern 1977, 265). Perhaps the most heated battle was fought over the issue of human rights. Radical Democrats wanted the platform to reflect the dependency-driven expansive view of human rights, which favored leftist regimes. However, conservative "Jackson Democrats" vehemently objected. Jeane Kirkpatrick (1979; 1986, xii-xiii) subsequently explained that the New Left adopted the Marxist-Leninist definition of human rights in order to legitimize the Communist dictatorships that they had sponsored. She also accused the New Left—who targeted the right-wing allies of the United States but downplayed human rights violations in Communist regimes—of a double standard. Kirkpatrick, Daniel Patrick Moynihan and other conservative Democrats urged to extend the human rights crusade to left-wing regimes. Without a consensus, both sides were forced to tolerate each other's human targets, or as Moynihan put it, "we'll be against the dictators you don't like the most, if you'll be against the dictators we don't like most" (Dumbrell 1993, 117; Muravchik 1986, 2).

With the shaky blessing of his divided party, Jimmy Carter began to campaign as a "moral crusader" ready to usher in a new era of global moral righteousness. As one observer noted, "Carter seemed to believe that the global community was waiting for America's signal to" lift the world's poor and attend to human rights and global plenty (Spanier 1992, 188). To accomplish this ambitious task the new administration had to purge American foreign policy of the realpolitik of the Nixon and Ford administrations and recast it in a moralpolitik mode.

Institutionalizing New Internationalism required a thorough "cleansing" of the foreign policy community. During the campaigning Carter often repeated Brzezinski's line about the "Waterloo of the WASP elite," railed against the "elitism and arrogance of the State Department" and promised "new faces, new ideas" (Kaufman 1993; Meyer 1978, 155, 171; Serfaty 1978). The task of recruiting a foreign policy cadre in tune with New Internationalism fell to Vice President–elect Mondale, David Aaron and Anthony Lake. While the top jobs of secretary of state and national security adviser went to two trilateralists—Cyrus Vance and Zbigniew Brzezinski—numerous second and third tier appointees were drafted from the McGovern faction and the New Left lobbies. Many of them became known as the "Mondale Mafia" and formed the core of the moralpolitik group in the administration.

A large number of moralpolitikers had ties to the IPS, the Center for International Policy (CIP) and other left-wing groups; others worked for leftist and liberal legislators. Warren Christopher, an associate of McGovern, was appointed deputy secretary of state. David Aaron, a protégé of Mondale became an assistant to the national security advisor, Anthony Lake was put in charge of the Policy Planning Staff in the State Department and Leslie H. Gelb headed the Bureau of Political-Military Affairs. Lake hired Richard Feinberg who was linked to the Castroite NACLA and Gelb was close to Morton Halperin from the CNSS. Thomas Ross, a leading detractor of the CIA, was made assistant secretary of defense for Public Affairs. Paul C. Warnke, a supporter of IPS, became the director of the Arms Control and Disarmament Agency (ACDA). Critics described this group as "soft-line ideologues who earned the blessing of McGovern" and passed the muster of the New Left (Franck and Wiesband 1979, 239; Powell 1987, 23; Lasky 1979, 333–3334; Muravchik 1986, 119).

Rounding out the New Internationalist contingent were third-tier appointees like Rick Inderfuth; Gregory Treverton; Robert Hunter, a policy adviser to Ted Kennedy; and Jessica Tuchman from the staff of Morris Udall. All in all, the administration had an unprecedented number of first-time appointees: in the State Department alone, out of the thirty senior positions, twenty-two were filled with political nominees, up from twelve in the Ford administration (Johnson 1978). This influx was described as a "take-over of the Vietnam War critics, advocates of arms-control agreements with the Soviets, and those who felt strongly that the power of the United States should be used to affect human-rights issues in other countries" (Destler, Gelb and Lake 1984, 97, 136, 138).

Some of Carter's appointees proved to be controversial. Warnke, a former official in the Johnson administration implicated in the Pentagon Papers, was close in thinking to the CDI, which downplayed Soviet threats. Shortly after taking office Warnke abolished ACDA's Verification and Analysis Bureau, infuriating critics who accused him of strategic complacency. Designating Andrew Young as the American ambassador to the UN turned out to be even more contentious. In what amounted to a mixture of American civil rights philosophy and radical New Internationalism, Young became a leading advocate of an expansive definition of human rights and regionalism. On one occasion he asserted that civil rights constitute a "luxury" for poor people. On another occasion he stated that Cuban forces in Angola were "helping to provide order and stability" and advised Americans not to get "paranoid" about it (Gershman 1978, 20; 1979, 17, 20). Following America's protest against trials of Soviet dissidents, Young announced that there were thousands of political prisoners in the United States. Young's deputy, Brady Tyson, who was involved with NACLA, publicly apologized to the UN Commission on Human Rights for bringing Pinochet to power in Chile (Powell 1987, 225).

Patricia Derian, Assistant Secretary of State for Human Rights, was perhaps the most controversial nominee. Derian, a former civil rights worker and a lecturer at the IPS Washington School, was deeply involved with the leftist human rights network. Mark Schneider, her deputy came from the staff of Edward Kennedy, and had ties to Letelier. Stephen Cohen, a deputy in charge of Iran's human rights policy, was a strict McGovernite. John Salberg joined the Bureau from the staff of Donald Fraser and Robert Cohen worked previously for the leftist International League for Human Rights (ILHR). Derian was the chief architect of the "disassociation" policy which called for the United States to distance itself from allies who violate human rights. Derian won the right to review U.S. arms sales and aid and recommended punishment for countries suspect of human rights violation. Not surprisingly, she targeted a number of right-wing regimes, including Iran, South Korea and Argentina. Governments like Nicaragua and El Salvador, that fought Marxist insurgencies, incurred a particular censure of the Human Rights Bureau. While Derian commented that "no description of hell touches the bestiality of what is happening to the people of El Salvador," she was reticent to speak out against Pol Pot's Cambodia and Vietnam's boat people (Muravchik 1986, 146–147).

A number of insiders noted the left-wing bias of the human rights activists in the administration. David D. Newsom, Carter's undersecretary for Political Affairs, described them as people who "came into the Department dedicated to the idea of seeing the overthrow of rightist regimes." Richard Holbrooke, an assistant secretary, testified before Congress that "in the name of human rights, a small but vocal group of people . . . sought to carry out far-reaching change in the world structure . . . their targets were almost without exception regimes of the right which happened to be anti-Soviet" (quoted in Muravchik 1986, 11–12, 114–115, 133, 138–139; Donovan 1985, 165). A 1979 congressional report found that the bureau rarely mentioned human rights abuses in Communist-controlled countries (Heginbotham and Bite 1979).

Along with changes in foreign policy personnel, Carter made an effort to diversify the decision-making process. Reacting to Kissinger's virtual monopoly on foreign policy, New Internationalist critics embraced the so-called "multiple advocacy" model of decision making. George (1972, 751), a leading authority on foreign policy, was a major booster: He asserted that "multiple advocacy" would "harness diversity of views and interests in the interest of rational policy making." Initially, Carter gave Vance, Brzezinski and Young almost equal input into foreign policy and even welcomed the inevitable tensions between the various policy centers.

Theoretical assumptions notwithstanding, the reality of "multiple advocacy" had proved problematic. There were well-publicized clashes between the State Department, the NSC and the Young contingent. Compounding interagency tension were the deep fissures within the foreign policy bureaucracies. The clash between the moralpolitikers and the career diplomats beholden to realpolitik and a globalist view of international relations turned the State Department into a battleground. Brzezinski complained that Carter failed to maintain discipline, but others noted that the team was unmanageable because of the large ideological contractions "that run between Brzezinski to Pat Derian or UN Ambassador Andrew Young" (Destler, Gelb and Lake 1984, 119).

It was within this web of structural contradiction that Carter translated New

Internationalism into a number of applied policy imperatives. The most dramatic was the human rights crusade. In his inaugural address the President pronounced that "our commitment to human rights must be absolute" and followed it up with a directive that made promotion of "human rights around the world" a major objective of American foreign policy (Crabb and Holt 1980, 162; Carter 1979; Stoessinger 1985, 247, 265). What is more, the administration seemed to have adopted the dependency inspired definition of human rights. To this effect, the president pronounced himself cured of the "inordinate fear of communism" and ready to build a new and more just global order, an apparent allusion to the New International Economic Order. Vance, who worked with McNamara in a group dedicated to eradicating global poverty, added such "vital needs as shelter, health care and education" to the list of human rights (Dumbrell 1993, 119; Stoessinger 1985, 263).

While Carter wanted to extend his human rights standards to the Soviet Union, other officials were far more forgiving of the communist record. Vance (1986) adopted the argument of his adviser, Marshall Shulman (1977), that the United States should learn to live with Russia because of its nuclear capability. More significantly, he argued that the United States should not automatically support anticommunist revolutions under the banner of human rights, because anticommunism cannot always be equated with democracy. Showing its New Internationalist bias, the brunt of the human rights campaign fell on right-wing American allies. In May 1977, Carter declared that in pursuance of containment, the United States had betrayed her own principle by supporting dictatorships and alienating "progressive" forces around the world. Soon after, he announced a plan to withdraw 32,000 troops from South Korea to signal his displeasure with the human right record of Park Chun Hee. In September, Jeffrey Hall Stein, an IPS associate, organized a conference of Parliamentarians on Korean Problems to popularize the issue of withdrawal from the peninsula (Braley 1984, 589; Rees 1983).

Carter was also eager to reconfigure American foreign policy in the regionalist mold. In a show of publicity, the administration denounced Kissinger's philosophy of linking regional conflicts to Soviet machinations and proclaimed itself satisfied with Moscow's global standing. To show its regionalist mettle, the administration downplayed communist involvement in civil conflicts in Africa and South America, while Young and Vance advocated a warmer embrace of the Marxist regimes in Angola and Mozambique. When Katangan rebels, supported by Cubans in Angola, launched an incursion into the Shaba province of Zaire in 1977, the administration did not react. The State Department studiously overlooked Castro's efforts to create a Marxist federation in the Horn of Africa (DeJames 1994). African policy was greatly influenced by Young, but Vance was also anxious to put America on the "right" side of history. He explained that "change was and is sweeping through Africa, and those who identify with it will be able . . . to influence its direction" (quoted in Dumbrell 1993, 192–193). This stand delighted the New Left. IPS's Barnet (1977, 173) praised the administration for "correctly" seeing "that the so-called North-South problem ... poses far greater challenge to the survival of the American way of life than the Kremlin's master plan whatever it may be."

Kirkpatrick would later note the "affinity between the foreign policy establishment and the New Left," and criticized the ease with which "categories of the new liberalism could translate into those of revolutionary socialism." She denounced the administration for double standards and charged that its policy was driven by a "quasi-Marxist theory of historical development" in which "history is on the side of the opponent" (quoted in Powell 1987, 225; Dumbrell 1993, 192). Robert Gates (1996, 126–127), the former CIA director who was on Carter's National Security Council (NSC), agreed with Kirkpatrick. He described as ironic the fact that while "members of Congress, Secretary Vance, others in the administration and various pundits were stressing the importance of not turning local or regional conflicts into . . . East-West conflict," the Soviet Union was deeply committed to global intervention.

Another major mission of the administration was to make American foreign policy more "humane" and less militaristic. The antimilitaristic imperative had three goals. First, Carter was reportedly intrigued by the New Internationalist idea of "minimal deterrence" and instructed Secretary of Defense Harold Brown to look into its feasibility. While nothing came out of the review, the administration decided to cut defense spending and eliminate a number of weapon systems. In addition to the B-1 bomber, Carter offered to scrap the Trident missile system and defer the production of the neutron bomb, which was greatly opposed by the New Left (Dumbrell 1993, 210–211; Bell 1980, 31).

Second, the administration announced that it would limit arm sales. The president explained that he was "particularly concerned by our nation's role as the world's leading arms salesman"; a May 19 memorandum pledged that arms transfers would be "an exceptional foreign policy instrument." Observers claimed that Washington's share of the $200 billion arms trade did not fit Carter's view that America should be the world's moral beacon and breadbasket, not its gun shop" (Bill 1988b, 229; Vance 1983, 319; Stoessinger 1985, 278).

Third, the administration was eager to curtail the intelligence community. While campaigning, Carter referred to the CIA as a "disgrace" and promised that when the agency makes a mistake "I will call a press conference and tell the people" (Ameringer 1990, 357; Meyer 1978, 18). Vice President Mondale (1976), a vociferous critic of intelligence on the Church committee, was put in charge of reforming the CIA, helped by Aaron, Treverton and Inderfuth. Carter's nominee to head the agency was Theodore C. Sorenson, a conscientious objector and a harsh critic of intelligence. After the Senate rejected Sorenson, his replacement, Admiral Stansfield Turner, was charged with restructuring the agency according to the "New View" guidelines favored by the New Internationalists. The new Director curtailed covert operations and human intelligence (HUMINT) in favor of the "cleaner" technical intelligence. As a Turner loyalist explained, HUMINT was likely to be suspect on moral grounds and do moral damage to the collector (Godfrey 1978). A subsequent study noted that the "New View" "equates intelligence with a sort of universal predictive science . . . diminished the role of secrecy, espionage and counterintelligence" (Shulsky 1993, 169).

Mondale and his group also supported the intelligence charter favored by CNSS and other anti-intelligence lobbies. The legislation, known as S.2525, was defeated in Congress, but Carter gave it a new lease on life in his Executive Order 12036. Written with the help of the staff of the Senate Intelligence Committee, the order incorporated many of the ideas of Halperin's *Lawless State*. Yet other legislation—the 1978 Foreign Intelligence Surveillance Act (FISA)—restricted the ability of intelligence to cover foreigners and instructed that all electronic intercepts not clearly related to specific violations of law be destroyed.

In incorporating so much of New Internationalism, the former governor of Georgia went further than any contemporary president in redefining the principles of American international conduct. One historian aptly commented that "the Carter administration attempted to promote a new system of world order based upon international stability, peace and justice" (Rosati 1987, 42). While it was not realized at the time, the new direction had a profound impact on a number of American right-wing allies, especially Iran. Iran, long considered a prize in American foreign policy, became a testing ground for the new paradigm.

A COAT OF MANY COLORS: THE SHAPING OF THE ADMINISTRATION'S IRANIAN POLICY

The premises of containment that drove Washington's Iranian policy had changed little over time. As long as the Soviet Union was perceived as a major threat, Iran's role as an anticommunist bulwark remained unchallenged. Carter's embrace of New Internationalism threatened to alter this approach in a number of dramatic ways.

The most immediate change stemmed from the newly minted regionalist creed. The Nixon and Ford administrations, which made Iran into one of their "Twin Pillars" in the Gulf, enlisted the shah's help in countering Soviet advances in South Yemen, the Horn of Africa and Ethiopia. Iran became a crucial player in the Red Sea Entente—known as the Safari Club—which also included Saudi Arabia, Morocco and Egypt. In the early seventies the shah put down a leftist rebellion in Dhofar and helped Morocco fight Polissario guerrillas in Western Sahara. However, when the shah moved to help Somalia in its struggle with Marxist Ethiopia, the Carter administration rebuffed his effort, signaling that the Entente was dead.

The administration seemed equally dismissive of the Nixon-Ford effort to secure a sympathetic government in Afghanistan. The shah, along with Pakistan, was the key supporter of the pro-Western Mohammed Daoud Khan who came under increasing pressure from the Afghan Communists. When, with Russian help, Daoud Khan was overthrown, Washington, bound by the theory of indigenous revolution, did not protest (Scott 1996, 41–42; Ledeen and Lewis 1981,

95). Moreover, to demonstrate that globalism was truly a thing of the past, Carter proposed to demilitarize the Indian Ocean, a step favored by McGovern and Kennedy (1975), who wrote that Washington should abandon its fear of Soviet aggression in the Gulf. The initiative was cancelled only after the Soviets, in an effort to help Ethiopia, increased their naval presence in the region.

The erosion of Iran's perceived strategic position gave the moralpolitikers in the administration an opportunity to question the shah's human rights record. In addition to Derian and her deputies, the circle included Mondale, Young, Lake, Gelb and Henry Precht from the State Department. In the NSC David Aaron, Jessica Tuchman and Robert Hunter were all unhappy with the monarchy. As a rule, Vance and Warren Christopher, and, occasionally, David Newsom supported the hard-core moralpolitikers. When serving as the president of the New York Bar Association, Vance encouraged efforts of William Butler from the International Commission of Jurists to liberalize the regime (Sale 1980; Ledeen and Lewis 1981, 75, 145; White Paper, 03564).

There is little doubt that Iran was a crucial test for the moralpolitikers in the administration. Both Mondale and Aaron had contacts with the Iranian opposition in the United States and were persuaded that the shah was a highly illegitimate ruler, whose behavior should be modified. Other moralpolitikers wanted to oust Reza Pahlavi, a goal that was vigorously pushed by the leftist lobby. Congressman David Bowen (D-Miss.) accused Derian and her colleagues of following the "McGovernite prescription" and complained that "opportunists" in the State Department were trying to out-Carter Carter" (Dumbrell 1993, 181). The shah would later charge that the "McGovernites in the second echelon of the State Department were anxious to see me go" (Pahlavi 1980b, 221). One study concluded that the moralpolitikers saw the shah as "a tyrant who was building up the military by using anti-Soviet rationale" and concluded that he "had to be removed" (Sale 1980, 81).

On the other side of the divide were the realpolitikers such as Brzezinski, Brown, senior officials in the State Department and the CIA Directorate of Operations. They argued that Iran's geopolitical importance overrode the human rights imperative, adding that military sales helped to recycle petro-dollars and help to defray research and development costs (Ledeen and Lewis 1981, 76; Milani 1988, 183).

With positions staked out so early, the discourse on Iran became one of the most entrenched foreign policy disagreements in the administration. One scholar familiar with the situation explained that the two sides "talked past each other" (Cottam 1988, 292–293). To bolster their cases, both sides lobbied Carter using the Iran estimate as ammunition. Even before taking office, the transition team solicited a report from the Intelligence and Research (INR) of the State Department. The report was mildly critical of the shah's style of governance, but concluded that, in spite of some challenges, Iran would remain stable under the shah, who was said to enjoy excellent health (White Paper, 03564: Bill 1988a, 423).

The moralpolitikers seized upon the report to make the "Diem argument"; the shah was losing legitimacy and had to liberalize or be replaced. The realpolitikers warned that a sudden liberalization would destabilize the country. Brzezinski asked Samuel Huntington and Colonel William Odom, two of his appointees to the NSC, to study the issue. As political scientists Brzezinski and Huntington were worried about the volatile nature of liberalization in authoritarian regimes known as "dismantling the tiger." Brzezinski, citing local customs, was convinced that Iran was not ready for democratization (Hargrove 1988, 154; Orme 1988). Others shared this view. Jack Miklos, the chargé d'affaires in the American embassy in Teheran, cautioned in a May 4, 1977 report against applying Western political concepts because there was a "wide gap between some Western images of current day Iran" and the Iranian culture (Documents, vol. 8, 160–162; Miklos 1983, 64–65). He and other critics would later argue that the administration failed to discuss the consequences of liberalization, mainly because the moralpolitikers denounced such efforts as a conservative ploy to protect the shah. Harold Saunders (1987, 221) the then-head of the INR wrote that human rights activities focused on the surface question of "how many political prisoners were let out" rather that on the dynamics of the situation.

Faced with a divided bureaucracy, Carter vacillated between the realpolitik and the moralpolitik approach. In spite of his early enthusiasm for the "multiple advocacy" model, the President seemed to be befuddled by the competing voices. Studies have suggested that Carter had a weak sense of leadership, which was exacerbated by an apparent discomfort with power and a "trauma of execution." This trait was compounded by an apparent tendency toward inconsistency, vacillation and "zigzagging," earning him the sobriquet "Lon Chaney." As a result, the president seemed to agree to contradictory advise proffered by his aides, and occasionally reversed himself, both in public and private (Davis 1980; Smith 1988, 16; Hoffman 1977–78; Sarkesian 1984; Glad 1980, 476, 441; Hinckely 1994, 138–139; Hargrove 1988, 111; Donovan 1985, 235; Salinger 1981, 3; Mazlish and Diamond 1979, 11; DeMause 1977; Haas 1992, 115; Hartman 1977). In his own memoires, Carter (1982, 143; Carter and Carter 1987, 7) described the difficulties of choosing between "idealism and realism," or between morality and the exertion of power.

Still, the need to appoint a new ambassador to Iran forced the president to make a decision. The Human Rights Bureau wanted to replace the outgoing Richard Helms, a former CIA director, with someone who would share the New Internationalist vision. However, Carter, acting on the advice of Dean Rusk, picked William H. Sullivan, who served in Laos and the Philippines. The moralpolitikers accused Sullivan of "bombing Laotian peasants" and described him as "security minded" and "pro-council." The Human Rights Bureau apparently conveyed its disappointment to Iranian dissidents (Sullivan 1987; Albert 1980, 8; Cottam 1980; Stempel 1981, 79).

To forge a consensus, the INR commissioned several studies by outside experts. In May some scholars were invited to brief the departing Sullivan. The

State Department account of the meeting indicates that most scholars anticipated "business as usual." Only one paper raised some tentative questions about the trends in Iran and the durability of the shah's regime (White Paper, 03564). The State Department did not list the name of the scholar, but a perusal of the literature in 1977 should be informative, even if the inevitable lag in publications is taken into consideration.

Marvin Zonis (1971, 5, 270–271), a leading expert, found that in spite of his achievements, Reza Pahlavi "had not located the majoritarian political base he so ardently sought." But Zonis was skeptical of democratic reforms, because of the political culture permeated by "Machiavellian traits" such as *taqieh* (dissimulation), lack of loyalty and mistrust. Another leading expert, James Bill (1977, 166) noted that the Iranian political process is "magnificently resistant" to outside analysis and warned about the darker side of Iranian culture, notably the penchant to blame all problems on the West (Taheri 1987, 79, 84). Some scholars raised specific concerns about imbalances in the economy, but there was no sense of alarm (Weinbaum 1977; McLachlan 1977; Askari, Cummings and Isbudak 1977; Fischer 1977). Indeed, many experts were upbeat about future prospects. Looney (1977, 89), an economic adviser to Teheran, made the "optimistic assumption" that the regime would prosper, a view shared by a number of economic publications and area studies (Campbell 1977; Elkan 1977; Rustow 1977; Amuzager 1977; *Major Companies of Iran* 1977; Nyrop 1978).

While outside experts could afford a leisurely debate, the administration was faced with the urgent problem of arms sales to Teheran. In May, Vance reassured the shah that Washington would honor a previous agreement to sell 160 F-16 planes and pledged to seek congressional approval for 10 AWACS (Airborne Warning and Command Systems) aircraft that Iran had requested. However, shortly after the White House issued a Presidential Directive (PD-13) that limited American arms sales, "except to countries of strategic importance." Iran was not mentioned, leaving commentators to wonder about the shah's position. The AWACS request was especially controversial since it promised to introduce new technology into the region, an outcome the directive sought to avoid.

Given the administration's ambivalence about the Iranian procurement policy, such speculations were not entirely misplaced. While Carter reassured Sullivan of his support for the sale and confirmed the importance of a stable Iran, he abandoned Nixon's policy of virtually automatic supplies in favor of a review process. When the AWACS request reached the White House, Carter approved it, but reduced the number of airplanes to seven. Gary Sick (1985, 24, 26), an Iran specialist on the NSC, explained that this maneuver was intended to send a signal that the "days of the blank check are over."

The review process triggered by the arms deal exposed the deep divisions in the administration. Frustrated by what they saw as too many concessions to the national interest, the moralpolitikers, including Derian, Lake and Gelb, decided to make a stand on the AWACS issue. Aaron was quoted as saying, "we are not going to be as open-ended" and that the "shah has to learn that is not the Nixon-Kissinger administration anymore" (Sale 1980, 80; Rubin 1980b, 196).

The Human Rights Bureau tried to block the sale on the ground that Iran violated human rights, and Policy Planning raised concerns that the shah would not be able to absorb yet another large shipment of arms.

Deriving from New Internationalism, such reservations reflected the view that arms sales are at the root of many of Iran's social and economic ills. Indeed, Michael T. Klare, an IPS fellow and the head of the Military and Disarmament Project that castigated right-wing American allies, propagated many of these views. Among others, Klare (1975; 1976) wrote that military transfers prevent a "meaningful distribution" of political power in Iran.

The realpolitikers in the State Department, Brzezinski, the Defense, Treasury and Energy Departments and Sullivan, who disliked the human rights activists, lobbied equally hard for the sale. They reiterated all the stock arguments about Iran's strategic importance and listed the added benefits: stabilizing oil prices and reducing per unit cost of manufacturing of the expensive system (Ledeen and Lewis 1981, 76; Bill 1988a, 231; Milani 1988, 183).

While the outcome of the review was never in doubt, the process set the standard for decision making on Iran. On the surface, the AWACS request was quite reasonable, given Iran's vulnerable borders and mountainous terrain. It was nonlethal and comparatively cheap compared to a traditional air-defense system. Yet the controversy was described as "passionate" and "bitter." What is more, the debate took on a life of its own, preventing any objective evaluation of the situation in Iran. John Stempel (1981, 295), a political officer in the embassy, wrote: "Aggressive advocacy by one group immediately triggered a reflex response in the other." The differences in opinion, which should have led to reanalysis of the situation, "became conflicts between true believers . . . the one side lauding the opposition, the other defending the shah's value to the United States."

The convergence of the arms sales request and the publication of PD-13 made matters worse. Sick (1985, 27) attributed the poor timing to the administration's failure to reconcile conflicting policy imperatives and insensitivity to public perceptions. Others pointed to Carter's habit of making discrete decisions without the ability to see their cumulative impact (Gates 1996, 73; Hunt 1987, 186; Saunders 1987; Glad 1980; Falkowski 1978, 128; Davis 1980). Whatever the reason for the contradictory polices, the White House linkage of the sales to the domestic record of the shah created an impression that Iran's strategic value had declined. The administration's failure to comprehend the symbolic ramifications of its Iran policy was amply demonstrated during the congressional debate on AWACS.

THE RESURGENT CONGRESS: THE AWACS SALE AS A REFERENDUM ON THE SHAH'S LEGITIMACY

Carter's victory encouraged the leftist network to redouble its efforts to oust the shah. Various groups intensified the campaign to expose the "political holocaust" in Iran, and stories of torture and political oppression proliferated. Reza

Baraheni, an Azerbaijani-Iranian poet who testified about torture in Congress in the fall of 1976, had a particular impact. Shortly thereafter, the anti-Vietnam journalist, Frances Fitzgerald, confirmed his report and, on January 5, 1977, the *New York Times* weighed in with a highly critical editorial. By mid-1977 SAVAK, the secret police in Iran, became a household name. A study of media coverage found that a "full year before the revolution began the best American newspapers were clearly telling a story of a country with a harsh dictatorial government, severe economic difficulties, and an unhealthy emphasis on importing weapons" (Rubin 1980b, 348; Radji 1983, 41).

Writing in the introduction to Baraheni's (1977b) book, *The Crowned Cannibals*, E. L. Doctorow compared the poet with Alexander Solzhenitsyn and called upon churches, colleges and politicians to speak out against the shah's cruelty. Baraheni told of thousands executed and more than three hundred thousand imprisoned and accused the United States of participating in the oppression (Baraheni, 1977a). Other opponents charged that there were 70,000 SAVAK agents (Hanrahan 1977). Although the real numbers were much lower—putting Iran well behind Cuba, Ethiopia, East Germany, Syria and Iraq—the shah's regime outscored others in notoriety. Anthony Parsons (1984, 330), the British ambassador to Teheran, commented that "SAVAK became one of the principle bogeys of the Western press." Manheim and Albritton (1986) found that Iran's public image in the United States had deteriorated rapidly and acutely.

Helping to create the publicity were the various antishah committees, which proliferated in academia. In one celebrated case, two University of Kansas professors, Norman Forer and Don Brownstein, co-founders of the American Committee for Iranian Rights (ACIR), went to Teheran to search for some allegedly missing writers (Dreyfuss 1980, 189). Ramsey Clark's Committee for International and Artistic Freedom published a poster that depicted the shah as a "killer" (Zonis 1991, 241). Thomas Ricks, a Georgetown professor who founded the U.S. People Committee on Iran, and Richard Falk helped to monitor human rights in Iran. Falk and a Stanford professor, H. Pierre Noyes, were involved in the Bay Area Conference, a large gathering of antishah forces on July 19. Noyes, who went to Teheran to watch a political trial in May, and Falk created the Support Committee to Send A Legal Medical Team of International Observers to Iran. After his return, Noyes wrote to Senator Alan Cranston (D-Calif.) complaining about the "sham" trials (State Department, 01173, 01180). During the Senate confirmation hearings for Sullivan, Falk, Ricks and Raskin testified against him. To emphasize the human rights plight, fifty masked students sat in the audience (Sullivan 1981, 33–34).

Using the human rights theme paid off in Congress. The powerful Human Rights Working Group of the CNFMP urged sympathetic congressmen to get involved, a call that was taken up by the ACFPC. Donald Fraser urged Carter to deliver on his promise to conduct a more humane foreign policy. Lest the administration miss the hint, Fraser publicized the December 1976 report on human rights abuses in Iran and other countries. William Miller, the staff director of the Senate Intelligence Committee, was also deeply engaged. Miller, a former Foreign Service Officer, who had served in Teheran, was strongly opposed to the shah. According to an embassy memo Miller "became so emotionally involved with the National Front that he had to be sent out of the country for his blatant and outspoken antishah criticism." The memo also noted that as chief of staff of the Intelligence Committee, Miller "found an outlet for his crusader zeal" (Documents, vol. 20, 1). Miller was credited with introducing Mehdi Haeri, a visiting professor at Georgetown University and a friend of Ayatollah Khomeini, to Henry Precht, the would-be director of the Iran Desk in the State Department (Taheri 1988, 78; Godson 1979, 83; Sale 1980; Ledeen and Lewis 1981, 130, 144).

When the administration submitted the AWACS request on June 16, the human rights activists used their links to sympathetic staffers to encourage resistance (Sullivan 1981, 114–115). In the Senate, Church, McGovern, Kennedy, Eagleton, John Culver and Gaylord Nelson led the fight against the sale. In the ensuing debate, Eagleton argued that Iran was not stable enough to be trusted with sophisticated weapons and Culver questioned whether Iran should be exempted from PD-13 "before the ink is dry on that piece of paper" (Bill 1988b, 19, 229–230; Dreyfuss 1980, 186; Purvis, Opperman and Campanella 1984). The House International Relations Committee—dominated by such leftists and liberals as Fraser, Michael Harrington, Helen Mayner, Leo Ryan, Gerry Studds and Diggs—was even more hostile. Diggs, chairman of the Subcommittee on African Affairs, resented the shah's help for South Africa and the anticommunist crusade of the Safari Club. Studds, an enthusiastic supporter of Carter's policy of limiting arm sales, introduced a resolution to register his disappointment (*Congressional Quarterly Weekly Review*, Sept. 3, 1977).

The leftist-liberal coalition saw the AWACS case as a major test for New Internationalism. Fraser acknowledged that human rights considerations are countervailed by strategic and economic considerations and that in Iran "we have them all in one place" (quoted in Dumbrell 1993, 161). Church, who described sales to Iran as the most rapid military peacetime buildup "in the history of the world," argued that it was immoral to supply arms to dictators "guilty of egregious violations of human rights" (Ioannides 1984, 20; Sullivan 1981, 116; Ledeen and Lewis 1981; Mofid 1987, 193).

To be sure, there were other motives involved in the AWACS showdown. It was a signal to Carter that the left wing of the Democratic Party, now led by Ted Kennedy, would closely scrutinize his steps. Congress was also asserting its newly found power to challenge the institution of the "imperial presidency." As one observer put it, "Congress has gotten used to kicking Presidents around, and they don't care whose President it is" (Abshire 1979, 60). Aggravated by Carter's celebrated reluctance to cultivate relations with Capitol Hill, the AWACS request was doomed, prompting the administration to withdraw the proposal (Jones 1985; 1988). It was later resubmitted and, after an intensive lobbying campaign by defense and aerospace corporations, oil interests and the Jewish lobby which was grateful for the shah's support of Israel, Congress passed the request in September.

In spite of the victory, the AWACS episode was costly in terms of the larger issue of the shah's legitimacy. The theoretical chapter suggested that public discourse, where perceptions of legitimacy are shaped, is rich in symbolic overtones whose implications go beyond the issue at hand. Under the best of circumstances, a congressional review process was not a pleasant experience for the country involved. In the case of Iran, the shah's regime was virtually put on trial, with Frank Church and other hostile legislators aggressively questioning hapless State Department officials sent to defend the sale. To make matters worse, Fraser decided to hold hearings on human rights abuses in Iran. Although the State Department argued that torture was abandoned and the number of political prisoners declined, the bad publicity only intensified. When Vance tried to defend the sale on national interest grounds, the *Washington Post* called it "an embarrassment to Mr. Carter's professed intention to reduce the American role as the leading arms merchant in the world" (quoted in Rubin 1980b, 199).

The raucous debate in Washington was watched carefully in Iran. It is a truism that international relations rest on a system of expectations among states, which are sustained by a complex array of signals, not all of them deliberate or purposeful. Whether Washington understood it or not, the implications of the public discourse in America had a profound impact on the political dynamics in Iran.

BACK HOME: THE SHAH AND THE OPPOSITION TAKE MEASURE OF THE "CARTER REVOLUTION" IN FOREIGN POLICY

Doubts about the legitimacy of the shah's regime preceded the Carter presidency. In fact, ever since a CIA operation code-named "Ajax" helped to depose the nationalist Prime Minister Mohammed Mossadeq in 1953, observers have been divided over the extent to which the monarchy's ambitious plan to modernize Iran, known as the White Revolution, was representative of the collective belief system. Many scholars, reflecting the developmental paradigm, argued that the shah had secured a substantial constituency for modernization. But some of their colleagues accused them of financially motivated bias and denounced them as "Pahlavites" (Bill 1988a, 174–175, 334, 372–373). Those critics argued that the true repository of legitimacy was Mossadeq's National Front (NF). However, even those who touted the NF were wedded to the linear view of history, which gave them the confidence to predict that, once repression lifts, Iran would evolve into a Western-type of democracy.

With the benefit of hindsight it is clear that all Iran watchers overlooked the emergence of a fundamentalist challenge belief system. Tehranian (1980, 13) explained that Iran was composed of two "epistemic nations" with two belief systems and two parallel communication systems. With only limited intercourse between them, it was easy for American observers, largely attuned to the epistemics of modernization, to overlook the growth of the fundamentalist movement.

For all of Mossadeq's nationalism, the NF was a Westernized institution with little appreciation for Islamic piety. As it disintegrated in the sixties, religious and radical groups filled the political vacuum. The Liberation Movement of Iran (LMI), under the leadership of Mehdi Bazargan appealed to the bazaar merchants and moderate clergy. The Iranian People's Fedaii Guerrillas better known as Fedayeen Khalq, was a Marxist movement, which attracted the same elements as the communist Tudeh party. Bridging the religious-socialist divide was the People's Mojahedeen Organization, or Mojahedeen Khalq (Abrahamian 1989; Alaolmolki 1987).

In a noticeable departure from the NF philosophy, those groups questioned Iran's Western orientation. Jalal Al-e Ahmad (1984), an iconoclastic intellectual with ties to the Tudeh; accused Iranians of "Westoxication," a form of corrupt Western identity. The growing popularity of the dependency paradigm brought more anti-Western critique. In a mirror image of the developmentalists who saw Iran as a "modernizing miracle," Iranian neo-Marxists argued that Iran represented everything that was wrong with Western capitalism. In searching for a new direction, some, and most notably Ali Shariati, developed a unique synthesis of Islam and socialism. In his numerous writings Shariati proposed a new concept of historical change; a return to a genuine Islamic identity and an egalitarian society based on the Koran. The highly popular philosopher inspired a whole generation of Iranian intellectuals, including Abolhasan Bani Sadr who developed his own model of the so-called Third Way economy (Salehi 1988, 124; Alger 1983, 76; Dorraj 1990; Chehabi 1990, 186–187; Keddie 1981, 225; Katouzin 1983; Farhang 1979).

There is evidence to suggest that American dependency advocates helped to impart anti-Western themes. Many of them, like Barnet (1968, 226–229), Chomsky (1969, 60), Joyce Kolko and Gabriel Kolko (1972, 414–419) and Fred Halliday (1975), a British Marxist and a TNI fellow, had for years castigated American "colonial" role in Iran, fueling anti-Western rage (Chubin and Zabih 1974, 87–88). The Iranian Marxist Bahman Nirumand (1969, 8, 90–91, 114) acknowledged his debts to the "teaching of those Americans like Paul Baran, Herbert Marcuse, Paul Sweezy."

In attacking the West, the challenge belief system also questioned the values of democracy. Some studies have blamed the secular leaders of the NF for showing an "elitist distaste" for democratic mobilization, but the Iranian demographics were not auspicious. By 1970, half of the more than 30 million people were less than twenty years old and many were deeply impressed by the revolutions in Cuba, Algeria and China. Others were yearning for a strict religious commitment, but wanted Islam to address the issue of distributive justice (Siavoshi 1990, 158, 162; Dorraj 1990, 113–114).

It was Ayatollah Ruhallah Khomeini who managed to synthesize these two strands and produce a challenge belief system. In spite of his involvement in the 1963 antishah riots, the marja from Qom had remained an isolated figure until the early 1970s. Khomeini developed his views on Islamic governance in *Kashef-ul-Asrur* (Revealing the Secrets), an obscure 1942 tome which proclaimed that the Hidden Imam was the ultimate source of authority in Shiite Islam. Even so, it was only in his 1971 book *Velayat-e Faqih: Hokumat-e Islam* (The Jurist's Guardianship: Islamic Government) that the ayatollah, by now exiled by the shah to Najef in Iraq, advocated a theocratic government. Still, the rather esoteric book could hardly serve to mobilize a following large enough to challenge the regime.

There is reason to believe that, while in exile, Khomeini was apprised by his followers of the popularity of dependency themes. A number of them, including Mohammed Beheshti and Hashemi Rafsanjani, urged the ayatollah to respond to the Mojahedeen and other neo-Marxists, a message repeated by Khomeini's younger students who were likewise influenced by revolutionary Marxism. In what became a pattern for his future actions, the ayatollah decided to "pre-empt" this challenge by incorporating many of the themes of Shariati and the Mojahedeen into his own philosophy (Maddel 1993, 144–145; Rajaee 1982, 22).

Khomeini's teachings, together with the writings of Al-e Ahmadi, Shariati and Western dependencistas, were changing the political discourse in Iran. Rather than blaming Iran's underdevelopment on clerical influence, as the shah and other modernizers had asserted, the new theory held Western economic and cultural dominance responsible for the country's backwardness. For many of the shah's critics, India, which was said to emphasize human needs over economic growth, was a preferred model of choice. As long as Iran enjoyed prosperity, the challenge belief system was limited. However, the economic slowdown in the mid-1970s gave the critics an opening. While the monarchy and the developmentalists saw the difficulties as a transitional but normal part of the modernization process, the dependency advocates felt vindicated in their forecast. Many also saw an opportunity to move against the regime.

In addition to the fundamentalists under Ayatollah Khomeini, the LMI, the remnants of the National Front and the guerrilla groups decided to step up their operations. The opposition was greatly encouraged by the "Carter revolution" and hoped to use the human rights issue to maximize its advantage. In March, in an effort to test the limits of liberalization, a prominent intellectual wrote an essay critical of the regime. More criticism followed in May and June, including an open letter by Bazargan, Karim Sanjabi, Shapour Bakhtiar and Dariush Foruhar who accused the shah of despotism and urged application of the Universal Declaration of Human Rights. When the government failed to react, a virtual floodgate of activity followed; the Writers Association, the Association of Iranian Lawyers and the National Organization of University Teachers were all mobilized. The traditional merchants, the *bazaaris*, seized upon the perceived liberalization to revive the Society of Merchants, Guilds, and Artisans of the

Teheran Bazaar (SMGATB). The merchants printed antigovernment material and collected money to support students and clerics, including the fundamentalist followers of Khomeini. In what would later become an effective revolutionary tactic, the bazaaris shut down the Teheran market to protest the government.

Political parties, long suppressed by the regime, had also blossomed. First to act were the remnants of NF. Dariush Foruhar revived the Party of the Iranian People (PIN) and the Iran Party was reconstituted under Shapour Bakhtiar. The old Third Force of Khalil Maleki became the Society of Iranian Socialists. The veteran politicians set out to create the Third National Front, but the new organization was seriously weakened because Bazargan's LMI refused to join. In spite of its impressive pedigree, the NF lacked mass support and a national infrastructure. Less radical than the religious camp and the Marxists, the NF wanted a political reform under the slogan "The Shah should reign, not rule" (Parsa 1989, 172; Chehabi 1990, 228–229).

Whatever their differences, the NF, the LMI and other groups decided to pursue a common human rights strategy. In December the Iranian Committee for the Defense of Freedom and Human Rights (ICDFHR) was created; Mehdi Bazargan served as the Executive Council and two prominent lawyers, Abdolkarim Lahiji and Hasan Nazih were included, along with politicians and activists. Even before its official debut, the committee was involved with Martin Ennals from Amnesty International (AI) and William Butler from the International Commission of Jurists (ICJ), who together with the International Association of Democratic Lawyers (IADL), a Soviet front, increasingly targeted right-wing authoritarian regimes. Iranian human rights activists were also advised by Richard Falk, who was associated with the IADL, Ramsey Clark and the American Friends of the Revolution in Iran, an organization which supported the Tudeh (Muravchik 1984–85; Klehr 1988, 49; Ferguson 1983).

Although the seculars and religious moderates took the lead in the mobilizations, the radical elements were equally elated by Carter's victory. The Tudeh and its Russian patrons were eager to act after years of suppression. In fact, the Soviet leadership had been increasingly alarmed by the anticommunist crusades of the shah; Andrei Gromyko and Aleksei Kosygin apparently pressed for his removal. Tudeh, which opposed the growing arsenal of the shah, joined those who criticized the regime for squandering resources (Hoveyda 1980, 110; Singh 1980, 332, 366–367). The Marxist Fedayeens who bore the brunt of repression, became convinced that liberalization would further their cause. In December the group published a lengthy analysis which claimed that Carter was bound "to pressure the shah to wear a liberal mask" (Taheri 1988, 90).

The fundamentalists were equally aware of the opportunity created by the "Carter revolution." Ibrahim Yazdi, who coordinated the Muslim Students Association in the U.S., had previously alerted Khomeini that "the shah's friends in Washington are out" and advised action (quoted in Taheri 1988, 90). In September the Ayatollah circulated a letter to the *ulama* (clergy) urging them to protest the injustice of the regime (Milani 1988, 187). More to the point, Ayatollah Beheshti, who founded the Organization of Militant Clergy in 1976, stepped up his activities.

While the moderates had little public following, the fundamentalists were able to cash in on a seeming explosion of religious sentiments. More new mosques were built between 1968 and 1978 than in the previous two centuries and the number of pilgrims to Mecca reached some one hundred thousand in 1977. The number of theology students quadrupled and private donations to clergy reached an estimated $200 million, a sevenfold increase from the previous decade (Taheri 1988, 44; Arani 1980). Beginning in June, the mosque network began distributing Khomeini's tapes and other material (Stempel 1981, 57). What was more intriguing, fundamentalism, once a preserve of illiterate peasants and urban poor, had spread to the middle class. As one observer noted, Western educated men and women "were undergoing a subtle change in self-perception and rediscovering their religious-cultural roots . . . pilgrimages to Meshad and Mecca became socially in" (Bashiriyeh 1984, 74).

The fundamentalists were also able to profit from a shift in the political allegiance of the bazaaris. Initially the merchants supported moderate clergy, but as the turmoil grew, the fundamentalist camp came to be perceived as a more authentic vehicle for antiregime activity. Khomeini, always quick to spot a new mobilization opportunity, urged the clergy to pick up the pace of protest. It was a measure of his popularity that, by 1977, a prophecy, which told that a man from Qom "will summon people to the right path," circulated widely among the population (Mackey 1996, 277).

In contrast to the opposition, the shah dreaded the prospect of a Carter White House. Asadollah Alam (1992, 500), the court minister and the shah's confidant, wrote in his diary that if Carter wins "who knows what sort of calamity he may unleash on the world." According to Mansur Rafizadeh (1987, 248), the SAVAK representative in America, General Nematollah Nassiri, the SAVAK chief, predicted that if Carter is elected "the shah is sure to collapse." After Carter's victory, the monarch was reported to have commented that "it looks like we are not going to be around much longer" (Ashraf and Banuazizi 1985, 4).

To begin with, the shah was greatly disturbed by Carter's embrace of the regionalist philosophy. He had seen Iran's position as a Gulf "influential" undermined and his anticommunist crusade in Africa curtailed. The monarch was also upset that his protest against Moscow's shipment of large quantities of arms to Iraq went unheeded by an administration committed to a favorable view of the Soviet Union. He became truly alarmed when Washington asked Iran to recognize the Communist regime in Afghanistan (Pahlavi 1980a, 135; Scott 1996, 41–44; Ledeen and Lewis 1981, 95). Equally disturbing was the issue of arms sales. The AWACS debate in Congress, where the regime was savaged, was particularly humiliating. Reza Pahlavi vented his anger during an August 1 meeting with Sullivan; he told the ambassador that Iran had reached a "turning point" and warned that the issue of future relations with the United States would have to be studied (White Paper, 03556, 61). In public, he warned that only a strong Iran could provide security in the Gulf and the Indian Ocean (Mackey 1996, 250).

Looming even larger on the monarch's horizon was the human rights issue. A number of accounts describe him as "nervous" about possible pressure from the administration and sensitive to the hostility emanating from Congress (Bill 1988b, 17). Alam met in September 1976 with Uri Lubrani, the Israeli representative in Teheran, and other Israeli officials who tried to help Iran to change its image in the United States. They recommended the pollster, Daniel Yankelovich, who produced a two-volume report, "A Study of the Attitudes of the American Public and Leadership toward Iran." Urged by Yankelovich and others, the shah met, in May and June, with Ennals and Butler (Alam 1992, 500, 507, 517, 535, 538; Radji 1983, 42–47, 88, 129; Ghani 1987, 407).

The government also launched a limited liberalization program dubbed "unity without uniformity," after the shah asserted that the "people of Iran have now reached the required degree of political maturity." A law that prohibited the holding of political activists for more than twenty-four hours without charges was promulgated. In a bow to the international human rights lobby, the trial of political prisoners was moved to civilian courts (Radji 1983, 97; Taheri 1988, 88; Cottam 1988, 157; Saikal 1980, 191; Tahir-Kheli 1980).

Privately, the shah was apparently toying with the idea of a gradual transition to a constitutional monarchy. The so-called "King Carlos scenario" was modeled on the Spanish monarchy, and was designed to ensure the succession for the crown prince and please the Carter administration. Vance (1983, 346), who wrote that "without doubt the shah wanted to be perceived by us as a progressive, human reformer," felt that the shah was sincere. His fight with cancer might have also motivated the plan. By 1978, the shah, who was diagnosed with lymphosarcoma in 1974, was suffering from adverse effects of chemotherapy. However, the monarch and his advisers were not sure that an immediate election would produce a result favorable to the monarchy.

In spite of the fact that the country was slowly recovering from the recession, the government continued to be besieged by problems. Workers, upset by a rising cost of living, stepped up their strike activities, disrupting important sectors of the economy. The regime responded by accusing the workers of not working hard enough and of raising the cost of labor; it also decreed that wage increases should be linked to a rise in productivity. The army was frequently called in to take over striking facilities, inflaming passions (Parsa 1989, 142). The bazaari sector of the economy, which was hampered by the antiprofiteering campaign of the government, was even more turbulent. By the end of 1977, some 20,000 merchants were jailed or fined for price-control violations. The problem of peasants who streamed into the cities and the pressure on housing and services added to the climate of political agitation (Arani 1980; Bashiriyeh 1984, 103; Parsa 1989, 103–109; Katouzin 1978).

Many of the economic grievances were grounded in perceptions of relative deprivation. Although in absolute terms Iranians were quite reasonably well-off for a developing country, the regime suffered from the J-curve effect, a psychological reaction to a sudden economic decline (Moshiri 1985, 115). Relative deprivation was compounded by a growing egalitarian ethos: Once norms of what was considered an acceptable level of equality had changed, the government found itself on the defensive. The mix of Shariati-style neo-Marxism and Khomeini's teachings turned the issue of inequality into a major rallying cry among the urban poor. The middle classes, which benefited greatly from the shah's modernization, seemed to be caught up in the same psychological process.

Unsure how to handle the cascading demands, the shah appealed to Sullivan, who advised him to expand his public relations campaign in the United States. Alam (1992, 550–551) met again with Yankelovich to work out an Information Plan headed by Kalman Druck, a public relations consultant in the Ford administration. The Iranian government was particularly worried about rumors that Senator McGovern planned to investigate SAVAK activities in America and upset that Kermit Roosevelt, the CIA operative who helped to remove Mossadeq, was about to publish a book about the Ajax exploits.

Besieged by protest at home and bad publicity abroad, the regime became increasingly inconsistent in its policies. Bowing to public pressure, in August, the shah replaced his long-time prime minister Amir Abbas Hoveyda with Jamshid Amuzegar, a technocrat favored by the Carter administration. On August 5, Constitution Day, the king proclaimed that Iran "will have as much political freedom as the European democracies." But two weeks later he added: "Only by supporting the monarchy can people attain political freedom." The government released more political prisoners and there was a public show of denouncing torture. In a telling sign of the times General Nassiri was forced to adopt a low profile. However, there was no change in the monopoly of the official Rastakhiz party and selective harassment of opposition leaders continued. Ayatollah Mahmud Taleqani, a leading opposition figure, was sentenced to a long prison term; SAVAK agents broke up a NF meeting; lawyers who signed protest letters were blacklisted; and the bazaaris found no relief from the antiprofiteering campaign (Parsa 1989, 185; Chehabi 1990, 226, 229).

By fall of 1977, the turmoil became so pervasive that it threatened to overshadow the shah's planned November visit to Washington. The meeting was designed to smooth the relations between the monarch and Carter and improve Iran's image. However, the opposition mobilized some 4,000 students in order to disrupt the White House ceremony. When the police used tear gas, televisions captured Carter and the shah wiping away tears; in the background, the protesters shouted "down with the fascist shah." Back in Teheran, these images were interpreted through Persian cultural lenses. Convinced that such an embarassing incident could not have taken place without the permission of the administration, the shah's enemies concluded that Carter had abandoned the

Pahlavis. Buoyed by the so-called "Washington tears" misperception, activists launched a series of demonstrations (Rafizadeh 1987, 271; Sick 1985, 31).

That such a misperception could take hold was symptomatic of the political discourse in Iran. But the administration, guided by New Internationalism and insensitive to cultural realties, did not make a connection between events in Washington and Teheran. On the contrary, as the year progressed, the finer points of Iranian politics were totally overshadowed by the internal dynamics of the divided administration.

WASHINGTON'S CHALLENGE: THE POLITICS OF THE PREDICTIVE PROCESS

Well before the shah's visit, the administration began a new review of Iran's stability. Sullivan, who was caught between the moralpolitikers and the realpolitikers, triggered this round by developing an independent opinion of the shah's problems. To begin with, the ambassador did not share the view of liberal critics who described the monarch as a "harsh, vain, unreasonable tyrant." He found the shah to be a "timid, insecure and indecisive man" (Sullivan 1984, 268). Sullivan was also aware of the complexities of liberalization. On July 25, the ambassador sent a lengthy cable "Straws in the Wind: Intellectual and Religious Opposition in Iran," in which he detailed the shah's efforts to liberalize. He noted that, paradoxically, intellectual and religious dissent had grown, and listed a number of puzzling phenomena such as educated women who took to wearing chadors and growing resistance to women's rights legislation. The envoy concluded that Washington should lower its profile on the human rights issue. Instead, he and Charles Naas, the chief of station, wanted quiet diplomacy, an approach that put them on a collision course with Derian who advocated open and vigorous pressure (Documents, vol. 8; 173–180; David 1993, 52; Ghani 1987, 418; Bill 1988a, 247).

The ambassador was also worried about the economy, which he blamed on the poorly performing agricultural sector and the uneven development of industry. He asked the State Department to send a research team to Teheran, but the human rights group wanted to tag onto the project a number of sensitive issues, including military sales. Unwilling to give the moralpolitikers more ammunition, Sullivan (1981, 68–69) shifted the review to the CIA, where it was quietly shelved.

Valiant as Sullivan's attempts to ascertain the depth of discontent in Iran were, he was confounded by the embassy's inability to read popular opinion. In hindsight, one diplomat allowed that "in 1977, many of us were aware that something was wrong." Yet, as another admitted, "America did not realize what was happening in Iran" (Kennedy 1986, 196; Stempel 1981, 79). Richard Helms added that the embassy had a general sense of "dissatisfaction and disaffection of various elements," but no one person "Persian or foreigner, came forward or even secretly indicated that these elements are strong enough to destroy the government" (quoted in Herz 1979, 23). Indeed, the theoretical analysis demonstrated that discerning delegitimizing changes is enormously difficult; a vague sense of "things being wrong" does not translate into a successful prediction.

Some of the misperceptions stemmed from cultural ignorance. Only ten percent of diplomats spoke fluent Farsi, limiting others to contacts with the small English-speaking elite. Many of the embassy workers were Armenians, knows as the "Armenian Mafia," who were hostile to the local population. One observer called the embassy the "Golden Ghetto," progressively encrusted by a ring of Westernized Iranians. For instance, in spite of the immense popularity of Ali Shariati, by 1977 only a handful of embassy officials had heard about his writings. More generally, Americans serving in Iran were contemptuous of the native culture and often used derogatory terms to describe the locals (Anderson 1992; Bill 1988a, 381, 386, 398, 437).

Under normal circumstances, the embassy would have been able to rely on the CIA. But the "New View" Carter-Turner reform complicated matters. S. Turner (1991a) fired some eight hundred agents from the Directorate of Intelligence, whom he described as the "most recalcitrant of the old boys." Among them were political specialists needed to penetrate the political vortex of an impending revolution. The complicated rules for recruiting agents adopted by the Agency—summed up in a 130-page manual—made it hard to draft foreign nationals. Veteran chiefs of stations who were associated with the "old regime" were often replaced with people who had no knowledge of the language and culture of the country. There was a serious slump in morale, leading Gates (1996, 136–137) to observe that the "CIA was not a happy shop under Turner" whom he described as "leading with his chin and with a chip on his shoulder."

Among the departing agents was the veteran Iran analyst Earnest R. Oney, whose absence was felt particularly because Charles C. Rudolph, another leading Iran specialist, had retired in 1973. Sick (1985, 123) contended that the United States approached Iran from a position of "almost unrelieved ignorance." Much of the slack was picked up by SAVAK, but Sullivan (1981, 99) described this information as not "of the highest professional caliber." Washington analysts considered Iranian reports to be of the Chicken Little variety—a reference to the shah's allegedly alarmist views about communist subversion in his country.

Some academics, including Bill (1988a, 423) maintained that using Iran experts would have enhanced prediction. However, a perusal of the literature does not support this contention. By 1977, the dependency driven politicization thoroughly affected Iran studies with the "Pahlavites" and "anti-Pahlavites" reaching diametrically opposed conclusions about the legitimacy of the monarchy. Only a few studies, mostly by anthropologists, dealt with the religious belief system and the clerical class. Keddie (1972) was one of the few to discuss the ulama, but she predicted that the hold of Islam would erode. The most prescient was Alger (1972) who concluded: "It would be rash to predict the progressive disintegration of the political role of the ulama." In a more general way, Lewis

(1976) warned about the "return of Islam." Yet hardly anyone paid attention to these warnings.

Even as events in Iran unfolded in the summer of 1977, academics remained divided on the chances of the monarchy. Many of the scholars who participated in the October symposium on "Iran in the 1980s" were convinced that the "Shah-People" revolution was on the right track (Amirie and Twichell, 1978). Some, like Lenczowski (1977) and Berger (1977), felt that the human rights campaign might threaten the monarchy. Bill (1977, 166), who came to question the legitimacy of the regime, warned that the pendulum swung to "participation, individual rights and social justice." Still, both the defenders and the detractors of the shah did not notice the challenge belief system.

The predictive record of the business community was marginally better. By 1977, U.S. direct investment in Iran approached $1 billion and there were some 50,000 expatriates working in the country. Nevertheless, executives who did business in Iran were somewhat anxious during a briefing for Sullivan in May. The ambassador was amazed to discover that few corporations made long-term investment in Iran, normally a sign of low business confidence. By mid-1977, there was a growing reluctance to engage in new ventures. Some businessmen noted that Iranians were sending out record amounts of money. Political risk analysis services picked up the social tremors in Iran. Business International (BI), which used the Delphi technique, gave Iran a score of 10, a midpoint between "long term stability" and "active factionalism." Business Environment Risk Index (BERI) rated Iran's stability at 43 out of a possible 100 abroad (Kennedy 1991, 2, 7–8; Gillespie 1990; Sullivan 1981, 31; Hoveyda 1980, 101; Hulbert 1982, 100).

Whatever the level of confidence in the monarchy's stability, the administration intensified its review after the shah requested 140 F-16 planes in the fall. In anticipation of a new congressional debate, the State Department decided to prepare an official estimate. The moralpolitikers used the occasion to reiterate the view that Iran was run by a shaky and illegitimate government. On November 2, Theodore Moran from the Policy Planning Staff wrote a memorandum highly critical of Iran's capacity to absorb sophisticated weapons and warned about political implications; two junior CIA staffers supported these findings. In spite of the objections of the Near East Bureau, these misgivings found their way into the Policy Planning Staff report to Congress (Armstrong 1980a; Moran 1978–79; David 1993, 62).

The congressional-mandated State Department's report on human rights triggered more bureaucratic strife; according to one record, Iran was "fought over" more than any other country (Rubin 1980b, 193). Sullivan (1981, 21–23) confirmed that State officials linked to the left wing of the Democratic Party used the occasion to openly defy the White House. Brzezinski (1983, 526) alleged that there was a breakdown of political discipline in the State Department where "anti-Carter gossip and barely masked sympathy" for Edward Kennedy was common.

The infighting reached a high pitch before the shah's visit to Washington. The moralpolitikers wanted to use the occasion to pressure Iran to carry out political reforms. Whether by coincidence or not, Warren Christopher (1979, 261) publicly affirmed that Washington was prodding governments to improve their human rights record. However, Brzezinski and fellow realpolitikers argued that Iran was an important bulwark against what they saw as increased Soviet expansionism in the Horn of Africa and the Gulf. Indeed, Brzezinski was so worried about Moscow's involvement in Ethiopia and South Yemen that he began pushing for a Rapid Deployment Force (Moens 1990, 97). Brzezinski and the Pentagon felt that, in view of Soviet behavior, the shah's arms requests were fully justified. Moreover, the shah "should be encouraged to do whatever was necessary to preserve the control of the country" (Ledeen and Lewis 1981, 144; Teicher and Teicher 1993, 34).

Accounts of the shah's visit indicate that Carter was inclined to follow the advice of the realpolitikers. At a state dinner he referred to "unbreakable ties of friendship" between America and Iran. During a cordial private meeting the shah, in return for a promise to work against an Organization of Petroleum Exporting Countries (OPEC) plan to raise the price of oil, extracted a promise from Carter that the "special relations" of the Nixon era will continue. The president was so nervous about raising the human rights issue that he had re-hearsed the brief statement. The official communiqué noted Iran's interest in American nuclear energy and its unique position in the Gulf (Ioannides 1984, 25; Alexander and Nanes 1980, 448–449; Sale 1980).

The violent clash outside the White House cast some doubts on the shah's legitimacy. An October 5 report noted that the "shah seems to have no health or political problems . . . that will prevent him from being the dominant figure in Iran into and possibly throughout the 1980s" (State Department, 012290). After the shah departed, Sick (1985, 30–31) wrote a memo pointing to the systematic intimidation in Iran, but did not question the stability of the regime. Sick later explained that talks with several experts and briefing material "re-flected the unspoken but unanimous view of virtually all observers at the time that the "shah was Iran and Iran was the shah."

The mixed imperatives of the administration continued to color the Iran es-timate. A December 1 National Policy Paper reiterated that the monarchy was the "only sole element of continuity," but also asked the embassy to take up human rights and discussed the orderly transfer of politics (Documents vol. 12, 1–7). On December 10, Christopher sent a cable to Sullivan outlining American foreign policy goals including human rights. The message was an apparent bow to the moralpolitikers who kept pressuring for more reforms (Ioannides 1984, 31).

The administration was also keenly aware of the realpolitik "bottom line." When Teheran stalled the proposed oil price hike at an OPEC meeting, Carter, who faced a slumping economy, decided to include Iran among the countries scheduled for his New Year's trip. During a banquet on December 31, the president discarded a rather "anodyne toast" prepared by the embassy, and proceeded to effusively praise Reza Pahlavi. He described their talks as "priceless," their friendship as "irreplaceable," applauded the shah's concern for human rights, and concluded that the monarch is "dearly beloved by his people and sustaining an island of stability in the region." One participant described the diplomats as "dumfounded" (Salinger 1981, 5).

The toast provoked outrage in Iran and criticism in Washington. If anything, Carter's hyperbole deepened the cleavage between those who wanted to protect the monarchy for realpolitik reasons and those who wanted the shah sacrificed on the altar of moralpolitik. As Iran entered 1978, a divided administration faced the unenviable task of predicting a revolutionary change.

4

In the Eye of the Storm: The Carter Administration and the Iranian Revolution

Even by the standards of the turbulent twentieth century, a radical revolution is a relatively rare event. The likelihood that it would strike a strategically located American ally is even smaller. While no administration is prepared for dealing with a revolutionary situation, the Carter team was particularly ill-suited for the task.

To understand how the administration perceived the rapidly changing political scene, the following chapter will present the developments in a chronological-thematic manner. The situation in Iran will be presented first, followed by American analysis, predictions and policy initiatives. To facilitate the analysis, the events of 1978 will be broken down into four stages: the cyclical riots from January to July, the mass demonstrations of August and September, the mass strikes and disturbances in the fall and the collapse of the shah's regime in December.

THE CYCLICAL RIOTS: THE VIEW FROM TEHERAN

The tumultuous events of 1978 have been widely chronicled and are well known. Shortly after Carter's visit, the country erupted in a cycle of upheavals and repression that shook the regime to its core. On January 7 the *Ettela'at* newspaper published an unsigned article "Iran, and the Black and Red Reactionaries," which accused Khomeini of being a traitor, a foreigner and a homosexual, among others. It was followed by a two-day riot of some 4,000 religious students in Qom. Far from discrediting Khomeini, the article helped the fundamentalist camp. The three grand ayatollahs, Kazem Shariatmadari, Mohammed Reza Golpayegani and Najafi Ma'ashi demanded a retraction. When the authorities refused, the relatively moderate clerics were forced to support their more radical colleagues (Milani 1988, 11). Khomeini seized upon the incident to mount a huge effort to destabilize the regime.

Even before his exile to Najef, the Ayatollah had been building a revolutionary network. Helped by his close aides—Ayatollahs Mohammed Beheshti and Morteza Motahari, and Hojjatalislams Mohammed Javad Bahonar and Mohammed Mofateh—he formed the Combatant *Ulama* Society (*Ruhaniyat-e Mobarez*). The Consolidation Groups, also known as the Coalition Societies (*Mei'at hay-e Motalefa*), were another important part of this network. The secret societies included clerics and laymen, mostly bazaaris, schoolteachers, university professors and students, who opposed the shah's efforts of secularization. Many of them were able to propagate Khomeini's messages in the mosques and the *hayats*, local religious groups (Ioannides 1984, 51).

Additional Khomeini followers were trained by Syria, Libya, the Palestine Liberation Organization (PLO) and other radical organizations. Some of these activists, including Sadeq Gotbzadeh, Mustafa Ali Chamran and Ibrahim Yazdi, traveled as his emissaries to Europe and the United States (Ledeen and Lewis 1981, 111; Alpher 1980). After Iran signed a treaty with Iraq in 1975, Khomeini was able to send emissaries from Najef and receive a growing stream of pilgrims. His couriers and visitors carried large numbers of taped messages, which attacked the shah. By the end of 1977, helped by liberalization, the sermons were selling in the millions and even long-distance buses and taxis carried them (Alger 1983, 105). Amir Taheri (1985, 17–19, 212–213), the editor of *Kayhan*, recalled that the cassettes were extremely crude, appealing to the "basest sentiments of fanaticism among illiterate masses." In fact, he and other journalists believed that the sermons were SAVAK forgeries designed to discredit Islamic preachers.

Although the initial round of opposition to the shah was secular, the religious impact was felt in the streets and on the campuses. By 1976, many women at the universities voluntarily segregated themselves and started wearing the chador (Helms 1981, 125). During the October 1977 riots at Teheran University, masked students distributed leaflets demanding segregation by gender. Others demonstrated on behalf of Sayyed Mehdi Hashemi, an obscure *mullah* (cleric) and a follower of Khomeini, who was sentenced to death for murdering several moderate clerics in Isfahan. Public outcry intensified after Khomeini's oldest son Mustafa died suddenly on October 21, 1977. His death was widely attributed to SAVAK, and memorial services for Mustafa at the Jam mosque—Teheran's cathedral—and other cities turned into large demonstrations. The mass outpouring apparently convinced the exiled cleric that it was time to act; he sent some four hundred messages to his followers around Iran asking them to activate the antishah network.

More than a month later, a number of Teheran newspapers received a handwritten letter signed a "*fitwa* (eolict) from Imam Khomeini." Claiming to exercise his religious authority, the ayatollah declared the shah to be a "usurper" and a "rebel" and called for his removal. At the time the importance of the fitwa was not recognized and many of the newspaper editors dismissed it as a crude fabrication of the SAVAK (Taheri 1985, 170–172). Later in December, Khomeini ordered a number of his close followers under the leadership of Morteza Motahari to create a special secret committee to supervise the "defense of the faith." The committee, chaired by Motahari, included Ayatollahs Beheshti, Mohieddin Anvari, Ali Golzadeh-Ghafouri and Ahmed Mowla'i, as well as Hojjatalislams Bahonar and Ali Akbar Hashemi Rafsanjani, and became the nucleus of the *Sharay-e Enqelab-e-Eslami*, the Islamic Revolutionary Council (Taheri 1985, 172, 179, 180–181). Beheshti, a seasoned organizer, was also planning a political party; he later sent a number of Combatant Ulama activists to North Korea to study the mass mobilization techniques of the Communist party there (Hiro 1985, 158; Siavoshi 1990, 157; Fischer 1980a).

The newly activated network was at the core of Khomeini's efforts to delegitimize the monarchy. The initial stage featured a savage personal campaign against Mohammed Reza. The shah was accused of being a womanizer, a heroin addict, a homosexual, a secret convert to Judaism, Zoroastrianism or Mithraism and a cross-worshipper, an allusion to the Catholic conversion of the Shah's sister, Princess Shams. These allegations blended with rumors about the Shah's promiscuous lifestyle, and were publicized in thousands of leaflets and repeated from the pulpit by pro-Khomeini clergy, who also painted the monarch as *Shah-e-Emrika'i* and *Shah-e-Esraili*, the "American Shah" and the "Israeli Shah." Declared a *mahdur ad-damn*, an imposter, the shah was described as a "bastard," "dog," "lackey," "traitor," "rascal" and "jackass." Empress Farah was also vilified and sexually linked to President Carter. According to one inside observer, this highly delegitimizing language was needed in order to "demystify" the shah in the eyes of the largely illiterate but reverent Iranian masses (Taheri 1985, 174, 194–195, 199–200).

Another effective tool for destabilizing the regime was the skillful use of the forty-day cycle of mourning. Building upon the tradition commemorating the martyrdom of Hussein during the month of Moharran, fundamentalist activists organized public commemorations of people killed by the security forces. The January disturbances in Qom led to the February riots in Tabriz, which were followed by strikes and demonstrations in Yazd, Shiraz and Isfahan during the month of March. The cycle of mourning culminated in a large demonstration on May 9 in Teheran. Since the police sometimes followed the demonstrators into holy places, long considered out of bounds, the disturbances aroused the moderate clergy and secular public opinion. The leader of the moderate religious camp, Kazem Shariatmadari, was reported to have turned against the shah after troops killed a follower in his own house in Tabriz (Singh 1980, 370–372). Overall, compared to 1976, the cycles tripled the number of antiregime actions and quadrupled the number of participants (Ashraf and Banuazizi 1985).

In their quest to unsettle the regime, the fundamentalists were helped by the continuous economic turmoil. As indicated, the economic setback alienated a number of important constituencies, including the urban poor, the bazaari and the ulama (Walton 1980). By 1978, doubts about the possibility of quickly modernizing the Iranian economy had emerged on both sides of the political divide. Westerners and many of the shah's economic advisers complained about the poor political and business culture of the Iranians. They decried the lack of trust; the "bazaar" mentality of excessive, short-term profiting and low productivity. One business survey found widespread corruption, profiteering, and other forms of self-serving manipulation of the economic process (Richardson 1979; Miklos 1983, 50; Graham 1979, 196). The Business Council for International Understanding doubted whether American-style economic development, with its emphasis on the latest "in gold plated technology," was appropriate for a profoundly underdeveloped country like Iran (Sale 1981–82).

Left-wing critics continued to hammer at the social and economic disparities between the urban and rural sectors and between the poor and the well-to-do. Long-suppressed studies, publicized under liberalization, showed that the gap between the rich and the poor was growing. Dependency advocates attacked "foreign manipulation" and alleged that Iran was a virtual "agricultural protectorate" of the United States and a dumping ground for "capitalist products" (Parvin and Zamani 1979; Kadhim 1983, 7; Cockcroft, 1980). The critique of the military procurement program, which was first highlighted by the IPS Militarism and Disarmament Program, achieved a particular resonance.

In seizing upon these themes, Khomeini was able to tap into the Iranian mistrust of foreigners. He and Abolhasan Bani Sadr, who served as Khomeini's economic spokesman, explained that Western capitalists mismanaged the Iranian economy in order to maximize their profits. Bani Sadr also called for the removal of multinationals and the decentralization of large industrial units in order to restore the "humanistic dimension" and Islamic character to the economy (Bani Sadr 1978; Bani Sadr and Vielle 1978; Alpher 1980).

Khomeini's use of the "time-honored ploy" of blaming foreigners was part of a broader appeal crafted with Iranian political culture in mind. Observers have noted Iran's xenophobia—hatred and dislike of foreigners—and a suspicious view of the outside world (Graham 1979, 193; Rubin 1980b, 7; Fuller 1991, 19–20, 255–256; Abrahamian 1993, 112, 120; Azimi 1989, 30). Khomeini was especially adept in communicating in Manichean terms, where symbols count as much as substance and the political realm is divided into the forces of good and evil. By painting the United States as the "Great Satan," the ayatollah positioned himself as the defender of goodness (Mottale 1987, 12). Fundamentalists were also skilled in using the Islamic-Shiite idiom of political repression; the masses were mobilized to defend the righteous Hussein from the cruel and oppressive Yazid, the shah. Thus, the shah's "detour to the secular West" could be portrayed as "betrayal of their most sacred ideals and traditions, rather than as a mistaken turn" (Rosen 1982, 42; Fischer 1980b, 185).

All alone, the fundamentalists were making good use of the Persian love of rumors and conspiracy theories. They were fed by an alternative communication channel based on audio-cassettes, leaflets, and visual material devoted to commemorating the young "martyrs" of the revolution (Taheri 1985, 195; Sreberny-Mohammadi and Mohammadi 1988; Ram 1994; Green 1980). This system replaced the official channels as the most credible source of information in the eyes of the masses. Powerful rumor mills in the bazaar and the mosques accused the shah of "every sin in the book" and alternative interpretations of events eroded whatever little credibility the government had possessed (Taheri 1985, 194). As the Prime Minister Sharif-Emami would notice in the fall, "if we say it is daytime when its is daytime, people will deduce it is nighttime" (quoted in Tehranian 1980, 17; Pilskin 1980).

It was already noted that regime legitimacy rests on an interaction of three elements: symbolic, that is, diffuse respect for the authority system; exchange, that is, economic benefits derived from submitting to an authority system and coercive, that is, fear of violating the rules of the authority system. The economic decline helped Khomeini and the leftist opposition to discredit the validity claims on which the modernizing market-oriented distributive system rested. Since neopatrimonial regimes are exceptionally vulnerable to a symbolic assault, the personal attacks on the shah hurt the symbolic part of the legitimacy construct. Equally important, the cycle of violence, in which the security services were repeatedly challenged, began to erode the coercive part of the legitimacy nexus. (Cottam 1980, 297) argued that the riots undermined the image of the security forces and especially SAVAK: It "was revealed as bungling, inefficient and badly led, eroding its coercive mystique." Sick (1985, 34) credited "doing the 40–40" with undermining the legitimacy of the military and civilian authorities and others commented on the decline of the myth of terror (Salehi 1988, 101; Arjomand 1986).

However, the success of the fundamentalists would not have been possible without a skillful manipulation of the larger dynamics of political change. Of utmost importance in this context was Khomeini's progressive monopolization of the leadership and symbolism of the opposition. The National Front had little popular following and even less aptitude for political mobilization. Its three constituent parties—the Iran Party of Shapour Bakhtiar, the Iranian Nationalist Party of Dariush Foruhar and the Iranian Socialists of the National Movement led by Reza Shayan—were hardly more than personalized groupings clustered around veteran politicians (Abidi 1979). These men had an "elitist distaste" for political mobilization and shared the Western-educated elite's "liberal distaste for Iranian people whom they considered not sufficiently developed to participate in politics" (Siavoshi 1990, 158).

The leftist opponents of the regime, the Fedayeen Khalq, the Mojahedeen Khalq and the Tudeh also lacked in popular following and, sensing Khomeini's power, decided to work with the fundamentalists. Nuradin Kianuri, the incoming head of Tudeh, appreciated Khomeini's advocacy of social justice, and his anti-Western and anticapitalism crusade (Cottam 1988, 201). The Communists, with the help of the Soviet embassy in Teheran, played an important role in the psychological warfare against the shah. The Mojahedeen and the Fedayeen contributed to the destabilization by attacking police stations around the country and targeting American personnel (Lenczowski 1979a; 1979b; Taheri 1985, 216–217; Mottale 1987, 35).

With political groups expediently lining up behind the fundamentalists, the ayatollah had gradually emerged as the sole symbol of the opposition, a position that enabled him to dominate the discourse in the critical liminal period of the revolution. The concept of liminality, described in chapter 1, indicates a point of transition where all previous legitimacy claims are subject to a comprehensive critique. The malaise was so profound that even regime stalwarts were seized by a sudden sense of doubt (Pilskin 1980). The shah's ambassador to London confided to his diary that he could no longer defend SAVAK and wondered about his sense of "sudden revulsion" toward this long-entrenched institution (Sick 1985, 162).

At the same time, liminality reduces the political discourse in the society to a few simple and emotionally charged claims. By vocalizing an early demand to remove the shah, Khomeini came to represent the symbolic alternative to the regime without having to undergo a close scrutiny of his Islamic vision. Indeed, commentators have noted that many Iranians simply wanted to get rid of the shah without much thought about the successor regime (Pesaran 1985, 36; Limbert 1987, 119; Green 1982, 88–89; Katouzin 1981, 354). Other Iranians projected onto the elderly cleric their own political dreams, ranging from Mossadeq-type nationalism, to liberalism, socialism and Marxist radicalism. As one observer put it, "the Islam that they were now seeking, salvation was all things to all people" (Rosen 1982, 48; Foran 1994, 175). Whatever the roots of his appeal, the exiled cleric managed to turn economic or social deprivation into "ethic deprivation," defined as a stage when an individual finds that the dominant values of the society no longer provide him with a "meaningful way of organizing his life" (Dorraj 1990, 163).

Driven by liminality, the distaste for the shah helped the fundamentalists to mobilize the educated middle class. The overnight politicization of cultural identity made Khomeini the new embodiment of Iranian tradition. Quite possibly, the crisis of prosperity generated a Durhkeimian-like cultural disorientation among the more affluent Iranians. After more than a decade of Western style materialism, the question of "who am I?" was answered in spiritual-national terms of Islamic identity and "Iranianness." In other words, the Iranian intelligentsia shifted from an early identification with constitutional liberalism to a stage of moral and religious renewal (Arani 1980; Arjomand 1988, 110–111; Bashiriyeh 1984, 74). Such a shift can explain why the 1906 revolution, based on a limited knowledge of the West, led to a Western-style constitution; but in 1978, the upheaval fueled a widespread anti-Western backlash (Keddie 1986, 7–14). This type of psychological dynamics can also explain the apparent paradoxical behavior of middle class Iranians noted by lay observers and scholars alike. Ambassador Sullivan (1984, 271) and the journalist, Joseph Kraft (1978), reported that many Westernized professionals expressed a passionate desire to see the shah go and a matching conviction that Islam is the only path to happiness. Studies of women described how educated women translated their antishah sentiment into support for Khomeini; in the process they came to emphasize their "cultural," as opposed to their gender, identity. Many middle class Iranian women, otherwise secular, took to wearing the veil as a sign of revolutionary fervor (Nima 1983, 91; Shoaee 1987; Sansasarian 1982; Azari 1983; Nashat 1983). Still, other scholars interpreted the surrender of the middle class to Khomeini as a form of self-deception in exchange for an "instant gratification of regicidal vengeance" (Arjomand 1988, 109).

Even if self-deception played a role in Khomeini's following, the fundamentalists took steps to disguise their ultimate goal of an Islamic republic. Initially, the Islamic Revolutionary Council and the Combatant Ulama Society acted in total secrecy. Motahari and Beheshti organized "spontaneous" crowds outside the residences of long-forgotten Mossadeq-era politicians, including Karim Sanjabi, the shy and retiring NF leader. Demonstrations were launched to enhance the visibility of Mehdi Bazargan and others. Motahari called this tactic "leading from behind"; a part of a larger campaign designed to assure the middle classes and the Western media that "Iran was experiencing a democratic revolution against a medieval and tyrannical regime" (Taheri 1985, 198–199). Camouflage and denial were part of the time honored Shiite strategies of taqieh, khod'eh, tanfih, ketman and other forms of dissimulation developed to fight a powerful enemy. Taken together, these tactics created a "*nebuleuse*," a screen behind which the fundamentalists could promote their agenda (Cogan 1990; Miklos 1983, 57, 59–60; Kapuscinski 1985, 73; Zonis 1971, 46; Taheri 1985, 229; Rafizadeh 1987, 362; Helms 1981, 135).

In retrospect, the revolutionary potential of the cyclical disturbances and Khomeini's strategy should have been more obvious to the shah's government and to American Iran watchers. However, at the initial stage of a revolution the challenge belief system and the countermobilization that it drives are largely subterranean. The crucial period when fermentation occurs looks much more obvious in retrospect. In this sense, revolutions are like erupting volcanoes: "they are noticed and taken seriously by observers after they have erupted" (Salehi 1988, 61; Kazemi 1980b). Indeed, neither the Iranian government nor the Americans seemed to understand the liminal importance of the cyclical riots.

Initially, the regime was acting as if the main problem was economic. When the shah picked Amuzegar as his new prime minister, he followed the American prescriptions for handling the economic crisis. Amuzegar, an American trained engineer who lacked political experience, adopted Carter's favorite "zero-based budgeting" and other anti-inflationary measures. Although the economy began to improve, Amuzegar further alienated critical constituencies, including the clergy, whose long-standing government stipend was cut.

Khomeini's fitwa presented the government with a new challenge. In December the shah ordered the creation of a special committee to fight the growing militancy of Khomeini and his followers. According to one source, the committee prepared a draft of the article that appeared in *Ettela'at*, which the shah personally approved (Taheri 1985, 172, 200). General Robert E. Huyser (1986, 9–10), the deputy commander of NATO forces, who visited Teheran in April 1978, recalled that the monarch told him that the ayatollah had a "blood vendetta" against the royal family. Other observers argued that Amir Abbas Hoveyda, who became the Imperial Court Minister, passed on the article to the Minister of Information Dariush Homayun, in an effort to unsettle his rival, Amuzegar (Forbis 1980, 3; Milani 1988, 190–191). Mehdi Pirasteh, a former Minister of Interior, supported this version in his conversation with a political officer in the American embassy (Documents, vol. 25, 72–74). More generally, the festering rivalry between Hoveyda and Amuzeger was said to have played a role in the government's difficulty in handling the revolutionary situation (Pipes 1981).

Whatever the origin of the *Ettala'at* initiative, the extent and the ferocity of the riots clearly took the regime by surprise. Governmental response followed a pattern that would be repeated throughout the year: sporadic and indecisive security measures against the protestors intermingled with conciliatory gestures towards the opposition. Fereydoun Hoveyda (1980, 24), the brother of the court minister who had an audience with the shah in April, asserted that Mohammed Reza was determined to pursue liberalization and viewed the disturbances as a price to be paid. However, at the beginning of May the monarch became shaken enough to postpone a scheduled visit to Hungary and Bulgaria. During a May 13 news conference, the shah accepted part of the blame for the casualties and pledged to continue the liberalization process (Singh 1980, 372).

According to Hedayat Eslaminia, the former head of the Majlis, the shah's inner circle fought bitterly over the proper response to the upheaval. During a May 13 gathering of security and police officials, General Nassiri, demanded to use decisive force. He was overruled by General Hossein Fardoust, a childhood friend and confidant of the shah, who argued that the army draftees could not be counted upon to quell the rebellion (Documents, vol. 25, 23–26). On June 6, Nassiri, the hated symbol of SAVAK and his deputy, General Ali Mo'tazed were dismissed. General Nasser Moghadam, an outspoken critic of Nassiri and chief of military intelligence who was credited with introducing democratic reform in the armed forces, replaced him.

The halfhearted policy of conciliation backfired on the government. The level of repression was high enough to fuel public rage, but the concessions did not mollify the more moderate groups in the society. Cottam (1988, 186–188) and Arjomand (1988, 133) are among those who maintain that the revolution would not have occurred, or would not have taken the radical turn it did, had it "not been for the regime's entirely avoidable failure to maintain coercive control" at this early stage. Interestingly, both supporters and detractors of the shah have shared this conclusion. Miles Copeland (1989, 250–254) a former intelligence operative who traveled to Iran in June at the behest of the hard-line Iranian ambassador to Washington, Ardershir Zahedi, was of the same opinion. Copeland met with both Moghadam and Nassiri, who complained about the softness of the shah; Nassiri warned that the situation was "beyond salvation," and, barring a crackdown, the regime was doomed.

The government's reluctance to take harsh measures was at least partially related to the American and Western stand on human rights. On February 17, the administration issued a Presidential Directive (PD) that pledged, among other things, to cooperate with nongovernmental organizations in order to further human rights. The PD also detailed the measures that the United States took to "encourage" the Iranian government to improve human rights conditions (White Paper, 03564, 10–12). In March a Committee for the Defense of Rights of Political Prisoners in Iran was formed. The committee, which had some 500 members, worked with William Butler from the ICJ and was regularly consulted by foreign journalists. The shah conveyed his misgivings about the human rights issue to Nelson Rockefeller, who visited in May (Sick 1985, 33; Thornton 1991, 248). According to Huyser (1986, 11), the shah expressed fear that he might fall into disfavor with President Carter. In his memoirs, the monarch bitterly accused America of trying to remake the rest of the world in its image, "no matter what the history . . . of other nations may be" (Pahlavi 1980a, 27–28). The British ambassador, Anthony Parsons, reinforced American pressure, which was behind the decision to sack Nassiri (Ledeen and Lewis 1981, 97, 103). Ironically, Parsons (1984, 144) later concluded: "if the shah had not 'liberalized' at the end of 1976, he would still be on his throne, or rather his son."

While Western pressure was apparently foremost on the shah's mind, there could have been additional factors involved. Since Mohammed Reza's cancer took a turn for the worse in early 1978, he might have been trying to ease the way for Prince Reza Cyrus (Hiro 1985, 94; Zabih 1979, 48–49). It is also quite possible that the shah was simply not ruthless enough to deal decisively with the opposition, a belief that Sullivan (1984, 260) seemed to harbor when he spoke about the "private humanity" of the monarch. Parsons (1984, 156) noted that even at his height he was not "ruthless" enough to destroy the clergy.

Even without these complicating factors, deciding on whether to pursue coercion or compromise was not an easy task. An appropriate governmental strategy would have to be based on an evaluation of the relative strength and position of the opposition groups. However, after the revolution it became clear that SAVAK knew precious little about the secret network established by Khomeini and his dissimulating tactics. The security services arrested Karim Sanjabi and harassed other moderates without finding the real culprits. There was even a faction in the SAVAK that argued that Khomeini would be a potential counterpart for the Communists. Overall though, the government shared the entrenched contempt that the ruling class had toward the mullahs, thus overestimating the power of the moderates (Sick 1985, 165; Taheri 1985, 186). What is worse, this type of miscalculation was reinforced by American Iran watchers.

THE CYCLICAL RIOTS: THE VIEW FROM WASHINGTON

The riots in Qom had a limited impact on the administration's discourse on Iran. Dispatches from the American embassy in Teheran noted the disturbances, but there was little alarm. A January 14 briefing mentioned the "growing restiveness in Iran over the past several months." A longer January 26 piece commented that Qom riots elevated the religious opposition to a major player. A January 29 summary argued that "traditional Islamic groups are stronger than anytime since 1963." A February 1 report tried to provide a more detailed look at the opposition groups, but admitted to limited information. It speculated that the moderate Ayatollah Shariatmadari may not be in control (Documents, vol. 12, 16–20, 24–30, 31–38; White Paper, 03564, 6; Armstrong 1980b; David 1993, 62). There was more concern after the Tabriz riots. The Farsi-speaking American consul in Tabriz, Michael Metrinko, began to report on the alliance between the clergy and the bazaaris. The Tabriz riots were also discussed during the weekly country team meeting at the embassy (Documents, vol. 12, 72–75). Gary Sick (1985, 35) Brzezinski's aide, warned in a February 24 memorandum about the "reactionary Muslim right wing" sustained by a network of mosques.

Still, there was no sense of foreboding. On the contrary, the human rights activists saw the disturbances as a sign that the pressure on the shah was working and tried to push further (Vance 1983, 323). In a February 13 speech before the American Bar Association, Warren Christopher (1979) reaffirmed American commitment to human rights, a message he repeated in a directive to the embassy in Teheran (Documents, vol. 12, 10–15). A month later, Patricia Derian (1979) urged "constant, unrelenting pressure" by lawyers, academics, jurists and clergy to achieve improvement in human rights. Sullivan reassured Washington that he was working through an intermediary from an international organization. This was an apparent reference to William Butler whom the embassy preferred to the more aggressive Martin Ennals from AI (Documents, vol. 12, 16–20).

As usual, human right activists could count on congressional opponents of the shah, who were eagerly awaiting the State Department's human rights report due in early February (Alexander and Nanes 1980, 454–460). On February 28, Fraser held hearings during which a representative from AI denounced the regime. An Iranian request for weapons and tear gas gave the human rights lobby additional leverage. Sullivan (1981, 147–148) recalled that the issue split the State bureaucracy: The Near East and South Asian Affairs Bureau favored the request, but Anthony Lake from Policy Planning Staff, Leslie Gelb from the Political-Military Bureau and Patricia Derian were opposed (Sullivan 1981, 147–148; Rubin 1980b, 208). Sullivan (1980, 177) contended that there were "those" in the State Department "who were so strongly opposed to the shah because of the human rights abuses of his regime that they wished to see him collapse no matter what the consequences for the United States or its allies."

The shah's academic opponents were also involved in the discourse. In March several Iran experts managed to persuade George Griffin, the officer in charge of Iran in INR, that the shah was losing support among his traditional followers. Griffin, already uneasy about the events in Qom and Tabriz, organized an academic seminar for middle-level State officials. James Bill, who had visited Teheran in December 1977 and met with some religious leaders, including Ayatollah Taleqani, believed that the "educated professional middle class" represents the greatest danger to Iran's monarchy. In his paper, "Monarchy in Collapse," Bill warned that the shah's future would be grim, unless the cycle of violence was broken. He and other academic advisers argued that time was running out for the shah and urgently recommended further democratic reforms (Sale, 1980; Bill, 1988a, 245; Armstrong 1980b; Rubin 1980b, 208).

But many practitioners disagreed with the seminar's conclusion. The embassy in Teheran felt that the shah was firmly in control and, as Sullivan later put it, "most of us . . . saw the events in Qom and Tabriz . . . as growing pains of a society" that modernized too fast. The CIA and the DIA were also optimistic. However, the embassy admitted that it had no communication with the less educated and poorer sectors of the Iranian society, making its analysis less than stellar (Sullivan 1981, 142; Armstrong 1980b; Documents, vol. 12, 79–83). When, in March, Turner ordered a National Intelligence Estimate on Iran, the disagreements between the INR and the CIA-DIA analysts could not be bridged.

It was already noted that the CIA reform made it harder to penetrate the underground fundamentalist network or analyze the extent of public discontent with the regime. There were also major structural changes in the analytic division: The Greece/Turkey/Iran branch was eliminated and a new Persian Gulf/Iran branch was established, but the new unit lacked Persian specialists. Because of political reasons, experienced operatives like Richard Helms and Kermit Roosevelt were largely ignored. So was Archibald Roosevelt, the political adviser to Chase Manhattan Bank, who warned about the danger to the shah (Bill 1988a, 418; Sick 1991, 23; Ledeen and Lewis 1981, 132; Stapenhurst 1992, 141).

By May, the disturbances in Iran, dubbed the "Teheran spring," began to raise alarm at the highest levels of the State Department and the White House. On May 10 Vance (1983, 324) reported to President Carter that the upheaval amounted "to the most serious antishah activity since 1963." Around the same time, the American embassy in Teheran became aware of two reports predicting that the shah would be deposed within a year. A junior intelligence officer of the French Service de Documentation Extérieure et de Contre-Espionnage (SDECE) wrote one, and Uri Lubrani, the unofficial Israeli envoy in Teheran and Reuven Merhav, a Mossad operative, authored the other one. The Israelis based their conclusion on an extensive network of contacts around the country and on Lubrani's audience with the shah in April. In June, Lubrani followed up his report with a long cable to Tel Aviv; the Israeli authorities became concerned enough to urge Iranian Jews to leave the country (Sullivan 1987; Ledeen and Lewis, 1980; Ledeen and Lewis 1981, 126; Black and Morris 1991, 330; Salinger 1981, 35). According to Shlomo Gazit (1988), a former head of Israel's military intelligence, Jerusalem passed on Lubrani's report to the CIA, but the agency deemed both the French and Israeli conclusions "alarmists." The CIA had little faith in French intelligence and the Lubrani report was suspect because the Carter administration assumed that Menachem Begin, facing intense American pressure to negotiate with the Arabs, was trying to scare Washington.

Even so, the embassy intensified its own efforts to evaluate the situation. In May, John Stempel, a political officer, tried to improve contacts with the dissidents and began meeting with Mohammed Tavakoli (Tavassoli), a leader in the Liberation Movement of Iran. The embassy forwarded, without comments, a May 20 cable from Metrinko in which the Armenian Archbishop of Tabriz, Diyair Panossian, was quoted as warning that the Pahlavi regime would not survive the trouble. But the diplomatic traffic did not exhibit any great sense of alarm; The cables in May and June argued that in spite of a serious challenge, the shah "remains master of all necessary instruments of power," as one dispatch put it. Sullivan and George Lambrakis, a political officer, who drafted many of the cables, were apparently confident that moderate religious leaders would not follow the more radical Khomeini. In a June 21 dispatch, Lambrakis reported that Shariatmadari broke with Khomeini because of his extreme antishah position. To be on the safe side, the embassy advised not to push the human rights issue (Documents, vol. 12, 91–93, 97–98, 103–128; vol. 25, 39–42; Bill 1988a, 248; Armstrong 1980b).

The deep divisions in the administration exacerbated the normal difficulty of following the rapid changes in Iran. In the first quarter of 1978, the realpolitikers in the NSC and the State Department scored a victory when they managed to nudge Carter toward a more globalist position. Brzezinski believed that Moscow was set on challenging the United States in Africa. In spite of Vance's bitter opposition, the President, already under relentless attacks for his confused and weak foreign policy, chose a March speech at Wake Forest University to send a stern message to the Kremlin. Many commentators interpreted Carter's denunciation of Soviet and Cuban intervention in Africa as a tentative retreat from his regionalist approach, a view that was confirmed by Robert Gates (Shoup 1980a, 128; 1980b; Davis 1980; Gates 1996, 73–74).

This switch put Brzezinski and other realpolitikers in a better position to control the debate on Iran. According to a former State Department official, the realpolitikers "panicked" when the liberalization produced the "Teheran spring" (Mansur 1979, 31). The National Security adviser, who had independent contacts with the Iranian ambassador Zahedi, sought to reduce the human rights pressure. Brzezinski took to citing Crane Brinton's *The Anatomy of Revolution* and the work of Harvard historian William Langer to underscore his thesis that revolutionary opportunities are increased when the state fails to apply coercive measures. Brinton stressed that liberalization in the middle of a violent upheaval would only encourage the opposition to demand more and ultimately doom the regime (Smith 1986, 189; Ledeen and Lewis 1981, 33). According to the realpolitikers, the best strategy was to support the shah and avoid "alarmist" predictions, at least publicly. Testifying in June before a congressional committee, Assistant Secretary of State for Near East and South Asian Affairs Harold Saunders seemed to follow this line. He claimed that the "majority of Iranians thoroughly approve of the very substantial improvements" during the past three decades (Rubin 1980b, 210).

The moralpolitikers, supported by some academic experts, saw in the cyclical riots a confirmation of their long held conviction that liberalization was the only way to proceed. What is more, many of them viewed the shah as a major liability and hoped that he might be toppled. As one commentator summed it up, "the shah's continued existence constituted an affront to civilized morality" of some powerful personalities in the administration (Spencer 1983, 77). The Human Rights Bureau, distrustful of official channels, sent its own representatives to closely monitor the shah's handling of the opposition (Prados 1991, 435–436; Copeland 1989, 250). The antishah group used a combination of modernization and dependency arguments to support the contention that, without the Pahlavis, Iran would evolve into a democracy sensitive to social needs of the underprivileged. Some like Moran (1978/79) continued to hammer at the military sales. Others like Cottam (1978a) advocated "political engineering" to turn Iran into a more liberal state. Not surprisingly, this group assumed that the belief system represented by the National Front—a blend of secularism, democracy and economic nationalism—was fairly representative of the population at large.

Those who wanted to see the National Front prevail, either ignored Khomeini's fundamentalist agenda or subsumed it under Bazargan's LMI. This view prevailed in spite of some reports from the embassy that showed unease with Khomeini. A February 12 dispatch quoted Parviz Raein, an AP correspondent, who complained that the international press portrayed Khomeini as a great libertarian (Documents, vol. 12, 70–71). On April 11, George Lambrakis reported that Hedayatollah Matin-Daftari, a NF leader, told him that Ayatollah Shariatmadari had been overshadowed by the much more political Khomeini and that Shariatmadari's followers "do not dare to stand up to the edicts from Khomeini" (Documents, vol. 23, 32–36). Even though the fundamentalist deception might have blurred the picture, the optimistic forecast could not have prevailed without the paradigmatic expectation of the moralpolitikers.

With Brzezinski gaining ascendancy over the State Department, the antishah lobby feared that its input into the discourse on Iran would be limited. However, a combination of factors gave the group a big boost. In early 1978, Henry Precht, one of Gelb's senior assistants in the Bureau of Political-Military Affairs, replaced Charles Naas as the head of Iran Desk. Precht, who served a tour of duty in Teheran, came to believe that the Pahlavi regime was seriously endangered, if not mortally wounded. Bill (1988a, 246) claimed that Precht arrived at this realization as a result of "an honest analysis of day-to-day events," but others have argued that he was a core member of the moralpolitikers (Sick 1985, 69; Muravchik 1986, 211; Milani 1988, 182; Moens 1990, 128). As Brzezinski (1983, 355) put it, Precht "was motivated by doctrinal dislike of the shah and simply wanted him out of power altogether."

Under normal circumstances, Precht would have been relegated to a relatively minor role in policy making (Esterline and Black 1975, 61–63). However, since senior state officials were involved in the intense SALT and Camp David negotiations, Precht, with the tacit support of Vance, became the virtual "overlord" of Iran's policy. He later recalled that "this was one of those happy occasions on which a desk officer can have a major impact on policy" (Ledeen and Lewis 1981, 170; Salinger, 1981, 22–23; Follet 1983, 74). Precht utilized his position to push the theory that, without serious reforms, the Pahlavi dynasty would collapse. He was credited with pressuring Teheran to relieve Nassiri from his SAVAK post (Sale, 1980). Precht ardently believed that the shah's demise would bring the NF into power (Ledeen and Lewis, 1981, 159). Without naming Precht directly, Sullivan (1981, 177) wrote that the antishah group in the State Department was so strongly opposed to the monarch "that they wished to see him collapse no matter the consequences for the United States or its allies."

As the revolution accelerated, both groups mobilized to influence the predictive process and the policy prescriptions that were based on it.

THE MASS PROTEST: THE VIEW FROM TEHERAN

Much to the relief of the administration, June and the beginning of July brought respite from the cycle of mourning riots. Many attributed the decline in tension to the limited political reforms, the change in SAVAK management and the public apology to Ayatollah Shariatmadari. There was some hopeful development in the economy as well. The Amuzegar government lowered the rate of inflation, bringing it down from a high of 35 percent in 1977 to just about 10 percent, and improved the performance of some key economic indicators. However, the credit squeeze upset the merchants and caused a slowdown in construction, particularly hurting the unskilled laborers in Teheran. The squatters in the slums of Teheran rioted after the government resumed efforts to clear them out. At the end of July, tales had spread that the shah was shot in an assassination attempt; on August 5, at the start of Ramadan, violent demonstrations broke out around the country. By August 11, Isfahan and other cities had to be placed under a curfew to control intense rioting and there were rumors that Israeli commandos disguised as police shot at the crowds.

Adding to the tension was a string of mysterious arsons in movie theaters and other public buildings. In the middle of Ramadan, on August 19, a fire in the Rex Cinema in Abadan killed about 400 people. The fires were apparently set by extremist fundamentalists protesting the showing of "sinful" movies, a fact that surfaced during a trial conducted after the revolution (Ashraf and Banuazizi 1985). However, the rumors, which quickly spread throughout Iran, blamed SAVAK for starting the conflagration and for locking the doors that trapped the victims, many of them women and children (Kazemi 1980a, 86–88; Rubin 1980b, 206; Hoveyda 1980, 40–41; Singh 1980, 373).

The new cycle of violence shook the monarchy badly. When calm returned after the cyclical mourning riots, the shah attributed it to the government's conciliatory actions, including his own pilgrimage to a religious shrine. To calm the waters, on August 5, the shah promised to hold free elections in less than a year and to relax the freedom of speech and press, but the disturbances, which culminated in the Abadan fire, continued. Faced with continuous turmoil, the government split over strategy; some ministers supported Amuzegar, but others, including the new head of SAVAK, General Moghadam, demanded the appointment of Jaafar Sharif-Emami. Moghadam, who had contacts with the opposition, was advised that Sharif-Emami, a pious person from a religious family, might be a good compromise candidate. Once appointed, Sharif-Emami called for a policy of "national reconciliation" and tried to appease the opposition by restoring the Islamic calendar, closing casinos and removing other offending symbols of Westernization. The media was allowed to discuss social and economic problems, and political activity was legalized. The moderate line had the blessing of Moghadam, who decided to tone down the government's opposition to Khomeini (Documents, vol. 25, 39–42). On August 31, the new prime minister initiated contacts with the opposition and was told by Shariatmadari that the 1906 Constitution should be used to create a strong parliament and a limited monarchy.

In spite of the concessions, the radicals decided to challenge Sharif-Emami by calling two large demonstrations on September 4 and 5. While the government had not authorized the demonstrations, it did not interfere. Emboldened by the victory, the fundamentalists and the left called for a general strike and more demonstrations. On September 7, half a million people marched in Teheran demanding death to the Pahlavis, the leadership of Khomeini and, for the first time, an Islamic Republic. In response, the government declared martial law, but the new rules did not receive much publicity. On September 8 about 20,000 people massed on Jalah Square, for what was billed as a religious celebration. When the security forces opened fire a large number of protesters were killed and wounded. The so-called "Black Friday" has been widely considered a turning point in the revolution. Government and independent sources put the number killed at 120 or less (Documents, vol. 25, 72–79). However, a popular rumor alleged that 50,000 people were murdered by Israeli soldiers firing on the crowd. As in the case of Abadan, the government version of events was rejected totally (Sick 1985, 50; Pilskin 1980; Cottam 1988, 176).

These remarkable revolutionary dynamics masked a bitter power struggle among the opposition forces. The secular grouping was too fragmented to formulate a coherent strategy and Karim Sanjabi, the nominal head of the NF, was not strong enough to calm the fratricidal struggles between his own cohorts and not popular enough to appeal to the masses mobilized by the fundamentalists.

One observer described the Mossadeq-era politicians as "seedy and senile" and another accused the secularists of "analytical weakness and destructive behavior" that played into the hands of the fundamentalist clergy (Arani 1980; Farhang 1987, 172). The LMI was in a better position to claim the mantle of leadership, not the least because of the support of Shariatmadari and other moderate religious leaders. The LMI had a relatively modest political agenda centered on the 1906 Constitution. It called for the legalization of political parties, free elections, abolition of military tribunals, the release of political prisoners and the dissolution of SAVAK. By early summer, Bazargan become increasingly uneasy about some of the more radical positions taken by Khomeini, whom he considered out of touch with the political reality in Iran (Sick 1985, 47).

In August, in an effort to settle the differences with Khomeini, Bazargan sent the ayatollah a message outlining the political strategy of LMI. Bazargan reiterated his general convictions that the shah would eventually have to go, but he urged the "bastion-by-bastion" approach of taking power gradually. In the meanwhile, Bazargan, Shariatmadari and other moderates were willing to work with Sharif-Emami. Both the secularists and religious moderates were convinced that the shah, pressured by the United States, had no choice but to pursue democratization (Chehabi 1990, 238–239; Ioannides 1984, 31–33).

Khomeini, who feared that a gradual approach topped by a free election would dissipate the revolutionary ardor building since January, vehemently disagreed with the "bastion-by-bastion" philosophy. Acting through the underground network, the Islamic fundamentalists, often helped by the Fedayeen and Mojahedeen, stepped up the pressure against the government. A standard tactic was to force bazaar merchants to close their stores; those who refused found their stores broken into or burned down (Parsa 1989, 106). Another strategy was to "persuade" moderate religious figures to radicalize and switch support to Khomeini (Taheri 1985, 215; Kraft 1978). There was also an increase in attacks on military installations, police stations and civilian supporters of the monarchy.

Unlike the moderate opposition, Khomeini showed great skill in mobilizing followers. When in August the newspaper *Kayhan* printed a picture of the exiled ayatollah for the first time, the circulation increased to over a million copies (Randal 1978). The fundamentalists were helped by the presence of a large number of unemployed young men who roamed the streets and provided the core of the demonstrators at any given event (Arani 1980, 13). Sullivan (1984, 265, 272) noted that "there was some inner fury in these men that appeared to need physical release." In view of the ambassador, these angry young men, augmented by new arrivals from the countryside, could not be placated by a rational democratic discourse.

The fundamentalists had additional reasons for rejecting the democratic agenda of their opposition partners. While publicly offering homage to human rights and democracy, Khomeini was laying the foundation for an Islamic republic. He quietly ordered a French translation of his book and, using a taqieh-style "doublespeak," began to distance himself from Western concepts of democratic governance. In a May 6 interview with *La Monde*, he rejected the monarchy and also demanded an amendment to the 1906 Constitution. In a June 5 speech, he took issue with Western notions of human rights; in a July interview with MERIP, he alluded to an Islamic state of the "Prophet and Imam Ali" (Taheri 1985, 197; Chehabi, 1990, 239; Moshiri 1985, 65; Khomeini 1978, 20; Ioannides 1984, 34).

As long as Shariatmadari and other moderate clerics were able to appeal for restraint, secular politicians and their counterparts in the LMI could delude themselves into thinking that they were leading the events. However, as the cycle of violence in August and early September intensified, the moderates lost control of the situation. Ironically, the lifting of political controls brought thousands of dissidents into the country, among them dozens of guerrillas trained in El Fatah camps in Lebanon who added to the turmoil (Taheri 1985, 221). Even before the "Black Friday" episode, it became clear that the other parties needed Khomeini's blessings for any new initiative. Things became much worse after Jalah Square; few opposition leaders had dared to engage in a dialogue with the monarchy for fear of being labeled traitors. One historian surmised that Jalah Square "must have convinced both government and opposition" that Khomeini was "indispensable" (Chehabi 1990, 241).

Harassed by the fundamentalists and the left, Sharif-Emami failed to quell the disturbances. The hardliners in the government, including a faction in the military and SAVAK, were unhappy with the liberalization program and advocated a crackdown. They argued that the "national reconciliation" policy was being perceived as a sign of weakness and asserted that it would spur even more demands. Shadowy SAVAK cells—the "Underground Committee for Vengeance" and the "Resistance Corps"—took to attacking opposition figures (Taheri 1985, 221; Sick 1985, 48; Armstrong 1980b). Even outsiders like Parvis C. Radji (1983, 228), Iran's ambassador in London, were skeptical about the policy of appeasing the opposition. He noted in his diary on September 9 that if the mullahs came to power, "the country will be set back a hundred years." The shah, depressed by illness and events, vacillated between the council of the hardline and moderate factions in his government. Ardershir Zahedi, who was summoned by the Empress concerned by the "drift of events," arrived in Teheran on September 5 and counseled the shah to take a tough stand. However, after the Jalah Square disaster Zahedi, who had hoped to replace Sharif-Emami as prime minister, could not prevail upon the shah to continue with the crackdown (Sick 1985, 49–50). On the contrary, the government decided to further placate the population. By October some thirty-four top-level SAVAK officials were accused of "deceiving the shah and exceeding their limits" and removed. A number of ministers and high ranking bureaucrats charged with corruption were also dismissed. The Pahlavi Foundation, long a target of the opposition, was curtailed and the royal family was barred by a September 26 decree from financial dealings with government agencies. By the end of the month, the shah took the unprecedented step of scaling down his military programs. In a highly symbolic gesture, the government diverted some $200 million to pay for the damages caused by the riots.

The shah's growing inability to control events and his psychological state were noticed by a number of insiders. Eslaminia told Lambrakis that in a July 21 meeting, Moghadam and Fardoust, a close friend of the monarch, found the Shah "down mentally" (Documents, vol. 25, 50–53). Sick (1985, 53) noted that the monarch, who spoke to Carter after "Black Friday," was in a seeming state of shock. Parsons (1984, 67) claimed that during an audience on September 16, the "shah was in bad shape" but determined to proceed with liberalization. In September, one of the shah's ministers saw what looked like French-speaking TV technicians coming out of a bedroom, where the shah was ostensibly re-covering from flu. In retrospect, the minister realized that these might have been French doctors attending to the shah's illness (Sick 1985, 53, 182). Manucher Farmanfarmaian, described an October audience as "tragic" and the shah as "shrunken" and "tired" (Farmanfarmaian and Farmanfarmaian 1997, 445–446). With the benefit of hindsight it is clear that the Mohammed Reza suffered from mood swings brought about by a combination of events and cancer therapy.

It remains in the realm of speculation whether a totally fit ruler could have handled the almost insurmountable policy dilemma any better. Antishah observ-ers and many academics have blamed the regime for practicing a policy of "too little, too late" which, in their opinions, contributed to the radicalization of the revolution. Bill (1988a, 240) argued that the regime's policies were "half hearted and poorly implemented." He quoted Fereydoun Hoveyda, who stated that "where immediate surgery was required, the shah used first aid." Implied in this critique is the assumption that a more timely process of liberalization would have enticed the liberal opposition to nudge Iran toward a true parliamentary democracy. There is undoubtedly some comparative empirical evidence to sup-port this assertion. But supporters of the monarchy and other scholars countered that it was the liberalization that expedited the revolutionary process.

As indicated, the direction of political change is hard to predict because of the bifurcation phenomenon. Timely liberalization may lead to a democratic outcome in some situations, but would not work in others. Most observers have come to believe that the "point of no return" was reached during "Black Friday" but it is theoretically possible that the process bifurcated into a radical channel even earlier. If this was the case, liberalization only emboldened the fundamen-talists and their leftist allies and, paradoxically, undercut whatever standing the moderates had.

The Iranian demographics provide a clue to the real direction of the revolu-tionary process. By 1978, nearly half of the population was under the age of sixteen and two-thirds under thirty. According to the 1976 census, 70 percent of Iranians were illiterate; some 80,000 mosques, 1,200 shrines, 100 ayatollahs, 5,000 hojjatalislams, 180,000 mullahs and 11,000 theology students served the population. In terms of Weber's elective affinity, Khomeini's use of the Karbala metaphor—where the shah was compared to the tyrant Yazid—fitted quite well the belief system of a large cultural subgroup. An anthropologist pointed out that the "Karbala paradigm was a highly effective technique for maintaining a high level of consciousness about the injustices of the Pahlavi regime" (Fischer 1980b, 183–185). Although Khomeini did not explicitly claim the mantle of the redeemer, by late summer his followers began referring to him as the Imam (Willner 1984, 87; Zubaida 1989, 72–77). Other observers noted that "unlike the simple appeal of communism . . . democracy could never muster grassroots enthusiasm in places like Iran," because it was a "complicated creed" (Farman-farmaian and Farmanfarmaian 1997, xxiii).

Fischer and other academics have argued that the Islamic idiom triumphed because the alternative civic idiom was repressed by the shah's autocracy. However, other scholars have contended that the political culture of Iran (and Arab countries) was fundamentally inimical to the emergence of a civic society. Indeed, one argued that the Iranian culture was easily moldable into a proto-fascist belief system led by a religious divine (Arjomand 1988, 204, 1986). Another asserted that fundamentalism was permeated with "nativism," an "amalgam of feelings" experienced by those who sense that their way of life is "being threatened by another culture" (Jansen 1997, 16). Mottale (1987, 22–23) used Weber's notion of patrimonial systems to argue that personalistic legitimacy was more in tune with Iranian culture than with the impersonal legal-rational validity claims of democracy. Indeed, one moderate cleric, Ayatollah Ustad Ali Teherani would later blame the hero worship and personality cult in Iran for the fundamentalist victory (Irfani 1983, 182).

Since a collective belief system is hard to measure, scholars tried to model the relative strength of a number of "belief profiles." One study suggested that at the start of the revolution there were five identifiable belief systems: Khomeini's militant Islam, Bazargan's liberal democratic Islam, secular nationalism of the NF and the Marxism-socialism of the Tudeh and the guerrillas. Sometime around the Jalah Square incident, fundamentalist Islam began gaining on its rivals (Foran 1994). However, few in Teheran were aware of the shift in legitimacy. The idea that political change was headed into a fundamentalist direction was even less apparent in Washington.

THE MASS PROTEST: THE VIEW FROM WASHINGTON

Well before the outbreak of mass protest, the bureaucratic infighting in Washington was in full swing. In June, Iran presented the Carter administration with a large request for military hardware. Several items on the list were potentially in violation of Carter's weapon sales policy, rekindling the struggle of the previous year. The request was debated in a number of adversarial meetings and policy papers, which Sick (1985, 45) likened to a "controversy of medieval scholastics in their fervor and parsing of different texts."

It took a Policy Review Committee (PRC) of July 5, chaired by Vance, to settle the dispute. Among the advocates of a liberal sales policy were the regional bureaus of the State Department, the Pentagon, the national security adviser and Ambassador Sullivan, who was spending an extended vacation at home. During several meetings with Brzezinski the ambassador delivered upbeat reports about the ability of the shah to survive the troubles. David Newsom, the undersecretary of state for political affairs, who traveled to Teheran on July 8, seconded Sullivan's opinion. Newsom reported that the shah was determined to liberalize and pass on a modern system as part of his political legacy. Newsom and his assistant, John Forbes, mentioned the tension in Teheran but felt that the shah "is a strong presence" (Shaplen 1980a, 50).

However, the lower level bureaucrats questioned the arms deal as well as the optimistic forecast. Theodore Moran from Policy Planning and Stephen Cohen from the Bureau of Human Rights felt that the shah was in deep trouble and suggested that the United States engage in a "zero base assessment" of its ties with Iran. In State's lingo, such an assessment was a prelude for a policy of "distancing" the United States from a dictatorial regime. Moran's boss, Anthony Lake, approved the project, but higher level officials stopped it (Armstrong 1980b, 18; Prados 1991, 435–436). Henry Precht was also in favor of "distancing;" he criticized the arms deal and disputed Sullivan's suggestion that the United States publicly encourage and support the shah (Rubin 1985, 189–190; Sick 1985, 69).

The bureaucratic infighting impeded the drafting of the National Intelligence Estimate (NIE) "Iran: Prospects Through 1985" ordered by Turner in March. Precht and George Griffin from the INR claimed that the CIA and DIA were too optimistic about the shah; in turn, the agencies accused the INR of being unduly pessimistic (David 1993, 73). Griffin issued a dissenting note when, in August, the CIA published an interim report which stated that "Iran was not in a revolutionary or even a pre-revolutionary state" and that the "shah will be an active participant in Iranian life well into the 1980s." The DIA backed the CIA, stating, on August 16, that although the "months ahead" are likely to be turbulent ones, "there is no threat to the stability of the shah's rule" (Documents, vol. 63, 1–9). On September 1, the INR responded that there is a "basic unresolvable conflict between the shah's liberalization program and the need to limit violent opposition" and predicted that there are "some chances that the shah will be forced to step down" (White Paper, 03564, 7–8). In a September 28 report, the DIA argued that the "shah is expected to remain actively in power over the next 10 years." Failing to achieve consensus, Turner quietly abandoned the NIE. It was replaced by an INR-drafted Interagency Intelligence Memorandum (IIM) which incorporated the views of the different agencies. The September 29 document held that, while the shah no longer appeared to be in immediate danger of being overthrown, "there was still considerable question . . . of his ability to survive in power over the next 18 to 24 months" (Bill 1988a, 258; Sick 1985, 92; Jeffreys-Jones 1989, 221; Armstrong 1980c; Ledeen and Lewis 1980).

Commentators have used the finding that Iran was "not in a revolutionary state" to heap scorn on the CIA. As already noted, the agency lacked both undercover capacity and analytical skills to follow a complex and quickly changing political situation. But there were additional psychological and political factors that contributed to the infamous claim. First, the CIA had to contend with what is known as the "cry wolf" syndrome. Predictions about the imminent demise of the shah had been a constant feature of the discourse on Iran for some three decades. Regime opponents used alarmist forecasts to publicize their case, matched by scholars who filled pages with writings on the "forthcoming crisis" of the royal family. Indeed, Bill (1988a, 424), a harsh critic of the CIA, noted that "there had always been someone somewhere predicting the fall of the shah." Rubin (1980b, 149–150) observed that "the shah's downfall had so often been predicted and his survival so often observed that warning about his imminent downfall had gradually lost credibility." Worse, it made the various experts sound like "Chicken Little when the sky had not fallen."

Second, unlike outside experts, the CIA had to thread a very thin line between alarm and complacency. It is a well-known fact that if the alarm threshold is set too low, the system runs the costly risk of repeatedly responding to false alarms. If the threshold is set too high, a real threat may be missed. Moreover, past false alarms can contribute to a situation where the threat potential becomes a "steady-state." Under such circumstances, the likelihood that a true deviation from the pattern would be detected is reduced. According to some sources, the CIA considered the shah to be a "professional worrier" and an alarmist. Added to the long history of pessimistic forecasts about the monarchy, it made intelligence analysts highly reluctant to predict the demise of the Pahlavis (Cable 1991; Shiels 1991, 121; Jeffreys-Jones 1989, 221; Ledeen and Lewis 1981, 58). One way to overcome the pitfalls of the "steady-state" fallacy is to use probability estimates to rate all incoming threats. However, as Turner (1985, 121) admitted, he was reluctant to use such estimates because the agency lacked familiarly with probabilistic methods and was sensitive to past criticism of "waffling" in its conclusions.

Third, Iran constituted a "high stakes country" for the United States. Foreign policy and intelligence bureaucracies operate under a tacit assumption that the international environment changes in incremental ways: Although there is a theoretical recognition that radical political transformations do occur, the bureaucracy tends to "panic" when faced with a catastrophic change in a high stake country. Sick (1985, 41) likened such an occurrence to a hurricane that "can demolish the elaborate policy structure erected over more than a decade." The NSC specialist felt that there was considerable reluctance to "make the call," even among those who had been in charge of "hurricane warning," that is, the intelligence community and Sullivan. Had the revolution occurred in a low-stake country, there would have been an extensive debate with estimates of different outcomes. But in the Iranian case the bureaucracy procrastinated, waiting for some "incontrovertible" evidence before proclaiming the shah lost.

Under the best of circumstances searching for definitive evidence of change can be excruciating. What in retrospect seems like a clear signal is rarely perceived as such during a crisis. There are thousands of signals that are ambiguous or contradictory, making the ratio of "signal to noise" very high. The failure to heed Lubrani's warning is a case in point. Reports by Metrinko were also consigned to the "noise" category, not the least because they went against the traditional perception of power in Iran. As Sick (1985, 41) noted, the shah "had thirty-seven years' experience on the throne and had survived crises which, by appearance, were no less severe than the riots of 1978." He had vast wealth, a large army and international influence and was facing "an aged cleric . . . congeries of aging Mossadeghists, village ecclesiastics and disgruntled job seekers."

Fourth, the administration could hardly afford a premature declaration of the shah's demise. As Brzezinski and other realpolitikers argued, firm American support was an important element in the power equation in Iran. Moreover, Brzezinski had repeatedly warned that there was no viable liberal democratic alternative to the monarchy. This view was supported by Sullivan, who asserted that the secular opposition was hopelessly fragmented, if not fratricidal (Chehabi 1990, 247–248). Brzezinski, Sick and some Pentagon officials tended to side with Zahedi, the shah's ambassador, who had little faith in a liberal democratic option. In August, Zahedi met with Carter, Mondale, Brzezinski and Turner to appraise them of the situation in Iran. But it was only Brzezinski who signed on to Zahedi's view that the real powerbrokers—the radical ulama—would not tolerate a compromise with the monarchy. When Zahedi traveled to Teheran at the beginning of September to counsel the use of force, he had the apparent blessing of the national security adviser (Rubin 1980b, 214; Hoveyda 1980, 59–60).

Finding a credible solution to the turmoil had also preoccupied Sullivan who was in touch with representatives of Ayatollah Shariatmadari and Bazargan. However, Stempel, the political officer, had doubts about the ability of LMI to lead the opposition. During a July 18 meeting with Bazargan and other LMI leaders, Stempel expressed his foreboding that the fundamentalist ulama would strive to control the political process. The LMI politicians reassured him that in the "Islamic East" there is no precedent of direct clerical involvement in politics. In their view, the mullahs "were only interested in seeking that civil law conformed with religious law." A skeptical Stempel cabled the State Department that LMI's confidence in being able to dominate a coalition "seems somewhat misplaced" (Ioannides 1984, 41–42).

While the bureaucracy was involved in an internal struggle, the violence in Iran had escalated. Sick was so concerned by the Abadan riots that he discussed the situation with a number of academics and government specialists. On September 7, he reported to the president that the situation in Iran "could be ripe for full-scale revolution" (Sick 1985, 50). The Jalah Square massacre had shaken the entire administration. Harold Saunders briefed the president, who was otherwise preoccupied with the Camp David negotiations. Carter (1982, 438) was apparently not aware of the intense infighting at the lower levels of his bureaucracy and, according to his memoir, had faith in the CIA's sanguine reports. At the urging of Brzezinski and others, the president called the shah on September 10, and the White House released a statement reaffirming its close relations with Iran.

"Black Friday" had also alarmed the Congress. The Senate Foreign Relations Committee held closed hearings on Iran on September 15. Jack Miklos, the former embassy deputy chief of mission, and Henry Precht had the unenviable task of explaining why the administration had failed to anticipate the events in Iran. The two officials admitted that the CIA relied too heavily on SAVAK for information, adding that the recent intelligence reform made it difficult for the CIA and the DIA to conduct covert operations. On September 27, Robert Bowie, the head of the CIA's National Foreign Assessment Center, testified before the same committee and argued that the new congressional guidelines made it hard for the CIA to penetrate dissident groups (Ledeen and Lewis, 1981, 124).

To improve prediction, in late September the administration established a Working Group on Iran, chaired by Warren Christopher. However, the group's meetings turned into yet another battleground for the contending approaches to Iran. Predictably, both the moralpolitikers and realpolitikers viewed Jalah Square as a confirmation of the correctness of their forecasts. The former argued that propping up the shah would be highly detrimental to future American interest and the latter contended that his demise would be a disaster. As a result, most of the sessions were spent debating whether public statements "would prove helpful or harmful" to the monarchy and Washington (Rubin 1980b, 216). Some State Department officials, frustrated by Brzezinski's perceived dominance of foreign policy and suspicious of the Zahedi channel, took to fighting their case in the press. The leaks further embarrassed an administration whose foreign policy had already been under withering criticism at home and abroad. Needless to say, the public brawling in Washington had sent confusing signals to the Iranian regime and its opponent (Ledeen and Lewis 1981, 169; Sick 1987, 1985, 61; Meyer 1978, 94).

On balance, the confusion had hurt the shah the most. Mohammad Reza was genuinely puzzled by the paradigmatic change in American foreign policy under Carter; the conflicting messages left him bewildered. The shah described Vance's demands that he both restore calm and proceed with liberalization as "Herculean fantasies that left me stunned" (Pahlavi 1980b, 185). Such advice was interspersed by calls from Brzezinski, who urged him to establish law and order first and then continue with liberalization. As his health and political situation worsened, the shah came to believe that Washington had resolved to get rid of him. He mentioned his suspicion to the visiting Rockefeller and many of the shah's other interlocutors noted his perplexity. In 1979, on his death bed, the monarch repeated the charge that the "Carter administration wanted him out and a new government more to its liking to replace him in Teheran" (Pahlavi 1980b, 185; Ashraf and Banuazizi 1985, 12; Helms 1981, 204).

However, in 1978 no one realized that disease was taking its toll on the shah. S. Turner (1991b, 25) admitted: "we were remiss in not knowing how ill the shah was." To confuse matters, the moralpolitikers described the shah as a tough and megalomaniac ruler, who had to be restrained from using coercion. In retrospect, it should have been clear that the shah, concerned about his own mortality and the legitimacy of the monarchy, was reluctant to exercise decisive force. Quant (1980), a NSC official, later wrote that the shah was psychologically dependent on the United States. Brzezinski (1983, 371–372) was almost alone in maintaining that, in order to save the regime, the United States had to pressure the shah to crack down on the opposition or even instigate a military coup.

Still, prompting the shah to be more forceful was unimaginable in an administration that epitomized the New Internationalist ethos (Smith 1984, 354). Nickel (1979) mused that after the lessons of Vietnam—the overthrow of Diem and the fall of Thieu—"there was a certain genuine modesty about our capacity to know what was right politically." Saunders (1987, 219) observed that in order to actively support the shah, the United States had to meddle preemptively in Iran, a stand that did not "come natural to American officials." Brzezinski (1983, 372) claimed that a such policy "went too much against the grain of the dominant value in the White House and the State Department."

More to the point, the administration was bitterly divided over what American responsibility should be. The realpolitikers were anxious to preserve the traditional American interests in the Gulf, but the moralpolitikers, who believed that America should play a lesser global role, were much more sanguine about the fortunes of the region. As Iran entered the last stage of the revolution, the former clamored to save the shah and the latter pressed to replace him with a progressive coalition.

THE GENERAL STRIKES: THE VIEW FROM TEHERAN

"Black Friday" accelerated the pace of the revolution. A series of progressively crippling strikes hit the country, affecting industry and services. Although the government caved in to most of the financial demands, the strikes, influenced by the Mojahedeen and the Tudeh, turned political (Parsa 1989, 157). The population responded with widespread panic buying and hoarding of goods. The more affluent fled the country or sent capital abroad. It was estimated that between October 1 and January 1979, some 100,000 Iranians left and some $2.6 billion were transferred abroad (Taheri 1985, 233; Wright 1989, 58).

The general strike was an important point in the revolution. It helped to crystallize the intense but sporadic protest of the previous months and fan out the unrest to smaller towns and the countryside. According to one estimate, between October and February 1, 1979 there was at least one antishah demonstration in each of some 130 cities and towns (Salehi 1988, 137; Kazemi 1980b; Green 1982, 143). The initially passive peasants had begun to switch their allegiance to the opposition (Hooglund 1982, 142, 146). New tactics for taunting the authorities were developed; in one highly effective measure the population was urged to climb on rooftops in the evening and chant *Allah Akbar* (God is Great). The strikes had created a good deal of solidarity; bazaar merchants set up soup kitchens to feed striking workers and volunteers delivered kerosene and staples to poor neighborhoods. As one commentator put it, "antigovernment activism now became a quotidian affair for most of the population" (Chehabi 1990, 237).

The strikes offered the Tudeh and the Soviet Union an opportunity to get closely involved. There is circumstantial evidence to indicate that, by 1978, the Soviets had developed a real interest in getting rid of the shah who threatened their interests in Afghanistan (Lenczowski 1979a; 1979b; Taheri 1985, 216–217; Motalle 1987, 35). In fact, Afghanistan became a center of Soviet activity against the shah, with KGB and GRU operatives freely crossing the border and mingling with the large number of Afghan refugees and workers. The Soviets activated the National Voice of Iran (NVOI) based in Baku and the Soviet embassy printed the Tudeh organ *Novin*. Both NVOI and *Novin* supported Khomeini and spread anti-American propaganda, often employing "the most blatant lies" (Rubin 1980b, 214; Moss 1978; Huyser 1986, 107). Moreover, in November, the Soviet government officially warned the United States not to intervene in the revolution, a move that was apparently urged by Nuradin Kianuri, the would-be Tudeh leader (Cottam 1990a).

Whatever the Soviet input, the Marxist and Muslim guerillas added weight to the strikes and other antigovernment actions. In addition to attacks on the police and the military, there was an increased campaign against Americans and other Westerners. Ayatollah Hossein Ali Montazeri, nicknamed "Ayatollah Ringo," created the clandestine *Sazami Towhidi e Saff* (Unitary Organization of the Line) which specialized in harassing Americans around Isfahan. In November Habibollah Payman, the veteran antishah activist, was released from jail and founded the clandestine Movement of Militant Muslims, which collaborated with the Mujahedeen. Payman, later identified as a key player in the attack on the American embassy, devoted his energies to creating "revolutionary disturbances" that enhanced the growing chaos (Taheri 1985, 217; Hiro 1985, 136–137).

The fundamentalist network played a leading part in the wave of strikes. The strikes were part of Khomeini's strategy to establish an alternative network of authority, which included decrees and the creation of the so-called "Imam's committees" throughout the economy. The committees were also highly active among the military forces, long considered by Khomeini a vital link in his revolutionary blueprint. The followers of the ayatollah had also made good use of the ubiquitous Iranian rumor mill. One notorious rumor, attributed to Beheshti, held that the face of Khomeini will appear on the face on the moon on November 27, and all but "miscreants and bastards" would be able to see him. On the appointed night millions attested to seeing the apparition, a line that was supported by *Novin*. A widely circulated poem promised that Khomeini's return as the Imam would end all hardship and usher in a period of peace (Hoveyda 1980, 63; Taheri 1985, 236–238; Mottale, 1987, 5).

Fearful of Khomeini's role, the government decided to pressure Iraq to expel the troublesome mullah from Najef. After Kuwait denied him entry, Khomeini and his entourage flew to Paris on October 6. Iranian officials, who had assumed that France would be distant enough to silence the cleric, did not object to the move. In retrospect, this was a grave, if not fatal error. Khomeini settled in the Paris suburb of Nauphle-le-Chateau and established a revolutionary headquarters equipped with an elaborate information center and a recording studio, where thousands of tapes were manufactured and sent to Iran. Three of his aides, Abolhasan Bani Sadr, Sadeq Gotbzadeh and Ibrahim Yazdi, managed the relations with the Western media and telephone orders were send to Beheshti, Rafsanjani and other members of the clandestine Revolutionary Council. In due course, Rafsanjani was named the "Imam's representative to Iran."

In a testimony to the power of the fundamentalists, most of the senior opposition leaders visited Paris during October and November. They wanted Khomeini's support for a coalition government that would collaborate with the shah until the proposed election, a move that was also supported by Shariatmadari (Documents, vol. 25, 67–71). However, the ayatollah was adamant that revolutionary activity should go on until the destruction of the Pahlavis. Privately he demanded the elimination of the monarchy and expulsion of all high officials. He hinted at these plans in an October 18 interview, and, on October 26, he declared that Iran should progress according to it own "nationhood and religion." In November, he publicly announced a "three point program" that called for an Islamic Republic (Rajaee 1983, 97; Radji 1983, 243; Moshiri, 1985, 65).

The negotiations at Nauphle-le-Chateau established a pattern that reflected the growing veto power of Khomeini over Iranian politics. First, he rebuffed the veteran politician Ali Amini who had tried since August to obtain a blessing for a bid to become a caretaker prime minister. Second, he refused Karim Sanjabi's request to serve as the head of a proposed coalition that would include royalists. With little to show for his "pilgrimage" to Paris, Sanjabi was forced to publish a declaration calling for a referendum to establish a government based on the principles of Islam and democracy. Third, and most important, Khomeini put an end to Bazargan's gradualism. Though it was not widely known at the time, before Bazargan left Paris on October 31, Khomeini forced him to draw up a list of mostly Muslim politicians that would serve after the shah's departure. On November 6 the LMI issued a declaration titled "Is it not Time the Ruling Establishment Become Realistic?" that stated, among other things, that the majority of people rejected the shah and wanted an Islamic government.

Although it was not understood at the time, the "cave-in" of the NF and the LMI indicated the end of whatever control the moderates had over the course of the revolution. A historian would later point out that, like Lenin, "Khomeini steered the opposition on a maximalist line" (Rubin 1980b, 221). This development was especially painful for Ayatollah Shariatmadari and Bazargan, who subsequently explained to an American embassy official that the LMI had little independent power and could only hope to affect events within the fundamentalist framework (Chehabi 1990, 245).

In fact, Bazargan, whose moderate leadership came under attack within his own movement, had little personal wiggle room. When Bazargan was still in Paris, Sadeq Gotbzadeh declared that he, along with Ezzatolah Sahabi and Ayatollah Mahmud Taleqani—would form a new group. For their part, the fundamentalists strove to undermine the LMI from the outside. Taleqani, who wanted to turn his office into the nerve center of the revolution, was outmaneuvered by the Center for Welcoming the Imam, a Beheshti creation that later evolved into the Islamic Republican Party. The secularist-liberal elements were likewise overtaken by the fundamentalist juggernaut. When, in November, a group of professors at Teheran University wanted to establish a free speech society, fundamentalist students forced them to demand a republic (Irfani 1983, 141; Ledeen and Lewis 1980).

While Khomeini was consolidating his power, the shah was floundering. "Black Friday" left Mohammed Reza shocked, confused and unable to decide on a course of action. During an October 10 audience, the monarch complained to Sullivan about "bickering" in his inner circle and expressed concern that the political disarray might spread to the troops. He also mentioned the possibility of offering an unconditional return to Khomeini, a suggestion that horrified the ambassador. In a meeting with Parsons, the shah seemed to toy with the idea of letting Sharif-Emami co-opt the National Front. On October 24, when Sullivan and Parsons accompanied Deputy Secretary of Defense Charles Duncan to the Niavaran Palace, the shah cut the meeting short. He then beckoned the two ambassadors to stay and sought their advice on the possibility of a military government. In retrospect, the shah might have suffered from depression, due to an apparent increase in his chemotherapy medication (Sick 1985, 56–58; Parsons 1984, 89; Ledeen and Lewis 1980).

Even without the complicating illness, the shah had the unenviable task of choosing between two equally difficult courses of action. One option was to continue with liberalization. In spite of the tremendous upheaval in the country, Sharif-Emami was convinced that he could split the opposition and work with Shariatmadari and other "logical and sensible" elements (Kraft 1978; Rubin 1980b, 216). An alternative stand was urged on the shah by the hardliners in his government, notably the military commanders led by General Gholam Ali Oveissi and Ambassador Zahedi. They wanted a "Chilean-style solution" complete with a military crackdown, mass arrests and executions. According to observers, Mohammed Reza was keenly aware of the fact that a bloodbath might delegitimize his monarchy and not be effective, or as he put it, "you can't crack down on one block and make the people on the next block behave." Oddly enough, he still regarded himself as the symbol of national unity and the head of "the Iranian family," and dreamed of turning Iran into a "civilized" and respected country. As some of his visitors noted, the shah did not want to be viewed as "another Idi Amin" (Kraft 1978, 134; Stempel 1981, 135–136; Rubin 1980b, 219; Sullivan 1984, 270; Salinger 1981, 71).

International censure continued to be a major concern for the government. In addition to the United States, European politicians and the media were accelerating their criticism of the monarchy. In May, Sir Harold Wilson, the former prime minister of Britain, visited Iran on behalf of an obscure academic human rights group and Judith Hart, Minister for Overseas Development in the British government, became the sponsor of the British Committee Against Repression in Iran (CARI). In August, Willy Brand, the then–head of the Socialist International called for the shah's resignation. The British Broadcast Corporation established itself as a de facto watchdog of the revolution and made Khomeini a household name abroad. Inside Iran, mosque meetings were interrupted to let the faithful listen to the popular BBC commentaries. In spite of their suspicion of all things foreign, the "Iranians faithfully and utterly credulously listened to BBC broadcasts, learning from them of the daily riots and demonstrations in Iran" (Rafizadeh 1987, 281; Farmanfarmaian and Farmanfarmaian 1997, 444). It was also known that AI was in the process of preparing another critical report on Iran (Radji 1983, 180, 183, 280; Pahlavi 1980b, 163; Muravchik 1986, 113; Pilskin 1980).

The failure of Sharif-Emami to control the increasing chaos forced the shah's hand. On November 4, students at Teheran University tried to pull down a statue of the monarch and were attacked by the army. The next day the city witnessed the most serious disturbances of the revolution. After three days of mob rule, the shah appointed General Gholam-Reza Azhari as the head of a military government of national salvation. Still, the choice of the aging Azhari, a relative moderate hampered by a serious heart condition, over General Oveissi was an indication that the monarch was not willing to use the iron fist option.

Azhari, who took power on November 6, promised free elections and seemed to continue the course of liberalization. In a major concession to the opposition, the military government arrested Amir Abbas Hoveyda, Nematollah Nassiri and several senior officials on charges of corruption. To "balance" the move, many opposition leaders, including Sanjabi, Dariush Foruhar and Bazargan were arrested, but were released soon after. This type of political maneuvering shocked and demoralized the loyalists, but did not appease the foes of the shah (Taheri 1985, 237). On the contrary, it was widely seen as a sign of weakness of the regime. On November 17, the press declared a general strike that would last until January 8, 1979. Throughout this period, the LMI's *Akhbar-e Jonbesh-e Eslami* (News of the Islamic Movement), was the only available publication that gave regular accounts of the revolution.

The shah was trying to put a liberal spin on the new government. In the speech nominating Azhari he sounded surprisingly apologetic, a stand that was followed by a number of conciliatory gestures, including the release of more political prisoners. As for his new prime minister, the shah took to telling his visitors that he had appointed the ineffectual Azhari to show the generals that martial law government would not work (Rubin 1980b, 228). Mohammed Reza's hesitant and confused behavior during November heightened concerns about his mental state. For the first time ever, he skipped the Armed Forces Day ceremony on November 17, sending alarmed loyalists to beg the American embassy to "do something." Both Iranian and American visitors came away with the impression that the shah had suffered a failure of nerves and could not function. There was also growing evidence that the royal inner circle was falling apart, leaving the monarch with precious little support and guidance. Some among the ruling elite either hedged their bets or became openly contemptuous of Mohammed Reza, as Uri Lubrani found out during a visit to Niavaran (Sick 1985, 162; Shawcross 1988, 276). Whatever the reason, it was quite clear that the king could not settle on a coherent course of action and complicated his problems by pursuing contradictory policy imperatives (Shiels 1991, 100–101; Zonis 1991, 92, 98; Stempel 1981, 264).

Given the situation, the shah was urged by some to invite the opposition into a coalition government. There were even some favorable signals from the fundamentalist camp. Ayatollah Qazi Tabatabi held secret meetings with the minister of Endowment and Religious Affairs, Alinaqi Kani, and reassured him that the fundamentalists had to radicalize their stand in order to upstage the left, but wanted to collaborate with the regime. As noted, Khomeini had already vetoed such an option, but the dissimulation added to the confusion in Niavaran Palace. Indeed, the inner council of the shah was targeted by purveyors of all sorts of fancy schemes, ranging from an invasion of Afghanistan to distribution of money to the mullahs (Taheri 1985, 230, 233).

In retrospect, it is quite clear that there was no political authority in Iran after Sherif-Emami was forced out. General Azhari, who recited poems and wept in public, struck many as embarrassing and ineffectual; even the shah joked that it did not matter whether the prime minister was present or away from his desk (Rubin 1980b, 228). With Khomeini calling the shots and the conditions increasingly resembling a civil war, the regime was reduced to an uneasy defensive posture.

The "face on the moon" episode was followed by the religious excitement of the holy month of Moharran that started on December 2. On the eve of the holiday, Khomeini called on the people to "unite, arise and sacrifice your blood." After outlining a plan for civil disobedience, the Imam vowed that "blood will triumph over the sword" and promised that "the satanic government will be abolished" (Sick 1985, 101). A human rights march that coincided with Tasau'a, the ninth day of Moharran (December 9), was one of the largest in Iran's history. The following day, on the tenth of Moharran, the demonstrations were even bigger and acquired a more religious character. On December 17, all the political parties and the ICDFHR issued a joint declaration demanding the end of the monarchy. For all intents and purposes, the quest for a compromise solution was over. Even if the shah understood it, the Carter team was only slowly coming to grips with the situation.

THE GENERAL STRIKES: THE VIEW FROM WASHINGTON

The administration's response to the fall unrest was sporadic and fragmented. The Camp David negotiations, the SALT treaty and normalization of relations with China all but relegated the Iranian crisis to a back burner. Top foreign policy leaders were constantly preoccupied with those weighty issues, and even lower level practitioners found their time and energies diverted. With the president and the secretary of state keeping their distance, lower ranking bureaucrats were left to proffer their own estimates and peddle policy prescriptions. Within this policy vacuum, a number of issues had to be addressed.

One of them was the shah's mental health. By fall numerous reports about the shah's unusual behavior reached Washington, including a Mossad message conveyed by the Israeli Foreign Minister, Moshe Dayan (Sick 1991, 63). On October 10, Henry Precht forwarded to Sullivan a request from a CIA psychiatrist for a profile update. The questionnaire included references to depression and impaired leadership, but cancer was not considered (Documents, vol. 7, 233–234). On November 21, Treasury Secretary Michael Blumenthal who visited Teheran, reported that the shah seemed thoroughly depressed. Still, when one day later, the CIA issued an assessment of the shah's psychological behavior, it contended that "his mood is not inappropriate to this situation, that he is not paralyzed by indecision" (quoted in Brzezinski, 1983, 368).

There were also questions about the procurement program. On October 10, Sullivan sent a cable to Washington advising to "cool down" military sales, but General Philip Gast, the head of the U.S. Army Mission Headquarters–Military Assistance Advisory Group (ARMISH–MAAG) in Iran, objected (Ledeen and Lewis 1981, 187–188). The Pentagon supported the sales program, but assigned Howard Teicher, a defense analyst, to study the implications of a hostile Iran on American strategic interests (Teicher and Teicher 1993, 47). On October 24, Deputy Secretary of Defense Charles Duncan, during a fact-finding mission to the Gulf, had the ill-fated audience with the shah, a factor that featured in the subsequent decision to "postpone" the arms transfer (Sick 1985, 58).

At about the same time, the State Department completed a comprehensive analysis of Iran for the president. Bearing the imprint of Precht and the human rights lobby, the paper noted the grim situation and, for the first time, discussed the modalities of transition. Three strategies were mentioned: support for the shah as part of a broadly based government, a more active, "advisory" American role in the liberalization program and a strong opposition to a military government. The report expressed concern about expatriates, but did not recommend an emergency evacuation. On October 26, an informal interagency group met to consider U.S. options. The participants concluded that Washington had limited capability to influence events in Iran, but recommended supporting the shah's liberalization policy and steadfastly opposed a military takeover. The latter was an apparent response to the rumors that "certain circles" in the United States and Great Britain wanted General Oveissi to stage a coup and take over the government (White Paper, 03556, 62; Rafizadeh 1987, 280).

Meanwhile, Sullivan, who was asked to comment on the State Department's memorandum, cabled on October 27 and rejected most of its proposals. Sullivan was contemptuous of the liberalization policy, comparing such efforts to "feeding the crocodiles" (Armstrong 1980c). The ambassador acknowledged that a military intervention might be a "delayed disaster," but he feared that the deteriorating situation between "now and next June" (the date of the proposed elections) might make such an intervention inevitable (Sick 1985, 58–59).

On the day that Sullivan's cable arrived, the State Department was hosting a meeting of government Iran experts and outside academics. Many analysts felt that neither more repression nor more liberalization, which the Persians were bound to perceive as weakness, would save the shah. In a straw poll of some forty participants, only four believed that the Pahlavi regime would be around one year later (Armstrong 1980c). Bill (1988a, 246) warned that a military crackdown would not do and argued that the shah had to back off his "tiny plateau of absolute power." He and Marvin Zonis debated whether the situation in Iran represented an "avalanche" or a "raging forest fire," an analogy that apparently shocked some officials.

Sullivan's communications added to the sense of urgency in the State Department. The ambassador reported that, during an October 31 meeting, the shah gave the impression that he might abdicate over the issue of a referendum on the monarchy, which the opposition demanded. Using a top-secret channel, he told Secretary Vance that within forty-eight hours the shah would seek U.S. advice on whether to abdicate or impose a military government. Sullivan argued that the shah would stay only if assured of American support and asked for urgent guidance.

But, as noted, the Carter team was badly split over the issue of a military government. The moralpolitikers continued to use the State Department memorandum to lobby against such an option. Vance (1983, 328), who was initially somewhat ambiguous, became persuaded that "the autocratic regime" was over. On the other hand, Brzezinski argued vigorously that the shah "should stay in power and that the United States must make every attempt to keep him in power." According to Rafizadeh (1987, 275) Brzezinski and Zahedi favored a military coup in Iran. When Vance wanted to send a cable to Sullivan suggesting that the monarch relinquish some of his domestic authority and leave for a vacation, Brzezinski complained to Carter. According to Vance, the National Security Adviser was convinced that the State Department gave up on the shah and was too "soft" for a military government.

Brzezinski, with the help of Zahedi, David Rockefeller, Henry Kissinger and John J. McCloy, tried to convince Carter to press the shah for a military government. At this point, the balance of power did not favor the State Department and the assorted New Internationalists in the administration. As early as June 1, the intelligence community briefed Carter on Soviet expansionism around the globe. An August 15 Policy Review Committee emphasized Soviet aggression, followed by an August 24 Presidential Review Memorandum that reflected Brzezinski's view that the Soviet Union should be contained along the so-called "arc of crisis" line in Asia and Africa (Gates 1996, 75). Iran's instability clearly threatened the situation in the Gulf, a prospect that apparently alarmed the president. True to his academic character, Brzezinski copied a number of pages from Brinton's book and gave them to Carter to underscore his contention that successful revolutions are made by governments' failures to use force. Harold Brown, the secretary of defense, became so concerned that he joined the national security adviser in lobbying Carter (Armstrong 1980c; Ledeen and Lewis 1981, 33; Zabih 1979, 59).

The Safari Club countries, which shared Brzezinski's view, urged the president to mount an all-out effort to save the Pahlavis (Armstrong 1980c). November brought pressure from European countries, Israel and Japan, which all expressed grave concern about oil supplies should the monarchy fall. Even the Chinese voiced their misgivings when Schlesinger visited Beijing in late October. The Chinese viewed the shah as their ally against the Soviet Union and were worried about his possible downfall. Conservatives in and out of government were raising their own alarm. Kissinger took to emphasizing that it was too late to make concession when the "revolutionary train was galloping." Ironically, the *New York Times* and *Washington Post*, whose early criticism of the shah had contributed to the upheaval, were now openly worried about the possibility of an anti-American successor regime (Armstrong 1980a, 1980d; Aitken 1993, 352–353; Ledeen and Lewis 1981, 145; Moses 1996, x; Rubin 1980b, 355).

Brzezinski's gloomy prognosis was reinforced by news from Teheran. On November 1, the embassy's country team noted the "hordes of uncontrolled demonstrations"; the press attaché described the scene at Teheran University where "thousands and thousands of starry eyed youths" attended prayers and half of the women were clad in chadors" (Documents, vol. 7, 239–240). The following day Sullivan wrote that "some believe" that the test of strength between the shah and the Khomeini camp had "reached a point of no return." He did not rule out a military crack-down, but felt that the "long term cost would be very heavy." An INR report on the same day implied that the monarchy was on the ropes and that "only drastic measures by the shah hold any promise for staving off a descent into chaos" (White Paper, 03556, 8; Documents, vol. 13, 9).

When the Special Coordinating Committee (SCC) convened on November 2 to provide guidance to Sullivan, Brzezinski was able to control the debate. He wanted the ambassador to assure the shah of official American support for either a civilian coalition or a military government and, importantly, urge him to re-store order. Warren Christopher, who represented the State Department and Admiral Turner, on behalf of the CIA, questioned the ability of a military government to solve Iran's problems, but Brzezinski secured Carter's support for the draft. In order to impress upon the shah that the State Department was behind the message, Vance agreed to tell a press conference the following day that he strongly supported Teheran's efforts to restore order before moving on with liberalization.

However, the SCC decision did not help to turn the situation in Iran around. On November 6, the day when the military government was announced, the long-scheduled meeting of the PRC took place. The interagency body, chaired by Vance, focused on the poor quality of intelligence from Iran and discussed measures to improve communication with the embassy in Teheran. There was also some discussion of contingency plans for evacuating expatriates from Iran and enhancing American military presence in the Gulf, but no new initiatives were recommended. As a matter of fact, the realpolitik group was "stunned" at what Sick (1985, 75–77) described as the apologetic and "almost pathetic" tone of the shah's speech announcing the Azhari government. Indeed, the INR report of November 2 maintained that the shah "reversed to the moods of depression and vacillation" he had displayed earlier in his career. An embassy cable on the same day claimed that the shah cut off Zahedi who urged him to crack down with a comment that the situation was not amenable to drastic actions (Documents, vol. 13, 9, 21–23).

Sullivan's November 9 telegram "Thinking the Unthinkable" created a sense of panic. The envoy noted that the shah had lost most of his public support and could not even take the loyalty of the military for granted. He suggested a transition scenario that would reflect the new power configuration, identifying the military and the clergy as the two groups likely to assume control. But, in a statement that came back to haunt him, Sullivan wrote that Khomeini, whom he described as a "Gandhi-like" figure, would not get personally involved in politics. To minimize damage to American interests, the ambassador urged Washington to work with moderate religious figures like Bazargan (Sullivan 1981, 200–201; White Paper, 03556, 62).

The cable stunned Carter, who reportedly cancelled all his appointments for the rest of the day (Armstrong 1980d). However, the PRC that met at the White House on the same day focused only on the economic and security aspects of the situation. The modality of transfer problem was left for future deliberations, a decision that generated a flurry of visits and fact-finding missions to assess the situation on the ground. Brzezinski dispatched Arthur Callahan, a former CIA station chief in Teheran, and the president asked Michael Blumenthal, the secretary of the treasury to visit the shah. INR's Carl Clement and George Griffin traveled to Iran with Stephen Cohen from the Bureau of Human Rights. Robert Bowie, the head of the National Foreign Assessment Center, and General

E. T. Tighe, the director of Defense Intelligence, went on a joint mission, followed by Robert Byrd, the Senate majority leader (Sullivan 1981, 196; Rubin 1980b, 229; Bill 1988a, 250).

This feverish activity masked a virtual policy paralysis in the administration. To begin with, the intelligence bureaucracies failed again to reach a consensual reading of the situation. Sick (1985, 90) credited his memo, written for the November 6 PRC meeting, for signaling problems with intelligence. Following the Sullivan cable, an angry Carter complained to Brzezinski, Vance and Turner about the poor quality of intelligence. On November 13, the president met with Brzezinski, Turner and Hamilton Jordan, his domestic adviser, to review the performance of the intelligence community. In retrospect, Carter was right: The House of Representatives Select Committee on Intelligence, which later investigated the effectiveness of the CIA prior to November 1978, issued a scathing critique (Flanagan 1985).

According to documents seized in the embassy, the United States had about 5,000 "sources of information" from all walks of life. However, many of these informers signed up to advance their own careers and provided information that was unreliable, biased or deceptive. Intelligence forwarded by SAVAK was also of poor quality (Shiels 1991, 108; Taheri 1985, 267). Without undercover capacity, the CIA could not penetrate the fundamentalist circles and pierce the screen of dissimulation. Turner all but admitted to the shortcomings. As he put it: "we did not known beans about who made up the Revolutionary Council" (quoted in Moses 1996, 89; Armstrong 1980d). In a remarkable turnabout, S. Turner (1991b, 208–209) later acknowledged that a stronger espionage branch would have been useful in assisting the analysis of political change in Iran and elsewhere.

Even if more information on the challenge belief system had been available, the intelligence bureaucracy and the foreign policy community would have had a difficult time conceptualizing a complex revolutionary change. Traditionally, American foreign policy has focused on political elites. As the case of Ali Shariati demonstrated, the mood of ordinary people or the intellectual pulse of the country was noticed by the embassy officers, but attracted little attention of the CIA director, let alone the secretary of state. The president's daily Top Secret Current Intelligence Bulletin was too brief to be of much use in this respect. Material that might have helped to understand groups that were outside the official power structure were either lost or misplaced in the sprawling intelligence complex. Jesse Leaf, a former chief CIA Iran analyst, compiled material on the precariousness of the shah's public support, but his reports were apparently not available when the trouble started (Bozeman 1979; Bill 1988a, 418–420; Rovere 1979).

The multifaceted effort of intelligence gathering was also detrimental to forging a consensus. As noted, information and analysis on Iran arrived in Washington from a variety of sources. The embassy in Teheran, including the CIA operatives, was the dominant purveyor, but military intelligence, mostly through

ARMISH-MAAG was also an important player, along with Iranian sources such as SAVAK and Zahedi. Adding to the cacophony of voices were the numerous special envoys, a multitude of business and academic intermediaries and other self-appointed emissaries to Iran. There was even disagreement among the personnel at the embassy. Sullivan's doomsday "Thinking the Unthinkable" cable was followed on November 15 by an upbeat report from George Lambrakis, who found that moderates in Iran were willing "to live with the shah" (Armstrong 1980d).

In the case of Iran, the organizational diversity of the intelligence gathering effort, theoretically a source of strength had turned into a weakness. Evaluation of the shah's mental state attests to this problem. Fed by conflicting reports, the CIA, after months of deliberation, failed to reach a consensus on whether the shah was "operational" (Brzezinski 1983, 361). Normally, it takes a bureaucratic focus and strong leadership to process the conflicting points of view and forge a consensus. As Stempel (1981, 307) noted, "coping with increasing complexity and speed of change requires strong organization leadership, particularly at the highest levels of government." Otherwise, such diversity "breeds different points of view leading to policy immobilization." But, as the reaction to the Sullivan cable illustrates, it was precisely the infighting among the foreign policy bureaucracy that created the "immobilization." Brzezinski, who considered the report an implied attack on his hard-won policy of support for the shah, was confirmed in his early suspicion that the ambassador avoided following official instruction. He also took issue with Sullivan's policy analysis; he later described the prediction that Khomeini will be "Gandhi-like" and the successor government will be pro-Western as a "Pollyanna prospect." The precarious situation conveyed by Sullivan's reports strengthened his belief that only a massive crackdown by the military could save the regime (Brzezinski 1983, 368, 355).

The State Department viewed Sullivan's analysis as a vindication of its position that Iran should move on to a moderate government with or without the shah. The human rights advocates in the State Department, Andrew Young and other moralpolitikers were particularly eager to see a transition to a democratic republic. Operating under the banner of "no more Pinochets"—a reference to American association with unpopular dictators—they argued that Sullivan's recommendations did not go far enough (Muravchik 1986, 212). Stempel (1981, 298), described Derian and "the committed ideologists around her" as highly hostile to the shah and confrontational toward the embassy officers, whom they saw as "hopelessly stuffy and retrogressive fascists."

It is not entirely clear whether Vance shared this hostility toward the shah. In his memories, the secretary distanced himself from some of the extreme positions of the moralpolitikers in his department. But Sick (1985, 71–72) noted the secretary's "conspicuous absence from interagency meetings on Iran" and Brzezinski (1983, 43, 355, 368, 396) placed Vance, along with Christopher and Mondale, in the camp of the shah's opponents. At the very least, Brzezinski accused them of "playing for time, always arguing that the next concession to

the shah's opponents was less dangerous that the difficult and dangerous decision for Washington to stage a coup." He scoffed at their "contractual-
litigational" style and noted his own lack of faith in the "quaint notion favored
by American lawyers of liberal bent" that a coalition of contending parties motivated not by a spirit of compromise but "by homicidal hatred" could be brought
together (Brzezinski 1983, 355, 368).

The tension between the State Department and the NSC affected Iran policy
making in the last crucial months of 1978 in a number of ways. First, there was
considerable personal animosity and little communication between the players
who dealt with Iran. Sick (1985, 69–70, 91) spoke of a "gradual choking off of
any useful communication" with Henry Precht, his counterpart in State, and
disclosed that, on one occasion, Precht watched him with "baleful eyes." The
NSC had to rely on Precht's superior, Harold Saunders, to coordinate the day-
to-day business. For his part, Precht complained that top secret communication
between the White House and Teheran was not made available to the State
Department. He surmised that this was due to the "level of distrust that exists
in the White House towards the State Department (and egotistically, I feel,
towards myself)" (Documents, vol. 13, 16–18).

Second, the distrust affected the overall process of policy formulation. Brzezinski (1983, 43) complained that Vance had failed to engage in a broad-ranging
historical and doctrinal debate on Iran. One observer affirmed that the adviser
was "contemptuous" toward Vance, whom he allegedly regarded as part of the
discredited "WASP elite" (Smith 1984, 360). However, Hodding Carter, the
State Department's spokesman and Patricia Derian's husband, called Brzezinski
a "second rate thinker in a field infested with poseurs and careerists" who "never
let consistency get in the way of self-promotion or old theories impede new
policy acrobatics" (quoted in Bill 1988a, 257). In the absence of a debate and
agreement, the administration messages on Iran, let alone its forecasts, tended
to contradict each other. As Vance (1983, 35–36) wrote in his characteristic
understated style, "his [Brzezinski's] policy utterances and my public statements
did not match." Stempel (1981, 307) stated the obvious when he noted that a
comprehensive debate would have "promoted a more complete understanding
of various options and their possible consequences."

Third, the two factions resorted to a public campaign replete with leaks to
bolster their views. By far, the worst offenders were the moralpolitikers, who
felt frustrated by a perceived inability to influence the president. Sick (1985,
71) compared it to a "kind of bureaucratic guerrilla warfare" whose primary
target was Brzezinski and to a lesser extent Sullivan. Sullivan (1981, 207) disclosed that his top-secret cables would appear almost verbatim in the *New York
Times*. David Newsom, the undersecretary for political affairs, explained that
some officials used the leaks to force the administration into a Vietnam-style
public discourse on Iran (Shaplen 1980a; 1980b). Carter (1982, 449), in a bid
to stop the leaks, summoned a group of state department officials to the White
House, where "he laid down the law to them" in the strongest possible terms.

However, far from solving the problem, Carter's action only exacerbated the bitterness. Leslie Gelb and Anthony Lake later commented that Carter "humiliated ... those people in the State Department who were most loyal to him," signaling that the president was now looking to "his courtier Brzezinski, not his baron Vance" for support (Destler, Gelb and Lake 1984, 222).

Fourth, there was mutual suspicion about raw intelligence data, analysis and forecasts. At one point, Brzezinski, who did not trust the State Department, sent Sick to review stacks of cables from the embassy. Brzezinski was so skeptical of the State Department and CIA analysis that he used Zahedi and his circles as an alternative source of information. After Blumenthal's gloomy report from Teheran reached the State Department, David Newsom assembled three analysts who had traveled to Iran on fact-finding missions—Stephen Cohen, George Griffin and Carl Clement—to brief David Aaron at the NSC. Aaron, who was apparently quite skeptical of what he considered "alarmist" analysis, demanded to know who the opposition was, prompting a reply, "the people, David, the people" (Armstrong 1989d, 10).

Fifth, and most important, the opposing groups tended to cancel each other's policy initiatives. On November 21, a mini SCC meeting found the situation in Iran to be extremely dangerous. It identified three options: to push the shah into a more active role, to "hunker down" until the crisis dies down or to actively promote a moderate coalition, which would rule under a limited constitutional monarchy (White Paper, 03556, 64). The State Department decided to instruct Sullivan to advise the shah to establish a broader coalition government. The cable, sent on November 22, apparently reflected the view that the shah was "damaged goods." But Brzezinski, in an internal power struggle, managed to cancel the message (Ledeen and Lewis, 1980). As Vance (1983, 330) later argued, this was part of the "intense" pressure from the White House to get the State Department behind the plan to encourage the shah to use force. It reflected Brzezinski's skepticism about the opposition and his conviction that the United States should provide a clear and decisive signal to break the shah's equivocation.

Brzezinski sought to include this so-called "iron fist" message in a letter to Teheran but when a draft was sent to the State Department, Vance warned the president that a military crackdown would lead to a large number of casualties or even a civil war followed by Soviet intervention. Not incidentally, the New Left groups, including the various antishah committees aggressively pushed such views. Falk and a delegation from the U.S. Peoples' Committee on Iran, which visited Teheran in October, sent a memo to the State Department warning of a "bloodbath worse than in Vietnam" (State Department, 01737; David 1993, 92–93). Vance wanted to modify the text, but the initiative was subsequently abandoned. According to some observers, this and other interventions by Vance were critical in withholding more active support for the shah (Armstrong 1980d; Shiels 1991, 98).

The target of much of the struggle between the two factions was the president.

The bureaucratic model of policy-making postulates that during a severe crisis the internal conflict decreases and the players line up behind a consensual policy. As the chief executive, the president is in charge of formulating and enforcing this policy consensus. However, in the case of Iran, Carter fell short of the theoretical expectations. As already noted, both in terms of personality and political beliefs, the president was ill-equipped to break the stalemate. Much to the dismay of those who bashed the "WASP elite," studies found that Carter and his foreign policy team were less capable of holding a "course in adversity" than their WASP predecessors (Liska 1975, 138; Falkowski 1978, 128).

Others have pointed out that Carter was caught in a dilemma largely of his own making. On the one hand, he was pressured by Brzezinski and realpolitikers like Harold Brown and James Schlesinger, his secretary of energy, to view Iran through global and Sovietcentric perspectives. As the crisis deepened, this view was reinforced by a large number of American allies. On the other hand, the new internationalists continued to insist that local problems, even as serious as Iran, should be viewed in a regional context. In his memoirs, Vance (1983, 246, 386) argued that the Soviets did not want to destabilize the shah because they "always wanted stability on their borders" and "feared Islamic revival." Vance took to repeating this line during speeches, forcing Carter to support his secretary of state in public. In a November 13 television broadcast, the president declared that "we don't have any evidence that the Soviets . . . are trying to disrupt the existing government structure in Iran" (in Ledeen and Lewis 1981, 134).

However, the administration was deeply divided on the nature of the Soviet threat in Iran and Afghanistan. Brzezinski used the article of a British journalist entitled "Who is Meddling in Iran" to support his contention that Moscow was a major player behind the unrest (Sick 1985, 106). A journalist, who interviewed David Newsom, and other commentators argued that Carter, Turner and the State Department did not want to publicize the Soviet connection because it did not fit their foreign policy doctrine (Shaplen 1980a; Ledeen and Lewis 1981, 116; Negaran 1979).

Faced with these powerful competing pressures, Carter seemed immobilized. Psychologically, the president was neither forceful nor experienced enough to preside over the "bureaucratic democracy" he sought to create. Even if he instinctively tended to heed the counsel of Brzezinski, he was also beholden to the powerful moralpolitik constituency that had helped to elect him. In the end, as Gelb (1988, 237) noted, "President Carter proved unable either to make a choice between the two [Brzezinski and Vance] or to blend the two views into a coherent approach." Gelb argued that Carter should have either found an organizational way to contain the conflicting views, or fire one or both men. But the "president chose to do nothing, and his administration fell into obvious disarray."

The mixed signals from Washington further confused the shah, already undermined by events and his illness. Those who have argued that the monarchy could have been saved by a strong and steady signal from Washington blamed the policy muddle for "losing Iran." For instance, David C. Scott, a senior executive from Allis Chalmers who visited Niaravan Palace at the end of November, reported that the shah bemoaned the fact that he had not received any firm commitment from the United States (Documents, vol. 7, 247–248). But even those who, like Prados (1991, 434), argued that "there was no constellation of forces in Washington that could have prevented the Iranian revolution," agree that a different bureaucratic set-up would have made handling of the crisis easier. At the very least, a different foreign policy team might have been more successful in analyzing the nature of the successor regime.

THE ENDGAME: A VIEW FROM TEHERAN

If the fundamentalists had any doubts about their chances, the massive demonstrations of Moharran convinced them that victory was at hand. According to Khomeini's revolutionary blueprint, in the last and decisive stage of the revolution the country had to be paralyzed and the military demoralized (Zabih 1979, 53; Taheri 1985, 196). In December the strikes intensified and bloody confrontations between the authorities and assorted opposition forces and guerrilla groups became a daily occurrence. Acts of sabotage on military bases and desertion from the ranks had also increased, especially among the low paid and poorly trained conscripts who had been a major target of fundamentalist activists.

By the end of December, Iran was veering towards chaos. On December 25, the guards at the American embassy had fired tear gas to repel a large student demonstration and the offices of the Iran-American Society in Shiraz were burned to the ground. The acts of revolutionary violence became ubiquitous, with smoke from burning cars and the sound of automatic weapons and tear-gas grenades filling the air in Teheran and other large cities. Merchants shuttered their stores and hid their inventories to prevent looting. Since the oil strike left the country with only one week's reserve of oil, power was cut and oil was rationed during what turned out to be an exceptionally cold winter. Industry and commerce came to a virtual standstill and the exodus of affluent Iranians reached furious proportions.

Meanwhile, the fundamentalist headquarters near Paris was engaged in a wide-ranging effort to make Khomeini the inevitable leader of the opposition. Three closely interrelated strategies were particularly effective. First, Khomeini and his chief representative in Iran, Ayatollah Beheshti, continued to categorically oppose any compromise with the monarchy. This strategy all but paralyzed any moderate initiative at the end of the year, including the effort of a number of professors and government ministers to form a new civil party. A group of bazaaris who planned to breach the gap between the fundamentalists and the shah by pleading with Khomeini was similarly rebuffed. Khomeini vowed to fight any coalition government, calling such a prospective body illegal (Documents, vol. 25, 137–143; vol. 26, 12–18; Pilskin 1980).

Second, the ayatollah and his advisers began to draw the contours of the successor regime. Perhaps the clearest indication of the radical political change in store came from the writings of Bani Sadr, the self-appointed Khomeinist ideologue. In a collection translated into English in December and a number of articles in the Western press, Bani Sadr (1978), in his signature combination of dependency thinking and Islamic populism, called for a more egalitarian economy, a smaller industrial base and a separation from worldwide "capitalist domination." Like Khomeini, he maintained that the political, social and cultural problems in Iran could only be addressed within the proposed Islamic republic. Such a republic was expected to reflect a combination of "authentic" Iranian and Islamic values that had been tarnished by the pro-Western monarchy. This was the clearest sign yet that, in order to implement the challenge belief system, a radical restructuring of the political system was planned. Most ominously, the anti-Western stand was an integral part of the new ideology. As one observer put it, "hostility to the United States was not something marginal for the Khomeinists but stood at the center of their thinking." Friendliness to the United States was equated, as Bani Sadr argued, with "subservience," and any compromise smacked of treason (Rubin 1980b, 234).

Third, the fundamentalists tried to reduce the cost of resistance to their plans through the use of dissimulation. In one successful ploy Ayatollah Motahari encouraged contacts with the shah's representatives to discuss a Regency Council, a scheme that would have eased out the shah without unduly alarming the military and other loyalists (Taheri 1985, 239). The fundamentalists were also busy building a veneer of moderation when dealing with the foreign press. Ibrahim Yazdi, Sadeq Gotbzadeh and Hassan Ibrahim-Habibi cautioned Khomeini to tone down his radical messages and avoid the sticky issue of a literal implementation of the Shari'a law, women rights and the role of the *faqih* (guardian). As a result, Khomeini took to pledging full freedom of press but qualified it with phrases such as "in accordance with Islam," or "on the basis of the Koran." One study found that Khomeini actively encouraged the "illusion that the mullahs will return to the mosques." He told a number of reports and Western visitors that neither he nor other religious leaders would hold top positions in the Islamic government (Benard and Khalilzad 1984, 39; Taheri 1985, 229; Katouzin 1981, 355; Bill 1982).

Much of the propaganda effort was directed at the United States. Yazdi was dispatched on a tour to reassure the public and the administration about the reasonableness of his boss (Taheri 1985, 227, 239). On December 12, Yazdi appeared in a televised discussion with Henry Precht and promised that the Islamic Republic would offer free election and freedom of speech and the press. According to Cottam (1988, 176), who had contacts with the fundamentalists, Yazdi "in particular was appraised of the situation in the administration" and was in a good position to fashion his messages accordingly. Evoking the language of the civil rights movement, the emissary painted a picture of a peaceful opposition brutalized by a tyrannical regime. He also claimed that the Islamic Republic would fight all efforts by Communists to take over and predicted the continuation of cordial relations with the United States (Sick 1985, 111). These reassurances were so effective that even astute observers were taken in. Clark Clifford, a former secretary of defense and one of the "wise men" of American foreign policy, expressed alarm at the prospects of a fundamentalist government in a November 29 memo to Brzezinski. However, after meeting with Khomeini's representatives in Paris, he was reassured that the ayatollah wanted to set up a government of secular moderates and that the Islamic clergy would stay in the background (Frantz and McKean 1995, 305–307).

As already indicated, mixed signals and rumors are an integral part of the liminal stage of political change. They add to the highly difficult problems of estimating the *motives, credibility* and *political power* of the various contenders. In Iran, the ratio of signal to noise was so high that both the shah and the moderate opposition found the situation confusing and fluid. Rafizadeh (1987, 263, 309–310), who visited Teheran in December, found the shah visibly sick and deeply depressed, adding that the monarch was "gaunt, his eyes huge, protruding, and unfocused, heavy rales produced by his breathing shaking his chest and shoulders." A month earlier, the shah, fearing that his father's grave would be desecrated, ordered the bones transferred to Cairo in a top-secret mission. Rafizadeh noted that the shah "did not see any future for himself and his family in Iran."

By early December, Mohammed Reza was ready to discuss devolution of power. His new strategy was to enlist a number of moderate opposition politicians to run a transitional government until the June elections. On December 18, the shah told Sullivan that he was trying to persuade Gholam Hossein Sadiqi to form a new cabinet. Sadiqi, a septuagenarian NF politician, had worked with Ali Amini behind the scenes to affect a face-saving constitutional formula for the monarchy. On December 26, the shah informed Sullivan that Sadiqi had located a few prospective ministers but that he needed an additional six weeks to form a government. Sadiqi's difficulties stemmed from the fact that no major opposition figure, including Karim Sanjabi, was willing to join a government linked to the shah and risk the wrath of Khomeini. Still, the shah decided to continue his search and, on December 27, he announced that Bakhtiar would form a new government.

Bakhtiar, a sixty-two-year-old deputy minister in the Mossadeq government and a co-leader of Iran Party, conditioned his acceptance on a number of guarantees. He demanded a free hand in running the country, dissolution of SAVAK, freedom of speech and press and the shah's departure. Neither the shah nor Bakhtiar had any illusions that the new government would be acceptable to Khomeini and the opposition, which was toeing the fundamentalist line. When John Stempel met Bakhtiar, the veteran politician was skeptical of the mullahs but felt that the NF could stand up to Khomeini (Documents vol. 20, 88–89). He believed that if his government could be credited for the shah's departure, the support for Khomeini would decline. This was apparently a popular theory among some secularists in Iran. Mohammed Derakhshesh, the head of the teachers union, told Sullivan on December 27 that, after the shah's departure, the support for Khomeini would decline by 50 percent (Documents, vol. 26, 87–88).

However, when Bakhtiar was sworn in on January 6, 1979, even the secularists hurriedly dissassociated themselves from the "traitor." Bakthiar was expelled from the NF and the Iran Party which replaced him with Abolfazl Qasemi, an obscure librarian and his alleged links to SAVAK during the 1961 upheaval were exposed (Chehabi 1990, 165, 249). Although Bazargan, who was close to Bakhtiar, was supportive, others in LMI followed the uncompromising line of Khomeini, who declared that the new prime minister was illegitimate (Chehabi 1990, 248). Bazargan had tried to mediate between Bakhtiar and the Islamic Revolution Council, but was rebuffed.

The shah's departure on January 16, 1979, did not improve the standing of the new government and, after negotiations with the council failed, Bakhtiar offered to resign. But Khomeini and Yazdi, who were apprehensive that a premature collapse of the government might trigger a military intervention, instructed the council to prolong the negotiations. They asked Bakhtiar to offer his resignation to Khomeini in Paris and get a new appointment as head of a transitional administration. However, Ayatollah Sadeq Khalkhali, who represented the extremist Fedayeen Islam, scuttled the deal. Bakhtiar refused to resign and tried to block Khomeini's planned return to Teheran at the end of January, a ploy that failed in the face of the overwhelming public support for the Imam.

The endgame in Iran presented the already bitterly divided Carter administration with a new set of challenges. Whatever its opinion of the monarchy, Washington was forced to focus on the successor regime. In an ironic twist, the wishful thinking and unrealistic expectations about the shah came to match, if not exceed, the wishful thinking and unrealistic expectations about Khomeini.

THE ENDGAME: THE VIEW FROM WASHINGTON

A month before the events in Iran reached a climax in late December, the Carter administration made a feeble attempt to break the policy paralysis. After his return from Teheran, Michael Blumenthal suggested that George Ball do an outside review of the shah's prospects. Ball, who started on November 30, was a former deputy secretary of state under Johnson and a vocal critic of American policy in Vietnam and the Middle East. Ball was well acquainted with Iran from his frequent business trips there and had a highly negative opinion of the shah, whom he described as suffering from "imperial megalomania" (Ball 1982, 453, 454–455). Since Ball was a friend of Vance, some observers claimed that the review amounted to a sophisticated effort to bring the president closer to the State Department (Thornton 1991, 259). Brzezinski (1983, 370) who apparently did not know about the connection, wrote later that he had come to regret the whole exercise.

The personal antipathy between Ball and the national security adviser was running high from the very beginning. Ball (1982, 458) found Brzezinski to have a facility "for inventing abstractions that sounded deceptively global and profound," at least to the inexperienced Carter. Ball was said to be "horrified by Brzezinski's bureaucratic imperialism" and reported to Vance that there was a "shocking unhealthful situation in the National Security Council with Brzezinski doing everything possible to exclude the State Department" (Bill 1988a, 249; Destler, Gelb and Lake 1984, 222). For his part, Brzezinski (1983, 370) complained that Ball was talking to the press and portraying the administration as "hopelessly split."

The substance of the review sparked more bureaucratic infighting. Ball ruled that the shah's regime was mortally wounded and, as he told Carter, "like Humpty Dumpty, could not be put together because there had been a national regurgitation by the Iranian people." He recommended a Council of Notables to be drawn from a list of about fifty, mostly elderly NF politicians. The State Department welcomed Ball's conclusion that the shah was "a goner," a view echoed in an INR memorandum of December 5. The memo found that "the shah was unable to provide the leadership that was necessary and he and the institutions he had built were rapidly becoming more a part of a problem than a force that can help resolve it." It referred to the shah as "a spent force" and predicted that, "sooner or later he will be replaced by others, no matter what we do" (White Paper, 03556, 9). Still, the department was unhappy with Ball's recommendation that the shah retain some authority alongside the proposed Council of Notables (Armstrong 1980d).

Brzezinski, on the other hand, was convinced that the NF leadership was weak, divided and had no popular following. Cottam (1990, 277) described Brzezinski as "contemptuous of the view" that secular and moderate religious leaders like Bazargan could remain in power, a view that was reinforced by a top secret CIA report of November 30. The agency argued that the NF lacked popular support and was too divided to be effective, and correctly predicted that Khomeini was the leader most likely to command the revolution (Armstrong 1980d). For once in agreement with Brzezinski, Sullivan scorned the Ball recommendations. The ambassador argued that the individuals on the list "would not be found in the same room with each other" and that, even if a Council of Notables was to be established, it would succumb to calls for the shah's abdication (Sick 1985, 118). Brzezinski (1983, 373) worried that, given the feebleness of the moderate opposition, the Ball plan would create a "Kerensky-like" slide, a reference to the ill-fated moderate Russian government that was steamrolled by the Bolsheviks in 1917. To avoid such an outcome he wanted to urge the shah to proceed with a military crackdown and, only after stabilizing the situation, "the military government can be progressively civilized like in Turkey or Brazil."

Because of the divisions in the administration, the December 13 meeting of the SCC called to review the Ball plan ended inconclusively. In a separate meeting with Carter, Ball failed to persuade the president to push the shah to embrace the Council of Notables. Carter was said to argue that the United States could not tell the head of another state what to do. What is more, Carter apparently succumbed to Brzezinski's pleas for a decisive American move, but as always, bureaucratic infighting prevented any action (Armstrong 1980d).

As already pointed out, Carter's ability to provide decisive leadership had not improved as the crisis deepened. His reluctance to use military force was especially profound. Although the president seemed to have accepted Brzezinski's arguments at the cognitive level, emotionally he could not bring himself to advise the shah to use force (Moens 1990, 158; Zonis, 1991, 251). Sullivan (1984, 270) observed that Carter had invested too much in his human rights policy to "officially convey the suggestion that military force be used, no matter how desperately he might have wished that consummation." Vance noted that the "President refused to give American blessing to the iron fist" strategy (quoted in Smith 1984, 363). Carter was equally uneasy about enforcing American will on another country. On December 7, Carter told reporters that the shah's fate is "in the hands of the people of Iran" and that "we have never had any intention and don't have any intention to intercede in the internal affairs of Iran" (Alexander and Nanes 1980, 463).

The president continued to vacillate on the use of force to the very end. On December 26, the shah asked the administration point blank whether it "would support a policy of brutal repression." Vance drafted a cable instructing the shah that the United States would not abide by an "iron fist" strategy. On the same day, Sullivan conveyed to the monarch Washington's concern about the chaos, but informed him that the responsibility for establishing "law and order" was entirely his (White Paper, 03556, 66). Two days later a White House meeting came close to accepting a military option. However, when the decision was sent to the State Department, Vance persuaded the President to remove any strong elements from the new cable. He wrote to Sullivan informing him that "Washington believed that the shah's uncertainty and wavering was undermining the morale of the army" and that the United States preferred a civilian government (Thornton 1991, 261–262; Sick 1985, 125; White Paper, 03556, 66).

It would have been even more inconceivable for Carter to back up the shah with American military presence, an option which Brzezinski, Duncan and Schlesinger were said to prefer. The president was quick to dispel any such notion and proclaimed that "we have no desire nor the ability to introduce massive forces into Iran or any other country to determine the outcome of domestic political issues" (quoted in Rosati 1987, 77). Even a seemingly minor military gesture fell prey to this psychology. A December 27 meeting of the

SCC attended by Brzezinski, Vance, Brown and Turner authorized the Seventh Fleet carrier *Constellation* to prepare for a possible deployment in the Indian Ocean. Because of the routine nature of the order the president was not notified. When the plan was leaked to the press, Mondale persuaded Carter that such a show of force might alienate the successor regime in Iran. The exercise was aborted and neither Brzezinski nor Brown challenged the decision (Lasky 1979, 382). As the press pointed out, the *Constellation* fiasco was a symbolic remainder of irresolution in high places.

In the absence of a consensus, various players were left free to vent their grievances and promote diametrically opposed strategies. In a December 19 letter to Sullivan, Henry Precht implied that Vance and Christopher were concerned about the Brzezinski-Zahedi channel. Precht described Zahedi as a "disastrous counterpart" in dealing with the crisis in Iran and expressed his regret that the counsel of the Iranian ambassador is "one of the strongest factors working on opinion in the White House" (Documents, vol. 13, 16–18). Precht wrote to Saunders that "there is general agreement that the shah has only a marginal chance to survive as a constitutional monarch"—a forecast included in an INR memorandum of the same day—and urged to "move now with definite steps toward a post-Shah future in Iran" (State Department, 01939; White Paper, 03556, 6–7). The State Department found it encouraging that the shah was negotiating with Sadiqi, Amini, and Bakhtiar, but felt that the preservation of the monarchy should not be an American absolute.

In contrast, Brzezinski and Schlesinger strongly rejected the notion that the crisis could be resolved by the departure of the shah. At the beginning of December, Schlesinger, a former CIA director, launched a belated but vigorous initiative to avert a Pahlavi collapse. He lobbied Carter's close aides, Hamilton Jordan, Jody Powell and Charles Kirbo as well as others in the foreign policy and defense bureaucracy. His message that "the linchpin of the Northern Tier [Turkey, Iran, Pakistan] would be removed" underscored the catastrophic consequence of Iran's fall (Sick 1985, 114). The energy secretary advocated the strengthening of the American base in Diego Garcia and wanted a number of carriers moved to the region. Brzezinski was also concerned with the strategic implications of the turmoil in Iran. In his December 20 "arc of crisis" speech, the security adviser warned that the "fragile political structure" in the region was collapsing and "the resulting chaos could well be filled by elements hostile to our values" (Rubin 1980b, 235).

To avert such an outcome, Brzezinski was apparently ready to engage in an Ajax-style operation. According to S. Turner (1991b, 77–78, 88) the adviser favored an undercover effort to strengthen the opposition to Khomeini and bolster politicians that would be able to work with the Pahlavis. In early December, Brzezinski wrote a memorandum to Vance asking him to drum up allied support for the scheme. However, Turner professed to be "dumbfounded" at the possibility of what he described as a Mossadeq era covert effort to provide advice and financial support to "so-called moderate political elements." Brzezinski's proposal did not receive much support in the administration and neither was there any enthusiasm for it in Europe. In any case, the CIA director claimed that the agency had no infrastructure for a covert action in Iran (Ranelagh 1987, 649).

Meanwhile, Sullivan was developing his own plan of action. The ambassador, long skeptical about the efficacy of the secular opposition, doubted the wisdom of American support for Sadiqi or Bakhtiar. In a cable to Washington, Sullivan (1981, 323) described how, in a meeting, Bakhtiar spoke with ebullience about "winning the revolution from the ayatollah." The ambassador noted that the NF leader was a "quixotic" character who failed to realize that his government would be swept away by the political tide. He added that the CIA sources in Iran viewed Bakhtiar as an "adventurer who is suspected of secret ties to the shah" (Bill 1988a, 263; Documents, vol. 20, 93–95). Thus, while sharing Brzezinski's doubts about the moderate opposition, Sullivan decided to fashion a diametrically different strategy.

Unauthorized by Washington, the ambassador began to negotiate with Mehdi Bazargan and other leaders of the LMI, in an effort to create a coalition government that would be able to retain power after the departure of the shah. Although Sullivan knew that Bazargan did not have a popular following, he hoped to "empower" the LMI and secular moderates by negotiating an agreement with the military. According to this plan, one hundred senior military officers would leave the country with the shah, making room for more junior and "opposition friendly" commanders (Huyser 1986, 17). Concurrently, Sullivan wanted the U.S. government to start negotiations with Khomeini and proposed to Vance, Newsom and Saunders to send Theodore L. Eliot, the Farsi-speaking inspector general of the Foreign Service, to Paris.

By January 3 the State Department worked out the details of the Eliot mission, which was set for January 6, the same day that Bakhtiar was scheduled to present his government to the Majlis. President Carter was notified of the plan just before his departure, on January 4, for a meeting with European leaders in Guadeloupe. Brzezinski criticized the idea on the grounds that the United States needed to show full support for the Bakhtiar government. Even though Vance confirmed that the shah did not object to Sullivan's scheme, the Eliot mission was aborted. On January 10, the White House decided to use the French government as an intermediary to Khomeini. Two days later, Sullivan (1981, 232) responded with a highly agitated cable. He argued that "our national interest demand that we attempt to structure a modus vivendi" between the military and the religious camp in order to preempt Tudeh. Brzezinski (1983, 381) revealed that Sullivan had called the White House decision "insane," prompting the adviser to describe Sullivan's message as "hysterical." In his memoirs Carter (1982, 446) claimed that "Sullivan lost control of himself" and described the cable as "bordering on insolence." Sullivan's often-sarcastic messages had irritated the president in the past. One staffer described Carter as tired of "smartass attitude and smartass cables" (Armstrong 1980d). On a number of occasions

Carter had wanted to fire Sullivan but Vance had persuaded him that it would be detrimental to the American image in Iran.

With tension between the State Department, the NSC and the embassy running high, important decisions about the crisis went unattended. In a December 26 meeting, Vance declared that Iran did not receive enough high level attention and ordered David Newsom to create a coordinating committee. The committee, which included representatives from some twelve different State Department bureaus and eight other agencies, was too unwieldy to be effective (Shaplen 1980a). Participants were also afraid to share sensitive information because there were so many leaks that the *Washington Post* routinely published detailed summaries of the meetings (Shaplen 1980a). Sick (1985, 123–124) described the atmosphere of mutual suspicion as almost "paranoid."

The three problems most affected by the bureaucratic infighting were the future of the military procurement, the safety of Americans in Iran and efforts to stabilize the shah-sanctioned Bakhtiar government. All three issues were part of a larger question of finding a balance between showing support for the monarchy and protecting American interests in the revolutionary aftermath. As Sullivan (1983–84) later argued, in a potentially revolutionary situation, the administration had to know when to "bail out." In his view, Carter stuck to the shah too long, dooming the moderate opposition, but in Nicaragua he moved so fast that the moderates did not have a chance to organize.

By mid-December, the administration dispatched Eric Von Marbod, the deputy director of the Defense Security Assistance Agency, to negotiate a memorandum of understanding that terminated some $10 billion of military sales. Brzezinski, who was concerned about undermining the shah, held up the agreement for a week, but Brown prevailed and the agreement was signed at the last moment, three days after the arrival of Khomeini. The issue of evacuating expatriates was even more sensitive. By December, there were still some 20,000 Americans in Iran. Since a mass exodus of Americans would have demonstrated a lack of American confidence, Sullivan (1981, 208–209) sent most of the dependents on an "early Christmas vacation." On December 25, Marines used tear gas to prevent a student demonstration from taking over the embassy and Americans were attacked around the country. On December 31, Sullivan denied that there was any planned evacuation, but with the chaos growing daily, many of the remaining Americans left even before Vance ordered the official evacuation on January 29, 1997.

The issue of supporting Bakhtiar proved even more complex. Sullivan, who was contemptuous of Bakhtiar, viewed his government as purely transitional. However, Brzezinski persuaded the president that it would be best to back the new prime minister, at least until a more stable pro-Western government could emerge. In the view of the NSC, Bakhtiar could only survive if he had the backing of the military. On January 3, General Robert Huyser, the deputy commander of NATO, was dispatched to Teheran to secure the cooperation of the armed forces. Huyser was familiar with top Iranian commanders but otherwise had little experience with the domestic politics of the country. An Iranian insider called him "ill-informed and politically inept" (Farmanfarmaian and Farmanfarmaian 1997, 451). Contrary to Sullivan's plan, Huyser was instructed to persuade the top military brass to stay put and work with Bakhtiar against the fundamentalists and their left-wing allies.

Huyser, whose main source of information was the military, was optimistic about the stability of the armed forces and their loyalty to the Bakhtiar government. Sullivan, who vehemently disagreed with this view, had to share with Huyser the embassy facilities for daily reports to Washington. Reflecting on this experience, Sullivan (1981, 230) observed that "there were times when we felt we must have been talking to two different cities." In retrospect, Huyser might have been putting too much faith in his military sources. According to a number of accounts, the top Iranian command was splintered into a number of factions. The hardliners like General Gholam Ali Oveissi, Admiral Habib Alahi and General Manuchehr Khosradad were apparently ready to stage a proshah coup, but other officers were hedging their bets. When the shah relieved General Azhari, he named General Abbas Karim Gharabaghi as the new chief of staff. General Hossein Fardoust, the shah's confidante, recommended Gharabahgi, an Azerbaijani outsider unpopular with many of his fellow officers. Since both Fardoust and Gharabaghi escaped the subsequent purge by the fundamentalists, some observers suggested that they might have been part of a faction in the royal entourage that had switched sides ahead of time. Cynthia Helms (1981, 204) recalled that, shortly before he died, the shah accused Fardoust of outright treason. While Fardoust's motives have remained a mystery, his defection virtually sealed the fate of the monarchy (Rubin 1980b, 239–240; Saidi 1993). At the very least, Fardoust's and Gharabaghi's contacts with the opposition encouraged the clergy to continue their uncompromising posture toward the monarchy.

Even if there was no overt treason, the military was not unified enough to justify Huyser's optimistic forecasts. The rank and file was deserting in great numbers and, by early January, Gharabaghi and SAVAK's Moghadam were negotiating with the deputies of Beheshti and Bazargan. While the Carter administration was apparently not aware of all this backstage maneuvering, there was an increasing recognition that any successor regime would need the blessing of Khomeini. However, as in the case of the shah, the perception of Khomeini and the challenge belief system was filtered through the paradigmatic lenses of practitioners and academic observers.

Quite naturally, the moralpolitikers regarded Khomeini as a reasonably moderate leader with whom the United States could do business. Precht, who participated in the Iran Working Group of the State Department, was particularly active in propagating this view. In a December 13 memorandum, Precht related that Ibrahim Yazdi had assured him that the Islamic republic would have free elections and would guarantee full freedom of speech and press, including the "right to attack Islam." Interestingly though, Precht wrote off as "naïve" Yazdi's plans for an Islamic economy and concluded that the Khomeini organization was "very amateurish in handling" its public relations efforts (Documents, vol. 18, 115–119). Precht and other like-minded officials directed journalists to what they described as "positive developments" in Khomeini's thinking. Taking a cue from Sullivan's reference to Khomeini as "Gandhi-like," some moralpolitikers took to painting the ayatollah as a moral figure who raged against a corrupt and tyrannical regime. Andrew Young compared the Iranian case to the American civil rights movement and predicted that, once the revolution was completed, Khomeini would be recognized as "some kind of a saint." When critics and some journalists expressed concern about Khomeini's teachings, Precht complained that his writings were misunderstood (Spencer 1983, 96; Taheri 1985, 289; Stempel 1981, 291; Rubin 1985, 190; Ledeen and Lewis 1980; David 1993, 71; Ledeen and Lewis 1981, 212).

Those who regarded the shah as indispensable to American interests pointed out that Khomeini was implacably opposed to the West and no friend of democracy. Sick (1985, 55) was among those who professed profound skepticism about Khomeini's intentions, and warned on a number of occasions that the moderates would be swallowed by the fundamentalists, a view shared by Brzezinski, Schlesinger and Brown. They all worried about American future relations with a fundamentalist Iran. In a January 12 memo, Brzezinski (1983, 381) called attention to the fact that Khomeini was extremely hostile, adding that the situation was becoming chaotic to the point where the Tudeh could utilize the political vacuum.

In fact, the debate in the administration reflected a larger American puzzle of how to relate to a hitherto little understood religious movement. Because of the sheer novelty of the situation, academics experts came to play a prominent role in the discourse. Rubin (1980b, 80) wrote that journalists had to call Middle East specialists for an "instant education" on the difference between Shiites and Sunnis and other intricacies of Islam. From his vantage point as an expert, Bill (1978/79, 321–322) criticized the coverage of the major newspapers as "especially superficial." As the monarchy teetered on the brink, it was the human rights community and the scholars who had first sounded the alarm about the shah that came to dominate the discourse on Khomeini.

Richard Cottam, who met Khomeini in August, was among the first Americans to speak to the ayatollah. He asserted that the religious leader has no interest in running the government and planned to retire to Qom (Ledeen and Lewis 1981, 129). In an October 2 letter to the editor of the *Washington Post*, Cottam (1978b) described Khomeini as a "moderate and centrist" who is strongly in favor of land reform, welfare and an improved role for women. Cottam also took umbrage at the suggestion that people in Iran and the Middle East were not ready for liberal democracy. In a veiled criticism of the journalist, Joseph Kraft, who earlier expressed doubts about Khomeini's commitment to democracy, Cottam called such views "contemptuous" and "self-serving."

In a widely read article published in early December, Bill (1978/79) asserted that the clerics, who were described as "the guardians of social justice and morality," "would never participate in the formal government structure." The article mentioned Khomeini only in passing and never used the term Islamic Republic, creating an impression that the opposition wanted to restore the liberal and Western-inspired Constitution of 1906. Sick (1985, 113) pointed out that the "appeal of such an analysis was powerful." It implied that "if only we would disengage ourselves from the evils of the shah's rule, we could have a progressive, nationalist regime run by moderate, middle class professionals whose respect for individual freedoms and human rights was closer to U.S. values than the manipulative and repressive rule of the shah."

Richard Falk, another academic critical of the shah, was also spreading the message of Khomieni's moderation and humanity. In December, Falk and Ramsey Clark traveled at the head of a delegation to Teheran and Nauphle-le-Chateau, where they met the ayatollah. In subsequent interviews with the press, the duo criticized American official policy and praised the Iranian cleric (Sullivan 1981, 206). Falk (1978) who lambasted American foreign policy as "set by the military and the right" was particularly vociferous in extolling the virtues of a Khomeini-led government. Early in 1979 he expressed the opinion that Iran "may yet provide us with a desperately needed model of a humane government" (quoted in Sick 1985, 166). Another member of the delegation, James D. Cockcroft, a professor of sociology at Rutgers University, wrote a letter to the *New York Times* (January 3, 1979) denying that the fundamentalists would actively participate in the political realm.

Not all scholars shared this rosey assessment of Khomeinism. In a March testimony to the Joint Economic Committee of the Senate, Leonard Binder asserted that, if victorious, an Islamic state would turn against middle class intellectuals and it's leftist allies in the revolution. He even predicted a "Cultural Revolution" in which "students, workers, and soldiers were encouraged to bring pressure to bear on bureaucrats, professors, and military administrators." In mid-December Marvin Zonis had an interview with Khomeini and found him to be rigid and highly irrational (Ledeen and Lewis 1981, 212). Laqueur (1978) warned that the Ayatollah was a dangerous enemy of liberalism and, should the shah fall, the next regime or the one after next "is bound to be worse." However, many of the scholars who had serious reservations about the fundamentalists were discredited because of their developmental view that accorded the monarchy popular legitimacy. For instance, in an edited volume published while the revolution reached its peak, Lenczowski (1978, 475) found that "half a century after the installation of the Pahlavi dynasty, this ancient legacy was being revived in its full dimension." Even with delays in publication, such a conclusion seemed far-fetched.

As indicated in the theoretical section, predictions tend to follow the conscious or subconscious norms of legitimacy harbored by observers. A number of Marxist scholars saw in the unfolding events a sign that Iran was moving toward a "workers revolution." They confidently predicted that the workers and the Tudeh would have a major role in the successor regime. For obvious reasons they either ignored or underplayed Khomeini's role (Abrahamian 1978a; 1978b; Halliday 1978a; 1978b).

Regardless of their ideological persuasion, the academics that shaped the Iran discourse were all too steeped in linear thinking to envisage what one commentator called a "regressive revolution," that is, one where people want less freedom rather than more (Taheri 1988, 97). There was also little modern precedent for what another observer described as "massive redefinition of Islam from a religion promising worldly salvation to an ideology harboring . . . a worldly utopia" (Dubashi 1988, 11). Indeed, some of the scholars seemed to have subsequently admitted to misjudging the true nature of the fundamentalist ulama. Falk would later describe the Khomeini regime as "the most terroristic since Hitler," a radical departure from his earlier assessment (quoted in Sick 1985, 166).

Whatever their predictions, academics and journalists are not held responsible the way intelligence officials and policymarkers are. As Shlomo Gazit (1980), an Israeli intelligence chief put it, after misjudging a situation, scholars proceed "to draft a new paper." Normally, academic failures have little immediate impact on official intelligence estimates. However, the Iran experts who pioneered the theory of Khomeini's moderation left a more permanent mark. Cottam and Bill were among the select groups of scholars who had been consulted by the State Department, the White House and the CIA (Sale 1980; Ledeen and Lewis 1981, 129). Sick (1985, 94) reported that, in mid-November, he had met with a U.S. academic) who assured him that the ulama would not assume direct leadership (S. Turner 1991b, 119; Sick 1985, 55; Dreyfuss 1980, 46; Copeland 1989, 254; Saunders 1987; Ledeen and Lewis 1981, 129)

These experts, in conjunction with the moralpolitikers in the State Department, contributed to a serious misreading of the successor regime in Iran. Sick (1985, 113) described their views as a "body of rosy doctrine which, in its determined rejection of unpleasant realities, could only be compared with the institutional myopia of the U.S. government in persuading itself of the 'stability' of the shah." As the next chapter will illustrate, these unrealistic perceptions hampered the administration's dealings with the postrevolutionary dynamics and, ultimately, led to the hostage crisis.

5

Dealing with Chaos: The Carter Administration and the Successor Regime in Iran

When Ayatollah Khomeini made his triumphant return to Teheran on February 1, 1979, the moralpolitikers were ready to welcome a liberal and democratic regime. To the realpolitikers, the tone and the direction of fundamentalist politics looked worrisome. However, this group was all but silenced by the defeat of the shah. Even if the realpolitikers harbored personal doubts, they found it expedient to get behind the winning view that the Iranian moderates were destined to prevail. There was also a domestic imperative to show that American relations with Iran could prosper in a post-Pahlavi era. Early in 1979, President Carter, already besieged by criticisms of his leadership, came under a withering attack for "losing" Iran and mishandling Nicaragua. Facing the prospect of defending his record in the forthcoming election, the President was eager to show that Iran and, for that matter, Nicaragua were not total losses. If the administration could normalize relations with the new rulers in Teheran, Carter would be in a better position to vindicate his foreign policy record.

As a result, Washington had little recourse but to bet on the political viability of the moderates. This imperative colored the Iran estimate for most of 1979 and led to policies designed to help them win the power struggle with the fundamentalists. In hindsight, this considerable and well-publicized effort might have helped the latter to vanquish their opponents. This moment came after the occupation of the embassy, which ushered in the Second Revolution and enabled Khomeini to institutionalize the challenge belief system.

The radical turn in Iran and the prolonged hostage crisis doomed Carter's chances for reelection. More significantly, together with the Soviet invasion of Afghanistan in December 1979, these events undermined the credibility of the foreign policy paradigm of the administration. Even before Carter left Washington, New Internationalism was discredited, ending one of the most unique experiments in American foreign policy. The following chapter will offer a thematic-chronological analysis of these events.

THE SHORT SPRING OF THE MODERATES: THE EMERGENCE OF A DUAL GOVERNMENT

When Khomeini arrived to a welcoming crowd of millions, he wasted little time in taking full credit for the revolution. Confounding the widely held expectation that he would depart to Qom, Khomeini turned the Refah girls' school into his new headquarters. He immediately called for a *jihad* against the Bakhtair government and, on February 5, he chose Bazargan to lead a new Provisional Government (PG). On February 13, Bazargan announced his cabinet, which was heavily weighted with LMI members; among the secularists, Karim Sanjabi served as a foreign minister, and PIN's Dariush Foruhar headed the labor and social affairs ministry.

In spite of its moderate facade, the PG served at the pleasure of the fundamentalists and more precisely, the shadowy Revolutionary Council. The fundamentalists enhanced their control through the *Hez-e Jomhuri-e Eslami*, the Islamic Republican Party (IRP), which was founded by Ayatollah Beheshti on February 19. Since Khomeini donated part of his religious tithes, the IRP, which was based on the mosque network, had considerable financial resources at its disposal. Beheshti also moved to consolidate the various secret Islamic societies that sprouted during the revolution. Many of these loosely structured groups attracted lower class supporters of the Imam, known as the *hizbollahis* (Ioannides 1984, 49; Siavoshi 1990, 144; Chehabi 1995).

Another important weapon in the fundamentalist arsenal was the *komitehs*, or revolutionary committees. As a rule, the komitehs were led by local mullahs and backed by self-appointed revolutionary guards, mostly teenagers armed with light weapons. While some komitehs dominated neighborhoods, others sprang up in factories, oil fields, government ministeries and even banks. There were some 1,500 committees in Teheran alone, and not even the fundamentalist leadership knew their exact number in the country. Many of the komiteh members were recruited to the Revolutionary Guard, the Pasdaran, officially established on May 5, 1979. Sick (1985, 200) described the move as a "brilliant political stroke" that enabled the fundamentalists to bypass the government structure and rule the country through an alternative system of power.

Controlling an alternative power center made it easier for the Khomeinists to dictate policy to the PG. Bazargan and his ministers found that Khomeini nullified many of their policy directives, most notably, a decree that legalized all political parties. Even more vexing for the PG was its failure to control the komitehs. Official orders were either ignored or had to be negotiated with each local group, prompting one minister to describe the government as a "knife without a blade" (Sick 1985, 200). Bazargan himself complained that "our country has become a city with a hundred sheriffs" (quoted in Siavoshi 1990, 146). In retrospect, they were right: Beheshti later revealed that Khomeini had never intended to give any power to Bazargan (Chehabi 1990, 275). Actually, the mullahs used the PG as part of their strategy of *howsaleh*, that is "taking no risk until the likely pattern of events has become clear" (Taheri 1988, 124). As a transitional institution, the Bazargan government helped the fundamentalists to continue their "leadership from behind" without unduly alarming those who might had been opposed to the Islamic vision. The alliance with the LMI helped the clerics in a number of specific ways.

First, the appointment of Bazargan served to split the ranks of the moderate camp. The NF secularists felt marginalized and humiliated by the treatment of their leader, Karim Sanjabi, who was denied real power and then unceremoniously replaced with Ibrahim Yazdi. Those nationalists who did not participate in the government fared even less well. The National Democratic Front of Hedayatollah Matin-Daftari, Mossadeq's grandson, was violently attacked by the hizbollahis, much to the chagrin of Bazargan who was powerless to stop the flagrant abuses. The secularists accused the PG of condoning these practices and, unwilling or unable to offend Khomeini, held Bazargan personally responsible (Chehabi 1990, 263).

Second, the fundamentalists used the legitimacy of the PG to fight the growing threat from the Left. After the departure of the shah, leftist guerrillas, strengthened by thousands of their comrades who returned from abroad, launched a major offensive. They attacked army and police arsenals and looted large amounts of equipment, including anti-aircraft guns and rocket launchers. The guerrillas also raided scores of banks and "confiscated" large sums of money in the name of the people. The Left's political demands—immediate nationalization of industry, land distribution and other radical reforms—were even more worrisome to the fundamentalists. Fedayeen and Tudeh members infiltrated public and private sector enterprises and urged the workers to demand prohibitive concessions. Banks refused to serve "capitalist" customers, a step that wrought havoc on the Iranian financial system (Taheri 1985, 251; Huyser 1986, 145).

Third, the seemingly moderate PG served to lull the military into submission to the new regime. As indicated in the previous chapter, the Khomeinists worked exceptionally hard to neutralize the armed forces. In the so-called "hearts and flowers" approach, civilians were urged to befriend conscripts and their officers (Zabih 1988, 340). These techniques proved so effective that, by the beginning of February, the defection from the ranks reached alarming proportions. On January 22, hundreds of *homafars*, air force technicians, mutinied and declared loyalty to Khomeini. When loyal units intervened, major clashes erupted. Given the growing chaos, the Chief-of-Staff, General Gharabaghi, and his Crisis Commission declared the "neutrality" of the armed forces on February 11 and sought Bazargan's protection (Enteesar 1988).

The PG welcomed this move and Khomeini personally reassured the military and other shah's officials that in Islam "repentance was accepted until the last moment" (Chehabi 1995, 134). Still, up to 12,000 officers were arrested, retired or cashiered. Of the eighty top generals, more than seventy were tortured and executed, along with hundreds of lower ranking officers. By one estimate, almost 75 percent of the shah's senior officers were killed by the end of summer. The government protested these often grisly executions, which were carried out after a perfunctory "revolutionary justice" hearing. The executions, coupled with the appointment of *mullahs* as military prosecutors, totally demoralized the military and sent a signal that the real power lay with Khomeini and his Revolutionary Guards (Chehabi 1995; Farhang 1987, 159; Taheri 1985, 257; Rosen 1982, 94). The PG was equally powerless to stop the purge and arrest of some 15,000–30,000 civilian members of the shah's regime. When Bazargan tried to protest, Khomeini called the PG "weak" (Documents, vol. 27, 8).

Fourth, the PG was forced to help Khomeini put down the growing ethnic rebellions. Initially, both the prime minister and his deputy Abbas Amir Entezam reassured the minorities that their rights would be respected. But when Khomeini rebuffed demands for autonomy, the Turkomans in Gorgan started an insurrection, followed by the Arabs in Khuzistan. The large Kurdish population, fearful of the increasing Islamization of the revolution, launched an attack under the leadership of the Kurdistan Democratic Party of Iran (KDPI). The Muslim People's Republican Party (MPRP), founded by the supporters of Ayatollah Shariatmadari, was making demands for greater autonomy in Azerbaijan.

Using the Pasdaran and regular army units, the fundamentalists crushed the rebellion in Kurdistan and oil-rich Khuzistan. The Azerbaijani demands were met with political intimidation and violence; on Khomeini's orders Shariatmadari's MPRP was disbanded. In Kurdistan, where Khomeini appointed the judges, Ayatollah Sadeq Khalkhali, known as "Judge Blood," presided and many of the locals were hanged. The brutality of the assault on the minorities took many of the supporters of the revolution aback. Ahmed Sadr Hajj Sayyed Javadi, Bazargan's minister of justice, protested the executions, but to no avail (Taheri 1985, 257). Even before the end of the PG tenure, the ethnic minorities had came to suffer a calamity far greater that Baraheni, the Azerbaijani poet, decried in his antishah manifesto, *The Crowned Cannibals*.

An initial coalition between moderates and radicals is not an unusual feature of a revolution. As Brinton (1965) pointed out, the former hope to gain enough power to stir the events into a moderate direction and the latter use their coalition partners to hide their true goals. Indeed, Bazargan himself used Brinton's argument to justify his alliance with Khomeini (Chehabi 1990, 277). But critics dismissed Bazargan and his colleagues as "idle talkers about the progressive spirit of Islam in American universities," who had never attempted to resist the mullahs (Arani 1980, 17). Their major test was the new constitution, a draft of which was proposed by a number of NF leaders, legal scholars and the ICDFHR. However, the fundamentalists ignored the draft, which was modeled on the 1906 Constitution, and insisted that the upcoming referendum would be limited to either a choice of a monarchy or an Islamic republic.

Sensing a trap, government members and the secular opposition protested the wording of the ballot. On March 5, a million people gathered to commemorate the death of Mossadeq and listen to his grandson, Hedayatollah Matin-Daftari, who blasted the Khomeinists. But the divisions in the National Front and the fractious nature of the opposition prevented a united action. In any case, the fundamentalists were taking measures to "discourage negative votes," a fact that undoubtedly contributed to the 98.2 percent support for the Islamic Republic in the March 30 referendum (Bakhash 1984, 73). The meaning of the term was left vague, but the Imam told his followers that a democratic Iran or even a democratic Islamic republic is not acceptable.

MAKING SENSE OF THE REVOLUTIONARY AFTERMATH: WASHINGTON'S GUIDE FOR THE PERPLEXED

The Carter administration proved to be as indecisive about the post-Pahlavi era as it had been about the shah. The immediate task at hand was to analyze the evolving power structure in Iran and identify those politicians that would be most amenable to American interests. But, as the attitudes toward the Bakhtiar government indicated, arriving at a new Iran estimate proved to be a highly contentious issue. The infighting over the issue prompted one observer to compare the administration to a "three-headed dog," with each head pulling in a different direction (Thornton 1991, 271).

During a January 11 mini-SCC meeting, Precht argued that Bakhtiar, like the shah before him, was a source of tension in Iran. But there was hope that other moderates would come to the fore, especially as the Ayatollah was expected to stay on the margins of the political process (Documents, vol. 26, 109–110). Harold Saunders testified before the House Committee on International Relations on January 17 that the situation in Iran was complex and that no quick solution could be expected. During a news conference on the same day, a defensive sounding president tried to justify his decision not to communicate with Khomeini (Alexander and Nanes 1980, 466–473, 476–478).

The issue of whether the United States should back a broader coalition was discussed again during a meeting on January 19. Vance pressured the president to make an overture to Khomeini, a strategy strongly advocated by Sullivan, who planned to affect an alliance between the military and the ulama. Mondale supported Vance and argued that Khomeini represented a strong political force but Carter objected on the grounds that the United States was not "going to accommodate the left anymore" (Thornton 1991, 269). Brzezinski (1983, 385) hoped that the collapse of the Bakhtiar government would prompt the military to stage a coup, an idea he raised a number of times with General Huyser after his return from Teheran at the beginning of February (Huyser 1986, 283; Thornton 1991, 273; Sullivan 1981, 249, 252).

Ironically, Huyser's famously optimistic reports that the generals had full control over the military might have contributed to Brzezinski's misperceptions. In reality, military power was already shifting to what would soon become the

Pasdaran (revolutionary militia), a fact that was mentioned in a Department of Defense memorandum (Teicher and Teicher 1983, 50). Robert Gates (1996, 128), affirmed that "there was enormous confusion in Washington at this point about who was in charge in Teheran."

The appointment of Bazargan gave Henry Precht and his fellow moralpolitikers a boost. The group was eager to vindicate its predictions that the brutal authoritarian regime of the shah would be replaced by a liberal democracy. At the end of February the Iran director wrote a report that laid the basis of what, in effect, became the "Precht doctrine." Although the paper was not coordinated with anyone outside the State Department, it was circulated to all NATO members for consideration (Sick 1985, 187). Precht asserted that the Iranians, an essentially pragmatic people, were fatigued by the turmoil of the revolution and were ready to return to normal conditions under a moderate anti-Soviet leader like Bazargan. To help the moderates, Precht insisted on an early normalization of relations with Teheran. This philosophy guided the Iran working group chaired by David Newsom. Even before Precht's paper was out, the Iran group came up with a number of proposals to normalize relations, including a radio broadcast and exchange of scholars and students (Ioannides 1984, 63).

Precht's views were at odds with the embassy dispatches. As early as January 7, Sullivan quoted a leading moderate politician to the effect that "Iran is moving from life under a dictatorship of the boot to life under a dictatorship of the sandal" (Documents, vol. 27, 49). Barry Rosen (1982, 62), a public relations officer, cabled a summary of a January 29 conversation with an *Ettala'at* journalist, who asserted that Khomeini would "remain inflexible" and "would reveal himself as an autocrat." Other reports indicated that moderate clergy, including Shariatmadari, were apprehensive about Khomeini and regretted the shah's departure. Writing at the end of February, Sullivan described the situation as "total chaos" and predicted that the "internecine warfare may keep Bazargan from ever functioning." A report in March argued that Bazargan government is not effective and that the situation is "schizophrenic and unstable" (Documents, vol. 13, 56–57, vol. 27, 20–21, 24–25). Around the same time the CIA reported that the fundamentalists initiated a virulent anti-American poster and cartoon campaign, but the administration made no serious effort to follow up on the issue (Fischer and Abedi 1990, 349–382). A report dated April 18, spoke of Khomeini's "anti-Western paranoia." Michael Metrinko suggested that the liberals were already disenchanted with the revolution, implying that they may be "peeled away" from the reactionary mullahs (Shaplen 1980a, 62; Documents, vol. 1, 507–508, 531–532; vol. 14, 30–39, 82–85; vol. 27, 12–13).

Much of the confusion in the administration stemmed from the analysis of the nature and strength of the Khomeini camp. Precht and like-minded officials, who wanted to see the moderates win, argued that Khomeini was neither anti-American nor antidemocratic and, more to the point, that he would become a figurehead. When the *Washington Post* (Randal 1979) questioned whether the shah was being replaced by an Islamic tyranny, Precht felt compelled to defend the ayatollah. He criticized Stephen Rosenfeld, the editorial columnist of the newspaper, who published excerpts from Khomeini's book *Velayat-e Faqih*. Speaking in early February at an open forum in the State Department, Precht accused Rosenfeld of using a book which, in his opinion, was either a collection of inaccurate notes taken by Khomeini's students or an outright forgery (Ledeen and Lewis 1981, 130, 20). When, in late February, the ayatollah moved to Qom, the moralpolitikers were quick to seize upon this "Gandhi-like" shift.

A number of complex institutional and psychological factors accounted for the optimistic assumptions that formed the "Precht doctrine." The revolution discredited Brzezinski who had bet on the shah's legitimacy, leaving the State Department to play a larger role. By the same token, Precht and others who pushed for the shah's ouster were basking in the triumph of their predictive success. They used their position to silence, or ignore those who were less sanguine about the chances of the moderates (Taheri 1988, 110). The decision to replace the diplomats who served during the Pahlavi era apparently enhanced the promoderate bias in embassy reporting. Some of the new staffers, including a commercial attaché, were eager to prove the "Precht doctrine" right and reported accordingly (Bill 1988a, 278; Kennedy 1986, 69).

There was also a great deal of receptivity to the "Precht's doctrine" at the higher echelons of the administration. The secretary of state had a deep commitment to the rule of reason and an equally passionate distaste for disorder and violence. He loathed confrontation and rationalized that a "cooperative attitude" toward Iran would disarm Khomeini (Sick 1991, 233; Mollenhoff 1980, 230). In spite of considerable provocation from the fundamentalists, Vance engaged in what one observer dubbed a "let's placate Khomeini policy" (Thornton 1991, 273). Like many well-meaning liberals, Vance could not envisage a political movement that would go against the Western notions of fair play and a Western view of rationality.

If anything, the president was even less prepared to deal with the tumultuous situation in Iran. Sick (1985, 218–219) noted that it was "one of the greatest ironies of history" that Carter, "a New Testament man" who "practiced tolerance as a positive virtue and sought peace through understanding and reconciliation" would have to face the confrontational Imam. The former engineer was hard pressed to realize that Khomeini was a "medieval prophet emerging from the desert with a fiery vision of absolute truth." What is more, in a mirror image of his own foreign policy vision, Carter tended to assume that Iran would exhibit such traits as humaneness and friendliness. However, Khomeini, who was told about Carter's preference for nonviolent protest lost whatever fear he might have had of the "nonagressive leader" (Rafizadeh 1987, 346).

Even if the administration harbored private doubts about the Iranian revolution, domestic policy made it imperative to play the moderate card. As early as January, the Republicans stepped up their attacks on the White House for "losing" Iran and later, Nicaragua. George Bush accused Carter of "pulling the rug out from under the shah" (Rubin 1980b, 256). Others invoked Jeane Kirkpatrick's argument, charging that the administration had helped to topple non-Communist regimes while staying passive in face of a major Communist expansion in Africa, Asia and Central America. There was also considerable alarm about the impact of the revolution on oil supplies, with several gloomy CIA reports leading the way (Hulbert 1982,126–127). Facing enormous pressure, Carter defended himself in a number of interviews and speeches and promised good relations with what he described as the evolving democratic Iran (Alexander and Nanes 1980, 478–480).

With the new orthodoxy established, the administration was bent on ignoring a number of worrisome developments in Iran. One of them was the growing anti-American propaganda of the Tudeh and their collusion with the fundamentalists. Nuradin Kianuri who assumed leadership of the Tudeh on January 4, decided to hitch his political wagon to the fundamentalists. The Tudeh downgraded its class struggle in order to concentrate on the fight against "imperialism," a strategy designed to drive a wedge between Iran and the United States and radicalize the revolution. In early February the Communist National Voice broadcast announced that the SAVAK archives had been transferred to the American embassy. On February 14, members of Fedayeen and Mojahedeen attacked the embassy but, after Bazargan's intervention, the diplomats were released. Charles Naas felt that Moscow might have been implicated in the so-called Valentine Day assault, but Stansfield Turner was on record downplaying the Communist propaganda (Stempel 1981, 54; Wright 1989, 60; Ledeen and Lewis 1981, 116; Shaplen 1980b; Documents, vol. 40, 6).

The "search for the center," which Sick (1985, 172) described as "classic U.S. response" to extremes, was bolstered by a number of academic experts on Iran and the human rights lobby. Dismayed over the failure of the intelligence community, Carter ordered the State Department and the National Security Council to enlist a number of leading Iranologists to help with the forecast. The task force on Iran consulted academic experts and Admiral Turner occasionally met with scholars (Taheri 1988, 108; Donovan, 1985, 182; S. Turner 1991b, 119). The media, which was similarly perplexed by the unprecedented turn that the revolution was taking, also turned to academics. Professor Richard Cottam, who had extensive contacts with the new regime, emerged as one of most authoritative voices in this group. Early in January, the State Department, unhappy with Huyser's reporting and anxious to discern the thinking in Khomeini's camp, send Cottam to Teheran. On January 7, Cottam reported to Vance that the military was planning a coup and gave details of the alleged plan. He predicted that Abbas Amir Entezam "will be a very important person" in the new government and asserted that Khomeini circles and the opposition in Teheran were "ready to think in sophisticated terms about future relations with the U.S." (Documents, vol. 10, no page number; vol. 14, 61–63; Abidi 1988, 19, 170–171).

Other scholars were also eager to dispel the "misperceptions" about Khomeini. Thomas Ricks protested the press treatment of Khomeini's book *Velayat-e Faqih* and denied the authenticity of the excerpts published in the *Washington*

Post (Ledeen and Lewis 1981, 131). Abrahamian (1979a, 15) stressed that the ulama supported the National Front's demand for constitutionalism. He argued that portraying Khomeini's circles as "Islamic reactionaries is a little like accusing liberal Catholic reformers in Latin America of wanting to bring back the Inquisition." Bill (1978/79) referred to the leading clerics as being "among the most democratically chosen grassroots leaders." Richard Falk, who visited Teheran with Ramsey Clark and two other human rights activists in January, was even more optimistic. In a discussion sponsored by the Institute for Policy Studies on February 1, Falk gave a very favorable description of Shiite Islam and praised its "amazing non-violent" spirit, which was "completely indigenous to Islamic and Persian culture" (Interview 1979). In a *New York Times* op-ed of February 16, 1979 Falk complained that the media defamed the ayatollah by "associating him with efforts to turn the clock back 1,300 years, with virulent anti-Semitism and with a new political disorder, "theocratic fascism." Falk also vehemently denied that the Ayatollah was engaged in taqieh calling such allegations "almost beyond belief." He reassured Americans that the "Shiite tradition is flexible in its approach to the Koran" and that Khomeini's entourage was "uniformly composed of moderate progressive individuals, who shared a notable record of concern for human rights." So much so, that "Iran may yet provide us with a desperately needed model of humane government of a third world country."

In any case, Falk asserted that Khomeini was ready to return to Qom to remove himself "from the daily exercise of power," a prediction echoed by Bill in a *Newsweek* interview on February 12, 1979 (Khomeini power 1979). Bill argued that "Khomeini is not a mad *mujtahid* [high-ranking clergyman]" but rather a "man of impeccable integrity and honesty." He predicted that the ayatollah, "who denied again and again that he will hold office," would be influential only in the short run (Khomeini's power 1979). Abrahamian (1979b) hoped that the "religious group will soon lose their hold over the labor movement" and make room in the political arena for the left. M. Reza Behnam (1979), castigated the media for an inaccurate depiction of Khomeini as a "man of violence, backward looking, irrational, and without prudent political policies." In a March article, the anthropologist Michael Fischer (1979, 5–6) stated that the revolution was remarkably protective of minorities" and noted that "Ayatollah Khomeini, conservative cleric, has helped to midwife the bourgeois revolution twice begun before." After discussing the progressive developments in Iran, Fischer concluded: "in the long run, the intelligentsia's democratic and open style . . . must succeed."

At the end of March, the State Department invited Cottam and Marvin Zonis for a group discussion about the unfolding situation in Iran. A March 29 memo of the meeting described Cottam as being more "favorably inclined" toward Khomeini and his people, adding that he assured the State Department that "in foreign policy Iran will be an 'Islamic messianic' activist in theory only." But Zonis was more "pessimistic about developments," especially about Sanjabi whom he called a "fool" and worried that Bazargan had failed to establish authority. Still, he felt that Bazargan has "some potential for becoming an eventual Mossadeq" (Documents, vol. 14, 61–63).

Other scholars were much less optimistic. Laqueur (1978) had warned for a number of months that the "ayatollahs are a backward reactionary lot" and that they could not be ignored. He also noted that "no gifts of prophecy are needed to understand that the next Iranian government—or at least the one after the next will rule the country more harshly than the shah." In a March article, Laqueur (1979) wrote: "the political elites which acted for the overthrow of the shah are not notable for competence or for their attachment to democracy." He also claimed that "Khomeini's ideal is to create an Islamic Republic" and that "fundamentalist Islam is xenophobic and intolerant toward infidels." He warned that "attacks on foreigners and minorities are intensifying," with Bahais and Jews expected to become the next target. Given this dynamic, Laqueur concluded that "it will be far fetched to assume" that the [fundamentalists movement] could be also a reformist or even liberalizing force."

Indeed, as the revolution entered its next stage, Laqueur's forecast came true.

THE HOT SUMMER: THE FUNDAMENTALIST TAKEOVER

Following the March referendum, the fundamentalists moved quickly to infuse the "Islamic republic" with specific meaning. They harshly attacked the PG sanctioned draft of a new constitution, which mentioned religion in the preamble, but was largely secular in nature. The IRP and an influential organization of radical clerics, the Congress of Muslim Critics of the Constitution, launched a campaign to discredit the proposal (Saffari 1993). Those who, like Hasan Nazih, the managing director of the National Iranian Oil Company and a longstanding human rights activist, spoke out against the Islamic vision were persecuted.

For its part, the IRP wanted to create a small (forty-member) heavily clerical body to draft a proper Islamic constitution. The plan, a clear violation of an early promise of a freely elected constitutional assembly, provoked intense opposition. Matin-Daftari's National Democratic Front (NDF) launched a series of rallies in June and a few high ranking ulama, including Ayatollah Shariatmadari and Ayatollah Hassan Tabatabi Qomi, who was rumored to be under house arrest, protested. Even the left leaning Ayatollah Mahmud Taleqani found the IRP manipulations objectionable. Bazargan, who was committed to an early promise to convene a constitutional assembly, sanctioned an election to a compromise seventy-three member Assembly of Experts (*Majles-e Khebregan*). The election that took place on August 3 was denounced by the NDF and eigthteen other parties as hopelessly rigged: The rules were devised by the IRP, and there was widespread fraud, corruption and intimidation (Rajaee 1983, 90; Saffari 1993, 67; Bakhash 1984, 80).

The newly elected assembly, which convened on August 18, had only a few secularists or lay members. Khomeini urged his handpicked mullahs to quickly rewrite the official draft and create "a 100 percent Islamic constitution" (Arjomand 1988, 138). The new guidelines, written by Hassan Ibrahim-Habibi, a protege of Beheshti, implemented Khomeini's concept of *velayat-e* faqih, giving the religious guardian a nearly absolute authority. Although Khomeini's writings were widely available by then, the prominence of the faqih created a political firestorm. As one observer noted, only a handful of theology students in Qom and Najf took it seriously, but "most secular and politically aware Iranians comprehended Khomeini's doctrine fairly vaguely, if at all" (Saffari 1993, 66). The outcry forced Beheshti to claim, somewhat ingeniously, that when Iranians voted for an Islamic republic in March they limited their future choice to a *maktab* [Islam]-based guardianship. Outmaneuvered, Bazargan and a majority of his ministers appealed privately to Khomeini to dissolve the Assembly, but their entreaties were to no avail (Milani 1993; Chehabi 1990, 265–267; Arjomand 1980).

In spite of the protest, the fundamentalists moved even more openly to seize complete power. Unleashing the hizbollahis on real and imaginary enemies of the revolution proved to be a highly effective tool. Key opposition leaders were often targeted; in one notorious case the sons and daughters-in-law of Ayatollah Taleqani were abducted. The Pasdaran, which grew to more than 7,000 by July, and was totally loyal to the Imam, could also be counted on as a revolutionary "watchdog." This group were augmented by the Iranian National Information and Security Organization (*Sazemaneh Eteiaat va Amniateh Mirian*), a new secret police known by its acronym SAVAMA and modeled on the old SAVAK. SAVAMA adopted the old terror and torture tactics of SAVAK and even took over the Committee Prison, the much feared interrogation center of the previous regime (Taheri 1985, 254; Afshar 1985; Fischer 1980b, 213; Irfani 1983, 189).

Khomeini's coercive apparatus was complemented by a growing number of revolutionary tribunals presided over by Ayatollah Khalkhali. "Judge Blood" was responsible for the brutal torture and execution of the former Prime Minister Amir Abbas Hoveyda, three SAVAK chiefs—Generals Nassiri, Moghadam and Pakrvan—and other prominent members of the shah's regime. These executions shocked many moderate Iranians but were apparently popular with the Left and the followers of Khomeini. In what became known as the "reign of terror," Khomeini loyalists killed, executed or imprisoned thousands of Iranians who were decreed the "enemies of the revolution."

When Bazargan tried to bring the tribunals under the jurisdiction of the Ministry of Justice, the Imam ignored him. Moreover, Ayatollah Ahmed Azari Qomi, the public prosecutor of the Islamic Revolutionary Tribunals, announced that, under an expanded jurisdiction, the tribunals would deal with "counterrevolutionary" activity in commerce and industry (Arjomand 1988, 138). As part of a campaign to "cleanse" the society, the tribunals also sentenced to death men and women accused of adultery, prostitution, homosexuality, drug dealering and addiction. In one incident, Khalkhali ordered the execution of half a dozen prostitutes in southern Teheran and homosexuals were publicly hanged from trees in a number of cities (Najmabadi 1987; Taheri 1985, 258). Amnesty International counted some 2,444 executions by 1981, but the number was apparently much higher. Ali Asghar Hajj Sayyed Javadi, the distinguished human rights activist, denounced the fundamentalists in an article "The Sounds of Fascism's Footsteps." According to one observer, this period amounted to "a reign of terror whose violence was unprecedented in twentieth-century Iran" (Chehabi 1995, 127; Simpson 1988, 204; Irfani 1983, 183–184).

Another powerful tool in the fundamentalist arsenal was the tight control of the media. In the initial euphoria following the departure of the shah, the Iranian press blossomed. By the spring of 1979, there were more than 360 titles on the newsstands, including papers in the long banned Kurdish and Azerbaijani Turkish languages. The fundamentalists, who became alarmed at the tenor of the mostly secular and leftist press, sent gangs of hizbollahis to terrorize editorial offices, newsstands and bookstores. In a more subtle technique, the Khomeinists pressured the major newspapers to change their coverage. In early May, the editorial board of the largest newspaper, the *Kayhan*, was purged and the new board apologized to the nation and the Imam for "not being revolutionary enough." Khomeini told the *Kayhan* journalists that "the nation wants a paper which conforms to its voice," and warned against editorial support for "criminals and traitors." One journalist complained that the pressure from the mullahs made him almost "nostalgic for the good old days of SAVAK (Rosen 1982, 62, 87). Khomeini also attacked *Ayandegan*, a prominent left of center paper and a favorite of the Iranian intelligentsia and the modern sector. On August 7, Azari Qomi shut it down and the following day the PG was forced to reinstate the shah's law curtailing press freedoms. Subsequently, the government ordered scores of newspapers and magazines closed. Many foreign correspondents were expelled, including the hitherto highly regarded BBC staff (White Paper, 035565, 5; Rosen and Rosen 1982, 99).

The International Committee of Jurists denounced the law and, on August 12–13, protest rallies were held by NDF. The hizbollahis attacked the demonstration and the NDF leader, Hedayatollah Matin-Daftari, was forced to go underground after the Islamic prosecutor, Ayatollah Azari Qomi, threatened to arrest him. Ayatollah Khalkali told a crowd that Matin-Daftari should be executed for "initiating anarchy." Although PG officials tried to intervene on behalf of the grandson of Mossadeq, he eventually fled the country (Documents, vol. 23, 48). Following the press protest on August 13, Khomeini banned all demonstrations against the government.

In another effective strategy, the Khomeinists were able to deny the PG access to electronic media. In a country where more than 50 percent of the population was illiterate, television and radio were vital links to the electorate. This fact was well recognized by the fundamentalists, who appointed Sadeq Gotbzadeh, a Khomeini aide, to head the National Iranian Radio and Television Organization. Gotbzadeh purged most of the Pahlavi-era workers and banned music and other forms of popular entertainment from the waves. When the fundamentalists increased their criticism of Bazargan, Gotbzadeh made it part of his broadcasts. Bazargan, who was left with no public outlet to defend his government, protested to Khomeini, but as usual, the Imam declined to intervene. The fundamentalist-run political and economic institutions provided another way to bypass the official power structure. The Foundation for the Disinherited, the Martyr Foundation, the Housing Foundation and the Imam Propaganda Office were all headed by individuals who had no allegiance to the PG and virtual autonomy in implementing the policies of the Revolutionary Council. When the more independent-minded ministers in the government protested, they were forced out.

While the Khomeinists were proceeding according to a blueprint, their opponents suffered from severe internal division. The National Front was affected to the point of disintegration: the Socialists headed by Reza Shayan followed Matin-Daftari who defected to form the NDF. On June 18, Dariush Foruhar, leader of the Iran Nationalist Party and one of the NF key leaders, departed as well, charging his colleagues with elitism and paralysis in face of dictatorships (Siavoshi 1990, 158). Ideological battles and personal disputes tore the Left as well, with the Mojahedeen Khalq and Fedayeen Khalq each splitting into rival factions and fighting bloody battles. The strain of ruling had affected Bazargan's own party, the Liberation Movement of Iran. Ezzatollah Sahabi who took over the party's leadership was sympathetic to the Mojahedeen and wanted to stir the party into a more fundamentalist direction. On June 17, Sahabi issued a document which declared that only those members who had evolved "parallel to the growth of the Islamic movement" represent the "new LMI" (Chehabi 1990, 244).

Lacking substantive unity, the various groups could only agree on attacking the PG. Ironically, the Bazargan government came to play a role not dissimilar to the shah who had provided the glue for the disparate opposition factions. The attacks from the left were especially brutal. Both the Mojahedeen and the "Bolsheviks" in the Fedayeen allied with the Tudeh accused the government of working in tandem with "reactionary forces" to hamper the revolution. The Tudeh, which made an early decision to support Khomeini, wanted to radicalize the revolution, a goal it shared with the Khomeinists (Moghadam 1988). In this sense, they both viewed Bazargan's efforts to normalize the situation as a major obstacle to their future plans. Bazargan seemed to realize his predicament when he complained in May to Eric Rouleau of *La Monde* that the revolutionary fever had not subsided yet (Ioannides 1984, 74). Bazargan later commented that "all the political . . . parties went to sleep after the revolution," enabling "the takeover by the clergy" (quoted in Ledeen and Lewis 1981, 196). By August the fundamentalists were ready to apply their norms to the membership, the authority system and the distributive justice dimensions of the collective belief system.

During the Pahlavi tenure, ethnic minorities, or about half of the population, were denied full membership rights in the name of greater Persian nationalism. Khomeini, who well before the revolution lashed out against the concept of nationalism and proclaimed himself to be in favor of the larger Muslim community, seemed to be unfettered by traditional notions of Persian nationhood (Benard and Khalilzad 1984, 147). Such proclamations notwithstanding, the fundamentalists brutally suppressed the autonomous movements. Khomeini's elevation of Shiite Islam to a dominant position explains this apparent contradiction. Since Persianism and Shiism overlap in Iran, the autonomy of the Sunni minorities was considered a major threat to the theocracy based on the faqih. Not surprisingly, the fundamentalists whipped up traditional Persian nationalism to gain support for the bloody treatment of the non-Persian minorities (Siavoshi 1990, 186–187; Sick 1985, 202–203).

The non-Moslems fared even less well. When the shah granted equal rights to religious minorities in the 1960s, Khomeini was outraged. As the revolution progressed, Christians, Bahais and Jews had come under increasing attack and their religious and civic rights were progressively curtailed. Much of their property was confiscated and many were either murdered or tried by the revolutionary tribunals and executed (Parsons 1989; Pilskin 1980). Khomeini attributed a particularly sinister role to the Jews, to whom he referred by the highly derogatory term *yahudi*. He called them "imperialist spies, agents and fifth columnists" and accused them of distorting Islam, plotting to take over the world and other crimes. Tying the Jews and Christians together, Khomeini forcefully asserted that the "Zionists allied themselves with the cross-worshippers in order to accomplish what the crusaders failed" (Abrahamian 1993, 123; Taheri 1985, 212; Curtis 1979).

Denying full membership rights to ethnic and religious minorities was justified by the numinous-traditional authority system proposed by Khomeini. The faqih rules by divine decree, but in a nod toward civic legitimacy, the guardian shares some of his authority with the "people." Described as a *dyarchy* or *clericy*, the hybrid system that the Assembly of Experts adopted gave popular sovereignty to an elected parliament and government, which were supervised by the faqih and the ulama. In an interview in February, the Imam declared that the parliament would be restricted to matters "beneath the dignity of Islam to concern itself with" (Arjomand 1980, 155). True to his writings, Khomeini was determined to use the position of the guardian to turn Iran into the "virtuous city," where the Islamic law is fully implemented and the citizens are expected to walk the "right path" (Chehabi 1991, 1995; Rajaee 1983, 94).

The guardianship-based authority system undermined any chance for political pluralism in Iran. In a democratic system, legitimacy is procedural, with free public discourse and periodical election serving to reaffirm the public will. In the Islamic dyarchy, public discourse and elections were limited to narrowly proscribed themes and, if necessary, manipulated to achieve the "right" outcome. Khomeini was described as having been particularly irritated by the intense political debates unleashed by the revolution. On August 24, he announced that, after allowing the opposition to show "their true face," the clerical party "would now break their poisonous pens and crush their conspiracies" (quoted in Arjom-

and 1988, 138). Islamic concepts, as interpreted by Khomeini, had also permeated the view of human rights in general and women's rights in particular.
Soon after returning home, Khomeini exhorted women to wear the veil (*hejab*);
in March, in spite of considerable opposition the *hejab* became mandatory. The
Revolutionary Guards and special "morality units" of the police were charged
with enforcing the new dress code. The Family Protection Law of 1975, which
gave women equal rights, had been gradually diluted and then scrapped altogether (Nima 1983, 92).

Undoubtedly, the use of political violence posed the most serious challenge
to Western notions of human rights. Bill (1988a, 267), argued that revolutionary
terror was personified in a number of renegade individuals such as "Judge
Blood" Khalkhali. However, violence was systemic in the Iranian theocracy.
Khomeini had always believed that Islam should be enforced through both "individual example and collective coercion." To turn individuals into "good Moslems," Islamic society had to be imposed from above, not merely recommended.
The Imam had often declared that the executed were *mutsed fel-ardh* (corrupters
of the earth) and had to be "eliminated like pests (Taheri 1985, 257, 261, Fischer
1980b, 216; Siavoshi 1990, 159).

Compared to the relatively straightforward blueprint for membership and authority legitimacy, the question of an appropriate distributive justice system was
less well defined. Beyond the Islamic concept of *adalah*, which forbids gross
disparities of wealth and privilege, Khomeini's understanding of economics was
limited. Forced to compete with the leftists, the ayatollah had incorporated some
of the more catchy notions of dependency and liberation theology, but at times
he gave the impression that the economy is an "evil force" destined to corrupt
the "pure Islamic nature of the revolution." Bani Sadr (1991, 56) wrote that,
"we were asking how can we increase production" and Khomeini was asking,
"how can we increase our faith." In lieu of specifics, the Imam regaled his
followers with the mantra that "conviction and ethical solutions" will lead to a
healthy economy (Kramer 1980, 11; Afshar 1985, 225; Limbert 1987, 14–15).

Such generalities were not enough for the Provisional Government, which
was under enormous pressure to reverse the economic free fall following the
revolution. By May, the economic situation in the country was chaotic: unemployment had reached 35 percent, industrial production was at a standstill and
the currency had lost 50 percent of its value compared to the previous year.
Many entrepreneurs and industrialists fled abroad and their enterprises were
either abandoned or bankrupt. With laws governing private property either suspended or ignored, land and commercial property were confiscated by the state,
the revolutionary foundations, workers councils or even private individuals. Restoring economic order was virtually impossible, as Bazargan discovered when
he tried to collect utility bills that had gone unpaid during the revolution (Bakhash 1989; Petrossian 1989).

How to address these issues and demonstrate that an Islamic model of economy was viable became the subject of a bitter power struggle among the fundamentalists, who discovered that it was easier to reject capitalism than to fashion an Islamic Third Way. Bani Sadr, Gotbzadeh and others with Marxist leanings advocated a collectivist economy. Bani Sadr asserted that labor was the sole justification for the ownership of material wealth and only those who labored "to transform God given recourse" were entitled to the fruits of their work (Valibeigi 1993; Behdad 1988; Hiro 1985, 150). They were supported by Taleqani and Hojjatalislams Ali Khameneh'i and Mohammed Khoiniha, who were in favor of large-scale nationalization. The populist faction in the IRP, known as the Imam's Line, wanted to add corporatism to the socialist mix (Hooglund 1986; Taheri 1985, 286–287; Bayat 1987, 155).

On the other side of the ideological divide were the affluent clerics, many of whom had substantial landholdings. They argued that, according to Islamic law, those who develop land cannot be dispossessed from it and were adamant that Islam guarantees the right to private property. Ironically, many landlords who capitalized on the revolutionary chaos to regain land forfeited during the White Revolution profited from this argument. The affluent ulama was strongly supported by the bazaaris, whose investment in land was also threatened (Afshar 1985).

The internal struggle in the fundamentalist movement forced the reluctant Khomeini to take a more specific stand. Ayatollah Montazeri and Hashemi Rafsanjani urged the Imam to neutralize the Left and placate the large number of the "dispossessed" whose normative expectations were raised by the revolution (Hassan 1984). In spite of Bazargan's bitter objection, Bani Sadr prevailed upon Khomeini to nationalize banks, insurance companies and large industrial enterprises in June and July. In fact, under the parallel government structure Bani Sadr had considerable authority over the economy; the governor of the Central Bank of Iran, Mohammed Ali Mowlavi was described as a "political prisoner" of Bani Sadr. As if to underscore the new line of authority, a mullah was installed in the bank to supervise the governor (Documents, vol. 27, 32–33). However, the wealthier clerics blocked a radical land reform and a wholesale expropriation of private enterprise. A committee of experts subsequently stipulated that an Islamic economy should have three sectors—public, private and cooperative—but, as Amirahmadi (1988, 231) observed, it was an eclectic program where "pieces from different strategies are juxtaposed to arrive at a workable model."

Having unveiled the blueprint for the new regime, the fundamentalists proceeded to cloak it in public legitimacy. In the absence of a procedural mechanism to measure popular support, the degree of legitimacy accorded to the new belief system can be only speculated upon. There is anecdotal evidence that Khomeini's charismatic leadership had attracted a large and genuine following, especially among the lower classes (Keddie 1981, 265). Rubin (1980b, 269) maintained that "millions of peasants who had historically looked up to the shah as an almost superhuman figure" simply shifted their allegiance to the ayatollah (Siavoshi, 1990, 164; Taheri 1985, 262; Farhang 1987, 172–173). Just to be on the safe side, the fundamentalists continued to manipulate public discourse through manufacturing or condoning rumors. Khomeini often warned about "Satanic agents" who were trying to destroy the revolution; American and foreign "agents" were his favorite targets. One scholar commented that in a cultural "mind-set within which every unpleasant problem or upheaval in the society is perceived as the work of foreign conspiracies" the fundamentalist propaganda faired quite well (Farhang 1987, 173; Taheri 1985, 242, 261–262; Ledeen and Lewis 1981, 199–200).

Even in such a favorable political culture, the legitimacy of the new belief system could not have been sustained without additional measures. Moshiri (1985, 123, 143) contended that the extent of support for Khomeini's vision of an Islamic Republic might have been overblown. In spite of all the public adulation of the Imam, the fundamentalists knew that they could fall short of achieving their true goal of an Islamic Republic. The historic memory of the 1906 Revolution, where the ulama helped to mobilize the masses only to end up as a footnote to a Western-style constitution, was still fresh in their memory. To further bolster their chances, the Khomeinists had to rely on two additional elements that sustain legitimacy of a dominant belief system: exchange and coercion.

There is little doubt that Khomeini understood the importance of the exchange elements in winning the allegiance of Iranians. The Imam was behind the large-scale welfare system for the poor, which operated through the state or special foundations (Abrahamian 1993, 61; Vali and Zubaida 1985). Khomieni also ordered some one hundred mullahs to travel to the provinces to disburse cash to the *mustaza'fin* (dispossed); Khameneh'i received about $1,75 million for Baluchistan alone. The Mustaza'fin Foundation (Foundation of the Dispossessed), established in March 1979, served as a clearinghouse for many of the programs targeting the poor (O'Kane 1991, 238; Taheri 1985, 250).

The Islamic welfare policy was achieved by favoring consumption over investment and productivity and by forcing the middle class to lower its standards of living. Over the repeated objections of the PG, the ayatollah rebuffed all those who wanted to moderate the revolutionary zeal in order to protect the country's infrastructure (Limbert 1987, 15). Ironically, what made this unwieldy economic model work was the fact that the revolutionary authority profited from the wealth of its predecessor. The Pahlavi Foundation contained 20 percent of the total assets of all privately owned firms and the government had also confiscated the property of those who were executed and jailed (O'Kane 1991, 238). In the long run, though, it was Iranian oil that helped to sustain the legitimacy of the new belief system. Scholars noted that the "rentier state," much maligned by dependencistas, was as helpful to Khomeini as it was to the shah (Farhi 1990, 118; Siavoshi 1990, 190).

The coercive elements in Khomeini's dyarchy were partially based on Islamic principles and partially a function of charismatic leadership. Islam requires a great deal of societal conformity of action and thought. The Islamization of the judiciary—a major goal of the fundamentalists—helped to carry out the Islamic injunction of "commanding the good and forbidding evil" (Najmabadi 1987). The Islamization of the universities served essentially the same role. But coercion is also required to sustain charismatic leadership, whereby all dissent is suppressed and the perception of mass legitimacy is sustained. One observer argued that because of political terror, it was virtually impossible to known how much of the support for Khomeini was due to "true feelings of support and how much of it is due to fear" (Irfani 1983, 202; Moshiri 1985, 150).

Since the new dominant belief system was such a mixed bag, scholars have had a difficult time classifying Khomeinism. Adding to Chehabi's dyarchy, Milani (1993) dubbed the new regime theocratic despotism and Arjomand (1988, 209) described it as fascist or proto-fascist. Benard and Khalilzad (1984, 68) used the term totalitarian democracy and Mottale (1987, 39) claimed that the new regime shared many features with the "reactionary, proto-fascistic and pro-tototalitarian features." Cottam (1990a) compared Iranian authoritarian populism to European fascism. These and other scholars have admitted that their analytic difficulties stem from the uniqueness of the Iranian case and from the fact that political science typologies reflect an essentially European experience. Even if Arjomand was right that Khomeinism was akin to the Rumanian Iron Guards or the Puritan revolution in England, these esoteric models would had been of little help to the Carter administration struggling to understand the nature of the political reality in Iran in the summer of 1979.

WHAT'S IN A NAME?: WASHINGTON BETS ON THE MODERATES

The March 30 referendum that established the Islamic Republic in Iran dealt a blow to the "Precht doctrine." Embassy cables indicated a persistent unease about the situation. Sullivan continued to complain about Bazargan's weakness and the overwhelming control that the mullahs had over the masses. There were also reports of renewed executions and extreme chaos. An in-depth analysis asserted that the PG "is not a repository of legitimate authority" and that Khomeini enjoyed a large popular following, but no universal legitimacy. Stempel noted that there was a growing anti-American campaign and harassment of American educated academics (Documents, vol. 14, 66–68, 71–73, 77–81, 82–93).

Yet these reports had seemingly little impact on the State Department's handling of a number of problems created by the change of regime. The most pressing issue was embassy security. Following the Valentine's Day attack on the embassy, a "bare bones" security plan featuring a "skeletal" crew was approved in March and embassy documents were moved to Washington (Shaplen 1980b). The precariousness of the embassy defense was underscored when, on May 24 and 25, some 100,000 protestors attacked the embassy and tore down the flag. The embassy guards, a motley assembly of Revolutionary Guards, *hom-afars* and strongmen provided little resistance. However, after Bazargan allocated a PG detachment, the documents were returned and there was an increase in embassy personal. Sick (1985, 190) attributed this bureaucratic "mission creep" to Precht's desire to encourage normalization in relations. There was also pressure to expand the consular section, so that Bahais, Jews and others fleeing persecution could get exit visas.

The fate of military supplies proved equally vexing. The bulk of the shah's procurement program was canceled before the PG came to power. According to Sullivan (1981, 274), Bazargan "pleaded" with the embassy not to liquidate the Military Assistance Advisory Group (MAAG) but, as with other issues, Teheran was sending mixed signals. On February 21, the Provisional Government announced that the United States would not be allowed access to the Kabkan and Behshar listening stations in northern Iran. Later on, some $12 million worth of military orders were canceled. These moves were apparently dictated by the Revolutionary Council, which tried to limit Iranian dependency on the United States. The new authorities were also reluctant to return the extra-secret Phantom jet training manuals; according to one version, the manuals were stolen by a Tudeh sympathizer and given to Moscow (Rafizadeh 1987, 296).

However, the Council changed its position when the upsurge in ethnic fighting made the issue of spare parts critical. The PG hoped to parlay its access to the United States into improving its position vis-à-vis the fundamentalists. On April 15, Vice Prime Minister Entezam complained to Charles Naas that Iranian helicopters were out of spare parts, and an equally urgent representation was made to the State Department. Sullivan (1981, 274) was critical of the proposed military sale because, in his view, the "army disintegrated and those who got the weapons were resentful to us." Others in the administration objected on the ground that the weapons would be used to slaughter the Kurds and other rebellious minorities. In an ironic twist, the moralpolitikers used the realpolitik argument that the procurement program would help U.S. interests in Iran. By July, the administration had agreed to enable Iran to purchase some non-sensitive military parts As Vance (1983, 368) contended, by August the relations between the two countries were "slowly improving" and a "limited supply" of spare parts resumed (Ledeen and Lewis 1981, 225).

Replacing Sullivan proved to be another delicate task. The ambassador, long frustrated by Washington, was increasingly vocal in his criticism. He began demanding "strategic guidance" rather than "tactical suggestions" and was virtually forced out (Sullivan 1981, 275; Stempel 1981, 301). With Sullivan's departure scheduled for April 1, Richard Cottam and William Miller were mentioned, but rejected. Instead, in a signal to Iran that relations were between equal sovereigns, the department chose Robert L. Cutler, a career officer with no known ideological leaning. Cutler was expected to assume office in May, but the Iranian Foreign Ministry asked to delay the appointment and, subsequently, rejected it. Yazdi explained that Cutler, who had served in Zaire, symbolized U.S. interference in Africa, a posting bound to offend Iran's newly acquired Third World sensibilities (Cottam 1988, 208; Abidi 1988, 39–40).

The real reason behind the scuttled nomination was the Revolutionary Council's unhappiness with American reaction to the human rights abuses in Iran. As Cottam (1988, 208) described it, "U.S. television viewers could expect an execution body count" on the evening news, adding that "journalistic accounts focused on the bizarre and excessive." While Cottam felt that the discourse was not balanced, the fundamentalists, who hired people to read foreign press, saw the Western coverage as part of a "careful plan to undue the revolution" (Rubin 1980b, 357). Ayatollah Montazeri called the media coverage part of a "Zionist cabal" to control the world. By June, the minister of information was urging expulsion all foreigners "on the grounds that the Western media was directed by international Zionism and imperialism." When the Congress became involved in the human rights debate, the worst suspicions of the Khomeinists were confirmed (Rubin 1980b, 290, 360).

The fundamentalist revolution created a backlash against the New Internationalists who had dominated the Congress for so long. The first issue on the congressional agenda was reexamination of intelligence and security needs. A January report on the intelligence failure in Iran was scathing; Senator Moynihan's subsequent comment that "there is no intelligence agency of any kind" were widely circulated (*Congressional Quarterly Weekly Review*, February 3, 1979; Cline 1981, 274). The Congress was also worried about the Soviet involvement in Afghanistan; the murder of U.S. ambassador Adolph Dubs in the spring raised more concerns about the stability of the Gulf region. Even among the advocates of regionalism there was a growing realization that the fall of the shah was advantageous to Russian designs in Afghanistan (Scott 1996, 44: Bell 1980, 63).

The anti-Israeli tenor of the revolution alarmed the large Israeli lobby. The PG cut off oil supplies to Israel, and Khomeini made little secret of his desire to force the inhabitants of the Jewish state out of the Middle East. As if to symbolize this vision, Yassir Arafat arrived in Teheran on February 17 and took over the building that housed the Israeli delegation. When the persecution of Jews, Bahais and other minorities intensified in the spring, the Senate decided to take up the human rights case. The execution of Habib Elghanian, a Jewish merchant and one of the wealthiest people in Iran triggered the hearings. Elghanian, one of the twenty-nine people executed between May 7 and 11, was charged, among other things, with treason for having close ties with Israel. During the debate, sponsored by Jacob Javits, Robert Byrd described Iran's human rights abuses as flying in the "face of all human sensibilities" and Abraham Ribicoff called them "barbaric and beyond imagination." In spite of intensive lobbying from the State Department, on May 17 the Senate passed a resolution expressing "abhorrence of summary executions" and urging Iran to moderate its behavior (Bill 1988a, 284).

The congressional action demonstrated the difficulties involved in betting on the moderates. The State Department knew that the Javits resolution would play into the hands of the of fundamentalists but, given the politicization of the human rights issue, to which the moralpolitikers themselves had contributed a year earlier, it had little room to maneuver. This time around, the realpolitikers could point to the exquisite irony of the State Department objecting to a human rights inquiry in the name of United States interests. The Republicans and pro-Pahlavite Democrats were quick to cry "double standards" at any attempt to soft-peddle what Precht and others somewhat euphemistically called "revolutionary excesses." The shah himself referred to the double standards: he accused the West of making him follow the ideas of democracy, while tolerating the new "morality" of the Islamic Republic (Pahlavi 1980b, 219). Those who agreed with him claimed that the administration was "resolutely insensitive to the barbarism of the new regime, acquiescing in human rights violations that would have been ground for angry protests" had they been committed under the shah (Ledeen and Lewis 1981, 221).

As predicted by the State Department, the resolution triggered a firestorm in Iran. Charles Naas, the outgoing charge d'affaires, commented that "the place went wild" (quoted in Bill, 1988a, 284). The PG issued a vitriolic protest and rejected the ambassador-designate, forcing the administration to deputize Bruce Laingen, the new chargé d'affaires, to run the embassy. Khomeini used the Senate resolution to hammer at the theme of "Zionist-American imperialism." To those who worried that the fundamentalist attack might damage relations with the United States, Khomeini replied "may God cause it to be endangered." The ayatollah and his followers began to routinely refer to the United States as the "Great Satan," "criminal America" "world devourers," the opposition was called "agents of America" (Miklos 1983, 57; Ledeen and Lewis 1981, 222; Rubin 1980b, 289–290; Benard and Khalilzad 1984, 151). On May 25, more than 100,000 people marched to the American embassy chanting "Death to the United States" and "Death to Carter." When Hashemi Rafsanjani, who delivered a major speech at the rally, was wounded that evening, Radio Teheran blamed the United States.

The Soviet Union had also utilized the Javits resolution to stir up anti-American sentiments. The Moscow-backed National Voice of Iran called the U.S. "the number one enemy of the people and the revolutionary government of Iran" (Rubin 1980b, 289). The broadcast drew the attention of its listeners to American reinforcements in the Persian Gulf, a fact that the Soviet ambassador had repeatedly emphasized to Yazdi. A leaflet entitled *America's Secret Plan*, attributed to the KGB, claimed that the American scholar, Bernard Lewis, had prepared a plan to carve up Iran and the whole of the Middle East into ministates representing various minorities (Taheri 1988, 121).

In spite of Yazdi's public efforts to explain that congressional censure is not part of a larger plot, Radio Teheran, controlled by Gotbzadeh, continued to propagate the theme of American "imperialistic duplicity." One broadcast claimed that there were eight American contingency plans to overthrow the new government. Another spoke of a multistage "imperialist" conspiracy; first, terrorist groups would carry out acts of murder, then false demonstrations would be fomented and finally, there would be a military intervention patterned on the anti-Mossadeq operation (Rubin 1980b, 294).

Observers have attributed some of the problems in U.S.–Iranian relations to mutual misperceptions. There is no doubt that cultural differences frustrated the Carter administration effort. As Halliday put it (1990, 249), "Iran has been one of the most difficult Third World countries to deal with, not least because the understanding of what constitutes 'reasonable behavior' or 'good intentions' notoriously differ." The cultural anthropologist Beeman (1990, 165) noted that the two nations lacked perspective "on the cultural basis for each other's political motivation and strategies in the international arena." In particular, Americans failed to understand the blend of Third Worldism and Khomeinism that guided the new Iranian foreign policy. Before his departure in June, Naas warned against drawing a conclusion that was too benign about Khomeini, adding that the ayatollah and his associates are "virtually paranoid about the United States" Taheri (1988, 109–110), who quoted Naas, noted that, almost to the very end, the Carter administration took "the middle-class fellow travelers" as the "real makers of history" and ignored the Imam and his foreign policy vision.

Had the administration analyzed the ideological underpinning of Khomeinism it would have found that the ayatollah and his followers described international relations as a struggle between the oppressed nations on the one hand and superpowers and their allies on the other. This struggle was said to be both economic and cultural. Bani Sadr, in his book *Oil and Domination* repeated the well-known dependency thesis that the United States and the West had subjugated the economies of developing countries. Culturally, the "Great Satan" was said to be a leader of a "materialistic" civilization without a "moral soul," which the West sought to impose on all countries (Benard and Khalilzad 1984, 96, 151, 155; Ramazani 1986, 205; Fischer and Abedi 1990, xxv; Hollander 1992, 364; Chubin 1994, 85). The fundamentalists regarded Islam, particularly "revolutionary Islam," as the appropriate ideology for the world's "deprived, oppressed and dispossessed." Immediately after coming to power, Khomeini urged to "export the revolution" and his followers set up the Revolutionary Foundation and a training center for would be revolutionaries (Behrooz 1990; Anderson 1992, 184; Ram 1994). As Rubin (1980a, 308) noted, "at a certain level," these people believed that their revolution would "furnish a model for a whole series of uprisings in the Third World, and particularly in the Islamic countries."

In spite of this radical foreign policy agenda, the virulent anti-Americanism, the human rights abuses and plans to establish an Islamic guardianship, the State Department was still clinging to the optimistic premises of the "Precht doctrine." Two Teheran-bound diplomats recalled that the Iran Desk had tried to sell the impression that "things were rapidly pointing to a return to 'business as usual' in Teheran." Charles S. Scott (1984, 149), one of the future hostages, was told that the "siege mentality," allegedly prevalent among the embassy staff, was caused by the failure to accept "the realities of post-revolutionary Iran." Moorhead Kennedy (1986, 62), another hostage, recalled being briefed by Mark Johnson, an economic expert at the Iran Desk, one of the few to hold the position that PG was just a "facade" and that "power resides in the Revolutionary Council and the religious authorities." Stempel (1981, 296) claimed that returning Farsi-speaking officers warned about the dangers of a process of normalization that was too speedy. They were discounted as "either soured by the revolution or insufficiently sympathetic to the tribulations of Iran's new government," because "for the Carter administration to back the moderates became an article of faith."

Such official optimism also belied the deteriorating position of American business in Iran. The Iranian revolution was a major fiasco for American firms: by one estimate 2,800 corporations and individuals filed claims against Iran, amounting to more than $10 billion dollars (Valibeigi 1988, 210–222). Major American banks like Chase Manhattan, Citibank and others that bought shares in Iranian banks were hurt when the government took over private banks in the summer. The revolution also put in jeopardy some $2.2 billion in loans that U.S. banks had made to the Iranian government and private individuals. Industrial concerns—among them Du Pont, General Motors, General Tire & Rubber Co., Flour Corporation Johnson & Johnson—lost their investments because the plants were either nationalized or abandoned. Others, like Electronic Data Systems of Dallas, Starrett Housing Corporation and David Lilienthall's Development and Resource Corporation, suffered when the government defaulted on payment for services rendered or canceled project. Suppliers and vendors, such as Beatrice Foods and the Singer Corporation who extended generous credits to the shah's government, went unpaid (Gillespie 1990; Kilborn 1976; 1979; Ebel 1979; Rush from Iran 1979).

The problems for American business actually began when, in January, Khomeini declared that business contracts that are against the "interests of our people" would be canceled (P. Lewis 1979). By June, expropriation and project cancellations in the civilian sector were in high gear, amounting to a policy of "cut, dismantle and destroy" (Ibrahim 1979). In the same month the government announced that it would seize "inefficient" and abandoned industries, followed in July by a formal nationalization decree of banks. The issue of compensation for the nationalized property was left murky. The government admitted that it confiscated shareholdings "closely tied to the shah" and promised to compensate unspecified "others." At the same time, the PG, under pressure from Khomeini and Bani Sadr, declared that factories taken over by Workers Councils—including a large General Motors plant—would not be considered seized (Gillespie 1990). The fundamentalist-run *Mustaza'fin* Foundation was exempted from paying compensation for the companies it confiscated on behalf of the poor (Kandell 1979). To add to the confusion, a number of delicate negotiations between

American firms and Iran all but collapsed. According to speculations in American business circles, the ayatollah singled out American firms for harsh treatment in a bid to rupture U.S.–Iran relations (Ill omen 1979).

In spite of these developments, the State Department was anxious to show that normalization can work. On June 3, the department distributed to various agencies its detailed Commercial Action Plan (CAP) for the year 1980. The document stated that the "country [Iran] planners must reestablish confidence, render priorities and began to lay the fundamentals for future economic growth." CAP stressed various investment opportunities; agribusiness and housing were seen as most promising (Documents, vol. 16, 18–21; Ioannides 1984, 64). The State Department was also upbeat about commercial prospects; a memo dated July 12 discussed the possibility of revitalizing the Iran-American Chamber of Commerce (Documents, vol. 15, 124–125 vol. 16, 18–21; Ioannides 1984, 64).

The embassy personnel split over the CAP directive. The commercial attaché, Andrew Sens, was convinced that the situation was "highly propitious" for investment. However, other officers disagreed vehemently. A June report on "Iranian Economic Trends" painted a gloomy picture of the revolutionary economy (Documents, vol. 63, 97–105). The recently arrived Moorhead Kennedy (1986, 91, 64–66) sent a telegram urging not to insure new American investment in Iran. Kennedy later described the commercial attaché as "naïve" and "ignorant" about the political culture of the Middle East. During a meeting with Bani Sadr, whom Kennedy described as "a nut," the two American diplomats were told that Iran would welcome investment, "if it would profit the Iranian people" rather than the multinational corporations. According to Kennedy, even this piece of dependency orthodoxy did not shake the optimistic Sens. Such optimism was quite startling, given the fact that an early embassy memo described Bani Sadr as a "radical economist" and a "fool" (Documents, vol. 27, 32–33).

In retrospect, Kennedy was right in his assessment of the situation, but the embassy as a whole was divided in its readings of the political situation in Iran. In June and July there was considerable worry about the PG-fundamentalist balance of power. Some cables reported "growing unhappiness with Khomeini's revolution" among the middle class and others noted that the fundamentalists had a large mass following. One report commented on Khomeini's hostility to the United States and the growing anti-American sentiment around the country, but another account gave the Islamic movement less than "50 percent of muddling through." A number of cables contained highly unflattering portrayals of the Iranian political culture. Iranians were said to exhibit "subline self-interest" and a "refusal to accept responsibility," which led them to a "cynical embrace of contradictions," a fact that, according to the American analysts, bode ill for the future (Documents, vol. 14, 110–116, vol. 15, 59–61, 79–85, 91–94).

The August dispatches took due notice of the fundamentalist efforts to set up an Islamic state. One cable claimed that "Khomeini openly exercises direct rule over Iranian domestic politics" and predicted that the Council of Experts would create a state in "which the influence of Khomeini and his allies" will predominate. Another dispatch reported that Vice Prime Minister Entezam was concerned with "radical religious influence around Khomeini." A report on violence between secular groups and the hizbollahis asserted that the Islamists would prevail, but at a cost of a "legacy of bitterness." Still, an August 8 cable stated that Iran "can no longer be characterized as being in crisis" (Documents, vol. 10, no page number; vol. 16, 27, 53–54, 57–59).

There was also concern about the lack of information on the revolutionary dynamics. On July 11, Vance requested the embassy to prepare a report on the political conditions in Iran. On July 20, Henry Precht wrote asking for "bios, inventory of political groups or current picturing of daily life" in Iran. A memo from the International Communication Agency (ICA) stated that "Americans have at present little ability to relate to the conceptual framework which informs the ulama." The ICA and the embassy worried about the communication gap and recommended an exchange of visits by acknowledged experts in the field of philosophy and religion (Documents, vol. 1, 515; vol. 15, 122–123, 127–129; vol. 16, 42–50).

Even though the embassy was divided and basic information on the fundamentalists was scarce, the State Department proceeded with its plans to normalize relations. This, in turn, generated a debate in the administration about whether the United States should adopt a low or high profile in Iran (Documents, vol. 15, 72–73). As before, estimates of the cost and benefits of proposed strategies reflected an underlying view of the legitimacy of the regime. Adherents of the "Precht doctrine" wanted to support the moderates in their struggle with the fundamentalists and felt that that U.S. skittishness would jeopardize the chances of the PG. This group was also eager to develop a more direct link to the circle surrounding Khomeini and, if possible, to establish a dialogue with the ayatollah himself. Their opponents felt that the fundamentalists were winning the battle and warned that a high-powered American effort on behalf of the PG would only serve to discredit the moderates and hasten their demise.

According to Kennedy (1986, 90), after the rigged elections for the Assembly of Experts, members of the political section in the embassy were planning to send a dissenting note to warn the State Department about the dangers of normalization. But even if such message had been sent, there probably would have been no change in the State Department position. Kennedy (1986, 69) and Sick (1985, 187) argued that normal checks and balances built into the policy analysis of the State Department had failed. The Bureau of Near Eastern and South Asian Affairs was still predominantly preoccupied with Camp David, leaving the Iran country director a lot of latitude. Precht, supported by Assistant Secretary Harold Saunders and Warren Christopher, had a relatively free hand in dictating small but cumulatively important policy decisions. One of them, a resolution to increase the embassy staff was taken without a major policy review. On August 17, Christopher recommended filling vacant position and staff and consider creating new ones" as well as reopening the consulates in Tabriz and Isfahan (Documents, vol. 16, 40–41).

Even Brzezinski, a major opponent of the State Department before the revolution, could not provide much of a counterbalance. The adviser, who was highly skeptical of the notion that Bazargan would prevail, became convinced that the ayatollah was "sincerely antiSoviet" and wanted to explore a direct approach to Khomeini (Cottam 1990b, 277). The absence of CIA input also hurt the deliberations. However, it was the psychological dynamics of the predictive process that hampered a reevaluation of the "Precht doctrine" most. Kennedy (1986, 69) described Precht as a "victim of the correctness of his party analysis" and a "partisan of the revolution whose inevitability he had so accurately foreseen." Sick (1985, 187) claimed that "Precht doggedly argued that Bazargan and company were steadily gaining strength" and that he "never wavered in his opinion," even though many of his colleagues disagreed. After the hostages returned, many of them blamed Precht for their ordeal (Kennedy 1986, 127).

Bruce Laingen had apparently helped to perpetuate the "Precht doctrine," mounting evidence to the contrary notwithstanding. Unlike the self-assured Sullivan, who had strong opinions and was willing to defend them in spite of considerable pressure from Washington, Laingen was a low-key official who tended to waver in his assessments. In a June 21 meeting, Entezam told Laingen that the PG had been constantly overshadowed by the fundamentalists and that Khomeini turned down hundreds of requests to interfere (Rubin 1980b, 291). However, it was not until August 20 that Laingen reported that "Khomeini and his entourage at Qom call all the shots" and that the election to the Assembly of Experts "symbolizes the essential rigidity of the Islamic forces in Qom" (Documents, vol. 16, 42–52). Still, the chargé d'affaires continued to be upbeat about the moderates. Kennedy (1986, 69) described Laingen as "one of these unusually fine people who see the best in everyone and everything," who wanted to see in Iran "the best." It is quite possible that, subconsciously, Laingen and others on his staff refused to acknowledge the logical implications of Khomeinism. Barry Rosen (1982, 97, 62), one of the diplomats taken hostage, attributed the summer optimism to the "failure to detect underlying realities." Rosen confessed that although he cabled the dire predictions of the *Ettala'at* journalist, he refused to take them "at face value."

The same psychological dynamics apparently blocked a fresh look at "moderates." The term, based on Western political convention, could have probably described Bazargan, Sanjabi and some of the original figures in the Provisional Government. But during the spring and summer most of these politicians were replaced by hardliners allied with the clerics. Foreign Minstser Yazdi, who distrusted the military, was instrumental in the formation of the Pasdaran. The would-be minister of defense, Mustafa Ali Chamran, was co-founder of the Pasdaran, and had led the firing squads that executed Nassiri and other of the shah's officials. Gotbzadeh, whose radio and television stations carried daily anti-American attacks, sent crews to film the executions (Taheri, 1985, 249). Bani Sadr, whom the CIA tried to recruit as a possible "moderate," was an ardent advocate of nationalization. Communication with some of the "moderates" proved to be difficult, if not impossible. Gotbzadeh refused to meet with the Americans in spite of the fact that the embassy tried for months to establish relations (Rosen 1982, 100). Saunders (1985, 55) revealed that he and Precht had difficulty relating to Yazdi, whom he described as "curiously obsessed with the past."

More important, there was no comprehensive effort to analyze the fundamentalist belief system. Part of the problem stemmed from a failure to grasp the importance of ideological factors in the fundamentalist movement. Kennedy (1986, 85) admitted that prior to the takeover, it was hard for the embassy staff to "grasp the depth of the revolutionary hatred for what we represented." Khomeini's utterances were dismissed as "rhetoric" and his writings on the role of the *velayat-e faqih* ignored. Making a comparison to *Mein Kampf*, Alpher (1980) pointed out that in the case of the 'other prophetic' book no one paid much attention to it while it still had operative value." Ledeen and Lewis (1981, 240) blamed the general debasement of language in the political discourse on Iran for misreading Khomeini's coming theocracy. Since the term "fascist" was used so loosely with regard to the shah, no one recognized it when it really appeared. Others noted that there was a tendency in the Carter administration to view Islamic extremism in terms of the American civil rights movement. Speaking in honor of Black History month, Andrew Young professed a close identity with the revolutionaries, who reminded him of the civil rights movement era. Later, Young compared Khomeini to Lester Maddox, the fundamentalist and segregationist governor of Georgia (Bozeman, 1979; Frady 1996, 318).

As before, the spring and summer discourse of the academic community exacerbated the failure to comprehend the nature of Khomeini's challenge to the PG. In an April news conference sponsored by Clergy and Laity Concerned, James D. Cockcroft, a Rutgers University sociologist, described his trip to Iran in glowing terms. He noted the liberation of women, free elections, flexibility in political life and the "control that people exercise over the clergy" (Klehr 1988, 145). In a May briefing paper prepared for a State Department colloquium on Iran, Michael Fischer noted that Khomeini's authority is in dispute and that "Iran has the potential, if it succeeds, in establishing a humane and modern Islamic republic" (Documents, vol. 15, 29–44).

The spring 1979 issue of *Foreign Policy* featured a symposium on the revolution by Iran observers. Among the scholars who participated, Falk continued to reassure that the "Islamic republic need not necessarily be inherently anti-American" and that the constitution proposed by Khomeini "has been drafted by political moderates with a strong belief in minority rights." Falk decried the fact that Americans do not understand Shiite Islam, which "is entirely different from the harsher Sunni variety" prevalent in Saudi Arabia and other Middle Eastern countries. As for the brutal executions, the human rights activist explained that they should be compared to the punishment of war criminals in Germany and Japan "who were killed for crimes against humanity" (Summary justice 1979). Cottam reiterated his position that Khomeinism was "a continu-

ation of the movement for fundamental change . . . to bring Iran genuine independence, free institutions, and a revival of Islamic and Iranian cultural values."
In a chapter written for the 1979 edition of his 1964 book, Cottam (1979, 360)
argued that Khomeini brushed aside "suggestions that he assume political office
in Iran" and asserted that, at the age of nearly eighty, Khomeini would assume
only a "boundary-setting" role.

Other scholars concurred with these assessments. Abidi (1979) claimed that
Khomeini's proposals showed pragmatism and clearly suggested an attempt "to
synthesize the traditional and modern concepts." Habiby and Ghavidel (1979,
16) argued that "it would be wrong to dismiss the wave of Islamic revival now
sweeping through the Islamic world as a reactionary religious movement." A
review of *The Illusion of Power* by Robert Graham, maintained that it was
doubtful whether Khomeini and his ministers could take the country back to its
Islamic past. Because the shah succeeded in shaking "traditional Iranian society," the new rulers "will have to face up to these challenges whether they like
it or not" (Books in Review 1979, 59). Ayoob (1979) ventured that after the
overthrow of the shah, "Khomeini has passed the peak of his influence and may
have passed the peak of his popularity as well." Armajani (1979, 16) chastised
"writers and reporters" because they "jumped to a conclusion" that the Islamic
government was going to be "reactionary." Keddie (1979, 55), who criticized
the shah's policies as "modernization from a myopic U.S. viewpoint," described
the appointment of Bazargan, a man "long involved in human rights" as a "hopeful sign" of true modernization.

Bill who was a featured speaker at a meeting of the American Management
Association held in New York on July 25–26 was equally optimistic. According
to a memo sent to Precht by a State Department participant, Bill argued that the
ulama would not provide "governmental leadership, or political leadership . . .
since they do not think positively enough to be political or governmental
leaders." Bill was also critical of what he called "fourth rate" press coverage of
Iran; he particularly objected to the way Khomeini had been presented, arguing
that "he is not nearly as bad as the press has made him out." Bill criticized the
administration's low posture toward Iran and urged to offer more aid. He concluded that there is a large reservoir of good will toward America, despite "universal animosity of Iranians towards our government" (Documents, vol. 16, 29–
36).

On the other hand, scholars, whom Bill called "Pahlavites," strongly disputed
these predictions. Lenczowski (1979a, 804, 808) warned that the ulama and the
bazaari are "not noted for their proclivity to democracy" and reminded his more
optimistic colleagues that "democracy is a system largely limited to the West."
Savory (1979, 10) noted that there are two governments in Iran and there is a
"complete breakdown of rule of law and suspension of human rights." He
claimed that "there is no theoretical basis in the Twelwer Shi'i state for an
accommodation between the *mujtahids* . . . and any form of polity be it mon-

archy or republic." He also warned that when Khomeini says "Islamic republic," he "does not mean it in a Western sense."

Other scholars had also developed serious doubts about Khomeinism. Zonis, in a May briefing prepared for ambassador-designate Cutler, argued that the revolution, although not religious in origin, was captured by "religious elements loyal to Khomeini." He also noted that, like the shah's, Khomeini's style of political leadership was "banal, vapid and authoritarian" and warned about xenophobia and antiforeign feelings (Documents, vol. 15, 25–28). Israeli (1979) predicted that "in Iran, Khomeini has been creating an Islamic Republic in which shi'ism will prevail and the guidance of government will remain the exclusive domain of the ayatollahs." Curtis (1979) anticipated that Khomeini's vision for an Islamic republic will "reach further into the social fabric than even Libya has yet traveled" and warned about the ayatollah's anti-Semitism. Menashri (1979) wondered about Khomeini's coalition "of strange bedfellows." Halpern (1979) chastised his colleagues for dismissing past fundamentalist movements as "atavistic," noting that "there was little apprehension that they might represent the wave of the future."

Bozeman (1979, 391, 400–401) argued that the revolution "as led by the mullahs should be seen, in essence, as a victory for the general cause of Islam." She criticized Carter's foreign policy paradigm for equating democracy with "just about anything that the 'people' or the 'masses' appear to want," rather than "government-by-the-rule-of-law." Bozeman noted that "the deferential trust in nomenclature," which made "monarchy" sound invariably bad and "republic" good, combined with the "blindness to the patterns of culture that set Middle Eastern societies from the American experience," prevented observers from noting that "people" were better off under the Islamic kings than "under those who slew the monarchs in order to establish their own lawless dictatorships under such titles as 'People's Democracy' or 'Islamic Republic.' " Cottrell and Hanks (1979) were among the first to warn that the new leadership in Iran might be detrimental to America's interests in the Gulf.

Though in retrospect such assessments were correct, at the time they were written off as "sour grapes" by antishah Iran experts. In fact, there was something of an academic "vendetta" conducted against the "Pahlavite" scholars. A special issue of *Race and Class* (1979), a journal of the leftist Institute of Race Relations and the TNI, accused many "orientalists," including Binder and Savory for being in the service of "imperialism." One contributor even chastised Zonis and Bill for failing to systematically analyze the "nature of dependency in Iran" and for "hedging their predictions" about the shah (Schaar 1979). In a June 1979 symposium at Centre College, Ricks (1981, 16, 43) criticized his peers for publishing research "favorable to Pahlavi dictatorship, to American imperialism, and the U.S. neocolonialism." He accused his colleagues of devoting "considerable research to justify both the Pahlavi monarchy and American modernization program." In a subsequent review article, Ricks (1980, 267–

268) repeated the claim that "Iranian revolution challenges the 'objectivity' and 'value free' theories of social science" and concluded that scholarship should be considered "either in the service of the Iranian struggle for national independence, or in the service of U.S. interventionist policies and the Pahlavi monarchy."

The failure of many academics to grasp the true nature of Khomeinism did not go unnoticed. The journalist Anthony Lewis (1979) described Falk's rosy depictions of Khomeini as "wishful thinking." Chehabi (1991) called such scholars part of a "small cottage industry" of observers and self-appointed mediators trying to identify the "moderates" with whom the United States could deal. Taheri (1988, 109) noted that the quest for "moderates" involved experts who "fantasized about the chances of their favorite heroes coming out on top."

Many of the antishah experts continued to urge the State Department to embrace the moderates to signal that the United States policy had been "purged" from royalist sentiments. Writing almost a decade later, Bill (1988a, 46, 279, 280, 282; 1988b, 46), admitted that the "moderate strategy" was "reinforced by the American Iran scholars" such as Cottam and himself. Bill, who described himself as a "leading proponent" of this strategy, explained that he made a "serious mistake" by assuming that Khomeini would return to Qom. Ironically, in another place in his book, Bill asserted that "America committed a number of major errors," including "the preoccupation with moderates," "pushing themselves too hard" and being "too visible." He described the embrace of the moderates as an "error of commission" that alienated the extremists and harmed the moderates.

Some of the same experts were also involved in the administration's debate over the proper American response toward revolutionary violence. Those who hoped that Iran was on a liberal-democratic path argued that any undue "harshness" would only radicalize the revolution. This argument was in line with the then-fashionable liberal view that Third World revolutions, including the Cuban one, were not inherently antidemocratic or anti-American. When the revolutionary regimes confounded these expectations, as they often did, liberals blamed the United States for "pushing" the revolutionary regime onto the path of extremism. Not surprisingly, the academics associated with the "Precht doctrine" blamed the Javits resolution for dooming the moderates. Cottam (1988, 209) felt that the United States effort to "reinforce Bazargan and his colleagues were largely counterbalanced" and that Yazdi's efforts to normalize relations with the United States received a "lethal setback." Bill (1988a, 47, 279, 281, 285) called the resolution "ill-considered and ill-timed."

However, other observers were skeptical that a more cooperative posture would have helped. Saunders (1985, 71) argued that "we tried to reach the Islamic centers of power earlier, but we failed." Rosen (1982, 100) asserted that "we were building bridges, but only to secondary—and reckless men . . . everyone everyone clever enough or close enough to Khomeini, knew to avoid us." Some scholars flatly asserted that the United States could do little to normalize relations. As Rubin (1980a, 313) put it, "it was not so much anything that U.S. did," but rather Khomeini's ideology that doomed these efforts. Thornton (1991, 273) argued that "there was nothing to support the American belief that Khomeini was a democrat, or that if only Washington 'came to terms with the revolution,' United States relations would not skip a beat." Benard and Khalilzad (1984, 104) concluded that "Khomeini's view of government was consistent from the start: "Governmental power was a moral prerogative and should belong to him and the fundamentalists"; the moderates were like "hired experts" to be disposed of at a convenient time. Kaufman (1993, 159) contended that the administration and most Middle East experts failed to realize that "Khomeini was bent on founding an Islamic theocracy in Iran" and that, in order to achieve this goal, he had to "discredit the moderates," using their contacts with the "Great Satan."

Of course, it is impossible to say whether the moderates would have prevailed had the Senate abstained from the human rights censure. It is a truism that complex or unexpected events can change revolutionary dynamics overnight. However, given the evidence about Khomeini's singular determination to establish an Islamic Republic, it is hard to imagine that a different American policy would have made much difference. Rubin (1980b, 302) asserted that the radical clergy manipulated the "moderates" against each other, but ultimately "the mullahs were not content to rule through even the most sympathetic" and compliant politicians such as Bani Sadr. In fact, as the fall approached, the fundamentalists were poised to make the final assault on their erstwhile revolutionary partners.

THE LONG FALL: THE PUSH FOR A FUNDAMENTALIST HEGEMONY

The final draft of the constitution, which the Assembly of Experts published on September 12, reflected Khomeini's vision of an Islamic Republic. Chapter One declared that government should be based on faith in one God and "man should submit to His will." In addition to the three customary branches of government there was a twelve-member Council of Guardians with veto power over all legislation. The faqih, the Supreme Jurisprudent, and a council of three to five ayatollahs considerably weakened the presidency, an elected office. The faqih, with unlimited tenure, was all-powerful; he appointed the Council of Guardians, the military and the judiciary and could dismiss the president.

The opposition reacted to the draft with vehemence. The NF liberals, who had done so much to undermine the Bakhtiar government, came to vindicate the much-despised politician. Cottam (1988, 196) would later note that "they saw him as a heroic and prescient figure who had understood early that, as bad as the royal dictatorship had been, a Khomeini dictatorship would be infinitely worse." In October, Bazargan publicly warned of "a dictatorship of the clergy" and Entezam charged that the Assembly exceeded its mandate by completely revising the document. Both tried to convince the ayatollah to dismiss the Assembly of Experts but were again rebuffed. The prime minister complained in an interview with the *New York Times* (October 28) that the clergy had "succeeded in taking over the country" (Wright 1989, 74; Rajaee 1983, 96; Saffari 1993). The Writers' Association announced a new round of poetry readings to be held from October 24 to November 4 to protest censorship and demand freedom of speech. Activists hoped that the readings, which were so effective against the shah, might move Khomeini to liberalize.

The fundamentalists were also facing increased pressure from other quarters. The bazaaris, which were highly instrumental in fomenting the revolution, had become increasingly disenchanted. In an ironic repeat of the shah's policies, the new authorities imposed stringent price controls and other antiprofiteering measures on the merchants. The revolutionary committees established the Headquarters for Combating Profiteering near the Teheran bazaar; sanctions against shopkeepers included monetary fines and public flogging. The committees also attacked moneylenders and a number of them were arrested. Small shopkeepers were hurt by food rationing or free distribution to the mustaza'fin. Many of the bazaaris joined forces with the NF affiliated Society of Merchants, Guilds and Artisans in the Teheran Bazaar or participated in other antifundamentalist activities (Parsa 1989, 275–279).

The restless Left presented even more of a threat. In addition to helping the ethnic uprisings in Kurdistan and elsewhere, the leftists were gaining an upper hand among the workers. The Fedayeen, Mojahedeen, the Workers' Path, the Maoist Paykar, the Tudeh, the Union of Communists, Union of Socialist Workers and the Toilers' Party all had contacts with the workers councils and planned to use them to affect a social transformation of the society. The councils instigated hundreds of strikes and sit-ins, virtually paralyzing industrial production in the country. The Left was making comparable strides in the universities, where Fedayeen and Mojahedeen had successfully competed with fundamentalist student organizations.

Faced with what seemed like a major assault on his revolution and a progressively chaotic situation, Khomeini chose to attribute it to American interference. The overthrow of Mossadeq in 1953 served as a bitter historic reminder of the capacity of the United States to meddle in Iranian affairs. American historic involvement in the Kurdish rebellion in Iraq and its links with other ethnic groups in the region added fuel to these concerns. The Moscow-inspired story about the "Lewis plan" to partition Iran along ethnic lines was made believable in this context. Things got worse when influential politicians in the Democratic Party, notably Frank Church and Gary Hart, called for an American military presence in the Gulf. After General Bernard Rogers, the newly appointed NATO commander commented that the Rapid Intervention Force was a partial response to the events in Iran, the alarm in Khomeini's circles reached a peak. Rafizadeh (1987, 346) claimed that Khomeini was too ignorant to understand the political process in the United States.

Rosen (1982, 100), who monitored the Iranian press, noted an increase in anti-American rumors in the fall; the IRP publications led the way in "attributing otherwise unexplained disruptions" to American saboteurs. Typically, articles accused the CIA—in conjunction with Israeli and Egyptian security services—of plotting to disrupt the Iranian economy. As always, there were the ubiquitous rumors about an American-backed counterrevolutionary effort (Taheri 1988, 113, 115). Paradoxically, the clerics perceived Washington's increasingly close relationship with the moderates as an equally serious threat. Voice of America, which reactivated its Persian language broadcasts as part of a series of "confi-dence—building measures," was particularly suspect because of its success with liberals and all those who found the new Iranian media too restrictive.

The fundamentalists were also unnerved by CIA collaboration with the PG, which received American data on Soviet activities gleaned from a secret listen-ing post at Kabkan (Bamford 1982, 200; Chehabi 1995). Among other things, the dossier included detailed information on Soviet fly-overs in Iranian air space and their airlifts to the Kurds. In one of the many ironic twists in American policy, the CIA's information apparently helped the regime put down the ethnic rebellions (Taheri 1988, 118–119). What looked to the Carter administration like a way to prove its a good faith in Iran, provided the Khomeini movement with "final proof" that the United States was set to repeat its 1953 performance. In this rather elaborate conspiracy theory, the shah's admission to the United States served as the last piece of evidence. Indeed, in the fall of 1979, the fate of the shah, already a highly emotional issue, acquired a huge symbolic meaning for the various forces jostling for power in the revolutionary vortex.

From the very beginning, punishing the shah was high on the political agenda of the fundamentalists. On February 17, the ayatollah told Yassir Arafat about his desire to see the shah "face trial for his crimes against Islam and the nation." On May 13 Ayatollah Khalkhali, a leader in the extremist Fedayeen Islam, announced that the Revolutionary Court condemned to death the exiled shah, his twin sister, Ashraf, and other members of the royal family. Later that month, a member of the group code-named "Mohammed Ali" tried unsuccessfully to assassinate the monarch who was staying in the Bahamas. On June 16, speaking on the anniversary of the execution of a Fedayeen Islam member accused of assassinating Prime Minister Ali Mansur in 1966, the "blood judge" announced new efforts to kill the shah. A day later, he promised that his organization would try to assassinate the shah in Mexico. On June 27, it was announced in Teheran that the effort had failed, but the Mexican authorities denied that there had been an attempt on the life of the exiled monarch (Ioannides 1984, 70, 72–73, 111).

The fate of the shah and, by implication, Iranian-American relations, was also at the center of a new Islamic society formed in early spring. The group, *Daanishjooyan-e Musalman Peyrov-e Khatt-e Imam* (Students Following the Line of the Imam [SFLI]) was recruited from students at Teheran University and the Polytechnic School in Teheran by Habibollah Payman. Payman, the leader of the Movement of Combatant Muslims, known by its Persian acronym JAMA (*Jonbesh-e Mosalmanan-e Mobarez*), was a strong advocate of dependency themes, calling for Iran's lead in a Third World anti-imperialist crusade. The SFLI attracted a number of Fedayeen and Mojahedeen supporters, some Tudeh sympathizers as well as strict fundamentalists with ties to IRP. Payman was in touch with Hojjatalislam Mohammed Mussavi Khoiniha, Imam's representative to the Revolutionary Committees on the Teheran campuses, whom he had first met during the 1963–64 struggle against the shah. There were rumors that Khoiniha, a member of the Central Committee of the IRP who attended Patrice Lumumba University in Moscow, was sympathetic to the Tudeh and the Fedayeen (Salehi 1988, 169; Ioannides 1984, 110–111, 113; Hunter 1987; Hiro 1985, 136–137; Shaplen 1980b).

The SFLI was looking for new ways to influence the revolution. After the assassination attempts failed, the SFLI, like most of revolutionary Iran looked with alarm at the prospect of the shah's relocation to the United States. Nor were these fears totally illusionary. The shah, in an apparent belief that he might be restored to power, decided to wait in Egypt instead of proceeding to the United States, where he was initially invited to stay. Even after Mohammed Reza left the Middle East, his twin sister, Ashraf, her sons and royalists still in Iran hoped for a monarchical comeback. An April 18 memo from Harold Saunders to Newsom mentioned that Princess Ashraf had not abandoned efforts to restore the regime (Documents, vol. 7, 268–269; Ioannides 1984, 107).

The Central Council of the SFLI was apparently well appraised about the negotiations over the shah's admission to the United States. In a bid to save his life, General Nassiri, the former SAVAK chief, divulged the name of a SAVAK agent inside the American embassy. The man, who was code-named Hafiz, agreed to work for the new authorities and, by September, the Revolutionary Council possessed many of the exchanges between Washington and the embassy. According to Mohammed Heikal (1981, 17), a leading Egyptian journalist, this correspondence formed the basis for the plans to seize the embassy. It is plausible that Khoiniha—who was close to Sayyed Ahmed Khomeini, the Ayatollah's son, as well as to Beheshti, Bahonar and Ali Khameneh'i—conveyed the essence of the embassy cable traffic to the SFLI activists (Hiro, 1985, 134; Ioannides 1984, 52, 92–93, 113).

According to Sick (1985, 197), there was "considerable evidence" to suggest that Khomeini himself knew about the SFLI plan and "openly encouraged" it. After the embassy seizure, Undersecretary Newsom stated to the International Court of Justice in the Hague that the large number of persons involved in the planning "made it questionable" whether the Revolutionary Council did not know about the plan in advance (Shaplen 1980b, 71). The hostage Charles Scott (1984, 151–153) claimed that Khoiniha told the radical students about American readiness to admit the shah on September 13. It was also around this time that the militants obtained a detailed layout of the embassy compound (Hiro 1985, 136–137).

It is not entirely clear what the students hoped to accomplish by attacking the embassy. The most reasonable assumption is that a number of motives, some only partially crystallized, were behind the takeover decision. First, there was the highly symbolic nature of such an act, originally planned to last a few days. The students and many regular Iranians viewed the embassy as the seat of American power and the center of the CIA 1953 intervention. That SFLI choice of November 4 as the day of the attack seems to point in this direction. The designated day was the first anniversary of the killing of several students at Teheran University and the fifteenth anniversary of Khomeini's exile. As a later editorial noted, "the taking of the American den of spies on November 4, 1979, logically ended a period of humiliation and outrage of the nation symbolized in the speech of the Imam before his exile" (Rubin 1980a).

Second, SFLI activists and their IRP mentors might have tried to preempt the Fedayeen and Mojahedeen, who were behind the "Valentine's Day" embassy attack. Given the extreme tension between the two groups, the clerics feared that the guerillas would profit politically from a long siege. As Bahonar later explained, "the February attack did not reflect the will of the Iranian people. Those who did it, did not represent . . . the people's Islamic revolution . . . they demanded a share of the Islamic revolution that was not theirs" (Ioannides 1984, 101; Irfani 1983, 191).

However, a new attack by the Fedayeen or Mojahedeen—which was widely rumored around Teheran—would have been much more difficult for the Revolutionary Council to handle. In the extreme anti-American agitation of the fall, the leftists, who were still reeling from the hizbollahis attacks in August, would have improved their revolutionary credentials. The same rumors had it that the guerillas were planning to seize documents and use them to discredit the moderates and fundamentalists that had contacts with the embassy. Dislodging the would-be assailants could have proved politically costly: The clerics were well aware that the PG, which took credit for settling the February incident, suffered a serious loss of revolutionary credibility. Conversely, a takeover by the SFLI would have bolstered the radical ulama and proved that Khomeini was the ultimate anti-imperialist, who "rubbed America's face in the dirt." Always quick studies, the fundamentalists, faced with a leftist challenge, apparently incorporated the strategy of the competition (Ioannides 1984, 102).

Third, the SFLI militants and the fundamentalists who guided them were eager to use the issue of the shah's admission to further undermine the PG and its policy of collaboration with the United States. Payman and his Movement of Combatant Muslims urged a complete break with the "American Satan" and a close alliance with the Third World. Severing relations with the United States was also very much in the interest of the Soviet Union and the Tudeh Party. According to James Angleton, the CIA counterintelligence chief, the SFLI was penetrated by a number of older professional ideologues, some of them actual KGB agents, who might have exerted influence in this direction (Copeland 1989, 254).

Plausible as this postfact reconstruction of the motives is, it should not be taken to mean that the militants and their fundamentalist patrons controlled the dynamics of the situation. As Stempel (1981, 191) noted, the "emergence of the religious extremists as the dominant force occurred as much by happenstance as by design." In this sense, the shah's admission issue played out against the background of a chaotic revolutionary process where "single issues," often of a symbolic nature, served to radicalize the society. The Iranian moderates were aware of the fact that the political energy released by the revolution was not yet spent and that "any issue could become that one that marked the moment at which the momentum to radicalization overtook them" (Benard and Khalilzad 1984, 164–165). By the fall, many of the American observers came to share this view, but the question of the shah's admission became enmeshed in the complex domestic politics in Washington.

THE UNWELCOME VISITOR: THE POLITICS OF THE SHAH'S ADMISSION TO THE UNITED STATES AND THE SEIZURE OF THE EMBASSY

Finding a safe heaven for the shah was part of an American policy to facilitate his abdication. Initially, the State Department was ready to accept the shah in the United States and Walter Annenberg, who was approached by Kissinger and Nelson Rockefeller, offered a sanctuary in his house in California (Isaacson 1992, 715). However, the shah, who hoped for a counterrevolution, stopped first in Egypt and then in Morocco, as the guest of King Hassan. When Hassan, under pressure from Iran, terminated his welcome at the end of February, the shah sent a message that he wanted to come to the United States.

The next day, the SCC chaired by Brzezinski, met to decide the request. Even though the adviser was sympathetic, the situation in Iran was too dangerous to consider the asylum request. Ambassador Sullivan, who was engaged in delicate efforts to secure the departure of Americans trapped in the Taksman II surveillance post in northern Iran, was adamantly opposed. He sent a very sharp personal warning to Washington and asked Charles Naas to reinforce the same point in a March 7 meeting with Newsom (Sullivan 1981, 277). The previous day, Henry Precht described the shah's proposed visit as a "disaster" for U.S.–Iranian relations. The memo also warned about security risks that Americans would face and mentioned a PLO effort to kidnap the shah (Documents, vol. 7, 267; Ioannides 1984, 83).

To defend its refusal, the administration decided to share these assessments with Kissinger and Rockefeller. As an interim solution, the exiled monarch flew to the Bahamas on March 30, where he stayed at the Paradise Island Resort. His overpriced villa was accessible from a public beach and provided little security from the assassination attempts of Khalkhali's emissaries (Hulbert 1982, 136). Meanwhile, Kissinger, Rockefeller, John McCloy and other "Pahlavites" had intensified their pressure to admit Mohammed Reza. Kissinger accused the administration of appeasing Khomeini and of letting the ayatollah intimidate America into abrogating its right to decide on asylum. In an April 9 speech,

Kissinger argued that, after years of loyal service to the United States, it would be morally wrong to turn the shah into "a Flying Dutchman looking for a port of call" (quoted in Ledeen and Lewis 1981, 219; Sick 1985, 180; Ioannides 1984, 81). The shah, who hired Robert Armao, a public relations consultant and a former aide to Nelson Rockefeller, mounted his own campaign against the administration. Around that time it became quite clear that the treatment of the shah, as part of the broader issue of "who lost Iran," would become a major theme in the forthcoming election. Still, in an April 18 memo, Saunders opposed granting visas to the shah and his entourage (Documents, vol. 7, 268–269).

There is little doubt that electoral considerations forced the foreign policy team to rethink its shah's strategy. The first to "convert" was Mondale, who discussed the issue with Brzezinski. On July 23, the adviser informed Vance and Brown that the vice president had "recommended that the time has come to review our policy on residence in the United States for the shah." At a July 27 foreign policy breakfast, the failure to admit the shah was compared to President Ford's refusal to meet with Solzhenitsyn; the general view was that the issue "would play very badly politically." Brzezinski added that the United States should not be "influenced by threats from a third-rate power," but Carter prophetically commented that "he did not wish the shah to be here playing tennis while Americans in Teheran were kidnapped or even killed." The participants agreed to reassess the situation after a new report promised by Vance. However, in a July 28 cable, Laingen warned Vance that the shah's admission "would endanger the situation of Americans" and pointed out to the skimpy Iranian defense of the compound (Brzezinski 1983, 473, 474; Bill 1988a, 333; Document, vol. 7, 241, 272).

In spite of Lanigan's warning, the White House estimated that the shah would have to be allowed in. Carter's secret directive to Vance and Newsom set the date for January 1980 or earlier. Henry Precht was ordered to write, on August 2, the ultrasecret "Planning for the Shah to Come to the U.S," memo, which recommended that the monarch should be admitted, but not before "a new and substantially more effective guard force for the Embassy" could be tested. The Iran country director predicted that the threat to the staff will "diminish somewhat further" by the end of the year, but did not rule out hostage taking (Documents, vol. 1–6, 10–17; Ioannides 1984, 77; Salinger, 1981, 22–23). Laingen, in spite of his concerns for embassy safety conveyed in a number of messages through the highly secret CHEROKEE channel, agreed that "we could eventually accept the shah." He told Washington twice in the summer that such a move would be possible after the appointment of a permanent ambassador—a sign of American acceptance of the revolution—and following the emergence of a stable Iranian government (Laingen 1992, 9; Ioannides 1984, 85).

The administration was right to anticipate more pressure. In mid-August, Princess Ashraf sent a personal letter to Carter which, according to Brzezinski (1983, 474), quite "literally begged" him to grant asylum to her brother. Under Carter's instructions, Warren Christopher drafted a reply which Brzezinski (1983, 474) found "curt and cold." He redrafted the letter to make it sound warmer but otherwise abstained from a more active posture. Although Brzezinski remained convinced that the exiled Iranian monarch deserved political asylum, he, like others in the administration, judged that the timing was not right. The rumors in Washington about the imminent arrival of the shah threatened to abort the all-out administration initiative to bolster the moderates. Vance informed Laingen to keep the issue top secret and Precht asked Laingen to inform the Iranians that "there has been no change in the U.S. Government's attitude toward a trip by the Shah to the US" (Documents, vol. 7, 276; Ioannides 1984, 79).

The cable traffic in September was unanimous in predicting dire consequences for the asylum policy. A report on September 2 stated that "any decision to allow the shah . . . to visit would almost certainly result in an immediate and violent reaction." But there was considerable confusion in evaluating the general political situation. Andrew Sens, the economic officer, attacked the notion that Iran had a dual government and gave the Khomeini revolution about six months to run. Sens argued that whoever was in charge of Iran would need revenues from oil and a working economy. Precht expressed optimism that the clerics would have to moderate because they could not run a "complex economy" without help from Westernized officials. R. T. Curran from the International Communication Agency proposed to build a communication network in Iran and sponsor an exchange program for scholars (Documents, vol. 1, 562, 574, 577; vol. 16, 60–64, 69–76, 109–111; vol. 27, 68–69). Others were less optimistic and warned against the "illusion that the Khomeini regime cannot survive without the Westernized elite." Some embassy dispatches expressed concern about the enthusiasm of the Assembly of Experts for the concept of faqih. John Graves from the ICA cautioned that Americans were too visible in Iran. Even the ever-optimistic Precht admitted to being confused about clerical politics and asked for more information (Documents, vol. 16, 77–78, 93–97; Bill 1988a, 280).

Kennedy (1986, 68) subsequently revealed that in September and October the Iran estimate polarized the administration. One school of thought maintained that the revolution took an implacably hostile turn. Even Saunders, who normally shared Precht's optimism, seemed to have developed some doubts. In a September 5 memorandum to Vance, the assistant secretary noted that Khomeini's hostility to the United States is unlikely to "abate significantly." He warned that a meeting with the ayatollah might appear as a "cave in to a man who hates us and who is strongly deprecated here and by Westernized Iranian" (in Bill 1988a, 281). But Precht and other moralpolitikers "preferred to assume" that conditions would improve and, given its geopolitical position, Iran would return to the Western fold. During a September visit to Washington, Laingen (1992, 9) professed to be "cautiously optimistic;" in speeches before academics and journalists the chargé d'affaires criticized those who described the situation in Iran as one of "extremism and chaos" (Rubin 1980b, 294). In a joint briefing with Precht, Laingen claimed that the press had exaggerated conditions in Iran and that articles critical of Khomeini were making the situation more difficult for the Americans. General Gast of MAAG, who was convinced that the need for American military supplies would moderate the revolution no matter who was in power, supported Precht and Laingen (Ledeen and Lewis 1981, 223).

To assure that the policy of normalization would not be derailed, Precht redoubled his efforts to delay the shah's admission. On September 17, Precht met with Mahmud Foroughi, a well-connected former official in the shah's government, who warned him that admitting the shah "would be very, very bad for the U.S. and for the West." Still, Foroughi assured Precht that the ascendancy of the mullahs was just a "passing phase," albeit a long one, and that the "moderate nationalists will prevail" (Documents, vol. 27, 78–81; Ioannides 1984, 84). Precht was also banking on the fact that the administration was worried about the growing influence of the Soviet Union in the region. To enlist the PG in the anti-Soviet bloc, Precht proposed to Laingen that Iran should assume control over the SALT monitoring posts, a step that would show American "sincerity" (Taheri 1988, 112). On September 27, in a speech before the Foreign Relations Council, Secretary Vance listed a long string of reasons why the shah should not be permitted to the United States.

However, just one day later, the administration came under renewed pressure to reverse its decision. An aide to David Rockefeller called Newsom to inform him that the shah, who was by then residing in Cuernavaca, Mexico, was seriously ill and might need medical attention in the United States. Newsom, well aware of Rockefeller's campaign on behalf of the shah, was highly skeptical. The State Department contacted Laingen who, in two strongly worded cables on September 30 and October 1, warned against admitting the monarch (Ioannides 1984, 86). The chargé d'affaires was particularly worried because news of an asylum for the shah would have jeopardized the upcoming meeting between Yazdi and Vance, the first high-level contact since the revolution.

The Iranian foreign minister was scheduled to arrive in New York at the beginning of October to attend the United Nations General Assembly. On October 4, Yazdi met with Precht and a number of officials from the Defense and Commerce Departments for preliminary discussions. Precht later reported that the "meeting was characterized by frank, sometimes bluntly-stated Iranian questions and objections," but felt that in spite of a heavy air of suspicion, there "was little acrimony." Two days later, Vance, accompanied by Newsom, Saunders and the UN ambassador Donald McHenry, met with Yazdi who, fresh from the Nonaligned Conference in Havana, was reported to be in a "prickly, provocative mood." He argued that the United States had not yet accepted the revolution and vowed that Iran would no longer condone "a big brother attitude," especially on the human rights issues (Shaplen 1980b, 58).

Nevertheless, Yazdi was interested in military purchases, and he and an Iranian general met the next day with Pentagon officials. Sick (1985, 188–189) described the Iranians as "totally uninformed but intensely suspicious" and Vance wrote that Yazdi put his desire for "self-satisfaction" and a demand to

discuss the causes of the revolution ahead of "whatever interests the new government may have in the . . . United States" (Documents, vol. 18, 135–136). But
Newsom argued that the "Iranian suspicions of us were only natural in the post-
revolutionary period." He added that after the transition period "common interests could provide a basis for future cooperation—not on the scale of before
but sufficient to demonstrate that Iran has not been "lost" to us and to the West"
(Shaplen 1980b, 61; Ledeen and Lewis 1981, 227). Even Sick, who, like Brzezinski was a skeptic, felt that there was "a genuine prospect for establishing
some limited but useful dialogue."

This prognosis was strengthened by academics, notably James Bill, who spoke
at a Middle East conference on October 15. According to a State Department
summary, Bill believed that the conservative clergy would not be able to retain
power for long and that a "triple alliance of the military, progressive clergy and
secular technocrats will emerge." He repeated his assertion that, in the long run,
"the ayatollahs do not have the ability to erect a new political structure" and
that "they are mentally and emotionally unprepared for the challenge of rebuilding Iran." The Iran expert urged the administration to "admit past errors" and
send a "new breed of representatives to Iran" as well as provide agricultural and
administrative aid that would reach "the people" (Documents, vol. 16, 135–141).

With the elections pending, the administration was eager to prove that, as
Newsom asserted, Iran was not totally "lost." The trump card in this new equation was Yazdi's alleged apprehension about the Soviet threat. On October 13,
the embassy reported that Yazdi had complained to George Cave, a CIA official,
that other leaders in the PG had failed to understand the need to preserve the
"delicate balance between [the] U.S. and USSR." Other dispatches showed that
the PG was anxious to obtain spare parts and reduce the American media criticism of Iran. An October 9 memo noted that Entezam urged a response to such
"current Iranian needs" as spare parts and the unlocking of Iranian funds in the
United States (Documents, vol. 10, no page number). In spite of the heavy
atmosphere during the Pentagon meeting, the administration decided to sell a
small quantity of military spare parts to Iran.

A week later—and just three weeks before the seizure of the embassy—
General Gast from MAGG met with an aide to Defense Minister Mustafa Ali
Chamran, who wanted to buy spare parts for helicopters used against the Kurds.
Gast, an energetic booster of the normalization theory, had developed an ambitious plan to restore some of the military procurement program. Gast, Precht
and other normalization advocates could also take heart from an ICA communication that found that the situation in Iran had stabilized. The ICA proposed
to establish an exchange program between the influential Fayziyeh School in
Qom and American theological students (Documents, vol. 1, 513–514, vol. 10,
no page number).

Given the growing anti-Americanism in October, this optimism seems quite
misplaced. Ironically, Khomeini used the Fayziyeh School for his constant attacks on the "Great Satan." On one such occasion, on September 8, the ayatollah

declared that the United States was the source of all evil (Moshiri 1985, 65). Some embassy dispatches in mid-October noted the increasing stridency of the fundamentalists and the drift toward theocracy. An October 10 report maintained that moderate Iranian parties were overshadowed by Khomeini (Documents, vol. 27, 89–90). In an October 15 cable, Abdolkarim Lahiji, a prominent lawyer and the vice chairman of the Iran human rights committee, was quoted as saying that moderates were "thwarted and he did not see how they could be put back on their track." Another cable cited a senior Iranian diplomat who asserted that "we traded an educated dictator for an uneducated dictator" (Documents, vol. 16, 137–141, 144–145; vol. 27, 80–82, 85–86). The reports on the economy were equally gloomy. Writing in response to a proposal that the Overseas Political Investment Corporation resume insurance for Iran, Laingen described the "revolutionary paranoia" toward investment, stemming from Khomeini's "own hostility to Western investment" (Documents, vol. 16, 166; vol. 63, 130–133).

All in all, the embassy cable traffic in October clearly indicated that Iran had a dual power structure and that the PG lost out to the increasingly dictatorial fundamentalists. However, there was no attempt to debate the issue at the highest levels of the administration and Precht's optimism prevailed. In an October 13 memo "Policy Initiatives," Precht noted that "we cannot bring down the present regime" but hoped to moderate its policies "and help to promote greater pragmatism" by building confidence measures, including the release of spare parts and sale of kerosene and heating oil. Precht also cautioned against contacts with the exiled Bakhtiar and other anti-Khomeini groups, which could be construed as "political endorsement." Closing a circle, the moralpolitikers who had criticized American reluctance to deal with the shah's opposition, wanted now to broaden a Carter executive order that banned contacts with Pahlavi officials (Documents, vol. 16, 129–133; Rafizadeh 1987, 312). Precht who mistrusted the "negative reporting" from the embassy, arrived in Teheran on October 20 on his own fact-finding mission. The visit was not devoid of irony; Precht, with his identity concealed, was taken to the Friday prayer meeting in a Teheran mosque where the crowd chanted "Death to America" (Rosen 1982, 77; Documents, vol. 16, 137–141, 144–145).

Even if there had been a willingness to engage in a high level debate about Iran, the shah's deteriorating health condition pushed the administration to the wall. On October 16, the French doctors in charge of the shah's treatment revealed his medical history to an American physician, Dr. Benjamin Kean, who was called to consult on the gravely ill Mohammed Reza. In an October 18 report to Secretary Vance, Kean stated that the shah, who had a malignant spleen and a malignant tumor in his neck, was no longer responding to chemotherapy and was suffering from complications from obstructive jaundice. The doctor strongly urged to be allowed to admit the shah to a medical facility in New York. The news was something of a bombshell; the panicked State Department scrambled to find a European country where the shah could be treated, but was rebuffed (Shaplen 1980b).

Carter's foreign policy team discussed the new developments during a break-fast meeting on October 19. Vance argued that the new circumstances made it imperative for the United States to admit the shah. On October 20, the State Department medical adviser submitted an appropriate report, which Warren Christopher forwarded to Carter at Camp David, along with a recommendation that the United States seek the approval of the Bazargan government for the shah's asylum. Vance wanted to gauge the reaction of the Iranians and, "if it was not strongly negative," let the shah come. Brzezinski (1983, 475) argued that the United States should simply inform the PG of its plans to admit the monarch, a suggestion that Carter reluctantly adopted. The president was re-ported to have asked "when the Iranians take our people in Teheran hostage, what will you advise me then?" (Shaplen 1980b, 66). One day later, Bruce Laingen and Henry Precht, who was still in Iran, informed Bazargan and Yazdi that the shah would be admitted to the United States on humanitarian grounds.

The decision to grant asylum has been extensively analyzed. Both Sick (1985, 185–186) and Brzezinski (1983, 475) claimed that the president felt compelled morally to change his position. Even Vance, the shah's main opponent, was forced to recommend temporary admission on humanitarian grounds. Carter and Vance were apparently convinced that the shah was dying and felt that it would be inhumane to deny him medical treatment. The question of treatment in Mex-ico apparently came up but, given the unanimous recommendation of the doc-tors, the option was discarded. At the same time, political expediency played a considerable role in these deliberations. As Sick put it, "it would be naïve to argue that President Carter and his advisers were oblivious to the political con-sequences of this decision." A denial of hospitality to a close ally of the United States in the name of realpolitik would have been a huge embarrassment for a president dedicated to the moral code of New Internationalism. Brzezinski (1983, 475) noted that the "president felt morally ill-at-ease over the exclusion of the shah." For better or worse, refusing entrance to the dying man was not an option that the administration could consider.

Bill (1984) and Hulbert (1982, 131) argued that Carter's decision might have been motivated by his primary race with Edward Kennedy, who at the time had a two to one lead. Hulbert (1982, 22–23) and to a lesser extent Bill (1988a, 339) have also subscribed to the so-called Manhattan Financial Theory. Ac-cordingly, Rockefeller, whose Chase Manhattan Bank loans to Iran were threat-ened when Teheran began withdrawing billions of dollars of financial deposits, manufactured a crisis around the shah's admission in order to freeze the money. Although Chase Manhattan benefited from the freeze on Iranian assets which Carter imposed in the wake of the embassy seizure, it is harder to prove that Rockefeller and Kissinger could have choreographed a complicated chain of events including the shah's acute illness or predict the hostage taking. A more plausible explanation is that Carter and his team had little illusion that the failure to admit the shah would have hurt Carter's reelection prospects. Brzezinski

(1983, 475) noted that Mondale's "election time conversion" helped to persuade the reluctant president.

The administration did not have to wait for the elections to find out how damaging the problem of the shah was turning out to be. A bipartisan group of Congress members—Jacob Javits, Barry Goldwater, Charles Percy, Richard Stone, Richard Brooke, John M. Murphy, William Lehman and John Brademas—had worked for a number of months to gain admission for the monarch. Senator Henry Jackson, another shah supporter, was publicly berating the new rulers in Iran and, in a "Meet the Press" interview, predicted that the revolution would fail and that the country would disintegrate. According to an embassy dispatch of October 28, Jackson's statement hit the Iranian Foreign Ministry like a "bombshell." Yazdi demanded a full transcript of the interview and wondered whether it contained "some kind of message" (Document, vol. 7, 290; Bill 1988a, 285).

Urged by the proshah politicians, the Congress compelled the State Department to investigate human rights violations of the new regime. In an October 18 report, Precht detailed numerous human rights abuses and Laingen delivered a formal U.S. protest to Interior Minister Hashemi Sabaqhian. Laingen's protest triggered vicious attacks in the Iranian media; the chargé d'affaires was accused of being part of a "satanic" organization set up by the CIA to rule Iran. In the eyes of many Iranians this pressure was part of a larger conspiracy to restore the shah to the throne "as in 1953" (Ioannides 1984, 118, 89; Bill 1988a, 364).

Given the heated anti-American climate in Iran, Bazargan and Yazdi were naturally upset about the news that the shah would be admitted. In what seemed like a major understatement, Laingen described Bazargan's reaction as "quiet but concerned acceptance of reality." The chargé d'affaires conveyed Yazdi's fear that the shah's arrival would be construed as a "symbol of Rockefeller and Zionism" and "open a Pandora's Box." Nevertheless, Laingen expressed his hope, based on Bazargan's solemn assurances, that the PG would protect the embassy against a mob attack (Documents, vol. 7, 281; Ioannides, 1984, 88; Vance, 1983, 372).

American diplomats in Teheran closely monitored the reaction to the shah's arrival in New York on October 23. Most of them shared Laingen's anxiety that their personal safety might be jeopardized. Barry Rosen, one of the hostages, was reported to have told a high administration official to "let me know a day in advance—so I can make a dash to the airport" (Ioannides 1984, 86). In his book, Rosen (1982, 102) described how, following the announcement of the shah's admission, "total silence followed. In time it was broken by a faint groan. Faces literally went white."

Still, the initial embassy dispatches showed a slight sense relief. On October 24, Laingen reported a relatively mild reaction. The press response was said to be "minimal," with most of the newspapers reporting the story in a "straightforward manner" (Documents, vol. 7, 283–285). Rosen (1982, 103), who monitored the Iranian media, noted that, initially, the response was "milder than anticipated," and that embassy officers congratulated themselves on "our seemingly safe passage." On October 28 the ICA noted that the "climate in Iran stabilized sufficiently to permit renewed program activity" (Documents, vol. 16, 156–157).

However, a few days later, Laingen wrote about a gradual build-up of fury and added that the "revolutionary radicals" and "unsophisticated clergymen" might pressure Bazargan into action (Documents, vol. 7, 288). The growing American anxiety reflected the fact that Khomeini and other fundamentalist leaders were intensifying their rhetoric against the United States. When the ayatollah first mentioned the issue on October 22, he expressed a desire to see the shah dead, and seemed to be mostly concerned with recovering the money that the Pahlavis allegedly plundered from Iran. However, over the next few days there was a gradual increase in clerically sponsored demonstrations in Isfahan, Qazvin, Mashad, Bonab and others provincial cities. On October 26, millions of Iranians marched in Teheran and the provinces to protest against the shah's admission. Three days later, Khomeini delivered a scathing anti-American attack at the Mofidi College in Qom (Documents vol. 16, 161–167; Miklos 1983, 57; Taheri 1988, 122; Ioannides 1984, 119–120).

Yet, much to the relief of the Americans, a mass rally on November 1, where Ayatollah Montazeri lambasted the United States for giving asylum to the "bloodthirsty shah," did not proceed to the embassy; the crowd chanting "Death to America" marched to Shush Square, some miles away. There was a smaller rally outside the embassy gates, apparently sponsored by Tudeh, but Laingen assumed that the Bazargan government would be able to protect the American diplomats.

In retrospect, this assumption proved to be highly flawed. A reconstruction of the events leading up to the embassy seizure indicates a different dynamic at hand. The SFLI and their IRP handlers knew from the Precht memo that the shah was not scheduled to arrive in the United States before the end of the year. In the meanwhile, the clerical leadership expected the United States to further destabilize Iran through ethnic rebellion and political unrest. According to this theory, the shah's admission, at the height of the unrest, would signal the beginning of a royalist revolution. Yazdi's meeting with Vance at the beginning of October added fuel to this conspiracy theory. When Yazdi subsequently conveyed to Khomeini Vance's assurances of good will, the ayatollah reportedly asked the foreign minister if he had not heard about the plans for the shah's admission.

This apparent double-dealing confirmed to Khomeini that America was using the moderates to mislead the ulama and cover up its preparation for a royal coup d'état. On October 27, Beheshti told Laingen and Precht that he was very concerned about such a scenario. In the eyes of the clerics, the shah's stay in New York was a logical choice to plot a counterrevolution. As Bahonar explained, "New York is the center of world Zionism. That is why the shah was taken there. To hatch conspiracies against the revolution with the CIA, imperialism and Zionism" (quoted in Ioannides 1984, 96, 116, 126). The fears that Americans were using the moderates as a "Trojan horse" to destroy the revolution from within were heightened when Bazargan and Yazdi, on a visit to Algeria, met Brzezinski on November 1. According to Gates (1996, 129) the Iranians requested the appointment, but the televised encounter outraged Khomeini, who had no prior knowledge about the move. Both in substantive and symbolic terms, the meeting could not have come at a worse time. Laingen (1992, 10) called it a "red flag" for the radicals. As one observer later put it, "the Prime Minister and the Foreign Minister were shaking hands with a top American official at a time when the Shah and the CIA were hatching plots in New York against the revolution" (Ioannides 1984, 124).

The fundamentalists were also concerned that the leftists guerrillas, long rumored to look for a pretext to attack the embassy, would utilize the shah's admission. Had the Fedayeen and the Mojahedeen succeeded in seizing the documents, it would have hurt Beheshti and other ulama that had contacts with the embassy. It is significant that after the embassy fell, the SFLI published documents that implicated members of the PG and moderate clerics like Shariatmadari, but spared the radical ulama. Besides, the SFLI planned to use the documents to prove the "CIA plot" against the revolution.

However, the SFLI had not finished training for the guerrilla attack, which it had planned originally. The students feared that a botched attempt would give the embassy staff time to escape or at least shred sensitive documents. To improve the odds, the SFLI decided to use the guise of a demonstration and a sit-in—a form of protest with which Americans were familiar. The new plan was to attack on November 4, after 300 participants were recruited to augment the 200 original members. Meanwhile, the SLFI and the IRP had created a "controlled environment" around the embassy to prevent random demonstrations or a leftist attack. Had the embassy been threatened earlier, diplomats could have been dispersed or documents shipped out. Thus the IRP routed the November 1 rally away from the embassy and the SLFI activists kept a constant watch over the embassy. They became anxious when a small pro-Communist crowd tried to put up a banner on the gates of the embassy, leading to a scuffle with the marines. Later that evening, Khomeini went on Radio Teheran to praise students who were killed a year earlier at the University of Teheran. He appealed to "the dear pupils, students and theological students to expand with all their might their attacks against the United States and Israel so they may force the United States to return the deposed Shah and to condemn this great plot." Khomeini urged students to intensify their protest on November 4 to honor their fallen comrades (Ioannides 1984, 126).

Writing on the same day to his wife, Bruce Laingen sounded quite discouraged. He mentioned the "growing irritation" over the shah's admission and predicted that "we are going to have some heavy weather for a while" (quoted in Ioannides 1984, 127). But neither Laingen nor the foreign policy team in Washington was prepared for what happened on Sunday morning of November 4. After the SFLI seized the embassy, Washington expected that the PG, in a repeat of the February incident, would intervene and release the captive diplomats. Amid the chaos of the early hours of the attack, the administration did not pay sufficient attention to a SFLI communiqué, which stated that the hostages would be released only after the shah was extradited. Nor did the State Department listen too carefully to an address delivered by Ayatollah Beheshti to the Council of Experts on the same day. In the speech, which was broadcast late at night by Radio Teheran, Beheshti stated that the release of the diplomats could be secured only when "the Shah was handed over to the Revolutionary Court" (Ioannides 1984, 128). The full scope of the problem became clear only after Khomeini refused to intervene, condemning the American diplomats to 444 days of captivity.

The unprecedented nature of the embassy takeover has led many observers to argue that the students had intended to seize the documents and release the diplomats soon after. Indeed, Abbas Abdi, one of the SFLI leaders, subsequently admitted that the plan was to hold the embassy for a few days (Burns, 1999). But Khomeini's refusal to intervene and the public adulation showered on the SFLI sealed the fate of the diplomats. According to this theory, even if Khomeini had no advance knowledge of the plot, he hardly could afford to order the students to release the Americans. As for holding hostages, Beheshti, Bahonar and other clerical leaders were apparently well aware that the act violated not only international law but also Islamic customs. However, from their perspective it was *remedium in extremis*, an extreme act of self-defense against a country that plotted to destroy the revolution. Again and again the clerics emphasized that they had moved to prevent a repeat of the 1953 CIA backed coup against Mossadeq (Ioannides 1984, 96–97). Not incidentally, dependency advocates and world theorists implied that the hostage taking was justified. For instance, Falk (1980, 92) claimed that the hostage issue should be viewed in the context of international laws created by powerful states, which "does not protect weak countries from intervention."

Whatever its legal status, the seizure of the hostages greatly helped the radical ulama: It removed the left as an effective competitor, energized the masses and launched the "Second Revolution." As Dr. Hadi Modaressi, a leading clergyman close to the Imam observed, the embassy was taken in order "to build this struggle against counterrevolutionary forces at home." He added that in order to accelerate the radicalization process of the masses, "we wish and we welcome military aggression against us because it strengthens the revolution and rallies the masses around it" (quoted in Rubin 1980b, 303). Soon after, Khomeini dismissed the PG and allowed the Revolutionary Council to take over.

Participants in the "postmortem" discourse have pointed to a number of underlying institutional imperatives and paradigmatic assumptions that contributed to the hostage crisis. Even those who accepted the argument that the dying shah had to be admitted questioned the safety precautions in the embassy. As was already noted, during the summer and fall, the "bare bones" plan was abandoned in order to pursue normalization. Critics argued that the embassy could have utilized the time between the shah's arrival in the United States and the attack to ensure its safety. At the very least, the documents should have been removed. Admiral Stansfield Turner (1991b, 24–25), who was ultimately responsible for embassy security, claimed that he had not been informed about the deliberations leading to the shah's admission. Still, he talked to David Rockefeller on October 23 and agreed with him that the United States has a responsibility for the monarch. At this point, Turner could have dealt with the files, but, as he admitted, "I overlooked the point about instructing the embassy to destroy documents." Sick (1985, 191) argued that Bruce Laingen "bears a heavy responsibility" for failing to destroy most of the papers after October 23. Consequently, "it was impossible to destroy all the files and large quantities of classified documents fell into the students' hands."

Reducing the staff was another option that could have been considered. As Bell (1980, 60) noted, the British, whose embassy was damaged badly in a 1978 mob attack, took such a step before expelling a number of Iranian students. But the administration was reluctant to move its diplomats out and disrupt the normalization process. Instead, it chose to rely on the security plan, which was geared toward fending off attackers until the arrival of reinforcements promised by the PG. In hindsight, both Vance (1983, 375) and Saunders (1985) claimed that no one, and especially Laingen and Precht, had realized the extent to which the authority of the PG was "diminished" and how "completely responsive" the mob was to the religious extremists. Stempel (1981, 302) added that, in relying on the security plan, too little attention was paid "to the less benign members of the revolutionary coalition." Needless to say, no one on the American team realized how powerful was the shadowy Revolutionary Council. Bani Sadr (1991, 31) would later comment that "Carter believed that we are a state, like any other, with a[n executive] hierarchy."

Perhaps the greatest obstacle was psychological, stemming from an abiding American belief in the universality of norms of international behavior. Rafizadeh (1987, 314), the SAVAK representative in America, maintained that the CIA had rejected his repeated warnings about hostage taking. Before the embassy seizure there were a number of assaults on American diplomats, but in none of the incidents was the host country in legal violation of the Convention on Diplomatic Relations that protects diplomatic envoys. As Sick (1985, 197) later emphasized, "until the incident in Teheran, there was no modern precedent for a nation renouncing its international obligation entirely and throwing its support for the mob. That was not expected even in nations where the veneer of civilization was thin and new." As for Iran, a country "with centuries of tradition in law and diplomacy" such behavior "was unimaginable." Saunders (1985, 51), who recalled "the utter frustration of not knowing what kind of political creatures" the fundamentalists were, added that they "marched to a code of behavior outside normal international law."

Even after the shock of the hostage taking the "comprehension gap" in Washington did not disappear overnight. Within a week of the assault, the INR prepared a highly pessimistic memorandum for Vance. The analysts argued that neither diplomatic action nor economic or military pressures were likely to budge the fundamentalists. Still, as Sick (1985, 221, 225) noted, there was "deep institutional reluctance," particularly in the State Department to "conclude that conventional diplomacy was of little value in dealing with the revolutionaries in Iran." This illusion was maintained in spite of the fact that the negotiations over the release of the hostages were not going anywhere.

Such observations underscored the underlying problems in comprehending the nature of the Iranian upheaval. At the very core, the failure to predict the revolutionary dynamics was paradigmatic. The unprecedented nature of Iranian fundamentalism confounded accepted notions of rationality, linear progression and other time-honored tools for peering into the future. American diplomats and intelligence officials as well as most of the Iran experts could not envision a country which would adopt a seemingly regressive collective belief system and proceed to institutionalize it amid breathtaking repression and violence. This paradigmatic difficulty was compounded by the inevitable personal, ideological and institutional power struggle in the American foreign policy community and Congress. Chapter 6 discusses this predictive failure in a systematic way.

6

Reflections on Predictive Failures

Efforts to understand the phenomenon of the Iranian revolution have continued to preoccupy scholars, foreign policy practitioners and intelligence officials. Despite the proliferation of explanations, there is little consensus on the causes and the dynamics of this remarkable "regressive" revolution and even less agreement on the causes that led to the predictive failure. Complicating the task is the fact that the debate has dealt with either policy or intelligence blunders, with little emphasis on the paradigmatic nature of the predictive endeavor. There has been virtually no attempt to present a systematic analysis of the synergistic impact of all three dimensions.

This book attempts to illuminate the complex nature of the predictive failure that caused the Carter administration to underestimate the fragility of the Pahlavi monarchy and overestimate the democratic nature of the successor regime. With this task now accomplished, it remains the burden of the concluding chapter to sum up the paradigmatic, policy and intelligence level failures. This analytic scheme allows us to reduce the realities of the predictive process to manageable categories and provide a certain coherence and economy to the discussion. However, the approach has some drawbacks. As was argued, the predictive endeavor is extremely complex and highly interactive, making any analytical distinctions somewhat arbitrary. Still, the use of clearly defined analytic categories can identify the web of factors that contributed to the administration's blunder. To the extent that problems of forecasting political change are comparable, these factors can provide an insight into other situations as well.

PARADIGMATIC FAILURE

The theoretical analysis makes clear that political change, whether incremental or revolutionary, is rooted in changing norms of legitimacy embedded in the collective belief system of a society. Ideally, any successful effort at predicting change in a closed society should follow its legitimacy discourse. However, a collective belief system is a theoretical construct that involves tracking numerous variables that are difficult to measure and embedded in a fluid and ill-defined discourse situation. While some of these variables can be approximated through concrete "look-see" measurements, others have to be inferred from certain indirectly observed properties at the individual or systemic level. To complicate matters, as was shown, legitimacy itself is a difficult and elusive concept that has defied an academic consensus.

To approximate the legitimacy discourse, political scientists have used the developmental and the neo-Marxist dependency paradigm to analyze change in Third World countries. Based on competing ontological and epistemic assumptions, the paradigms offered very different visions of the future. In spite of its claims of scientific universalism, the developmental paradigm was firmly rooted in the Western philosophy of Enlightenment and Newtonian physics. Using the linear law of change, developmentalists postulated that all societies are destined to move from a traditional to an advanced stage. Along the way, they were expected to legitimize a rational-legal authority system and a meritoriously based distributive justice system, which would propel them into a "golden age" of liberal democracy and market economy.

The contending dependency paradigm was equally firm in asserting that societies move along a linear path from tribal and other "backward" forms of affiliations into such "enlightened" states of existence as secularism, universalism and global equality. One axiom of *dependencia* held that this path is literally "wired" into the beliefs of humans who strive to liberate themselves from various forms of domination. Once multinational corporations and other tools of capitalism were eliminated, Third World societies were expected to adopt a secular-socialist and universalistic creed. Viewed from this perspective, the revolutionary struggles in Southeast Asia and Latin America were considered not only legitimate expressions of public will but inevitable stages of political change. In the dependency version of linear progression, these egalitarian strivings were moving societies toward the "right" side of history.

Both paradigms were extremely influential in coloring the perception of political reality of Iran. Such perceptions were amplified through "model fitting," that is, the tendency of observers to corroborate their paradigmatic assumption regardless of political reality. Since much of developmental and dependency writing was general in nature and deductive in character, predications were often based more on the belief in the logic of the paradigm that on the detailed knowledge of the situation.

The developmental paradigm viewed Iran as a modernizing country firmly embarked on the path of secularization and market rationality. The shah was perceived as the embodiment of these norms and a leader that could successfully inculcate such values in his traditional subjects. Indeed, developmentally inspired observers considered the belief system of the *ulama* to be a throwback to a "primitive" past and predicted that, as modernization and economic prosperity spread, such sentiments would either disappear or be drastically marginalized. Those who had doubts about linear progression were told that Iran was following the path of Turkey, the then-empirical Mecca of modernization studies.

Even observers who were not happy with the shah's rule did not question the assumption that a successor regime would become an embodiment of democratic legitimacy. It is within this perspective that the opposition was evaluated and its alleged dedication to norms of democracy was vouched for. In reality, the Iranian opposition was a mixed bag, with only some of the constituent groups of the National Front committed to a Western-style polity. Sympathetic scholars were willing to give the benefit of the doubt to the more authoritarian groups out of fear that to do otherwise would be "tantamount to supporting the existing regime" (Chehabi 1990, 33–45). Writing after the revolution, one critic sarcastically commented that some antishah Iranologists believed "that the main source of tension in Iran was a desire on the part of the middle class for more freedom" (Taheri 1988, 94).

The dependency paradigm presented Iran as a case study in the pathology of North-South relations. It decried the capitalist oppression and the widening inequalities between the poor and the rich. In line with their vision for Latin America and other Third World countries, the dependencistas wanted Iran to break its ties itself from the Western economic system, mostly by terminating relations with multinational corporations and the United States. Only then, Iran was expected to move into a socialist stage of development, as Fred Halliday (1979), a Marxist scholar at the Transnational Institute, predicted. Unlike the developmentalists who touted Turkey, the dependencistas pointed out that Iran was close to becoming another India. In spite of their differences, both paradigms expected the "progressive classes"—the middle class, the workers and even the peasants—to be the bearers of political change.

In retrospect, both paradigms missed the mark by linking change to a normatively defined view of "progress." Their ontological and epistemic assumptions minimized the role of religion and culture, a bias compounded by the "culture of disbelief" that was especially strong in the academic-diplomatic world. One observer noted that the "academic-diplomatic view of the of the world, which is secular through and through, is baffled and helpless wherever religious ideas become a serious factor in foreign policy" (Kristol 1987). Another observer explained that Western elites were ignorant of religion, which resulted in an "educated incapacity to take seriously reports dealing with religion from the Middle East" (Codevilla 1992, 17).

The role of culture was equally misunderstood, leading some commentators to accuse the paradigms of "cultural blindness." This type of misperception took a number of forms. First, there was a tendency to marginalize the role of culture in the process of political change. As already noted, the conventional models of revolution, especially the then-fashionable Marxist-structuralist model developed by Skocpol and other fourth generation scholars, tended to ignore human agency in general and the role of culture in particular. Skocpol (1982, 265) would later admit that the Iranian revolution "challenged the expectations about revolutionary causation that I developed through comparative-historical research on France, Russia and China."

Second, even when culture was incorporated into the discussion, it was presented in a comparative style that tended to universalize Western political experience. Setting the tone was the celebrated "civic culture" study of Almond and Verba that used a small number of empirically observable criteria to define the scope of political culture. Limited by the methodological requirements of behaviorism, scholars had little incentive to dwell on the more subterranean manifestations of cultural beliefs. There was a special reluctance to deal with questions of "national character." As one critic complained, such studies were considered unfashionable or even "politically incorrect" because of their association with stereotypes and racism (Fuller 1991, 9). Instead, there was a tendency to describe the Iranian political culture by using "comfortable," Western-sounding labels. Critics would later charge that such labels were simplistic, misleading and contributed to wishful thinking and "fond illusions" about the Iranian and other non-Western societies (Codevilla 1989; Codevilla 1992, 404; Godson 1988; Bozeman 1979; 1988). More generally, there was a paucity of insights into the role of culture in relations between states (Cohen 1991).

Given the complexities of the national character of Iran, Westernized views of political change contributed to the predictive failure. It made it harder to decipher the deeply seated religious idioms and the ingrained mistrust and dissimulation that pervaded the popular culture. In commenting on this failure, one observer described these beliefs as "centuries of tradition, superstition, magic and mythology, cocooned in a xenophobic and ritualistic Islam" (Mottale 1987, 25). Even if this depiction is too harsh, the inability to discern the discourse of the traditional "epistemic community"—the ulama, the bazaaris and peasant migrants—was costly. Deep cultural knowledge was essential because 1979 represented the "first modern revolution whose idiom of discourse is exclusively derived from native sources and whose moral claims are advanced in confrontation with the ideological and political currents of the modern world" (Farsoun and Mashayekhi 1992, ix; Moshiri 1991).

Third, cultural blindness resulted in a tendency to rule out certain directions of change on the grounds that they are "irrational." As noted, assumptions about rationality are critical in the predictive endeavor, but despite decades of research and a vigorous debate, no universally accepted definition or rationality has ever emerged. Assumptions about what is rational are still made on the basis of common sense or conventional definitions of what is "rational." This mode is highly susceptible to the interpretation of individual scholars and the schools of thought they subscribe to, whether consciously or subconsciously. Different paradigmatic assumptions yield different answers as to what is a politically feasible choice and how it would play out given a defined set of circumstances. What is more, assumptions of rationality are closely related to assumptions about risk taking among individuals and collectives.

Since the developmental paradigm tended to use secular-utilitarian criteria for defining what is a rational political belief, a religiously driven high-risk belief system and its attendant behavior were ruled out as virtually impossible. The dependency paradigm, using a form of secular-egalitarianism for assessing rationality, also ruled out the possibility of a purely religious transvaluation of the belief system. Indeed, the debate about the "rationality" of Khomenism has continued unabated to this day. While some observers have tended to view Iran's postrevolutionary behavior as "irrational," others have reluctantly admitted that such nonutilitarian elements as psychic satisfaction or lust for vengeance against the United States might have constituted "rational" behavior. The latter have normally pointed out that though the hostage episode was very costly to Iran both in financial and foreign policy terms, the Iranians considered it a worthy expenditure (Rezun 1990; Amirahmadi 1990, 39; Ioannides 1984, 106).

Fourth, in a religiously driven belief system, people do not always make a working distinction between fact and value. For many of the pious, such a distinction is irrelevant or even harmful (Carter 1993, 223). But for the academic observers, the refusal to make the evidentiary distinction that Western secular culture demands, has been yet another proof of "irrationality." This approach made it difficult to appreciate the popular discourse in Iran that was replete with myths, rumors, conspiracy theories and other fanciful interpretation of reality.

In what proved to be a related influence, paradigmatic thinking provided a misleading map of power in Iran. As will be apparent from the theoretical chapter, predictive efforts are directed at discerning changes in what is perceived as the centers of power in a society. The developmental paradigm, with its heavy overlay of functionalism-structuralism, is biased toward formal centers of power to the exclusion of informal channels and carriers of alternative beliefs. This oversight was compounded by the American tendency to concentrate on a narrowly defined political discourse to the detriment of politically covert venues and cultural themes. The contending dependency paradigm, informed by radical structuralism that offered a critique of the status quo, should have been more sensitive to the emergence of a challenge belief system. However, because of the Marxist focus on the "progressive" classes such as workers and peasants, the beliefs of "regressive" ideational bearers like the mullahs or bazaaris were overlooked. In the end, both paradigms failed to comprehend the ephemeral nature of power in Iran.

Perhaps more significantly, there was no model in Western political tradition that would have predicted the developments in Iran. It is easy to lapse into hindsight to conclude, as many have done, that a fundamentalist revolution was inevitable. This hindsight bias stems from the fact that all successful revolutions acquire an aura of inevitability. However, prior to 1979, there was virtually no scholarly indication that a Shiite theocracy was in the making. This book suggests that, with minor exceptions, students of Iran, like most other Western observers, could not envisage that an obscure cleric would succeed in implementing an equally obscure concept of *velayat-e faqih*. Even today, two decades after the revolution, the nature of fundamentalist Iran eludes easy categorization. As noted, some scholars have argued that it represents a novel form of fascism mixed with elements of the Puritanical revolution in Britain. Even if this diagnosis is correct, it forces the complex belief system of Iran into a Western taxonomic straightjacket.

A more important reason behind the failure to discern the direction of the revolution is related to the permeable boundary between observations on legitimacy and the sense of legitimacy of academic observers. In line with Majone and other students of policy communities, it has been a major assumption of this work that, far from being objective observers, scholars use their own sense of what is a legitimate political order in order to forecast future change. In the case of developmentalism, such a projection is mostly subconscious, formed by the paradigmatically driven tools of analysis. In the case of dependency, this type of projection is more overt and, indeed, mandated by the dictum of academic activism and the scholar's self-appointed role in changing society. Commenting on this phenomenon, one observer noted that "many regional specialists become intellectually and emotionally co-opted by the countries they study. . . . Some even seek to gain support for the country in the U.S. affecting what they write" (Marshall 1989, 121). Majone (1989, 38) argued that social scientists should be forced to advocate their values rather than allowed to hide behind the false pretenses of scientific objectivity.

Whatever the source of bias, this study presented abundant evidence that scholars expected Iran to follow a linear evolution into either a liberal democracy or socialist democracy à la India or Yugoslavia. Many of these observers continued to blame the shah's repressive and corrupt rule for thwarting the democratic impulse in the society. James Bill, Michael Fischer and other proponents of this view argued that the revolution resulted from repression of other modes of discourse rather than from an Islamic revival. Implied in this criticism was the notion that a more democratic system, or a less corrupt one prior to 1979, would have produced a different type of political change. But other observers vehemently denied that Iran could have evolved into a civic society. They pointed out that, given Iranian political culture, there was, as one of them put it, "precious little historically to assume so" (Miklos 1983, 63–64).

Of course, the claim that Iran could have turned out to be a democracy under a different set of circumstances is impossible to substantiate or reject. It is interesting that this question is part of the larger debate of whether Islam is compatible with validity claims that underpin a democracy. A current project on civic culture in Moslem countries identified only three countries in which "long term prospects for successful democratization" may be "better than is commonly assumed" (Norton 1993, 216). Ironically, some of the most vociferous critics of the shah have been forced to admit that Iran might have lacked in Western notions of civic culture. Falk (1980, 84), who had decried the shah's tyranny, subsequently defended the repressive regime of Khomeini on grounds that "human rights in Iran have to be understood within a regional and cultural context where levels of abuse are widespread and severe."

Scholars' tendency to project their own norms of legitimacy has often shaded into a more overt form of academic activism. In the Iranian case a close relationship between scholars and the policy community developed right after World War II and continued until the revolution. The substantial policy participation of academic experts at the policy-making level in evaluating and predicting political change in Iran has belied the often-heard complaint that foreign policy practitioners do not listen to the academy. Many academics advised the State Department and the intelligence community. Those who disagreed with the alleged "Pahlavite" bias of the developmentalists found other venues for influencing the discourse on Iran, including political protest and media influence. Overall, this considerable academic involvement augmented the paradigmatic influence on the predictive process and must share the blame for its failure.

The case of Iran raises a more general concern about the linkage between scholarly writings and the predictive effort. In the IR field scholars serve as "predictive experts," either by engaging in "informed commentary" or being part of more structured forms like Delphi, Baysian, or simulation analysis. But, whatever form they utilize, scholars have not achieved a satisfactory level of predictive success (Hopple and Kuhlman 1981). The detailed analysis of the Iranian evidence supports this finding. Depending on paradigmatic assumptions, personal ideology and professional background, different experts came up with different readings of the legitimacy of the shah's regime, and different scenarios for change. While the developmentalists overestimated the ability of the monarchy to survive, their intellectual opponents underestimated the ability of Khomeini to impose a strict theocracy. The failure to predict the nature of the successor regime was especially glaring in this context.

Indeed, Iran experts have remained divided in their assessment of the sources and causes of the revolution, not to mention the legitimacy of Khomeinism. Scholars have differed with regard to the nature and power of the fundamentalists and the standing of the opposition (Akhavi, 1989; Rezun, 1990; Ramazani 1982; 1986; 1990). With so much of American foreign policy in the post-Carter era focused on establishing a modicum of discourse with fundamentalist Iran, academic hairsplitting over "moderates" and "radicals" and dramatically different assessments on the balance of power in Iran have been less than helpful.

Even if a more consensual approach could emerge—an unlikely prospect given the continuing paradigmatic and ideological divisions in the discipline—there have been additional impediments to a truly fruitful linkage between scholarship and the predictive endeavor. Perhaps the most significant obstacle stems from the fact that scholarship is neither affected by actual political outcomes nor held accountable for forecasting errors. Betts (1982, 829), a leading intelligence expert, observed that "academics are comfortable with theory because they are not burdened with responsibility for political outcome." Unlike in the field of intelligence, in political science research, the stakes are low. Bernstein (1984, 38) commented that "nothing much happens when I misunderstand the causes of the French revolution." To restate Shlomo Gazit, the Israeli intelligence chief, academics, like journalists, even when wrong in their prognosis, do not suffer any consequences. They can change their minds and go on to write more books and articles. In the words of yet another critic, "we all know that the conclusions reached in an article or a book in the academic community may turn out to be completely wrong and have no impact at all anywhere, not even on the author's career." The question of whether the research is right or wrong "isn't necessarily one of the criteria used with respect to judging scholarship in the academic community" (Horowitz 1980, 180).

While it is impossible to prove that this generalized lack of accountability is behind a specific predictive failure, this study makes it clear that scholars who were part of the policy community on Iran experienced no professional consequences. On the contrary, most have contributed to the prodigious research effort to explain the sources of the revolution and evaluate the legitimacy and durability of the fundamentalist republic. Many have adjusted their views to suit the new political reality, reevaluating old assumptions or creating new theories. The most dramatic change occurred in the weight assigned to religion: whereas before the 1978 scholars paid only scant attention to Shiite Islam and the clerical class, religious factors have featured prominently in post-1979 explanations of the origins of revolution. Another interesting change occurred in the analysis of the "masses," often a reference to the collective belief system of Iranians. Whereas before the revolution, the masses were depicted in fairly enlightened terms, post-revolutionary scholarship has often referred to them as "fanatical" or mob-like.

Important as these sources of paradigmatic failures might be, they have to be directly related to the case of Iran. It will be clear from our theoretical discussion that broad intellectual themes are not readily identifiable in the beliefs of foreign policy practitioners or the policy decisions that they make. In fact, studies have demonstrated that Foreign Service officers, not to mention higher policy officials, only seldom follow academic writings. Nevertheless, paradigmatic assumptions are embedded in the intellectual milieu of the discourse community that forms around any given foreign policy issue. Academic writing that reflects paradigmatic lines form powerful, if diffuse channels of influence; policy makers, journalists and other lay observers use the past to interpret current realities. What they find depends to a large extent on "accepted history," a narrative that is "shaped by residues of post mortems and interpretation" (Bobrow 1989).

In the case of Iran, such diffuse paradigmatic impacts were amplified because scholarship was closely associated with applied concerns. What is more important, the dependency paradigm, elements of which were embraced by the New Left, shaped the tenets of New Internationalism that guided the Carter administration policy.

POLICY FAILURE

New Internationalism, with its blend of a moralistic foreign policy and egalitarian oriented regionalism, was a dramatic departure from the traditional realpolitik of Washington. For Carter to succeed in putting America on the "right" side of history, a number of New Internationalist assumptions had to come true. Foremost was the idealist belief in the perfectibility of human nature, which postulated a voluntaristic urge to share resources and a disposition to live in global harmony unmarred by dictates of power. According to this "therapeutic ethic," as one critic called it, "undisciplined" nations could be "chided" for their transgressions and "would learn to behave in a 'proper' and socially responsible way" (Kristol 1987). Another key belief was regionalism, an assumption that regional conflicts are not related to Soviet global ambitions but are "authentic" expressions of history's march toward an appointed egalitarian end-time.

However, once translated into applied policies by the administration, these assumptions run into serious problems. In particular, Soviet behavior in Africa and Latin America did not square with New Internationalist dictates. Still, the administration was reluctant to acknowledge it. To do so would have upset the New Left circles and the left wing of the Democratic Party, which were less than enthusiastic toward Carter. Such a stand would have also gone against the position of the strong New Internationalist contingent within the administration itself.

Assurances about Soviet good behavior were also forthcoming from lay and academic observers. Just before the Soviet invasion to Afghanistan, an article in *Foreign Policy* declared that "given the Soviet foreign policy and behavior during the two decades since Stalin, there is no reason to assume that the Soviet Union will attack a country situated outside its East European front yard" (Pryor 1978). This "conventional wisdom of most government officials, academic experts and others specializing in foreign relations" was only repudiated when Carter admitted that the Soviet action "taught" him to understand the real character of Moscow (Gershman 1980, 13).

The various policies originating in New Internationalism—restrictions on arms sales, efforts to demilitarize the Indian Ocean, mothballing the Safari Club—had eroded the standing of Iran as a regional influence. The human rights policy, the linchpin of Carter's vision for a new international order, had undermined the Pahlavi monarchy and contributed to the dynamics that brought Khomeini to power. This is not to say that a different approach would have prevented a radical change in Iran. The interminable debates among scholars and practitioners about whether the revolution could have been prevented are a testimony to the intractability of the issue. However, New Internationalism blinded the

Carter administration to the complexities of the Iranian political scene and paralyzed it in the face of fast developing realities. The policy failure had stemmed
from a number of sources and took a number of forms.

First, the moralpolitikers were ill-equipped to understand the human dynamics
of the revolution and even less prepared to deal with the deception strategy of
Khomeini. It is a point of considerable significance that questions of surprise
and deception have received more attention in a discourse inspired by realpolitik,
which, by definition, deals with the darker side of human nature (Handel 1981,
11). Indeed, studies equate governmental learning with a "growth of realism,"
that is a capacity to recognize the different elements and processes that are
actually operating in the world. Without such realism, the government is said
to be incapable of an intellectual integration and reflective perspective that are
essential to successful learning (Etheradge 1985, 66–67).

Second, the moralpolitik-inspired policies were opposed by a small but determined group of realpolitikers in the administration. Epitomized by Zbigniew
Brzezinski, the realpolitikers argued that applying New Internationalist policies
to Iran was misguided at best and dangerous at worst. Quite naturally, evaluation
of political reality in Iran became a casualty in the fierce battle between the two
groups whose vision of international reality was nourished by different ontolo-
gies and epistemics. Like hawks and doves in foreign policy debates, they differed in the reasons they gave for interpreting evidence and in the reasons for
expecting "that a course of action would lead to one result rather than another"
(Hollis and Smith 1986). Whereas moralpolitikers saw in the political dynamics
in Iran a reaffirmation that human rights pressures were successful in democ-
ratizing the regime, the realpolitikers warned that the situation was dangerously
unstable and worried that the shah might be replaced with a "greater evil."

Third, the disagreements undermined the ability of the administration to fashion a timely and consensual response to the evolving crisis. The squabbles between the State Department and the National Security Council took time to
resolve and, as a result, decisions became outdated by fast moving events. On
a number of occasions, Carter, under pressure from Brzezinski, seemed to agree
to a specific course of action, only to reverse himself after the intervention of
the State Department. In the meantime, proponents and opponents of a particular
policy were lobbying in public and trying to influence the situation through
unilateral channels.

Bureaucratic tensions in foreign policy making are not uncommon and have
been amply discussed in the bureaucratic model of decision making. The literature is virtually unanimous in holding that bureaucratic struggles often blur the
logic and consistency of key decisions. However, in the case of the Carter
administration, these problems were amplified by a decision to adopt the multiple advocacy model pushed by George and New Left critics of Kissinger's
foreign policy monopoly. The president, who tried to project a democratic and
populist image, embraced this strategy with enthusiasm. In retrospect, this was
a particularly poor choice because, in terms of personality, Carter was ill-suited

to handle conflicting advice. Whether a stronger president might have benefited more from multiple advocacy is impossible to determine. However, an intelligence expert, writing at the height of the Iranian revolution, noted that George's ideas might highlight ambiguity and fail to produce better results than the traditional model (Betts 1978).

The behavior of Carter's foreign policy team undermined another cherished academic assumption known as "groupthink." Developed by Janis (1972) in his classic study by the same name, groupthink postulates that decisionmakers that face a crisis adopt a shared perception of the situation. However, as this study makes clear, Carter's foreign policy team shared precious little perceptual ground. At least three distinctive perceptual foci held during the crisis: the moralpolitikers in the State Department; the realpolitikers in the National Security Council, the Pentagon and the Energy Department; and Ambassador Sullivan in Teheran. The gulf among these divergent perceptions deepened with the growing chaos in Iran. In fact, the differences recorded in the memoirs written by most of the participants, have continued well after the revolution, along with mutual recriminations characteristic of other debates about "losing country x."

Ironically, while the historic debate will undoubtedly continue, Carter himself settled the struggle between the moralpolitikers and the realpolitikers. A few months after the collapse of the Pahlavis, Carter took a number of tentative steps toward returning his foreign policy toward a realpolitik position. In a secret June 1979 meeting, the NSC affirmed American strategic interest in the Gulf and the Indian Ocean and elaborated upon ways to protect the supply of oil, including the creation of a Rapid Deployment Force (Klare 1989). The NSC decisions paved the way to what became known as the Carter doctrine, a reaffirmation of the superiority of American national interest. By his own admission, the holding of American diplomats in Teheran and, especially, the Soviet invasion of Afghanistan "cured" the president from the remaining vestiges of New Internationalism. In his State of the Union address on January 23, 1980, Carter called for protecting American national interest, stronger security measures and fewer restraints on the intelligence community (Woodard 1981).

Crucial as the impact of contradictory advocacy on the administration's policy in Iran was, it is also important to recognize the inherent limits of bureacratic structures to deal with a revolutionary situation. The State Department, and to a lesser degree the CIA and National Security Council, are guided by standard operating procedures (SOPs). Such routines are based on the tacit notion that political change is incremental rather than dramatic and sudden. As Sick (1985, 39) wrote, "the tacit but all pervasive assumption of all governments is that tomorrow will, by and large, be very much like yesterday." Two companion assumptions of SOPs are that the United States has partial control over events and that international relations are made up of rational actions. Such assumptions are geared toward routine diplomacy, or what Sick called the chess game model of international relations; SOPs are rational and cost-effective in the sense that a vast majority of events can be handled via routine diplomacy.

However, the standard approach is hardly adequate in situations that involve revolutionary change. Handel (1980b) used Kuhnian imagery to argue that "revolutionary" or "surprise" diplomacy necessitates radical changes in "well established policies," primarily because the tried and true assumptions of rational action, incremental change and partial control do not work. Sick, speaking from the vantage point of an insider, observed that managing change under revolutionary conditions can be captured best by the hurricane analogy. Indeed, the magnitude and speed of change overwhelmed Carter's foreign policy team and especially the State Department. Already overburdened by the Herculean effort to conclude the Camp David agreement, the State bureaucracy responded in routine and plodding ways, often missing critical opportunities. The tensions between moralpolitikers and realpolitikers exacerbated the problem, leading to heated battles within the State Department and the well-publicized quarrels between State and the National Security Council.

At minimum, the routine character of bureaucratic policy making contributed to the predictive failure in three subtle ways. First, standard thinking is partial to a strict definition of rationality. It was already noted that the underlying paradigmatic assumptions biased American Iran watchers to a utilitarian-rational view of reality. Presumptions about Western-style rationality were even more prevalent among foreign policy practitioners, whose analytic horizon was shaped by the rule-driven view of international relations. The preceding chapter detailed the "comprehension gap" of the State Department and the strong institutional reluctance to accept that the fundamentalist government in Iran was operating within a different rationality context. Years later such sentiments have still informed senior State officials. Harold Saunders (1985, 45) observed that "there was no unity and no leadership except of Khomeini, and I am not sure he had a rational scheme in mind." Warren Christopher (1985, 14) rejected the notion that hostage holding could be rationally explained in terms of psychic satisfaction. He wrote: "I still doubt that any nation would find such a psychic ride to be enough compensation for the massive losses Iran suffered."

Second, standard procedures encourage incrementalism, which one State Department insider defined "as a tendency to decide as little as possible," partially because of the difficulty or reluctance to give "rational considerations" to all alternative options and the myriad of "resulting consequences" (Hilsman 1967, 548). In the case of the Iranian revolution this natural reluctance was exacerbated by the ideological splits within the administration. As Brzezinski argued, the State Department tried to avoid a full-fledged debate out of a reluctance to expose the divisions and provide a platform for the realpolitikers to push for radical solutions. Whatever the motives, an incremental approach is highly detrimental to successful evaluation of revolutionary change.

Third, standard procedures impact the issue of relevance, defined as the process of deciding what elements are pertinent to understanding and predicting change in a given situation. Changing conditions are made up of hundreds of potentially relevant factors that a bureaucracy can consider; what is designated as relevant is normally a function of standard rules of international interaction. There is little doubt that the State Department had gravitated toward a formal definition of the political process and a legalistic approach to the domestic dynamics of foreign countries. Complaints about the lack of imagination, cultural parochialism and poor quality of its analysis were not new. The 1975 Commission on the Organization of Government for the Conduct of Foreign Policy named after its chairman, Ambassador Robert O. Murphy, emphasized the need to update general analysis and prediction. Peter Szanton, the chief researcher for the Murphy commission, and his academic colleague argued that improving State's capacity for foreign assessment should be made first priority (Allison and Szanton 1976, 137–138). Interestingly, Carter used the findings of the Murphy commission to argue that the State Department had not produced a "new idea in 20 years" (in Rubin 1985, 173).

The complexities of the Iranian situation accentuated these shortcomings. In addition to the legalistic approach in identifying relevant factors, there was an ideological emphasis on the supremacy of the human rights issue. Such a view fitted very neatly with State's notion that the Iranian drive to change the political system was fueled by a desire to institute a Western-style liberal democracy. There was a similar relevance bias in dealing with the successor regime. As detailed earlier, in deciding to normalize relations with the Provisional Government, the State Department drew on a number of limited economic factors such as the purported need of the Iranian economy for American goods and services.

What amplified this bias was the decision-making milieu during much of the Iranian revolution. Under normal circumstances, top-level bureaucrats influence the discourse on what constitutes a relevant factor in evaluating political change. However, because of systemic overload caused by Camp David and the reluctance of Secretary Vance to get involved in the Iranian issue, Henry Precht, aided by the human rights faction, was at liberty to impose his definition of reality. This was highly unusual, since country directors normally carry little policy weight (Bacchus 1974, 216; Esterline and Black 1975, 60). Precht used his unexpected influence to push the notion that the post-Pahlavi regime was moderate enough to warrant speedy normalization of relations.

Although the Carter administration bears the lion's share for the policy failure, the role of Congress in the Iranian debacle should not be overlooked. As noted, the Democratically controlled Congress was responsible for turning many of the New Internationalist imperatives into applied policy, most notably in the realm of foreign aid, military sales, human rights and intelligence. With the help of the Human Rights Group of the Coalition for a new Foreign and Military Policy, the Institute for Policy Studies and other like-minded groups, leftists and liberal members of Congress strove to put the United States on the "right" side of history. To do so they had to stop American anticommunist interventions around the world and terminate relations with right-wing authoritarian regimes, many of which faced leftist insurgencies.

The first imperative was addressed through an attempt to reform the CIA along the "New View" philosophy advocated by the New Left. The second goal was to be achieved through a policy of "disassociation" from right-wing governments friendly to the United States. Encouraged by the success of the crusade against the Saigon government, the New Left compiled a "short list" of other potential targets, including South Korea, Nicaragua, the Philippines and Iran.

Iran, which was high on the "short list," became an early test case in the battle between the regionalists and the globalists in Congress. While there were legitimate misgivings about Iran's ability to absorb advanced military equipment and its record on human rights, the debate offered many of the leftists and liberal congressmen an opportunity to show their New Internationalist stripes. In an ironic reversal, the congressional human rights resolution protesting the brutality of Khomeini's rule complicated efforts of the administration to portray the successor regime as moderate.

These actions should be judged in the larger context of the legislative struggle with the executive branch. After demolishing the "imperial presidency" of Nixon, Congress wrestled away a substantial amount of control over foreign policy from the presidency. However, the legislative body was too fragmented and decentralized to sustain a coherent plan of action. Congress was even less equipped to deal with the complex and subtle nature of managing political change; the ideologically heated debates tended to either oversimplify or dramatize the issues and obscured the difficulties involved in the solution that it proposed. William Fulbright (1979), the architect of congressional activism, professed shock at the transformation of Congress from a "hopelessly immobile herd of cattle" in need of prodding to a "stampede" and worried that the legislators went not only too far but in the wrong direction. Others blamed the "post revolutionary anarchic euphoria" for creating the proverbial "535 secretaries of state on the Hill," which left little consistency and predictability in American foreign policy. Even Donald Fraser, the erstwhile human rights crusader, complained that "human rights have gotten out of hand in Congress" (Crabb and Holt, 1980, 35; Franck and Wiesband 1979, 91, 211). It is significant that after the release of the hostages, Congress declined to pursue an inquiry. Hedley Donovan (1985, 170), a Carter adviser, suggested that Congress refused to investigate because there was "too much blame to go around."

Unlike the diffuse paradigmatic influence, the policy level explanations are easier to relate to the predictive failure in Iran. Moreover, policy decisions also had a major role in the intelligence level failure.

INTELLIGENCE FAILURE

In specifying the sources of the intelligence level failure a number of highly interrelated factors should be emphasized. Perhaps the most important one was the New Left–inspired reform of the intelligence community. The Carter-Turner restructuring affected the CIA's ability to discern the revolutionary dynamics in a number of ways. At the organizational level the "New View" reform dismantled much of the human intelligence operation that was considered "corrupt" and ideologically tainted. Among those who were fired or resigned were agents experienced in espionage, undercover and political work, a loss that deprived the agency of skills necessary to assess the balance of power in Iran. At the personal level, the administration's hostility toward the agency and Turner's management style triggered a sense of general malaise. Although it is impossible to assess the level of discontent, Mansur Rafizadeh (1987, 346), the SAVAK representative in the United States, was probably right when he argued that there "were very strong anti-Carter sentiments in the CIA."

The "clean" technical intelligence on which Turner planned to rely was poorly equipped to deal with the complexities and chaos of an esoteric revolution. The absence of political skills in the agency was subsequently acknowledged by the administration. In December 1978, Carter ordered a high-level interagency task force to recommend ways for increasing the CIA's ability to predict political instability in countries of vital importance to the United States. According to reports, the task force criticized the "reliance placed on technical means of intelligence collection" at the expense of human sources. It was also implied that there would be "sweeping changes in existing methods of intelligence collection and evaluation" (Burt 1979). Rebuilding intelligence become even more urgent after Carter shifted foreign policy gears in the wake of the Soviet invasion of Afghanistan. In his State of the Union message in January 1980 the president vowed to "remove unwarranted restraints on American's ability to collect intelligence" (quoted in Cline 1981, 275).

The realization that the New Left crusade against intelligence restricted American ability to evaluate potentially detrimental developments was not limited to the administration. The *New York Times*, which had played a pivotal role in spreading anti-intelligence sentiments, solicited an article on "Rebuilding American Intelligence" from a top expert (Cline 1981, 275). There was also a change of mood in Congress. Legislation aimed at creating an intelligence charter was abandoned; the Intelligence Oversight Act, passed in June 1980, reduced reporting requirements and relaxed standards for covert action. Indeed, the House and Senate intelligence committees called for improving collection and processing of intelligence data (Pickett 1985). Perhaps the best indicator of the declining fortunes of the anti-intelligence lobby was the defeat of many of its advocates, including senators Frank Church and Dick Clark.

While more difficult to assess, the intellectual impact of "New View" intelligence was probably more considerable. The Iranian political culture, not to mention the tactics of the fundamentalists, were permeated by taqieh and other tools of dissimulation and deception. Under the best of circumstances, detecting deception and concealment is not easy, a fact compounded by a paucity of research on the subject. One expert noted that the official school of American intelligence has paid little attention to the subject, although foreign regimes place a premium on dissimulation (Cohen 1989). This attitude was embedded in the intelligence doctrine developed by Sherman Kent, a dominant figure in the Directorate of Intelligence. The doctrine, which reflected many of the paradigmatic assumptions of developmentalism, exuded a strong positivist belief in a "rational" political universe which experts could objectively analyze. It relied heavily on predictions that were considered "objective" truths—derived from what was considered a detached and dispassionate parsing of political reality—and left little room for cultural difference.

The idealistic assumptions of New Internationalism, with its insistence on universal good will and honorable intentions, added to these tendencies. Critics pointed out that such "no fault" intelligence was ill prepared to cope with the fact that prediction involves a struggle with real human opponents who share a different cognitive and behavioral code (Cohen 1989; Shulsky 1993, 192–193). Robert Gates (1989, 114) argued that intelligence managers placed "little value on the idea that people of different cultures have different habits of thought, values and motivations." What is more, "New View" intelligence downplayed the "otherness" of the enemy, leading analysts to assume that the enemy is "like us."

Following the Iranian debacle there was increased interest in the study of deception and misinformation, including an effort to compose a theory of deception (Laqueur 1985, 286). One scholar argued that the intelligence agencies should employ philologists, textual critics and experts in semiotics to uncover misleading and esoteric realities (Bernstein 1984). At a more fundamental level, the intelligence community modified parts of its doctrine to incorporate the critique of Willmore Kendall, an intellectual rival of Kent. Kendall (1949) disputed the epistemic assumption that predictive "truth" can be separated from the values and outlook of analysts and doubted whether political reality is neatly packaged and universally rational.

Even without the impact of the New Left, predicting a revolution would not have been easy. Intelligence doctrine differentiates between two types of surprises—military and political. Political surprise results from a failure to anticipate domestic developments that result in an international change important to American national security. To avert such an outcome, the analytic branch of the CIA was charged with a number of tasks: recognizing early stirrings of change, making estimates of how the situation will develop and alerting policy makers in a timely fashion. While an impressive analytic apparatus was erected over the years, the CIA record of anticipating political change has been less than stellar. What is more, in spite of the fact that political surprise is much more prevalent that military surprise, it has been much less studied (Laqueur 1985, 256; Handel 1980a).

This study points to a number of reasons behind the CIA's difficulties in Iran. Like other cases of radical change, the fundamentalist upheaval was triggered by a *crisis of legitimacy*. Unlike a crisis of performance, a crisis of legitimacy is difficult to investigate not the least because it is conceptually less advanced. The legitimacy matrix of membership/authority system/distributive justice is essentially an analytic construct and cannot be readily identified in the continuous societal discourse. It was already noted that individuals have mixed and hazy notions of legitimacy, and observers called upon to evaluate the legitimacy of a regime tend to project their own sense of what is legitimate onto the situation. At the very least, such a complex situation demands a close examination of public opinion, normally a difficult feat in closed or traditional societies. However, as Razi (1987) pointed out, questions of legitimacy are not only more esoteric, but also peripheral to the interest of practitioners.

As detailed in the study, the intelligence community and the American embassy that supplied much of the daily evaluation focused for most the part on the analysis of the official power elite. There was little understanding of the legitimacy discourse and its key players and efforts to study religious leaders were dismissed as "sociology" (Bill 1988a, 414). That should not be surprising given the fact that the intelligence community tended to view social and economic changes as slowly developing and outside the realm of short-term forecasts. The infrequent forays into monitoring public opinion lacked depth and sophistication; little attention was paid to cultural and theological issues and the anti-Americanism of the core fundamentalist philosophy was not fully recognized until the attack on the embassy. In the words of one critic, the intelligence service was "ahistorical and anticultural" and given to an emphasis on materialism, economic determinism and current events (Bozeman 1988, 129). Stansfield Turner (1985, 125) subsequently acknowledged that the CIA did not have anthropologists and sociologists that could deal with the situation. Richard E. Bissel (1985, 256), a former high-level CIA official, would later comment that "the lessons of Teheran 1978 will long be burned in the minds of Washington policymakers," teaching them that inattention to public opinion could be very costly.

Even with a better understanding of the public discourse, there is no guarantee of a successful prediction. The theoretical discussion suggests that revolutionary change involves a dynamic interaction of a large number of factors that suddenly bifurcate into directions that are difficult to forecast. Statistically, forecasting involves an attempt to relate a stochastic variable (crisis or opportunity) to a dynamically evolving situation that is composed of a large number of highly correlated events. The occurrence of any of these events depends upon whether a number of other events are likely to occur or not (Moritz 1978). Although the CIA apparently developed cross-impact analysis, a forecasting tool that determines how a change in the probability of occurrence of one event affects the probability of all other events, such an analysis is confined to variables that are relatively easy to measure. The Iranian revolution was driven by hard-to-measure symbolic events and a mob dynamic that left observers and participants equally amazed at the outcome.

The sheer novelty of some of the situations had a profoundly adverse impact on the predictive process. It is well known that novel systemic arrangements may produce events that are totally unanticipated. Such occurrences destroy the usefulness of the existing empirical generalizations used for forecasting and can turn historical parallels into false and perilous analogies (Freeman and Job 1979; Brodin 1978; M. A. Turner 1991). The notion that some "lessons of history" may be misleading is especially noteworthy given the fact that intelligence officials, like other foreign policy practitioners, are inclined to filter new phenomena through the prism of past experience. This type of routine thinking is at the heart of the predictive blunder and undoubtedly accounted for the failure to understand the nature of Khomeinism and the hostage taking.

Using an established framework of analysis can create the "decoy effect," that is the danger of paying attention to a well-defined problem at the expense of an important but ill-structured problem in the background. The decoy phenomenon is common in organizations like the CIA where conceptual frameworks are translated into analytic routines and decision-making procedures, cementing the notion that some issues are important to the understanding of the problem at hand and others are not (Turner 1976). In the Iranian case, there was a strong partiality for the study of empirical indices of performance, but little inclination to follow the more esoteric field of normative judgment, culture and spirituality. The diffuse notion of legitimacy that was at the heart of the crisis was beyond the pale of the intelligence purview.

The fast-paced dynamics of revolutionary change posed additional problems for the intelligence community. The most difficult task in this context is to determine when political unrest is about to cross the threshold beyond which the regime loses control. Such thresholds can be identified only in retrospect since, as demonstrated in the theoretical part of this book, bifurcation can occur suddenly and randomly, pushed by cumulating events or by a singular dramatic occurrence. For example, the Black Friday incident has been normally viewed as the threshold event in the revolution, but in actuality the bifurcation might have occurred during the Abadan fire or in the course of the general strikes in the fall.

In speculating about the threshold condition, the intelligence community is invariably betting on certain patterns of power distribution. Here again, the fast-moving events made it hard to identify the real power holders and the likely coalition they would form. In the liminal stage of the revolution, power is diffuse and ever changing—not even the eventual winner or winners can be sure that their cause will prevail. A former American ambassador made the undoubtedly true observation that "not even Khomeini six months earlier could have predicted the force and rapidity of the uprising which ended with his assumption of power" (Herz 1979, 25).

This problem is compounded when clandestine or semiclandestine movements articulate and implement the challenge belief system. Under such conditions, the question of who speaks for whom and with what authority is hard to answer. The reports are fragmentary, anecdotal and, at times, misleading. When trying to build a political road map the intelligence community is at the mercy of these larger sociopolitical dynamics. One expert commented that under such circumstances the "light—or the darkness—must come from within the analyst" (Codevilla 1992, 21). But as this research repeatedly showed, the Iranian road map was lacking in good and reliable detail. Initially, the power and the representatives of the shah were overestimated and that of the opposition disregarded. Ironically, when the agency subsequently warned that the fundamentalists were in a position to overwhelm the moderate forces, its forecast clashed with official State Department doctrine that the Provisional Government was the legitimate repository of national power and legitimacy.

Given these difficulties and mindful of the high stakes involved, the intelligence community tends to err on the side of caution. Factors that can lead to revolutionary upheavals exist in many societies, but unlike scholars who can issue vague warnings, intelligence officials pay professionally for alarmist forecasts. Over the years, the shah had survived a large number of challenges; declaring his premature demise would have earned pessimistic analysts the unenviable title of "Chicken Little." Ironically, caution was also in order because the New Left chastised the CIA for producing alarmist reports. The intelligence agencies were accused of inflating danger either to bolster budgetary requests or to show that "they are doing a good job and that competing organizations in the intelligence field are less effective" (Halperin 1974, 145).

That consideration of the larger bureaucratic and political milieu play a role in the forecasting process points to another source of predictive failure. Left to their own devises, individual analysts could have probably produced more nuanced and intellectually sophisticated analysis. Many of them are trained academics whose natural inclination is to write in ways that reflect the ambiguity and complexity of political change. However, busy bureaucrats and politicians see ambiguity and complexity as irritants and impediments to good decision-making. There is even less tolerance for theoretically laden concepts such as discourse, legitimacy or collective belief system. In the words of one observer, "policymaking elites and intelligence bureaucracies are not readily disposed toward dealing with theories in a conscious, rigorous or sustained manner" (Intelligence and crisis forecasting 1983, 823). Experts have emphasized that the cognitive barriers of intelligence consumers are an important factor in intelligence failures (Betts 1978; Handel, 1988).

Focusing on the cognitive needs of intelligence consumers raises the broader issue of cognition and predictive failures. A large literature on heuristics indicates that people rely on suboptimal information processing techniques such as availability, representativeness, misguided parsimony and other biased assessments of information (Nisbett and Ross 1980). In spite of considerable training, intelligence analysts are not immune to such heuristic pitfalls. Perfecting norms and procedures for analysis or larger organizational reforms are only a partial answer to these problems. As leading experts on intelligence have argued, reforming and rehabilitating cognitive processes is next to impossible and may create a dangerous illusion that an analytic or systemic reform would guarantee good predictive scores (Hopple 1984; Betts 1978). Still, this study suggests that analysts and policymakers should adopt what one expert called "conscious epistemology" (Godson, 1989). In a nutshell, analysts have to be self-conscious about the paradigms that guide their work and have to ensure that policymakers understand the major premises that underlay forecasts. In Iran, conscious epistemology would have helped the analysts and their consumers to understand the implications of developmentalism and dependency on forecasting political change.

This is not to say that addressing this or other suggestions that were offered in this summary is easy or even possible. The dimensions that make up forecasting—the paradigmatic, the policy and the intelligence—harbor numerous potential pitfalls. Their interactive and interlocking nature makes predictive failures even more difficult to avoid. This conclusion is in line with the observations of intelligence experts and practitioners alike. Betts (1978) has spoken about the inevitability of intelligence failures and Jervis (1986) has noted that there are limits to predictability because the "world is not deterministic." Such limits are especially noticeable in a revolutionary situation that is driven by a legitimacy crisis. As John Stempel (1981, 263) the political officer in the embassy wrote: "politics in a situation so uncertain that the legitimacy of the entire system is called into question, is an essentially unpredictable art."

UNDERSTANDING THE "GREAT UNKNOWN": THE IRANIAN REVOLUTION AND PREDICTING POLITICAL CHANGE IN THE FUTURE

It is customary in the "summing up" chapter of a work such as this to offer some suggestions for improving the prediction of political change. Indeed, the post–Cold War period has presented unprecedented problems in this realm. The tried and true concepts of the past have been replaced with novel challenges of dealing with international terrorism and the danger of nuclear, chemical and biological warfare conducted either by terrorist groups or by renegade states. The growth of Muslim fundamentalism has spanned the New Islamic International, which is dedicated to challenging the United States and her allies. Last, but not least, economic issues have become vastly more important to national security considerations. In a world of economic interdependence, the economic stability and prosperity of any given country depends on a series of interlocking and incredibly complex equations that involve numerous markets. As the so-called "high politics" of diplomacy and military balance of power are being replaced by the "low politics" of trade, monetary policies and movement in global stock markets, much of the forecasting effort has become diffuse and multifaceted.

To the extent that this study offers more general insights into the predictive process in closed societies, the conclusions are sobering. To be successful, intelligence warnings have to be issued early enough to alert the administration and enable it to intervene effectively whether to avert a crisis or seize an opportunity. In cases of radical change, such a judgment can only be made by following the legitimacy discourse of a given society and determining whether a normative change is likely to occur in any of the three dimensions of the collective belief system and affect the political structure. Of utmost importance in this context is to follow potential challenges to the belief system and the elites that articulate it, even if they fall outside the accepted definition of power and influence.

The focus on a collective belief system also highlights the linkage between the legitimacy of the authority system and economic performance. Economic standards are important in maintaining the legitimacy of the authority system, whether it is totalitarian, authoritarian or democratic. At the same time this formula is not deterministic: Highly coercive regimes can survive serious performance crises by suppressing a challenge system and the elites that advocate it. Alternatively, regimes can manipulate nationalistic or religious feelings to survive economic hardship, as the case of Iraq and Serbia demonstrates. Policymakers who put faith in economic sanctions as an instrument of political change in foreign societies should be aware of such factors.

The absence of deterministic relations in the nexus of legitimacy and performance posits a challenge to any linear notion of future political change. The current wave of democratization around the globe has been underpinned by the allure of market economy. But performance failures can erode the legitimacy of a democratic authority system and even delegitimize market norms themselves. The halting progress of market democracy in Russia and other former Soviet republics underscores this theme.

The same formula explains why Islamic fundamentalism is still on the increase. Prevented by religious norms from embracing principles of market economy, many Muslim societies are locked in a circle of poverty and high demographic growth that reinforces the legitimacy of a distinctive non-Western and nonmarket belief system. Indeed, some futurologists have argued that in the twenty-first century there will be a clash between the Western and Muslim "civilizations."

While this study cannot confirm these predictions, it draws attention to the legitimacy formulas that drive change. This and other issues that the current analysis highlighted calls for theoretical developments that are at present rarely explored, and therein lie the challenges for future studies of predictive intelligence.

References

Abidi, A.H.H. 1979. The Iranian revolution: Its origins and dimension. *International Studies* 18: 129–161.

———. 1988. *The calculus of consent*. New Delhi: The Patriot Publishers.

Abrahamian, E. 1978a. Iran: The political challenge. *MERIP* 8, no. 69: 3–8.

———. 1978b. Iran: The political crisis intensifies. *MERIP* 8, no. 71: 3–6.

———. 1979a. The crumbling myth of the good shah. *The Progressive* 43: 14–16.

———. 1979b. Iran in revolution: The opposition forces. *MERIP* 9, nos. 75/76: 3–8.

———. 1989. *Radical Islam: The Iranian mojahedin*. London: I. B. Tauris & Co.

———. 1993. *Khomenism: Essays on the Islamic republic*. Berkeley: University of California Press.

Abshire, D. M. 1979. *Foreign policy makers: President vs. Congress*. Beverly Hills: Sage.

Adelman, I., and Minh, J. M. 1982. Politics in Latin America: A catastrophe model. *Journal of Conflict Resolution* 26: 590–620.

Afshar, H. 1985. The Iranian theocracy. In H. Afshar, ed., *Iran: A revolution in turmoil*. Albany: State University of New York Press.

Aitken, J. 1993. *Nixon: A life*. Washington, D.C.: Regnery Publishing.

Ajami, F. 1981. *The Arab predicament: Arab political thought and practice since 1967*. Cambridge: Cambridge University Press.

Akhavi, S. 1989. Reflection on a decade of scholarship on the Iranian revolution: Background to two recent perspectives in the literature. *Middle East Journal* 43: 289–295.

Alam, A. 1992. *The Shah and I: The confidential diary of Iran's royal court 1969–1977*. New York: St. Martin's Press.

Alaolmolki, N. 1987. The new Iranian left. *Middle East Journal* 41: 218–233.

Albert, D. H. 1980. Introduction: The text and the subtext of the Iranian revolution. In

D. H. Albert, ed., *Tell the American people: Perspectives on the Iranian revolution*. Philadelphia: Movement for a New Society.

Al-e Ahmad, J. 1984. *Occidentosis: A plague from the West*. Trans. R. Campbell. Berkeley, Calif.: Mizan Press.

Alexander, Y., and Nanes, A., eds. 1980. *The United States and Iran: A documentary history*. Frederick, Md.: University Publications of America.

Alger, H. 1972. The opposition role of the ulama in twentieth century Iran. In N. R. Keddie, ed., *Scholars, saints and sufis: Muslim religious institutions in the Middle East since 1500*. Berkeley: University of California Press.

———. 1983. *The roots of the Islamic revolution*. London: The Open Press.

Alker, H., Jr., and Russett, B. M. 1966. Indices for comparing inequality. In R. L. Merritt and S. Rokkan, eds., *Comparing nations: The use of quantitative data in cross-national research*. New Haven: Yale University Press.

Allison, G., and Szanton, P. 1976. *Remaking foreign policy: The organization connection*. New York: Basic Books.

Almond, G. 1966. Political theory and political science. *The American Political Science Review* 60: 869–879.

———. 1990. *A discipline divided: Schools and sects in political science*. New York: Basic Books.

Almond, G., and Verba, S. 1965. *The civic culture*. Boston: Little Brown.

Alpher, J. 1980. The Khomeini international. *Washington Quarterly* 3: 54–74.

Ameringer, C. D. 1990. *U.S. foreign intelligence: The secret side of American history*. Lexington, Mass.: Lexington Books.

Amirahmadi, H. 1988. Introduction: From ideology to pragmatic policy in post-revolutionary Iran. In H. Amirahmadi and M. Parvin, eds., *Post-revolutionary Iran*. Boulder: Westview Press.

———. 1990. *Revolution and economic transition: The Iranian experience*. Albany: State University of New York Press.

Amirie, A., and Twichell, H. A. 1978. Synthesis. In A. Amirie and H. A. Twichell, eds., *Iran in the 1980s*. Teheran: Institute for International Political and Economic Studies.

Amuzagar, J. 1977. *Iran: An economic profile*. Washington, D.C.: The Middle East Institute.

Anderson, M. 1986. Cultural concatention of deceit and secrecy. In R. W. Mitchell and N. S. Thompson, eds., *Deception: Perspectives on human and nonhuman deceit*. Albany: State University of New York Press.

———. 1992. *Imposters in the temple*. New York: Simon & Schuster.

Anderson, P. A. 1983. Normal failures in the foreign policy advisory process. *World Affairs* 148: 148–175.

Apter, D. E. 1965. *The politics of modernization*. Chicago: University of Chicago Press.

———. 1974. *Political change*. London: Frank Cass.

Arani, S. 1980. Iran: From the Shah's dictatorship to Khomeini's demagogic theocracy. *Dissent* 27: 9–26.

Argyris C., and Schon, D. A. 1978. *Organizational learning: A theory of action perspective*. Reading, Mass.: Addison-Wesley.

Arjomand, S. A. 1980. The state and Khomeini's Islamic order. *Iran Studies* 13: 147–164.

———. 1986. Iran's Islamic revolution in comparative perspective. *World Politics* 38: 383–414.

———. 1988. *The turban and the crown: The Islamic revolution in Iran.* New York: Oxford University Press.

Armajani, Y. 1979. What the U.S. needs to know about Iran. *Worldview* 22: 13–19.

Armstrong, S. 1980a. Carter held hope even after Shah had lost his. *Washington Post*, October 25.

———. 1980b. Failing to heed the warning of revolutionary Iran. *Washington Post*. October 26.

———. 1980c. U.S. urged "Crackdown on opposition." *Washington Post*, October 28.

———. 1980d. Vance deflects a call for toughness. *Washington Post*, October 27.

Ashraf, A., and Banuazizi, A. 1985. The state, classes and modes of mobilization in the Iranian revolution. *State, Culture & Society* 1: 3–38.

Askari, H., Cummings, J. T., and Izbudak, M. 1977. Iran's migration of skilled labor to the United States. *Iran Studies* 10: 3–35.

Ayoob, M. 1979. Two faces of political Islam: Iran and Pakistan compared. *Asian Survey* 19: 535–546.

Azar, E. E., and Burton, J. W. 1986. Lessons for great power relations. In E. E. Azar and J. W. Burton, eds., *International Conflict Resolution: Theory and Practice.* Boulder: Lynne Rienner.

Azar, E. E., and Farah, N. N. 1981. The structure of inequalities and protracted social conflict: A theoretical framework. *International Interaction* 7: 317–335.

Azari, F., ed. 1983. *Women of Iran: The conflict with fundamentalist Islam.* London: Ithaca Press.

Azimi, F. 1989. *Iran: The crisis of democracy.* London: I. B. Tauris & Co.

Bacchus, W. I. 1974. *Foreign policy and the bureaucratic process.* Princeton: Princeton University Press.

Bakhash, S. 1984. *Reign of the Ayatollahs: Iran and the Islamic revolution.* New York: Basic Books.

———. 1989. The politics of land, law and social justice in Iran. *Middle East Journal* 43: 186–201.

Ball, G. W. 1982. *The past has another pattern: Memoirs.* New York: W. W. Norton.

Bamford, J. 1982. *The puzzle palace.* London: Sidgwick & Jackson.

Bani Sadr, A. 1978. The present economic system spells ruin for the future: An interview. In A. Nobari, ed., *Iran erupts.* Stanford: The Iran-American Documentation Group.

———. 1991. *My turn to speak: Iran, the revolution & secret deals with U.S.* Trans. W. Ford. New York: Brassy's Macmillan.

Bani Sadr, A., and Vielle, P. 1978. Iran and the multinationals. In A. Nobari, ed., *Iran erupts.* Stanford: The Iran-American Documentation Group.

Banks, M. 1985. The inter paradigm debate. In M. Light and A.J.R. Groom, eds., *International relations: A handbook of current theory.* Boulder: Lynne Rienner.

Baraheni, R. 1977a. America in cahoots with Shah. *The Nation*, March 12.

———. 1977b. *The crowned cannibals: Writings on repression on Iran.* New York: Vintage Books.

Baran, P. A. 1957. *The political economy of growth.* New York: Monthly Review Press.

Baran, P. A., and Sweezy, P. M. 1966. *Monopol capital: An essay on the American economic order.* New York: Modern Reader Paperback.

Barnet, R. J. 1968. *Intervention and revolution: The United States in the Third World*. New York: The New American Library.

———. 1969. *The economy of death*. New York: Atheneum.

———. 1971. The illusion of security. *Foreign Policy* 3: 71–87.

———. 1977. *The giants: Russia and America*. New York: Touchstone Books.

Barnet, R. J., and Muller, R. E. 1974. *Global reach: The power of multinational corporations*. New York: Simon & Schuster.

Barnet, R. J., and Raskin, M. G. 1966. *After 20 years: The decline of NATO and the search for a new policy in Europe*. New York: Random House.

Barnett, M. N. 1996. Israel in the world economy: Israel as an East Asian state? In M. Barnett, ed., *Israel in comparative perspective: Challenging the conventional wisdom*. Albany: State University of New York Press.

Barron, J. 1985. *KGB today: The hidden hand*. New York: Berkley Books.

Bashiriyeh, H. 1984. *The state and revolution in Iran, 1962–1982*. London: Croom Helm.

Bay, C. 1965. Politics and pseudopolitics. A critical evaluation of some behavioral literature. *American Political Science Review* 59: 39–51.

Bayat, A. 1987. *Workers and revolution in Iran*. London: Zed Books.

Bazelon, D. T. 1963. *The paper economy*. New York: Random House.

Beauchamp, T. L. 1977. The justification of reverse discrimination. In W. T. Blackstone and R. D. Heslep, eds., *Social justice and preferential treatment*. Athens: The University of Georgia Press.

Becker, G. S., and Tomes, N. 1979. An equilibrium theory of the distribution of income and intergenerational mobility. *Journal of Political Economy* 87: 1153–1189.

Beeman, W. O. 1990. Double demons: Cultural impedance in U.S.–Iranian understanding. In M. Rezun, ed., *Iran at the crossroads: Global relations in a turbulent decade*. Boulder: Westview Press.

Beetham, D. 1991. *The legitimation of power*. Atlantic Highlands, N.J.: Humanities Press International.

Behdad, S. 1988. The political economy of Islamic planning in Iran. In H. Amirahmadi and M. Parvin, eds., *Post-revolutionary Iran*. Boulder: Westview Press.

Behnan, M. R. 1979. Misreading Iran through U.S. news media. *Christian Science Monitor*, March 12.

Behrooz, M. 1990. Trends in the foreign policy of the Islamic republic of Iran. In N. R. Keddie and M. J. Gasiorowski, eds., *Neither East nor West: Iran. the Soviet Union, and the United States*. New Haven: Yale University Press.

Bell, C. 1980. *President Carter and foreign policy: The costs of virtue?* Canberra: The Australian National University.

Bell, D. 1962. *The end of ideology: On the exhaustion of political ideas in the fifties*. Rev. ed. New York: The Free Press.

Benard, C., and Khalilzad, Z. 1984. *"The government of god"—Iran's Islamic republic*. New York: Columbia University Press.

Ben-Dor, G. 1974. Corruption, institutionalization and political development: The revisionist thesis revisited. *Comparative Political Studies* 7: 63–83.

Berger, P. L. 1977. Are human rights universal. *Commentary* 64: 60–63.

Bernstein, A. H. 1984. The academic researcher and the intelligence analyst: How and where the twain might meet. In B. W. Watson and P. M. Dunn, eds., *Military intelligence and the universities: A study of an ambivalent relationship*. Boulder: Westview Press.

Betts, R. K. 1978. Analysis, war and decision: Why intelligence failures are inevitable. *World Politics* 31: 61–89.

———. 1980. Intelligence for policymaking. *Washington Quarterly* 3: 106–117.

———. 1982. Warning dilemmas. Normal theory vs. exceptional theory. *Orbis* 26: 828–833.

Betts, R. K., and Huntington, S. P. 1985–86. Dead dictators and rioting mobs: Does the demise of authoritarian rulers lead to political instability? *International Security* 10: 112–146.

Bialer, S. 1983. The question of legitimacy. In D. Held et al., eds., *States and societies*. Oxford: Basil Blackwell.

Bienen, H. S., and Gersovitz, M. 1986. Consumer subsidy cuts, violence and political stability. *Comparative Politics* 19: 25–44.

Biersteker, T. J. 1987. *Multinationals, the state, and control of the Nigerian economy*. Princeton: Princeton University Press.

Bill, J. A. 1977. The American analysis of Iranian politics. *Iranian Studies* 10: 164–195.

———. 1978/79. Iran and the crisis of 1978. *Foreign Affairs* 57: 323–342.

———. 1982. Power and religion in revolutionary Iran. *Middle East Journal* 36: 22–47.

———. 1984. US foreign policy in Iran: A system of reinforced failure. In D. P. Forsythe, ed., *American foreign policy in an uncertain world*. Lincoln: University of Nebraska Press.

———. 1988a. *The eagle and the lion: The tragedy of American-Iranian relations*. New Haven: Yale University Press.

———. 1988b. *The Shah, the ayatollah, and the United States*. New York: Foreign Policy Association.

Billig, M. 1976. *Social psychology and intergroup relations*. London: Academic Press.

Billington, J. H. 1987. Realism and vision in American foreign policy. *Foreign Affairs* 65: 630–652.

Binder, L, et al. 1971. *Crisis and sequence in political development*. Princeton: Princeton University Press.

Bissel, R. E. 1985. Implication of anti-Americanism for U.S. foreign policy. In A. Z. Rubinstein and D. E. Smith, eds., *Anti-Americanism in the Third World: Implications for U.S. foreign policy*. New York: Praeger.

Black, I., and Morris, B. 1991. *Israel's secret wars: A history of Israel's intelligence services*. New York: Grove Weidenfeld.

Block, F. 1979. Trilaterism and inter-capitalism conflict. In H. Sklar, ed., *Trilaterate commission on elite planning for world management*. Boston: South End Press.

Bobrow, D. B. 1989. Stories remembered and forgotten. *Journal of Conflict Resolution* 33: 187–210.

Books in Review. 1979. *Middle East Review* 11: 59.

Bornschier, V., and Chase-Dunn, C. 1978. Cross-national evidence of the effect of foreign investment and aid on economic growth and inequality: A survey of findings and a reanalysis. *American Journal of Sociology* 84: 651–683.

Boulding, K. E. 1962. *Conflict and defense: A general theory*. New York: Harper.

Bozeman, A. B. 1979. Iran: U.S. foreign policy and the tradition of Persian statecraft. *Orbis* 23: 387–402.

———. 1988. Political intelligence in non-western societies. In R. Godson, ed., *Comparing foreign intelligence: The U.S., the USSR, U.K. and the Third World*. McLean, Va.: Pergamon Brassey.

Bradley G. W. 1983. Book review. *American Political Science Review* 77: 239–241.

Braley, R. 1984. *Bad news: The foreign policy of the New York Times*. Chicago: Regnery Gateway.

Bratton, M. 1982. Patterns of development and underdevelopment. *International Studies Quarterly* 26: 333–372.

Brecher, M., and Jones, P. 1986. *Crisis and change in world politics*. Boulder: Westview Press.

Brenner, P. 1983. *The limits and possibilities of Congress*. New York: St. Martin's Press.

Brinton, C. 1965. *The anatomy of revolution*. New York: Vintage Book.

Brodin, K. 1978. Surprise attack: The case of Sweden. *Journal of Sociological Studies* 1: 98–110.

Brown, M. B. 1985. *Models in political economy: A guide to the argument*. Boulder: Lynne Rienner.

Brzezinski, Z. 1968. America in the Technetronic Age. *Encounter* 30: 16–26.

———. 1970. *Between two ages*. New York: Viking Press.

———. 1971. Half past Nixon. *Foreign Policy* 3: 3–21.

———. 1972. How the cold war played. *Foreign Affairs* 51: 181–209.

———. 1973. U.S. foreign policy: The search for focus. *Foreign Affairs* 51: 708–727.

———. 1976. America in a hostile world. *Foreign Policy* 23: 65–96.

———. 1983. *Power and principle: Memoirs of the national security adviser*. New York: Farrar, Straus & Giroux.

Brzezinski, Z., and Huntington, S. P. 1971. *Political power: USSR/USA. Similarities and contrasts, convergence or evolution*. New York: The Viking Press.

Budge, I., Crewe, I., and Farlie, D. 1976. *Party identification and beyond: Representation of voting and party competition*. London: John Wiley & Sons.

Bull, H. 1966. A view from abroad: Consistency under pressure. *Foreign Affairs* 57: 441–462.

———. 1979. International theory: The case for a classical approach. *World Politics* 18: 361–377.

Burns, J. F. 1999. Iranian's career: From hostage-taker to reformer. *New York Times*, October 13, 1999.

Burrell, G., and Morgan, G. 1985. *Sociological paradigms and organizational analysis*. Portsmouth, N.H.: Heinemann.

Burt, R. 1979. U.S. seeks ways to gauge foreign national stability. *New York Times*, January 29.

Burton, J. W. 1979. *Deviance, terrorism and war: The process of solving unsolved social and political problems*. New York: St. Martin's Press.

———. 1985. World society and human needs. In M. Light and A.J.R. Groom, eds., *International relations: A handbook of current theory*. Boulder: Lynne Rienner.

Butler, D., and Stokes, D. 1971. *Political change in Britain*. Harmondsworth, England: Penguin Books.

Cable, L. 1991. Piercing the mist—limited and ambiguous conflict. *International Journal of Intelligence and Counterintelligence* 4: 59–78.

Campbell, J. C. 1977. Oil power in the Middle East. *Foreign Affairs* 56: 89–110.

Campbell, J. F. 1971. *The foreign affairs fudge factory*. New York: Basic Books.

Canetti, E. 1962. *Crowds and power*. New York: Viking Press.

Cardoso, F. H. 1973. Associated-dependent development: Theoretical and practical implications. In A. Stepan, ed., *Authoritarian Brazil*. New Haven: Yale University Press.

———. 1977. The consumption of dependency theory in the United States. *Latin American Research Review* 12: 7–24.

Cardoso, F. H., and Faletto, E. 1979. *Dependency and development in Latin America*. Berkeley: University of California Press.

Carter, J. 1979. Humane purposes in foreign policy. In B. M. Rubin and E. P. Spiro, eds., *Human rights and U.S. foreign policy*. Boulder: Westview Press.

———. 1982. *Keeping faith: Memoirs of a president*. Toronto: Bantam Books.

Carter, J., and Carter, R. 1987. *Everything to gain: Making the most of the rest of your life*. New York: Random House.

Carter, S. L. 1993. *The culture of disbelief: How American law and politics trivializes religious devotion*. New York: Basic Books.

Cauthen, K. 1969. *Science, secularization and God: Toward a theology of the future*. Nashville: Abindgdon Press.

Chalmers, D., and Robinson, C. H. 1982. Why power contenders choose liberalization. *International Studies Quarterly* 26: 3–26.

Chase-Dunn, C. 1975. The effect of international economic dependence on development of equality: A cross-national study. *American Sociological Review* 40: 720–738.

Chehabi, H. E. 1990. *Iranian politics and religious modernism: The Liberation Movement of Iran under the shah and Khomeini*. Ithaca, N.Y.: Cornell University Press.

———. 1991. Religion and politics in Iran: How theocratic is the Islamic republic. *Daedalus* 120: 69–91.

———. 1995. The provisional government and the transition from monarchy to Islamic republic in Iran. In Y. Shain and J. Lintz, eds., *Between states: Interim government and democratic transition*. Cambridge: Cambridge University Press.

Chomsky, N. 1969. *American power and the new mandarins*. New York: Pantheon.

Christian Science Monitor.

Christopher, W. 1979. The diplomacy of human rights: The first year. In B. M. Rubin and E. P. Spiro, eds., *Human rights and U.S. foreign policy*. Boulder: Westview Press.

———. 1985. Introduction. In P. H. Kreisberg, ed., *American hostages in Iran*. New Haven: Yale University Press.

Chubin, S. 1994. *Iran's national security policy: Intentions, capabilities & impact*. Washington, D.C.: The Carnegie Endowment for International Peace.

Chubin, S., and Zabih, S. 1974. *The foreign relations of Iran*. Berkeley: University of California Press.

Cline, R. S. 1981. *The CIA under Reagan, Bush and Casey*. Washington, D.C.: Acropolis Books.

Cnudde, C. 1973. Stochastic processes and political theory. *Comparative Political Study* 6: 255–260.

Cockcroft, J. D. 1980. On the ideological and class character of Iran's anti-imperialist revolution. In G. Stauth, ed., *Iran: Precapitalism, capitalism and revolution*. Fort Lauderdale: Breitenbach Publishers.

Codevilla, A. M. 1989. Political warfare. In F. R. Barnett and C. Lord, eds., *Political warfare and psychological operations*. Washington, D.C.: National Defense University.

————. 1992. *Informing statecraft: Intelligence for a new century*. New York: The Free Press.

Cogan, C. G. 1990. Not to offend: Observations on Iran, the hostages and the hostage rescue mission. Ten years later. *Comparative Strategy* 9: 415–483.

Cohen, E. 1989. The "no fault" view of intelligence. In R. Godson, ed., *Intelligence requirements for the 1990s: Collection, analysis, counterintelligence and covert action*. Lexington, Mass.: Lexington Books.

Cohen, R. 1991. *Negotiating across cultures: Communication obstacles in international diplomacy*. Washington, D.C.: United States Institute of Peace Research.

Colburn, F. D. 1994. *The vogue of revolution in poor countries*. Princeton: Princeton University Press.

Coleman, K. M. 1977. *Self delusion in U.S. foreign policy: Conceptual obstacles to understanding Latin America*. Erie: Northwestern Pennsylvania Institute for Latin America Studies.

Constantinides, G. C. 1993. *Intelligence and espionage: An analytical bibliography*. Boulder: Westview Press.

Converse, P. E. 1964. The nature of belief systems in mass public. In D. E. Apter, ed., *Ideology and discontent*. New York: The Free Press of Glencoe.

————. 1987. Changing conceptions of public opinion in the political process. *Public Opinion Quarterly* 51: 512–525.

Copeland, M. 1989. *The game player: Confession of the CIA's original political operative*. London: Aurum Press.

Coser, L. A. 1964. *The function of social conflict*. Glencoe, Ill.: The Free Press.

Cottam, R. W. 1978a. Arms sales and human rights: The case of Iran. In R. D. Gastill, ed., *Freedom in the world*. Boston: G. K. Hall.

————. 1978b. Letter to the editor. *Washington Post*, October 2.

————. 1979. *Nationalism in Iran*. Pittsburgh: Pittsburgh University Press. Updated through 1978.

————. 1980. American policy and the Iranian crisis. *Iranian Studies* 13: 279–305.

————. 1988. *Iran and the United States: A Cold War case study*. Pittsburgh: Pittsburgh University Press.

————. 1990a. Inside revolutionary Iran. In R. K. Ramazani, ed., *Iran's revolution: The search for consensus*. Bloomington: Indiana University Press.

————. 1990b. U.S. and Soviet response to Islamic political militancy. In N. R. Keddie and M. J. Gasiorowski, eds., *Neither East nor West: Iran, the Soviet Union, and the United States*. New Haven: Yale University Press.

Cottrell, A. J., and Hanks, R. J. 1979. The strategic tremors of upheaval in Iran. *Strategic Review* 7: 50–56.

Cox, H. 1965. *The secular city*. New York: Macmillan.

Crabb, C. V., and Holt, P. M. 1980. *Invitation to struggle: Congress, the president and foreign policy*. 2nd ed. Washington, D.C.: Congressional Quarterly.

Crozier, B. 1979. Power and national sovereignty. *National Review*, February 2.

Crozier, M. J., Huntington, S. P., and Watanuki, J. 1975. *The crisis of democracy: Report on the governability of democracies to the Trilateral Commission*. New York: New York University Press.

Curtis, M. 1979. Khomeini's thoughts on Jews and Israel. *Middle East Review* 11: 57–58.

Dahrendoff, R. 1959. *Class and class conflict in industrial society.* London: Routledge and Kegan Paul.

D'Amico, R. 1988. Relativism and conceptual schemes. *Philosophy of the Social Sciences* 18: 201–212.

David, C., with Carol, N. A., and Seldon, Z. A. 1993. *Foreign policy failure in the White House: Reappraising the fall of the Shah and the Iran-Contra affair.* Lanham, Md.: University of America Press.

Davies, J. C. 1962. Toward a theory of revolution. *American Sociological Review* 6: 5–19.

Davis, V. 1980. Carter tries on the world for size. In V. Davis, ed., *The post-imperial presidency.* New York: Praeger.

Deitchman, S. 1976. *The best laid schemes: A tale of social research and bureaucracy.* Cambridge, Mass.: MIT Press.

DeJames, R. B. 1994. Managing foreign policy: Carter and regional experiment toward Africa. January 1977–May 1978. In H. D. Rosenbaum and A. Ugrinsky, eds., *Jimmy Carter: Foreign policy and post-presidential years.* Westport, Conn.: Greenwood Press.

Dellums, R. V., with Miller R. H., and Hamilton, H. L. 1983. *Defense sense: The search for a rational military policy.* Cambridge, Mass.: Ballinger Publishing Company.

DeMause, L. 1977. Jimmy Carter and American fantasy. In L. deMause and H. Abel., eds., *Jimmy Carter and American fantasy: Psychological explorations.* New York: Two Continents/Psychohistory Press.

DeMott, B. 1989. Reading fiction to the bottom line. *Harvard Business Review* 67: 128–134.

Denitch, B. D. 1976. *The legitimation of a revolution: The Yugoslav case.* New Haven: Yale University Press.

———. 1979. Legitimation and the social order. In B. Denitch, ed., *Legitimation of regimes: International framework for analysis.* Beverly Hills: Sage.

Der Derian, J. 1996. Headley Bull and the idea of diplomatic culture. In R. Fawn and J. Larkins, eds., *International society after the Cold War: Anarchy and order reconsidered.* New York: St. Martin's Press.

Derian, P. M. 1979. Human rights: The role of law and the lawyers. In B. M. Rubin and E. P. Spiro, eds., *Human rights and U.S. foreign policy.* Boulder: Westview Press.

Destler, I. M., Gelb, L. H., and Lake, A. 1984. *Our own worst enemy: The unmaking of American foreign policy.* New York: Simon & Schuster.

Deutsch, K. W. 1953. *Nationalism and social communication: An inquiry into the foundation of nationality.* Cambridge, Mass.: MIT Press.

———. 1963. *The nerves of government: Models of political communication and control.* New York: Free Press.

Deutsch, M. 1975. *Distributive justice.* New Haven: Yale University Press.

———. 1985. Equity, equality, and need: What determines which value will be used as the basis of distributive justice? *Journal of Social Issues* 31: 137–149.

Dickson, P. 1971. *Think tanks.* New York: Atheneum.

Diggins, J. P. 1992. *The rise and fall of the American left.* New York: W. W. Norton.

Documents from the U.S. Espionage Den. 1980–99. *Muslim students following the line of Imam.* 70 volumes. Teheran: Center for the Publication of the U.S. Espionage Den's Documents; Washington, D.C.: National Security Archive.

Donovan, H. 1985. *Roosevelt to Reagan: A reporter's encounter with nine presidents.* New York: Harper & Row.

Doran, C. F. 1989. The globalist-regionalists debate. In P. J. Schroeder, ed., *Intervention in the 1980s: U.S. foreign policy in the Third World.* Boulder: Lynne Rienner.

Dore, R. 1983. Goodwill and the spirit of market capitalism. *British Journal of Sociology* 34: 459–482.

Dorraj, M. 1990. *From Zarathustra to Khomeini: Populism and dissent in Iran.* Boulder: Lynne Rienner.

Douglas, M. 1992. *Risk and blame: Essays in cultural theory.* London: Routledge.

Dror, Y. 1975. Some fundamental philosophical, psychological and intellectual assumptions of futures studies. In *The future as an academic discipline.* Ciba Foundation Symposium. Amsterdam: Elsevier.

Dreyfuss, R. 1980. *Hostage to Khomeini.* New York: New Benjamin Franklin Publishing Company.

Dubashi, H. 1988. Islamic ideology: The perils and promises of a neologism. In H. Amirahmadi and M. Parvin, eds., *Post-revolutionary Iran.* Boulder: Westview Press.

Dubnoff, S. 1986. How much income is enough? Measuring public judgments. *Public Opinion Quarterly* 49: 285–299.

Dumbrell, J. 1993. *The Carter presidency: A re-evaluation.* Manchester, England: Manchester University Press.

Dunn, J. 1972. *Modern revolutions: An introduction to the analysis of a political phenomenon.* Cambridge: Cambridge University Press.

Easton, D. 1953. *The political system.* New York: Alfred Knopf.

———. 1965. *A system analysis of political life.* Chicago: University of Chicago Press.

———. 1969. The new revolution in political science. *American Political Science Review* 63: 1051–1061.

Ebel, R. E. 1979. A postmortem for industry. In M. B. Winchester, ed., *The international essays for business decision making.* Vol. 4. New York: AMACOM.

Edelman, M. 1985. *The symbolic uses of politics.* Urbana: University of Illinois Press.

Elkan, W. 1977. Employment, education, training and skilled labor in Iran. *Middle East Journal* 31: 175–188.

Elliot, P., and Schlesinger, P. 1979. On the stratification of political knowledge. Studying Eurocommunism, an unfolding ideology. *Sociological Review* 27: 55–81.

Ellul, J. 1958. Modern myth. *Dogenes* 23: 23–40.

Elsenhans, H. 1983. Rising mass income as a condition of capitalist growth: Implications for world economy. *International Organization* 37: 1–40.

Enteesar, N. 1988. The military and politics in the Islamic republic of Iran. In H. Amirahmadi and M. Parvin, eds, *Post-revolutionary Iran.* Boulder: Westview Press.

Epstein, E. C. 1984. Legitimacy, institutionalization and opposition in exclusionary bureaucratic-authoritarian regimes: The situation of the 1980s. *Comparative Politics* 17: 37–54.

Esterline, J. H., and Black, R. B. 1975. *Inside foreign policy: The Department of State: Political system and its subsystems.* Palo Alto, Calif.: Mayfield.

Etheradge, L. S. 1985. *Can government learn? Foreign policy and Central American revolutions.* New York: Pergamon Press.

Etzioni-Halevy, E. 1985. *The knowledge elite and the failure of prophecy.* London: George Allen & Unwin.

————. 1986. Radicals in the establishment: Toward an exploration of the radical role of intellectuals in Western societies. *Journal of Political and Military Sociology* 14: 29–40.

Evans, P. B. 1979. *Dependent development: The alliance of multinational, state, and local capital in Brazil*. Princeton: Princeton University Press.

Fagan, R. 1978. A funny thing happened on the way to the market: Thoughts on extending dependency ideas. *International Organization* 32: 287–300.

Falk, P. 1988. The past to come. *Economy and Society* 17: 374–399.

Falk, R. A. 1975. Who pays for foreign policy: A debate on consensus. *Foreign Policy* 18: 92–95.

————. 1976a. CIA covert operations and international law. In R. L. Borosage and J. Marks, eds., *The CIA file*. New York: Grossman Publishers.

————. 1976b. *Future worlds*. New York: Foreign Policy Association.

————. 1977. Nuclear weapons proliferation as a world order problem. *International Security* 1: 79–93.

————. 1978. Panama treaty trap. *Foreign Policy* 30: 68–82.

————. 1980. Iran: Human rights and international law. In D. H. Albert, ed., *Tell the American people: Perspectives on the Iranian revolution*. Philadelphia: Movement for a New Society.

Falkowski, L. 1978. *Presidents, secretaries of state, and crisis in U.S. foreign relations: A model and predictive analysis*. Boulder: Westview Press.

Farcau, B. W. 1996. *The transition to democracy in Latin America: The role of the military*. Westport, Conn.: Praeger.

Farhang, M. 1979. Resisting the pharaohs: Ali Shariati on oppression. *Race and Class* 21: 31–40.

————. 1987. How the clergy gained power in Iran. In B. Freyer, ed., *Islamic impulse*. London: Croom Helm.

Farhi, F. 1990. *States and urban-based revolutions: Iran and Nicaragua*. Urbana: University of Illinois Press.

Farmanfarmaian, M., and Farmanfarmaian, R. 1997. *Blood & oil*. New York: The Modern Library.

Farsoun, S., and Mashayekhi, M. 1992. Introduction: Iran's political culture. In S. Farsoun and M. Mashayekhi, eds., *Iran: Political culture in the Islamic republic*. London: Routledge.

Feher, F. 1982. Paternalism as a mode of legitimation in Soviet type societies. In T. H. Rigby, and F. Feher, eds., *Political legitimation in Communist states*. New York: St. Martin's Press.

Feierabend, I. K., with Feierabend, R. L., and Nesvold, B. A. 1972. The comparative study of revolution and violence. *Comparative Politics* 5: 393–424.

Feldman, J. 1989. *Universities in the business of repression: The academic-military-industrial complex*. Boston: South End Press.

Ferguson, J. 1983. The left. *Review of the News*, May 4.

Festinger, L. 1957. *A Theory of cognitive dissonance*. New York: Peterson and Co.

Feyerabend, P. 1975. *Against method: Outline of an anarchistic theory of knowledge*. London: New Left Books.

Fischer, M.M.J. 1977. Persian society: Transformation and strain. In H. Amirsadeghi, ed., *Twentieth century Iran*. New York: Holmes & Meier.

———. 1979. Protests and revolution in Iran. *Harvard International Review* 1: 1–6.

———. 1980a. Becoming mullah: Reflections on Iranian clerics in a revolutionary age. *Iranian Studies* 13: 83–117.

———. 1980b. *Iran: From religious dispute to revolution.* Cambridge, Mass.: Harvard University Press.

Fischér, M.M.J., and Abedi, M. 1990. *Debating Muslims: Cultural dialogues in post-modernity and tradition.* Madison: University of Wisconsin Press.

Flanagan, S. J. 1985. Managing the intellectual community. *International Security* 10: 58–95.

Florig, D. 1986. The concept of equal opportunity in the analysis of social welfare. *Polity* 18: 392–407.

Follet, K. 1983. *On wings of eagles.* New York: William Morrow.

Foran, J. 1994. The Iranian revolution of 1977–79: A challenge for social theory. In J. Foran, ed., *A century of revolution: Social movement in Iran.* Minneapolis: University of Minnesota Press.

Forbis, W. H. 1980. *Fall of the peacock throne: The story of Iran.* New York: Harper & Row.

Frady, M. 1996. *Jesse: The life and pilgrimage of Jesse Jackson.* New York: Random House.

Franck, T. M., and Wiesband, E. 1979. *Foreign policy by Congress.* New York: Oxford University Press.

Frankel, F. R. 1978. Compulsion and social change: Is authoritarainism the solution to India's economic problem? *World Politics* 30: 215–240.

Frantz, D., and McKean, D. 1995. *Friends in high places: The rise and fall of Clark Clifford.* Boston: Little Brown.

Fraser, J. 1974. Validating a measure of national political legitimacy. *American Journal of Political Science* 18: 117–134.

Freeman, J. R., and Job, B. L. 1979. Scientific forecast in international relations. *International Studies Quarterly* 23: 113–143.

French, J.R.P., Jr., and Raven, B. 1959. The bases of social power. In D. Cartwright, ed., *Studies of social power.* Ann Arbor: University of Michigan Press.

Frey, F. W. 1985. The problem of actor designation in political analysis. *Comparative Politics* 17: 127–152.

Friedrich, C. J., and Brzezinski, Z. 1956. *Totalitarian dictatorship and autocracy.* Cambridge, Mass.: Harvard University Press.

Fuhrman, P. 1988. Another stake through Stalin's heart. *Forbes,* December 26: 34–35.

Fulbrigth, J. W. 1979. The legislator as educator. *Foreign Affairs* 57: 719–732.

Fuller, G. F. 1991. *"The center of the universe": The geopolitics of Iran.* Boulder: Westview Press.

Galbraith, J. K. 1957. *The affluent society.* New York: The New American Library.

———. 1985. *The new industrial state.* 4th ed. Boston: Houghton Mifflin.

Galston, W. A. 1980. *Justice and the human good.* Chicago: University of Chicago Press.

Galtung, J. 1964. A structural theory of aggression. *Journal of Peace Research.* 2: 95–119.

———. 1971. A structural theory of imperialism. *Journal of Peace Research* 8: 81–117.

———. 1976. Toward new indicators of development. *Futures* 8: 261–265.

———. 1990. U.S. foreign policy as manifest theology. In J. Chay, ed., *Culture and international relations.* New York: Praeger.

Gamson, W. A. 1975. *The strategy of social protest*. Homewood, Ill.: Dorsey.

Garson, M. 1996. *The neoconservative vision: From the Cold War to the culture war*. Lanham, Md.: Madison Books.

Garthoff, R. L. 1978. On estimating and imputing intentions. *International Security* 2: 22–32.

Gates, R. M. 1989. Discussion. In R. Godson, ed., *Intelligence Requirements for the 1990s: Collection, analysis, counterintelligence and covert action*. Lexington, Mass.: Lexington Books.

———. 1996. *From the shadows: The ultimate insider's story of five presidents and how they won the Cold War*. New York: Simon & Schuster.

Gazit, S. 1980. Estimates and fortune telling in intelligence work. *International Security* 4: 36–56.

———. 1988. Intelligence estimates and the decision maker. *Intelligence and National Security* 3: 261–289.

Geertz, C. 1964. The integrative revolution: Primordial sentiments and civic politics in the new states. In C. Geertz, ed., *Old societies and new states*. New York: Free Press.

Gelb, L. H. 1988. Why not the state department? In C. W. Kegley and E. R. Wittkopf, eds., *Perspectives on American foreign policy*. New York: St. Martin's Press.

Gendzier, I. L. 1985. *Managing political change: Social scientists and the Third World*. Boulder: Westview Press.

George, A. L. 1972. The case for multiple advocacy in making foreign policy. *American Political Science Review* 66: 751–785.

Gershman, C. 1978. The world according to Andrew Young. *Commentary*, August: 17–23.

———. 1979. Selling them the rope. *Commentary*, April: 35–45.

———. 1980. The rise and fall of the new foreign policy establishment. *Commentary*, July: 13–24.

Ghani, C. 1987. *Iran and the West: A critical bibliography*. London: Kegan Paul.

Gieryn, T. F. 1983. Boundary-work and the demarcation of science from non-science: Strains and interest in professional ideologies of scientists. *American Sociological Review* 48: 781–795.

Gillespie, J., and Nesvold, B. 1971. *Macro-quantitative analysis*. Beverly Hills: Sage.

Gillespie, K. 1990. U.S. corporations and Iran at the Hague. *Middle East Journal* 44: 18–36.

Glad, B. 1980. *Jimmy Carter: In search of the great White House*. New York: W. W. Norton.

Glazer, M. 1972. *The research adventure: Promise and problems of field work*. New York: Random House.

Godfrey, E. D. 1978. Ethics and intelligence. *Foreign Affairs* 56: 624–642.

Godson, R. 1979. The role of pressure groups. In E. Lefever and R. Godson, eds., *The CIA and American ethics: An unfinished debate*. Washington, D.C.: Ethics and Public Policy.

———. 1988. *Comparing foreign intelligence: The US, the USSR, the UK, and the Third World*. McLean, Va.: Pergamon-Brassey.

———. 1989. Intelligence for the 1990s. In R. Godson, ed., *Intelligence requirements for the 1990s: Collection, analysis, counterintelligence and covert action*. Lexington, Mass.: Lexington Books.

Goodin, R. E. 1981. Civil religion and political witchhunts: Three explanations. *Comparative Politics* 14: 1–16.

Gouldner, A. 1959. Reciprocity and autonomy in functional theory. In L. Gross, ed., *Symposium on sociological theory*. White Plains, N.Y.: Row, Peterson and Co.

———. W. 1970. *The coming crisis of Western sociology*. New York: Avon Books.

Gowa, J. 1985. Subsidizing American corporate expansion abroad: Pitfalls in the analysis of public and private power. *World Politics* 37: 180–203.

Graham, R. 1979. *The illusion of power*. New York: St. Martin's Press.

Green, J. D. 1980. Pseudoparticipation and countermobilization: Roots of Iranian revolution. *Iranian Studies* 13: 31–53.

———. 1982. *Revolution in Iran: The politics of countermobilization*. New York: Praeger.

———. 1984. Countermobilization as a revolutionary form. *Comparative Politics* 16: 153–170.

Gurr, T. R. 1968. A causal model of civil strife: A comparative analysis using new indices. *American Political Science Review* 1104–1124.

———. 1970. *Why men rebel*. Princeton: Princeton University Press.

———. 1973. The revolution–social change nexus: Some old theories and new hypotheses. *Comparative Politics* 5: 359–392.

Gurtov, M. 1974. *The United States against the Third World*. New York: Praeger.

Haas, C. A. 1992. *Jimmy Carter and the politics of frustration*. Jefferson, N.C.: McFarland & Company.

Habermas, J. 1975. *Legitimation crisis*. Boston: Beacon Press.

Habiby, R. N., and Ghavidel, F. 1979. Khumanyi's Islamic republic. *Middle East Review* 11: 12–20.

Halliday, F. 1975. *Arabia without sultans*. New York: Vintage Books.

———. 1978a. Iran: The economic contraindictions. *MERIP* 8, no. 69: 9–18.

———. 1978b. Iran: Trade union and the working class opposition. *MERIP* 8, no. 71: 7–14.

———. 1979. *Iran: Dictatorship and development*. Harmondsworth, England: Penguin Books.

———. 1990. The Iranian revolution and great power politics: Components of the first decade. In N. R. Keddie and M. J. Gasiorowski, eds., *Neither East nor West: Iran, the Soviet Union, and the United States*. New Haven: Yale University Press.

Halperin, M. H. 1974. *Bureaucratic politics and foreign policy*. Washington, D.C.: The Brookings Institution.

Halperin, M., et al. 1976. *The lawless state: The crimes of the U.S. intelligence agencies*. Harmondsworth, England: Penguin Books.

Halpern, B. 1979. Introduction. *Middle East Review* 11: 3–4.

Halpern, M. 1963. *The politics of social change in the Middle East and North Africa*. Princeton: Princeton University Press.

Handel, M. I. 1980a. Avoiding political and technological surprises in the 1980's. In R. Godson, ed., *Intelligence requirements for the 1980's: Analysis and estimates*. Washington, D.C.: National Strategy Information Center.

———. 1980b. Surprise and change in international politics. *International Security* 4: 57–85.

———. 1981. *The diplomacy of surprise: Hitler, Nixon, Sadat*. Cambridge, Mass.: Harvard University Press, Center for International Affairs.

————. 1988. Leaders and intelligence. *Intelligence and National Security* 3: 3–39.

Hanrahan, J. 1977. Foreign agents in our midst. *The Progressive* 41: 31–35.

Hargrove, E. C. 1988. *Jimmy Carter as president: Leadership and the politics of public good.* Baton Rouge: Louisiana State University.

Hartman, J. J. 1977. Carter and the utopian group-fantasy. In L. deMause and H. Ebel, eds., *Jimmy Carter and American fantasy: Psychological explorations.* New York: Two Continents/Psychohistory Press.

Hassan, R. 1984. Iran's Islamic revolutionaries: Before and after the revolution. *Third World Quarterly* 6:675–686.

Hatcher, P. L. 1990. *The suicide of an elite: American internationalists and Vietnam.* Stanford: Stanford University Press.

Heginbotham, S., and Bite, V. 1979. Issues in interpretation and evaluation of country studies. In B. M. Rubin and E. P. Spiro, eds., *Human rights and U.S. foreign policy.* Boulder: Westview Press.

Heikal, M. 1981. *The Return of the Ayatollah: The Iranian revolution from Mossadeq to Khomeini.* London: Andre Deutsch.

Helmer, O. 1986. The future relationship between the superpowers. *Futures* 18: 493–507.

Helms, C. 1981. *An ambassador's wife in Iran.* New York: Dodd, Mead & Company.

Herz, J. M. 1978. Legitimacy: Can we retrieve it. *Comparative Politics* 10: 317–344.

Herz, M. F. 1979. *Contacts with the opposition.* Washington, D.C.: Institute for the Study of Diplomacy.

Hilsman, R. 1967. *To move a nation: The politics of foreign policy in the administration of John F. Kennedy.* Garden City, N.Y.: Doubleday.

Hinckley, B. 1994. *Less than meets the eye: Foreign policy making and the myth of the assertive Congress.* Chicago: The University of Chicago Press.

Hiro, D. 1985. *Iran under the Ayatollah.* London: Routledge & Kegan Paul.

Hobbs, A. H. 1951. *The claims of sociology: A critique of textbooks.* Harrisburg, Pa.: The Stackpole Company.

Hoffman, S. 1977–78. The hell of good intention. *Foreign Policy* 29: 3–26.

Hollander, E. J., and Julian, J. W. 1970. Studies in leader legitimacy, influence and innovation. In L. Berkowitz, ed., *Advances in experimental social psychology,* Vol. 5. New York: Academic Press.

Hollander, P. 1981. *Political pilgrims: Travels of Western intellectuals to the Soviet Union, China, and Cuba 1929–1978.* New York: Oxford University Press.

————. 1992. *Anti-Americanism: Critique at home and abroad 1962–1992.* New York: Oxford University Press.

Hollis, M., and Smith, S. 1986. Roles and reasons in foreign policy decision making. *British Journal of Political Science* 16: 269–286.

Holsti, K. J. 1978. A new international politics? Diplomacy in complex interdependence. *International Organization* 32: 513–530.

Holsti, O. R. 1962. The belief system and national image: A case study. *Journal of Conflict Resolution* 6: 244–252.

Homans, G. C. 1961. *Social behavior: Its elementary forms.* London: Routledge and Kegan Paul.

Hooglund, E. J. 1982. *Land and revolution in Iran: 1960–1989.* Austin: University of Texas Press.

————. 1986. Social origins of the revolutionary clergy. In N. R. Keddie and E. Hooglund, eds., *The Iranian revolution & the Islamic republic*. New ed. Syracuse, N.Y.: Syracuse University Press.

Hopple, G. W. 1984. Intelligence and warning: Implications and lessons of the Falkland Island's war. *World Politics* 36: 339–361.

Hopple, G. W., and Kuhlman, J. A. 1981. Expert generated data: An overview. In G. W. Hopple and J. A. Kuhlman, eds., *Expert generated data: Applications in international affairs*. Boulder: Westview Press.

Horowitz, D. L. 1973. Direct, displaced and cumulative ethnic aggression. *Comparative Politics* 6: 1–16.

———. 1980. Discussion. In R. Godson, ed., *Intelligence requirements for the 1980's: Analysis and estimates*. Washington, D.C.: National Strategy Information Center.

Horowitz, I. L. 1977. *Ideology and utopia in the United States, 1956–1976*. London: Oxford University Press.

———. 1978. The Cuba lobby: Supplying rope to a mortgaged revolution. *Washington Review of Strategic and International Studies* 1: 58–71.

———. 1979. The norms of legitimacy—ten years later. In B. Denitch, ed., *Legitimation of regimes: International framework for analysis*. Beverly Hills: Sage.

Hough, J. F. 1973. The bureaucratic model and the nature of the Soviet system. *Journal of Comparative Administration* 5: 134–167.

———. 1977. *The Soviet Union and social science theory*. Cambridge, Mass.: Harvard University Press.

Hoveyda, F. 1980. *The fall of the Shah*. Trans. R. Liddle. New York: Wyndham Books.

Hudson, M. C. 1977. *Arab politics: The search for legitimacy*. New Haven: Yale University Press.

Hughes, H. S. 1983. Social theory in a new context. In J. C. Jackman and C. M. Borden, eds., *The muses flee Hitler*. Washington, D.C.: Smithsonian Institution Press.

Hughes, T. L. 1975. Liberals, populists and foreign policy. *Foreign Policy* 20: 98–137.

Hulbert, M. 1982. *Interlock*. New York: Richardson & Snyder.

Hunt, M. H. 1987. *Ideology and U.S. foreign policy*. New Haven: Yale University Press.

Hunter, S. T. 1987. After the Ayatollah. *Foreign Policy* 66: 77–97.

Huntington, S. P. 1968. *Political order in changing societies*. New Haven: Yale University Press.

———. 1991. *The third wave democratization in the late twentieth century*. Norman: University of Oklahoma Press.

Huyser, R. E. 1986. *Mission to Teheran*. New York: Harper & Row.

Ill omen. 1979. *Time*, July 2: 56.

Institute for Policy Studies. 1980. *Institute for Policy Studies Annual Report 1979–1980*. Washington D.C.: Institute for Policy Studies.

Intelligence and crisis forecasting. 1983. *Orbis* 26: 817–839.

Interview. 1979. *MERIP* 9, nos. 75/76: 9–12.

Ioannides, C. 1984. *America's Iran: Injury and catharsis*. Lanham, Md.: University Press of America.

Irfani, S. 1983. *Iran's Islamic revolution: Popular liberation or religious dictatorship*. London: Zed Books.

Isaac, R. J. 1980. The Institute for Policy Studies: Empire on the left. *Midstream* 26: 7–18.

Isaac, R. J., and Isaac, E. 1983. *The coercive utopians: Social deception by American power players*. Chicago: Regnery Gateway.

Isaacson, W. 1992. *Kissinger: A biography.* New York: Simon & Schuster.

Israeli, R. 1977. The new wave of Islam. *International Journal of Race and Religion* 34: 369–390.

Janis, I. L. 1972. *Victims of groupthink: A psychological study of foreign-policy decisions and fiascoes.* Boston: Houghton Mifflin.

Jansen J.J.G. 1997. *The dual nature of Islamic fundamentalism.* Ithaca, N.Y.: Cornell University Press.

Jasso, G. 1980. A new theory of distributive justice. *American Sociological Review* 45: 3: 32.

Jasso, G. A., and Rossi, P. 1977. Distributive justice and earned income. *American Sociological Review* 42: 639–651.

Jeffreys-Jones, R. 1989. *The CIA and American democracy.* New Haven: Yale University Press.

Jervis, R. 1986. What's wrong with the intelligence process. *International Journal of Intelligence and Counterintelligence* 1: 28–43.

Johnson, C. 1978. Carter in Asia: McGovernism without McGovern. *Commentary*, January: 36–39.

Jones, C. O. 1985. Carter and Congress: From the outside in. *British Journal of Political Science* 15: 269–298.

———. 1988. *The trusteeship presidency: Jimmy Carter and the United States Congress.* Baton Rouge: Louisiana State University Press.

Jones, R.J.B. 1981. Concepts and models of change in international relations. In B. Buzan and R.J.B. Jones, eds., *Change and the study of international relations: The evaded dimension.* New York: St. Martin's Press.

Judis, J. 1981. Setting the stage for repression. *The Progressive*, April: 27–30.

Kadhim, M. 1983. *The political economy of revolutionary Iran.* Cairo: American University in Cairo.

Kadushin, C. 1974. *The American intellectual elite.* Boston: Little Brown.

Kammen, M. 1980. The historian's vocation and the state of the discipline in the United States. In M. Kammen, ed., *The past before us: Contemporary historical writings in the United States.* Ithaca, N.Y.: Cornell University Press.

Kanbur, S. M. 1979. Of risk taking and the personal distribution of income. *Journal of Political Economy* 87: 769–797.

Kandell, J. 1979. Iran calls to its business exiles. *New York Times*, June 22.

Kapuscinski, R. 1985. *Shah of Shahs.* Trans. W. R. Brand and K. Mroczowska. San Diego: Harcourt, Brace, Jovanovich.

Katouzin, H. 1981. *The political economy of modern Iran: Despotism and pseudo-modernism, 1926–1979.* New York: New York University Press.

———. 1983. Shiism and Islamic economics: Sadr and Bani Sadr. In N.R. Keddie, ed., *Religion and politics in Iran.* New Haven: Yale University Press.

Katouzin, M. A. 1978. Oil versus agriculture: A case of dual resource depletion in Iran. *Journal of Peasant Studies* 5: 347–369.

Kaufman, B. I. 1993. *The presidency of James Earl Carter, Jr.* Lawrence: University Press of Kansas.

Kaye, D. G., and Solem, K. E. 1974. Future studies and conflict. *Futures* 11: 235–238.

Kazemi, F. 1980a. *Poverty and revolution in Iran: The migrant poor, urban marginality and politics.* New York: New York University Press.

———. 1980b. Urban migrants and the revolution. *Iranian Studies* 13: 257–277.

Keddie, N. R. 1972. The roots of the ulama's power in modern Iran. In N. R. Keddie, ed., *Scholars, saints and Sufis: Muslim religious institutions in the Middle East since 1500*. Berkeley: University of California Press.

———. 1979. Iran: Is "modernization the message." *Middle East Review* 11: 55–56.

———. 1981. *Roots of revolution: An interpretive history of modern Iran*. New Haven: Yale University Press.

———. 1986. Introduction. In N. R. Keddie and E. J. Hooglund, eds., *The Iranian revolution & the Islamic republic*. New ed. Syracuse, N.Y.: Syracuse University Press.

Kelley, D. 1976. For socialist alternatives: A radical think tank is working within the system. *Barron's*, August 23: 5, 12, 14.

Kendall, W. 1949. The function of intelligence. *World Politics* 1: 540–552.

Kennedy, C. R., Jr. 1991. *Managing the international business environment: Cases in political and country risk*. Englewood Cliffs, N.J.: Prentice Hall.

Kennedy, E. 1975. Persian Gulf: Arms race or arms control. *Foreign Affairs* 54: 14–35.

Kennedy, M. 1986. *The Ayatollah in the cathedral*. New York: Hill and Wang.

Key, V. O. 1955. A theory of critical elections. *Journal of Politics* 17: 3–18.

Khomeini, Ayatollah R. 1978. The start of a gigantic explosion. *MERIP* 8, no. 69: 19–20.

Khomeini power. 1979. *Newsweek*, February 12: 43–47.

Kilborn, P. T. 1976. Starret Risks Big Loss in Iran. *New York Times*, January 7.

———. 1979. Business lessons learned in Iran. *New York Times*, June 14.

Kimmel, M. 1990. *Revolution: A sociological interpretation*. Philadelphia: Temple University Press.

Kinder, D. R., and Kiewiet, D. R. 1979. Sociotropic politics: The American case. *British Journal of Political Science* 11: 129–161.

King, A. 1975. Overload: Problems of governing in the 1970s. *Political Studies* 23: 284–296.

Kirkpatrick, J. 1979. Dictatorship and double standards. *Commentary*, November: 34–45.

———. 1986. Forward. In J. Muravchik, ed, The uncertain crusade: *Jimmy Carter and the dilemma of human rights policy*. Lanham, Md.: Hamilton Press.

Kissinger, H. 1981. *For the record: Selected statements, 1977–1980*. Boston: Little Brown.

Klare, M. T. 1975. Petrodollars for phantoms: The arms build-ups in Iran and Saudi Arabia. In D. Mermelstein, ed., *The economic crisis reader*. New York: Vintage Books.

———. 1976. Hoist by our own Pahlavi. *The Nation*. January 31: 110–114.

———. 1989. The development of low-intensity conflict doctrine. In P. J. Schroeder, ed., *Intervention in the 1980s: U.S. foreign policy in the Third World*. Boulder: Lynn Rienner.

Klehr, H. 1988. *Far left of center: The American radical left today*. New Brunswick, N.J.: Transaction Books.

Kochanek, S. A. 1973. Perspectives on the study of revolution and social change. *Comparative Politics* 5: 313–320.

Kolko, G. 1969. *The roots of American foreign policy: An analysis of power and purpose*. Boston: Beacon Press.

Kolko, J., and Kolko, G. 1972. *The limits of power: The world and United States foreign policy, 1945–1954*. New York: Harper & Row.

Konrad, G., and Szelenyi, I. 1970. *The intellectual on the road to class power*. Trans. A. Arato and R. E. Ellen. New York: Harcourt Brace Jovanovich.

Kraft, J. 1978. Letter from Iran. *New Yorker*, December 18: 134–168.

Kramer, M. 1980. The ideas of an Islamic order. *Washington Quarterly* 3: 3–12.

Kristol, I. 1987. American foreign policy: A neoconservative view. *Jerusalem Journal of International Relations* 9: 68–84.

Kubalkova, V., and Cruickshank, A. 1981. *International inequality*. New York: St. Martin's Press.

Kuhn, T. S. 1970. *The structure of scientific revolutions*. 2nd ed. Chicago: University of Chicago Press.

Kuznet, S. 1955. Economic growth and income inequality. *American Economic Review* 45: 1–28.

LaBarre, W. 1971. Material for a history of crisis cults: A bibliographical essay. *Current Anthropology* 1: 3–44.

Ladd, E. C., Jr., and Lipset, S. M. 1971. The politics of American political scientists. *PS* 4: 135–138.

———. 1973. *Academics, politics and the 1972 election*. Washington, D.C.: American Enterprise Institute for Public Policy Research.

———. 1975. *The divided academy, professors and politics*. New York: McGraw-Hill.

Ladjevardi, H. 1983. The origins of U.S. support for an autocratic Iran. *International Journal of Middle East Studies* 15: 225–239.

Laingen, B. 1992. *Yellow ribbon: The secret journal of Bruce Laingen*. Washington, D.C.: Brassey's (US).

Lamber, R. D. et al. 1988. The social sources of political knowledge. *Canadian Journal of Political Science* 22: 359–374.

Landsberger, H. A., and McDaniel, T. 1976. Hypermobilization in Chile 1970–1973. *World Politics* 28: 502–541.

Lane, D. 1979. Soviet industrial workers: The lack of legitimation crisis? In B. Denitch, ed., *Legitimation of regimes: International framework for analysis*. Beverely Hills Sage.

Lane, R. E. 1979. The legitimacy bias: Conservative man in market and state. In B. Denitch, ed., *Legitimation of regimes: International framework for analysis*. Beverly Hills: Sage.

———. 1985. From political to industrial democracy. *Polity* 16: 623–648.

———. 1986. Market justice, political justice? *American Political Science Review* 80: 383–402.

Laqueur, W. 1978. Trouble for the Shah. *The New Republic*, September 23: 12–21.

———. 1979. Why the Shah fell. *Commentary*, March: 47–55.

———. 1985. *A world of secrets: Uses and limits of intelligence*. New York: Basic Books.

Lasky, V. 1979. *Jimmy Carter: The man & the myth*. New York: Richard Marek Publishers.

Lawler, P. 1995. *A question of values: Johan Galtung's peace research*. Boulder: Lynn Rienner.

Ledeen, M. A., and Lewis, W. H. 1980. Carter and the fall of the Shah: The inside story. *Washington Quarterly* 3: 3–40.

————. 1981. *Debacle: The American failure in Iran.* New York: Alfred A. Knopf.

Lenczowski, G. 1977. The Middle East. A political-economic dimension. *Columbia Journal of World Business* 12: 42–52.

————. 1978. Political process and institutions in Iran: The second Pahlavi kingship. In G. Lenczowski, ed., *Iran under the Pahlavis.* Stanford: Stanford University Hoover Institute Press.

————. 1979a. The arc of crisis: Its central section. *Foreign Affairs* 57: 796–820.

————. 1979b. Iran: The awful truth: Behind the Shah's fall and the mullah's rise. *American Spectator* 12: 12–15.

Lenski, G. E. 1966. *Power and privilege: A theory of social stratification.* New York: McGraw-Hill.

Lerner, D., and Laswell, H., eds. 1951. *The policy sciences: Recent development in scope and method.* Stanford: Stanford University Press.

Lewis, A. 1979. Trusting in illusion. *New York Times*, March 12.

Lewis, B. 1976. The Return of Islam. *Commentary*, January: 39–49.

Lewis, P. 1979. Khomeini's demands review of Iran's foreign deals. *New York Times*, January 22.

Lewy, G. 1992. *The cause that failed: Communism in American political life.* Oxford: Oxford University Press.

Lijphart, A. 1968. *The politics of accommodation.* Berkeley: University of California Press.

Lilienfeld, R. 1978. *The rise of the system theory: An ideological analysis.* New York: John Wiley and Sons.

Limbert, J. 1987. *Iran: At war with history.* Boulder: Westview Press.

Linton, R. 1945. *The cultural background of personality.* London: Prentice Hall.

Lipset, S. M. 1959. American intellectuals: Their politics and status. *Daedalus* 88: 469–486.

————. 1960. *Political man: The social basis of politics.* Garden City, N.Y: Doubleday.

————. 1979. The new class and the professorate. In B. Bruce-Briggs, ed., *The New Class?* New Brunswick, N.J.: Transaction Books.

————. 1982. The academic mind at the top: The political behavior and values of faculty elites. *Public Opinion Quarterly* 46: 143–168.

Lipset, S. M., and Dobson, R. B. 1972. The intellectuals as critics and rebels. *Daedalus* 101: 137–198.

Lipset, S. M., and Ladd, E. C. 1972a. The political future of activist generations. In P. G. Altbach and R. S. Laufer, eds., *The new pilgrims: Youth protest in transition.* New York: McKay Co.

————. 1972b. The politics of American sociologists. *American Journal of Sociology* 78: 67–104.

Liska, G. 1975. *Beyond Kissinger: Ways of conservative statecraft.* Baltimore: The Johns Hopkins University Press.

Little, R. 1985. Structuralism and neo-realism. In M. Light and A.J.R. Groom, eds., *International relations: A handbook of current theory.* Boulder: Lynn Rienner.

Looney, R. E. 1977. *Iran at the end of the century: A Hegelian forecast.* Lexington, Mass.: Lexington Books.

Lutz, M. A., and Lux, K. 1988. *Humanistic economics.* New York: Bootstrap Press.

McClosky, H. 1958. Conservatism and personality. *American Political Science Review* 52: 27–45.

McDounough, P., Barnes, S., and Lopez Pina, A. 1986. The growth of democratic legitimacy in Spain. *American Political Science Review* 80: 735–760.

McGovern, G. 1977. *Grassroots: The autobiography of George McGovern*. New York: Random House.

MacIntyre, A. 1973. Ideology, social science and revolution. *Comparative Politics* 5: 321–342.

Mackey, S. 1996. *The Iranians, Persia, Islam and the soul of a nation*. New York: Plume Books.

McLachlan, K. 1977. The Iranian economy. In H. Amirsadeghi, ed., *Twentieth century Iran*. New York: Holmes & Meier.

McNamara, R. S. 1995. *In retrospect: The tragedy and lesson of Vietnam*. New York: Times Books.

Maddel, M. 1993. *Class, politics, and ideology in the Iranian revolution*. New York: Columbia University Press.

Majone, G. 1989. *Evidence, argument, and persuasion in the policy process*. New Haven: Yale University Press.

Major companies of Iran. 1977. London: Graham & Trotman Limited Publishers.

Manheim J., and Albritton, R. B. 1986. Public relations in the public eye: Two case studies of the failure of public information campaigns. *Political Communication and Persuasion* 3: 269–291.

Mannheim, K. 1955. *Ideology and utopia*. San Diego: Harcourt Brace Jovanovich.

Manning, B. 1976. Goals, ideology and foreign policy. *Foreign Affairs* 54: 271–284.

Mansur, A. K. 1979. The crisis in Iran: Why the U.S. ignored a quarter century of warning. *Armed Forces Journal International*, January: 26–32.

Marshall, A. 1989. Discussion. In R. Godson, ed., *Intelligence requirements for the 1900s: Collection, analysis, counterintelligence and covert action*. Lexington, Mass.: Lexington Books.

Maruyama, M. 1973. A new model for future research. *Futures* 5: 435–437.

———. 1974. Endogenous research vs. expert from outside. *Futures* 6: 389–394.

Matheson, C. 1987. Weber and the classification of forms of legitimacy. *British Journal of Sociology* 38: 175–198.

Mazlish, B., and Diamond, E. 1979. *Jimmy Carter: A character portrait*. New York: Simon & Schuster.

Menashri, D. 1979. Strange Bedfellows: The Khomeini coalition. *Jerusalem Quarterly* 12: 21–34.

Merkl, P. H. 1967. *Political continuity and change*. New York: Harper & Row.

Meyer, P. 1978. *James Earl Carter: The man and the myth*. Kansas City, Kans.: Sheed Andrew and McMeel Inc.

Michael, D. N. 1985. Thinking about the future. *Futures* 17: 94–103.

Miklos, J. C. 1983. *The Iranian revolution and modernization: Way stations to anarchy*. Washington, D.C.: National Defense University Press.

Milani, M. M. 1988. *The making of Iran's Islamic revolution: From monarchy to Islamic republic*. Boulder: Westview Press.

———. 1993. The evolution of the Iranian presidency: From Bani-Sadr to Rafsanjani. *British Journal of Middle Eastern Studies* 20: 64–82.

Miller, D. W., and Starr, M. K. 1967. *The structure of human decision*. Englewood Cliffs, N. J.: Prentice Hall.

Misztal, B. A. 1996. *Trust in modern societies: The search for bases of social order.* Cambridge, England: Polity Press.

Mitchell, E. J. 1968. Inequality and insurgency: A statistical study of South Vietnam. *World Politics* 20: 421–438.

———. 1969. Some econometrics of the Huk rebellion. *American Political Science Review* 63: 1159–1171.

Moens, A. 1990. *Foreign policy under Carter: Testing multiple advocacy decision making.* Boulder: Westview Press.

Mofid, K. 1987. *Development planning in Iran: From monarchy to Islamic republic.* Wisebach, Cambridgeshire, England: Menas Press.

Moghadam, V. 1988. The left and the revolution in Iran: A critical analysis. In H. Amirahmadi and M. Parvin, eds., *Post-revolutionary Iran.* Boulder: Westview Press.

Mollenhoff, C. R. 1980. *The president who failed: Out of control.* New York: Macmillan Publishing.

Mondale, W. 1976. Reorganizing the CIA: Who and how? *Foreign Policy* 23: 57–61.

Moore, B., Jr. 1966. *Social origins of dictatorship and democracy: Lord and peasant in the making of the modern world.* Boston: Beacon Press.

Moran, T. H. 1978–79. Iranian defense expenditures and the social crisis. *International Security* 3: 178–192.

Moritz, F. 1978. Cross impact analysis: Forecasting the future of Rhodesia. In R. J. Heuer, ed., *Quantitative approaches to political intelligence: The CIA experience.* Boulder: Westview Press.

Moses, R. L. 1996. *Freeing the hostages: Reexamining U.S.–Iranian negotiations and Soviet policy 1979–81.* Pittsburgh: University of Pittsburgh Press.

Moshiri, F. 1985. *The state and social revolution in Iran: A theoretical perspective.* New York and Frankfurt am Main: Peter Lang Publishing.

———. 1991. Iran: Islamic revolution against Westernization. In J. Goldstone, T. R. Gur, and F. Moshiri, eds., *Revolutions of the late twentieth century.* Boulder: Westview Press.

Moss, R. 1978. Who's meddling in Iran. *The New Republic*, December 2: 15–18.

Mottale, M. 1987. *The political sociology of the Islamic revolution.* Tel Aviv: The Dayan Center for Middle Eastern Studies.

Muller, D. 1979. *Public choice.* New York: Cambridge University Press.

Muravchik, J. 1981. The think thanks of the left. *New York Times Magazine*, April 26.

———. 1984–85. Communophilism and the Institute for Policy Studies. *World Affairs* 147: 161–189.

———. 1986. *The uncertain crusade: Jimmy Carter and the dilemma of human rights policy.* Lanham, Md.: Hamilton Press.

Nagel, E. 1979. *The structure of science: Problems in the logic of scientific exploration.* Indianapolis: Hackett Publishing.

Najmabadi, A. 1987. Iran's turn to Islam: From modernism to moral order. *Middle East Journal* 41: 202–217.

Nash, G. H. 1975. *The conservative intellectual movement in America since 1945.* New York: Basic Books.

Nashat, G., ed. 1983. *Women and revolution in Iran.* Boulder: Westview Press.

Negaran, H. 1979. The Afghan coup of April 1978: Revolution and international security. *Orbis* 23: 93–113.

Newbury, M. C. 1983. Colonialism, ethnicity, and rural political protest in Rwanda and Zanzibar in comparative perspective. *Comparative Politics* 15: 253–280.

Nickel, H. 1979. The U.S. failure in Iran. *Fortune*, March 12: 94–106.

Nima, R. 1983. *Wrath of Allah, Islamic revolution and reaction in Iran*. London: Pluto Press.

Nimmo, D. D., and Sanders, K. R. 1981. The emergence of political communication as a field. In D. D. Nimmo and K. R. Sanders, eds., *Handbook of political communication*. Beverly Hills: Sage.

Nirumand, B. 1969. *Iran: The new imperialism in action*. Trans. L. Mins. New York: The Monthly Review Press.

Nisbet, R. A. 1969. *Social change and history: Aspects of the Western theory of development*. New York: Oxford University Press.

Nisbett, R., and Ross, L. 1980. *Human inference: Strategies and shortcomings of social judgment*. Englewood Cliffs, N.J.: Prentice Hall.

Norton, A. R. 1993. The future of civil society in the Middle East. *Middle East Journal* 47: 205–216.

Nyrop, R. F. 1978. *Iran. A country study*. Washington, D.C.: Foreign Area Studies, The American University.

O'Kane, R.H.T. 1991. *The revolutionary reign of terror: The role of violence in political change*. Aldershot, England: Edward Elger.

O'Neill, R. 1982. Strategic studies and political scientists of strategic studies and its critics revisited. In C. Bell, ed., *Academic studies and international relations*. Canberra: Australian National University.

Orme, J. 1988. Dismounting the tiger: Lessons from four liberalizations. *Political Science Quarterly* 103: 245–265.

Packenham, R. A. 1973. *Liberal America and the Third World: Political development ideas in foreign aid and social science*. Princeton: Princeton University Press.

———. 1992. *The development movement: Scholarship and politics in development studies*. Cambridge, Mass.: Harvard University Press.

Pahlavi, M. R. 1980a. *Answer to history*. New York: Stein and Day.

———. 1980b. *The Shah's story: Mohammed Reza Pahlavi*. London: Michael Joseph.

Paige, J. M. 1970. Inequality and insurgency in Vietnam: A re-analysis. *World Politics* 23: 24–37.

Palmer, M. 1985. *Dilemmas of political development: An introduction to the politics of developing areas*. 3rd ed. Itasca, Ill.: F. E. Peacock Publishers.

Parenti, M. 1983. *Democracy for the few*. New York: St. Martin's Press.

Parsa, M. 1989. *Social origins of the Iranian revolution*. New Brunswick, N. J.: Rutgers University Press.

Parsons, A. 1984. *The pride and the fall: Iran 1974–1979*. London: Jonathan Cape.

———. 1989. Iran and Western Europe. *Middle East Journal* 43: 218–229.

Parsons, T. 1951. The social system. Glencoe, Ill.: Free Press.

Parvin, M. 1973. Economic determinants of political unrest: An econometric approach. *Journal of Conflict Resolution* 17: 271–296.

Parvin, M., and Zamani, A. N. 1973. Political economy of growth and destruction: A statistical interpretation of the Iranian case. *Iranian Studies* 12: 43–78.

Payne, A. 1984. Introduction: Dependency theory and the commonwealth Caribbean. In A. Payen and P. Sutton, eds., *Dependency under challenge: The political economy of the Commonwealth Caribbean*. Manchester, England: Manchester University Press.

Pesaran, M. H. 1985. Economic development and revolutionary upheaval in Iran. In H. Afshar, ed., *Iran: A revolution in turmoil*. Albany: State University of New York Press.

Petrossian, V. 1989. Dilemmas of the Iranian revolution. *World Today* 36: 19–25.

Pettman, R. 1975. *Human behavior and world politics*. New York: St. Martin's Press.

Phillips, K. 1968. *The emerging republican majority*. New Rochelle, N.Y.: Arlington House.

Pickett, G. 1985. Congress, the budget, and intelligence. In A. C. Maurer, M. D. Tunstall, and J. M. Keagle, eds., *Intelligence: Policy and process*. Boulder: Westview Press.

Pilskin, K. 1980. Camouflage, conspiracy, and collaborators. Rumors of the revolution. *Iranian Studies* 13: 51–81.

Pipes, D. 1981. The culture gulf. *The New Republic*, April 25: 36–38.

Pipes, R. 1977. Why the Soviet Union thinks it could fight & win a nuclear war. *Commentary*, July: 21–34.

Popper, K. R. 1963. *The poverty of historicism*. London: Routledge and Kegan Paul.

Powell, S. S. 1987. *Covert cadre: Inside the Institute for Policy Studies*. Ottawa, Ill.: Green Hill Publishers.

Prados, J. 1991. *Keepers of the keys: A history of the National Security Council from Truman to Bush*. New York: William Morrow.

Prigogine, I., and Stengers, I. 1984. *Order out of chaos: Man's new dialogue with nature*. Toronto: Bantam Books.

Pryer, L. M. 1978. Arms and the Shah. *Foreign Policy* 31: 56–71.

Purvis, H., Opperman, J., and Campanella, T. 1984. Congress, country X, and arms sales. In H. Parvis, and S. J. Baker, eds., *Legislating foreign policy*. Boulder: Westview Press.

Quant, W. B. 1980. The Middle East crisis. *Foreign Policy*. 58: 540–562.

Race and Class. 1979. Special Issue. Summer.

Radji, P. C. 1983. *In the service of the peacock throne: The diaries of the Shah's last ambassador in London*. London: Hamish Hamilton.

Radosh, R. 1996. *Divided they fell: The demise of the Democratic Party 1964–1996*. New York: The Free Press.

Rafizadeh, M. 1987. *Witness: From the Shah to the secret arms deal: An insider's account of U.S. involvement in Iran*. New York: William Morrow.

Rajaee, F. 1983. *Islamic values and world view: Khomeyni on man, the state and international politics*. New York: University Press of America.

Ram, H. 1994. *Myth and mobilization in revolutionary Iran: The use of the Friday congregational sermon*. Washington, D.C.: The American University Press.

Ramazani, R. K. 1982. Who lost America? The case of Iran. *Middle East Journal* 36: 5–21.

———. 1986. *Revolutionary Iran: Challenges and responses in the Middle East*. Baltimore: The Johns Hopkins University Press.

———. 1990. Preface. In R. K. Ramazani, ed., *Iran's revolution: The search for consensus*. Bloomington: Indiana University Press.

Randal, J. 1978. Shah seems to prefer free press to protest in streets. *Washington Post*, October 28.

————.1979. Views differ on Islamic role in republic. *Washington Post*, February 4.

Ranelagh, J. 1987. *The rise and decline of the CIA.* Rev. ed. New York: Simon & Schuster.

Raskin, M. G. 1979. *The politics of national security.* New Brunswick, N.J.: Transaction Books.

Rawls, J. 1971. *A theory of justice.* Cambridge, Mass.: Harvard University Press.

Razi, G. H. 1987. The nexus of legitimacy and performance: The lesson of the Iranian revolution. *Comparative Politics* 19: 453–470.

Rees, J. 1981. How and why they nearly destroyed U.S. intelligence. *American Opinion*, November: 21–34.

————. 1983. How and why the Communists use radical lawyers. *American Opinion*, October: 45–54, 69.

Rescher, N. 1969. A questionnaire study of American values by 2000 A.D. In K. Baiter and N. Rescher, ed., *Values and the future, the impact of technological change on American values.* New York: The Free Press.

Rezun, M. 1990. Introduction. In M. Rezun, ed., *Iran at the crossroads: Global relations in a turbulent decade.* Boulder: Westview Press.

Ricci, D. M. 1993. *The transformation of American politics: The new Washington and the rise of think tanks.* New Haven: Yale University Press.

Richardson, P. 1979. Understanding business policy in Iran. *Journal of General Management* 4: 42–53.

Ricks, T. M. 1980. Iran and imperialism: Academics in the service of the people or the Shah? *Arab Studies Quarterly* 2: 265–277.

————. 1981. Background to the Iranian revolution: Imperialism, dictatorship, and nationalism, 1872 to 1979. In A. Jabbari and R. Olson, eds., *Iran: Essays on a revolution in the making.* Lexington, KY.: Mazda Publishers.

Rigby, T. H. 1982. Legitimation: Political legitimacy, Weber and Communist mono-organizational system. In T. H. Rigby and F. Feher, eds., *Political legitimation in Communist states.* New York: St. Martin's Press.

Root, E. M. 1955. *Collectivism on the campus: The battle for the mind in American colleges.* New York: The Devin-Adair Company.

Rosati, J. A. 1987. *The Carter administration's quest for global community: Beliefs and their impact on behavior.* Columbia: University of South Carolina Press.

Rose, R. 1969. Dynamic tendencies in the authority of regimes. *World Politics* 21: 604–628.

Rosen, B., and B. 1982. *The destined hour: The hostage crisis and one family's ordeal.* Garden City, N.Y.: Doubleday & Company.

Rostow, W. W. 1964. *The stages of economic growth: A non-Communist manifesto.* Cambridge: At the University Press.

Rothestein, R. L. 1972. *Planning, prediction, and policymaking in foreign affairs: Theory and practice.* Boston: Little Brown.

Rothman, S., and Lichter, S. R. 1996. *Roots of radicalism: Jews, Christians and the left.* New Brunswick, N.J.: Transaction Books.

Rothschild, J. 1979. Political legitimacy in contemporary Europe. In B. Denitch ed., *Legitimation of regimes: International framework for analysis.* Beverly Hills: Sage.

Rovere, R. 1979. Affairs of state. *The New Yorker*, January 22: 107–110.

Rubin, B. 1980a. American relations with the Islamic republic of Iran. *Iranian Studies* 13: 307–326.

―――. 1980b. *Paved with good intentions: The American experience in Iran*. New York: Oxford University Press.

―――. 1985. *Secrets of state: The State Department and the struggle over U.S. foreign policy*. New York: Oxford University Press.

The Rush from Iran. 1979. *Newsweek*, February 15: 64.

Russett, B. 1964. Inequality and instability: The relations of land tenure to politics. *World Politics* 16: 442–454.

Russo, A. J. 1972. Economic and social correlates of government control in South Vietnam. In I. K. Feierabend, R. L. Feierabend, and Ted R. Gurr, eds., *Anger, violence and politics*. Englewood Cliffs, N.J.: Prentice Hall.

Rustow, D. A. 1977. U.S.–Saudi relations and the oil crisis of the 1980s. *Foreign Affairs* 55: 494–516.

Saffari, S. 1993. The legitimacy of the clergy's rights to rule in the Iranian constitution of 1979. *British Journal of Middle Eastern Studies* 20: 64–82.

Said, A. A., ed. 1971. *Protagonists of change: Subcultures in development and revolution*. Englewood Cliffs, N.J.: Prentice Hall.

Saidi, M. F. 1993. All the Shah's men. *Middle East Journal* 47: 113–117.

Saikal, A. 1980. *The rise and fall of the Shah*. Princeton: Princeton University Press.

Sale, R. T. 1980. Carter and Iran: From idealism to disaster. *Washington Quarterly* 3: 75–87.

―――. 1981–82. Americans in Iran. *SAIS* 3: 27–39.

Salehi, M. M. 1988. *Insurgency through culture and religion; The Islamic revolution of Iran*. New York: Praeger.

Salinger, P. 1981. *America held hostage: The secret negotiations*. Garden City, N.Y.: Doubleday and Company.

Sansasarian, E. 1982. *The women's rights movement in Iran: Mutiny, appeasement and repression from 1900 to Khomeini*. New York: Praeger.

Santoro, C. M. 1992. *Diffidence and ambition: The intellectual source of U.S. foreign policy*. Boulder: Westview Press.

Sarkesian, Sam C. 1984. The president and national security: An overview. In Sam C. Sarkesian, ed., *Presidential leadership and national security: Style, institutions, and politics*. Boulder: Westview Press.

Saunders, H. S. 1985. The crisis begins. In P. H. Kreisberg, ed., *American hostages in Iran*. New Haven: Yale University Press.

―――. 1987. Iran: A view from the State Department. *World Affairs* 149: 209–213.

Savory, R. M. 1979. The problem of sovereignty in an Ithna Ashari (Twelver) Shii state. *Middle East Review* 11: 5–11.

Schaar, S. 1979. Orientalism at the service of imperialism. *Race and Class* 21: 67–80.

Schmitter, P. C. 1971. *Interest, conflict and political change in Brazil*. Stanford: Stanford University Press.

Schmookler, A. B. 1984. *The parable of the tribes: The problem of power in social evolution*. Berkeley: University of California Press.

Scott, C. W. 1984. *Pieces of the game: The human drama of Americans held hostage in Iran*. Atlanta: Peachtree Publishers.

Scott, J. M. 1996. *Deciding to intervene: The Reagan doctrine and American foreign policy*. Durham, N.C.: Duke University Press.

Selbin, E. 1993. *Modern Latin American revolution*. Boulder: Westview Press.

Seligman, D. 1982. Friendly fatuity. *Fortune*, June 14: 63.

Seliktar, O. 1986. Identifying a society's belief system. In M. G. Hermann, ed., *Political Psychology*. San Francisco: Jossey-Bass.

Serfaty, S. 1978. Brzezinski: Play it again Zbig. *Foreign Policy* 32: 3–12.

Sewell, W. 1985. Ideologies and social revolution: Reflection on the French case. *Journal of Modern History* 57: 57–85.

Sexton, D. J. 1986. The theory and psychology of military deception. In R. W. Mitchell and N. S. Thompson, eds., *Deception: Perspectives on human and nonhuman deceit*. Albany: State University of New York Press.

Shafer, D. M. 1988. *Deadly paradigms: The failure of U.S. counterinsurgency policy*. Princeton: Princeton University Press.

Shain, Y., and Linz, J. J. 1995. *Between states: Interim governments and democratic traditions*. Cambridge: Cambridge University Press.

Shapiro, M. A., Bonham, G. M., and Heradstveit, D. 1980. A discursive practice approach to collective decision making. *International Studies Quarterly* 32: 397–420.

Shaplen, R. 1980a. Profiles. Eye on the storm—I. *The New Yorker*, June 2.

———. 1980b. Profiles. Eye on the storm—II. *The New Yorker*, June 9.

Shawcross, W. 1988. *The Shah's last ride: The fate of an ally*. New York: Simon & Schuster.

Shiels, F. L. 1991. *Preventable disasters: Why governments fail*. Savage, Md.: Rowman & Littlefield.

Shirk, S. 1977–78. Human rights: What about China? *Foreign Policy* 29: 109–127.

Shklar, J. N. 1984. *Ordinary vices*. Cambridge, Mass.: Harvard/Belknap Press.

Shoaee, R. S. 1987. The mujahid women of Iran: Reconciling culture and gender. *Middle East Journal* 41: 519–538.

Shoup, L. 1980a. *The Carter presidency and beyond: Power and politics in the 1980s*. Palo Alto, Calif.: Ramparts Press.

———. 1980b. Jimmy Carter and the trilateralists: Presidential roots. In H. Sklar, ed., *Trilateralism: The Trilateral Commission and elite planning for world management*. Boston: South End Press.

Shulman, M. D. 1977. On learning to live with authoritarian regimes. *Foreign Affairs* 55: 325–538.

Shulsky, A. 1993. *Silent warfare: Understanding the world of intelligence*. Washington, D.C.: Brassey's (US).

Siavoshi, S. 1990. *Liberal nationalism in Iran: The failure of a movement*. Boulder: Westview Press.

Sick, G. 1985. *All fall down: America's tragic encounter with Iran*. New York: Random House.

———. 1987. Iran: A view from the White House. *World Affairs* 149: 209–213.

———. 1991. *October surprise: American hostages in Iran and the election of Ronald Reagan*. New York: Times Books.

Silvert, K. H., ed. 1964. *Discussion at Bellagio: The political alternative of development*. New York: American Universities Field Staff.

Simpson, J. 1988. *Behind iron lines*. London: Robinson Books.

Singer, J. D. 1961. The level-of-analysis problem in international relations. In K. Knorr and S. Verba, eds., *The international system*. Princeton: Princeton University Press.

――――. 1976. An assessment of peace research. *International Security* 1: 118–137.

Singh, K. R. 1980. *Iran: Quest for security*. New Delhi: Vikas Publishing House.

Sivin, N. 1966. Chinese conception of time. *Erlham Review* 1: 82–92.

Skocpol, T. 1979. *States and social revolutions: A comparative analysis of France, Russia and China*. Cambridge: Cambridge University Press.

――――. 1982. Rentier state and Shi'a Islam in the Iranian revolution. *Theory and Society* 11: 265–283.

Smelser, N. J. 1962. *Theory of collective behavior*. New York: The Free Press.

Smith, G. 1984. Ideas under siege: Carter's foreign policy. *Yale Review* 73: 354–366.

――――. 1986. *Mortality, reason and power: American diplomacy in the Carter years*. New York: Hill and Wang.

Smith, H. 1988. *The power game: How Washington works*. New York: Random House.

Smith, J. A. 1993. *Strategic calling: The Center for Strategic and International Studies 1962–1992*. Washington, D.C.: The Center for Strategic and International Studies.

Smith, T. 1985. Requiem or new agenda for Third World studies. *World Politics* 37: 532–561.

Smolensky, E. 1971. The past and the present poor. In R. W. Foge and S. L. Engerman, eds., *The reinterpretation of American economic history*. New York: Harper & Row.

Spanier, J. 1992. *American foreign policy since World War II*. 12th ed. Washington, D.C.: CQ Press.

Spence, L. D. 1978. *Politics of social knowledge*. University Park: Pennsylvania University Press.

Spencer, D. S. 1983. *The Carter implosion: Jimmy Carter and the amateur style of diplomacy*. New York: Praeger.

Sreberny-Mohammadi, A., and Mohammadi, A. 1988. The Islamic republic and the world: Images, propaganda, intentions, and result. In H. Amirahmadi and M. Parvin, eds., *Post-revolutionary Iran*. Boulder: Westview Press.

Stang, A. 1976. National security mousetrap. *American Opinion*, November 17: 41–54, 103.

Staniland, M. 1991. *American intellectuals and African nationalists 1955–1970*. New Haven: Yale University Press.

Stapenhurst F. 1992. *Political risk analysis around the North Atlantic*. New York: St. Martin's Press.

State Department, Declassified Documents on Iran. 1990. Published in Eric Hooglund, ed., *Iran: The Making of U.S. Policy, 1977–1980*. Alexandria, Va.: Chadwyck Healey and National Security Archive, 1990.

Stark, R., and Glock, C. 1968. *American piety: The nature of religious commitment*. Berkeley: University of California Press.

Stauber, L. 1975. The implications of market socialism in the United States. *Polity* 8: 38–62.

Stempel, J. D. 1981. *Inside the Iranian revolution*. Bloomington: Indiana University Press.

Stoessinger, John G. 1985. *Crusaders and pragmatists: Movers of modern American policy*. 2nd ed. New York: W. W. Norton.

Strumpel, B., ed. 1972. *Subjective elements of well being*. Paris: Organization for Economic Cooperation and Development.

Sullivan, W. H. 1980. Dateline Iran: The road not taken. *Foreign Policy* 40: 175–186.

———. 1981. *Mission to Iran*. New York: W. W. Norton.

———. 1983–84. Living without Marcos. *Foreign Policy* 53: 150–156.

———. 1984. *Obligato: 1939–1979: Notes on a foreign service career*. New York: W. W. Norton.

———. 1987. Iran: A view from Iran. *World Affairs* 149: 215–218.

Summary justice. 1979. *Time*, April 23: 23–36.

Sundquist, J. L. 1983. *Dynamics of the party system: Alignment and realignment of political parties in the United States*. Washington, D.C.: The Brookings Institution.

Swidler, A. 1986. Culture in action: Symbols and strategies. *American Sociological Review* 51: 273–286.

Taheri, A. 1985. *The spirit of Allah: Khomeini and the Islamic revolution*. Bethesda, Md.: Adler & Adler.

———. 1987. *Holy terror: Inside the world of Islamic terrorism*. Bethesda, Md.: Adler & Adler.

———. 1988. *Nest of spies: America's journey to disaster in Iran*. New York: Pantheon Books.

Tahir-Kheli, S. 1980. Proxies and allies: The case of Iran and Pakistan. *Orbis* 24: 339–352.

Tanter, R., and Ullman, R. H. 1972. *Theory and practice in international relations*. Princeton: Princeton University Press.

Tehranian, M. 1980. Communication and revolution in Iran: The passing of a paradigm. *Iranian Studies* 13: 5–30.

Teicher, H., and Teicher, Radley G. 1993. *Twin pillars to desert storm: America's flawed vision in the Middle East from Nixon to Bush*. New York: William Morrow.

Thoenes, P. 1966. *The elite in the welfare state*. New York: The Free Press.

Thompson, W. R. 1976. Organizational cohesion and military coup outcomes. *Comparative Political Studies* 9: 255–276.

Thornton, R. C. 1991. *The Carter years: Toward a new global order*. New York: Paragon House.

Tillich, P. 1977. *The social decision*. Trans. F. Sherman. New York: Harper & Row.

Tilly, C. 1973. Does modernization breed revolution? *Comparative Politics* 5: 425–447.

———. 1978. *From mobilization to revolution*. Reading, Mass.: Addison-Wesley.

———. 1984. *Big structures, long processes, huge comparisons*. New York: Russell Sage Foundation.

Train, J. 1980. The source (Institute for Policy Studies). *Forbes*, November 24: 50.

———. 1981. Invective from the left. *Forbes*, August 3: 110–111.

Tucker, R. C. 1961. Toward a comparative politics of movement regimes. *American Political Science Review* 55: 281–293.

———. 1981. *Politics as leadership*. Columbia: University of Missouri Press.

Turner, B. A. 1976. The organizational and interorganizational development of disaster. *Administrative Science Quarterly* 21: 378–397.

Turner, B. S. 1974. *Weber and Islam*. London: Routledge and Kegan Paul.

Turner, M. A. 1991. Issues in evaluating U.S. intelligence. *International Journal of Intelligence and Counterintelligence* 5: 275–286.

Turner, R., and Killian, L. 1972. *Collective behavior*. Englewood Cliffs, N.J.: Prentice Hall.

Turner, S. 1985. *Secrets and democracy: The CIA in transition*. Boston: Houghton Mifflin.

———. 1991a. Purge the CIA of KGB types. *New York Times*, October 2.

———. 1991b. *Terrorism and democracy*. Boston: Houghton Mifflin.

Tyler, T. R. 1990. *Why people obey the law*. New Haven: Yale University Press.

Tyson, J. 1981. *Target America*. Chicago: Regnery Gateway.

Valenzuela, J. S., and Valenzuela, A. 1978. Modernization and dependency. *Comparative Politics* 10: 535–558.

Vali, A., and Zubaida, S. 1985. Functionalism and political discourse in the Islamic republic of Iran: The case of the Hujjatiyeh society. *Economy and Society* 14: 139–173.

Valibeigi, M. 1988. U.S.–Iranian trade relations after the revolution. In M. Parvin, ed., *Post-revolutionary Iran*. Boulder: Westview Press.

———. 1993. Islamic economics and economic policy formation in post-revolutionary Iran: A critique. *Journal of Economic Issues* 27: 793–812.

Vance, C. R. 1983. *Hard choices: Critical years in American foreign policy*. New York: Simon & Schuster.

———. 1986. The human rights imperative. *Foreign Policy*. 63: 3–19.

Vargas Llosa, M. 1992. The Miami model. *Commentary*, February 21–27.

Visker, R. 1988. Marshallian ethics and economics: Deconstructing the authority of science. *Philosophy of the Social Sciences* 18: 179–199.

Vogelgesang, S. 1974. *The long dark night of the soul: The American intellectual left and the Vietnam War*. New York: Harper & Row.

Von Bertalanffy, L. 1956. General system theory. *General Systems* 1: 1–10.

Waddington, C. H. 1977. Stabilization in systems: Chreods and epigenetic landscapes. *Futures* 9: 139–48.

Wallerstein, I. 1975. *World inequality: Origins and perspectives on the world system*. Montreal: Black Rose Books.

Walton, T. 1980. Economic development and revolutionary upheaval in Iran. *Cambridge Journal of Economics* 4: 271–292.

Ward, M. D. 1983. Things fall apart: A logical analysis of crisis resolution dynamics. *International Interaction* 15: 65–79.

Warner, R. S. 1979. Theoretical barriers to the understanding of evangelical Christianity. *Sociological Analysis* 40: 1–9.

Weede, E., and Tiefenbach, H. 1981. Some recent explanations of income inequality: An evolution and critique. *International Studies Quarterly* 25: 255–283.

Weinbaum, M. G. 1975. Iran and Israel: The discreet entente. *Orbis* 28: 1070–1087.

———. 1977. Agricultural policy and development politics in Iran. *Middle East Journal* 31: 434–450.

Weinstein, B. 1979. Language strategies: Redefining political frontiers as the basis of linguistic choices. *World Politics* 31: 345–364.

White Paper on Iran. State Department. 1990. Published in Eric Hooglund, ed., *Iran: The Making of the U.S. Policy, 1977–1980*. Alexandria, Va.: Chadwyck Healey and National Security Archive, 1990.

Wiarda, H. J. 1985. *Ethnocentrism in foreign policy: Can we understand the Third World?* Washington, D.C.: American Enterprise Institute.

Wildavsky, A. 1987. Choosing preferences by constructing institutions: A cultural theory of preference formation. *American Political Science Review* 81: 3–21.

Williams, W. Applemen. 1969. *The roots of modern American empire: A study of the growth and shaping of social consciousness in a marketplace society*. New York: Random House.

Willner, A. R. 1984. *The spellbinders: Charismatic political leadership*. New York: Yale University Press.

Wise, D., and Ross, T. B. 1964. *The invisible government*. New York: Random House.

Wohlstetter, R. 1962. *Pearl Harbor: Warning and decision*. Stanford: Stanford University Press.

Wolfe, A. 1971. Unthinking about the thinkable: Reflection on the failure of the Caucus for a New Political Science. *Politics and Society* 1: 393–406.

———. 1978. Has social democracy a future? *Comparative Politics* 11: 100–125.

Woodard, K. 1981. The second transition: America in Asia under Carter. *SAIS* 3: 129–148.

Wright, R. 1989. *In the name of God*. New York: Simon & Schuster.

Wrong, D. H. 1980. *Power: Its forms, bases and uses*. New York: Harper & Row.

Wynn, M. 1972. Who are the futurists? *The Futurist* 4: 73–77.

Yanai, N. 1990. The political affair: A framework for comparative discussion. *Comparative Politics* 22: 185–198.

Yoffe, E. 1977. IPS faces life. *The New Republic*, August 6: 16–18.

Yunker, J. A. 1986. Would democracy survive under market socialism? *Polity* 18: 678–695.

Zabih, S. 1979. *Iran's revolutionary upheaval: An interpretative essay*. San Francisco: Alchemy Press.

———. 1988. *The Iranian military in revolution and war*. London: Routledge.

Zonis, M. 1971. *The political elite of Iran*. Princeton: Princeton University Press.

———. 1991. *Majestic failure: The fall of the Shah*. Chicago: University of Chicago Press.

Zubaida, S. 1989. *Islam: The people and the state*. London: Routledge.

Index

About the Author

OFIRA SELIKTAR is Associate Professor of Political Science at Gratz College in Pennsylvania.

DATE DUE

HIGHSMITH #45115